SCHOPENHAUER
AND THE WILD YEARS
OF PHILOSOPHY

SCHOPENHAUER AND THE WILD YEARS OF PHILOSOPHY

Rüdiger Safranski

Translated by Ewald Osers

Harvard University Press

Cambridge, Massachusetts

Copyright © 1987 by Carl Hanser Verlag München Wien
Translation © 1989 by Ewald Osers
Printed in the United States of America

This book has been digitally reprinted. The content remains identical
to that of previous printings.

First Harvard University Press paperback edition, 1991

Library of Congress Cataloging-in-Publication Data

Safranski, Rüdiger.
 [Schopenhauer und die wilden Jahre der Philosophie. English]
 Schopenhauer and the wild years of philosophy / Rüdiger Safranski;
 translated from the German by Ewald Osers.
    p.   cm.
 Translation of: Schopenhauer und die wilden Jahre der Philosophie.
 Includes bibliographical references (p.).
 ISBN 0-674-79275-0 (alk. paper) (cloth)
 ISBN 0-674-79276-9 (paper)
 1. Schopenhauer, Arthur, 1788-1860. 2. Philosophers—Germany—
Biography.   I. Title
 B3147.S2413   1990
 193—dc20
 [B]
                                                      89-29362
                                                         CIP

CONTENTS

TRANSLATOR'S NOTE

Where English translations of Schopenhauer's work exist, I have quoted from the most recent and authoritative translations by E. F. J. Payne, even though some of the terms used differ from the more familiar traditional ones. These new terms – e.g. 'Representation' instead of 'Idea' in *The World as Will and Representation* – have accordingly been used throughout the book.

References to Schopenhauer's works are given to these English translations where such exist; where there is no English translation, references are given to the original German. A full list of these sources will be found in the Notes at the end of the book.

The Hölderlin poem ('Andenken') and the passage from Goethe's *Prometheus* are quoted in Michael Hamburger's translation. The *Communist Manifesto* is quoted from the official English text, and the Bible in the Authorized Version. Hegel's *Phenomenology of Spirit* is quoted from A. V. Miller's translation, 1977, Oxford.

PREFACE

This book is a declaration of love to philosophy. Something that once upon a time existed: thought of God and the world, which came from a fervent heart; the great wonder that something is, instead of being nothing. This book looks back to a vanished world, when philosophy was once more, perhaps for the last time, in magnificent flower. The 'wild years of philosophy': Kant, Fichte, Schelling, the philosophy of the Romantic movement, Hegel, Feuerbach, young Marx. Such exciting and excited ideas never existed before. The reason was the discovery of the ego; whether it took on the role of the spirit, of morality, of nature, of the body, or of the proletariat, it produced a euphoric mood which gave rise to the most extravagant hopes. Man was claiming back for himself 'the riches squandered to heaven'. All these, it was realized, were things made by man. Man re-entered into his property, no matter to what distant shores he was setting out. For a while this was delightful, but soon it began to disappoint. As man discovered what he had himself made among the old riches of metaphysics, they lost their magic, their promise. They became stale and trivial. No one any longer knew what 'Being' was, even though one was told on all sides that 'Being determines consciousness'. What was to be done? If one was the maker oneself, then one must make as much as possible. The future was being sought through hectic accumulation. The happiness of knowledge disappeared; all that was left was its usefulness. 'Truths' only existed to be 'realized'. This released the secularized religion of progress and growth. The time soon came when man felt encircled by what had been *made*, and when he longed for what had *become*, a time when the appropriation of what was one's own became a problem. There was talk of alienation amidst a self-made world; the 'made' was overwhelming the 'makers'. Imagination discovered a new utopia: the 'made' could be controlled. When this utopia lost its power a new kind of fear arose, the fear of self-made history. This brings us to the present time. The 'wild years of philosophy' bear more than a little responsibility for it. A postdated declaration of love will therefore also have to be a corrective. This will be made easier by the other great subject of this book: Schopenhauer.

He came out of the 'wild years of philosophy' and yet he was bitterly hostile to them. He did not think much of the new secularized religion of reason. As a former apprentice merchant he regarded reason as a counter-jumper, scurrying wherever the principal, the 'will', commanded. 'Will' was neither spirit, nor morality, nor historical reason. 'Will' was, simultaneously, the vital and the fatal, causing death and ruin, and a host of enemies. Schopenhauer was at loggerheads with his period. He was inspired not by the thrill of 'making' but by the art of 'sitting back': this 'most rational philosopher of the irrational' (Thomas Mann) constructed a gripping philosophy of inhibition of action. His dream was a world transformed back into the 'disinterested' play of music, a dream of reconciliation which, concealed under all kinds of delicate formulations, was later also dreamed by Wittgenstein and Adorno. By dreaming, Schopenhauer was endeavouring to protect himself against a reality which had become a nightmare to him. He saved himself by incorporating the nightmare into the core of his philosophy. Towards the end of his life he said: 'A philosophy in between the pages of which one does not hear the tears, the weeping and gnashing of teeth and the terrible din of mutual universal murder is no philosophy.'

Kant, the *accoucheur* of the 'wild years', had written about the French Revolution: 'Such a phenomenon in the history of mankind *can never be forgotten* because it uncovered in human nature a talent and a capacity for improvement, such as no politician would have puzzled out from the past course of things.'

Our own events which can never be forgotten bear the names of Auschwitz, the Gulag archipelago and Hiroshima. Philosophical insight today needs to prove itself equal to what emerges from these events. We shall have to go back to Schopenhauer in order to measure up to our own time. Not only his pessimism, but also his philosophy of vigorous restraint and renunciation drives thinking forward.

Schopenhauer was a philosopher of the early nineteenth century. That is easily forgotten because his impact came so late.

He was born in Danzig in 1788. He spent his youth in Hamburg. He came to know Europe on his grand tours with his parents. His father, a wealthy patrician merchant, wanted to turn him into a merchant. But Schopenhauer, benefiting from his father's death and helped by his mother (to whom he later adopted a hostile attitude), became a philosopher. His passion for philosophy stemmed from his wonder at the world – the most ancient motive of philosophy. Thanks to his inherited wealth Schopenhauer was able to live *for* philosophy; he had no need to live *by* it. He had no prospects in the world of professional philosophers. In the end he abandoned the effort. That proved beneficial: the existential stimulus which drove him to philosophy was not blunted by social or professional considerations. He retained his acute vision: he saw the nakedness of the emperors in the German chairs of philosophy, he saw careerism, obsession with originality, and acquisitiveness showing through their finely spun philosophical systems.

His principal work, *The World as Will and Representation*, was written between 1814 and 1818. He completed this phase of his life convinced that he had accomplished his life's real task. Then he stepped out in front of his audience and, to his horror, discovered that no one had turned up. Without having played his scene he left the stage. He was not given the chance to be a thinker on stage. Yet he was in no danger of confusing glittering stage settings with truth; he had no time for philosophical masquerades. He was content with one mask: to be an uninvited observer of the often brutal carnival of life. And yet, more than he would admit to himself, he was waiting for a response. Too proud to seek an audience, let alone to woo one, he was secretly hoping that the public would seek *him*. What he tried to personify was the truth which withdraws. When eventually, towards the end of his life, he was 'discovered', he would, in retrospect, interpret his prolonged incognito as the long road to truth.

Arthur Schopenhauer had to be patient, throughout a long life, while in the outside world history was accelerating and the 'wild years of philosophy' were culminating in the revolutionary events of 1848.

The 'wild years' ignored this philosopher of 'weeping and gnashing of teeth', and of the ancient art of the contemplative life which is anxious to attain tranquillity. They ignored a philosopher who, far ahead of his time, brought together the three great affronts to human megalomania and thought them through to the end. The cosmological affront: our world is one of countless spheres in infinite space, with a 'mildew of living and sentient beings' existing on it. The biological affront: man is an animal, whose intelligence must compensate for a lack of instinct and for inadequate adaptation to the living world. The psychological affront: our conscious ego is not master in its own house.

I shall relate how Schopenhauer came to his philosophy, and what that philosophy then made of the philosopher.

I take the risk of reflecting on philosophy while relating it, just as I relate Schopenhauer's life and its cultural and historical background. The people who produced all these ideas then are dead, but their ideas live on – sufficient reason to let those ideas, which have survived them, appear here like living persons.

BOOK ONE

CHAPTER ONE

THE WAREHOUSE ISLAND

Arthur Schopenhauer was very nearly born in England. That had been his father's wish, to which his mother had submitted. His parents had travelled to England. The birth of the child was to have been awaited in London. Schopenhauer's father, an admirer of the English way of life, intended his son – he hoped it would be a son – to acquire British nationality in this way. But suddenly, during the dark foggy days of waiting, his father panicked. In exhausting day-long journeys he dragged his highly pregnant wife back to Danzig, where Arthur was born on 22 February 1788.

As a philosopher, however, and for the world at large, Arthur Schopenhauer was in effect born in England. He was sixty-four and his life's work, ignored by the public, had been completed, when in April 1853 an English periodical, the *Westminster and Foreign Quarterly Review*, turned its spotlight on this neglected waif of German philosophy.

The British public, which had always regarded the German fever of philosophical speculation as a curiosity, now had a hitherto obscure philosopher introduced to it with the following words: 'Few, indeed, we venture to assert, will be those of our English readers who are familiar with the name of Arthur Schopenhauer. Fewer still will there be who are aware that the mysterious being owning that name has been working for something like forty years to subvert the whole system of German philosophy which has been raised by university professors since the decease of Immanuel Kant, and that, after his long labour, he has just succeeded in making himself heard – wonderfully illustrating that doctrine in acoustics which shows how long an interval may elapse between the discharge of the cannon and the hearing of the report.'

The report of this article, on the other hand, was heard at once, even in Germany, where *Vossische Zeitung* published a translation. The praise ringing out from the British Isles was simply too shrill: 'And even still fewer will there be who are aware that Arthur Schopenhauer is one of the most ingenious and readable authors in the world, skilful in the art of theory building, universal in attainments, inexhaustible in the power of illustration, terribly logical and unflinching in the pursuit of consequences, and – a most amusing qualification to everyone but the persons "hit" – a formidable hitter of adversaries.' This article from England inaugurated what Schopenhauer caustically referred to as the 'comedy of fame'. Visitors, anxious to call on him in Frankfurt, were dismissed with the remark: 'The Nile has reached Cairo.'

But from Frankfurt and the Nile delta back to London. Arthur was yet to be born. His parents were waiting.

The couple had left Danzig on St John's Day in 1787. There was a double purpose to this journey of Heinrich Floris Schopenhauer. He wished to provide a pleasant change for his wife, who was twenty years younger than him and who had as yet seen nothing of the world. Two years earlier he had married Johanna Trosiener, a marriage of convenience, and so far childless. Johanna found it difficult to dispel her boredom in the splendid Danzig townhouse or at their idyllic country place, Oliva. Ill-humour and melancholy began to trouble their marital bliss, moderate as it had been from the outset. To Johanna the journey was a gift from heaven. 'I was to travel now! Travel! See England! . . . I am dizzy with joy, I thought I was dreaming when my husband informed me of this unsuspected good fortune,' Johanna wrote in her memoirs.

Heinrich Floris, however, did not intend it to be merely a present to his wife. He was considering a move to England and he wanted to make the necessary inquiries there, as Danzig, where the Schopenhauers had lived for generations as highly respected merchant magnates, was no longer the place it used to be.

Until as recently as the seventeenth century 60 per cent of the Baltic trade went through the ancient Hanseatic city. Under Polish patronage, Danzig preserved its political independence. But as the kingdom of Poland declined in the course of the eighteenth century, becoming the plaything of the competing power interests of the Habsburg empire, Russia and Prussia, Danzig's freedom increasingly came under threat. Other neighbours, admittedly, offered to be Danzig's protector, but Danzigers realized that this way lay not protection but extortion. Danzig was having to accustom itself to the idea that a proud trading city with a rich tradition had now itself become a trading object between the great European powers. A few decades before Arthur's birth the city's determination to preserve its status was formulated in a call for assistance addressed by the Danzig government to the Dutch States General: 'Here we stand, like a sandbank surrounded by the roaring sea, waiting for the moment when the waves will engulf us and bury us unlamented.' The Danzigers did not have to wait long for the wave that would bury them. In 1772 Prussia, motivated by the First Partition of Poland, advanced and seized the city in a stranglehold. Troops occupied the surrounding countryside and the Vistula estuary. Many country seats of rich Danzig burghers now found themselves in Prussian territory. Russian and Polish grain shipments down the Vistula were obliged to pay customs duty at the Prussian Excise, greatly to the detriment of Danzig trade. Frederick the Great's 'coffee snoopers' were even showing themselves within the Danzig city precincts. One of them was grabbed by the outraged populace and beaten to death.

Johanna Schopenhauer was a little girl when all this happened. One morning things were especially lively in the streets. Sailors, artisans and servants were standing around, debating loudly, among them a few more solid burghers in silk stockings. On the open terraces of the houses, known in Danzig as *Beschläge*, the women, still in their wrappers and slippers, huddled together. The young girl anxiously asked her Kaszubian nursemaid what had happened. 'Indeed a misfortune, and a great one,' Kasche replied, 'but you're too young to understand. The Prussians have come overnight – so you'd better behave.'

One who did not behave in this situation was Heinrich Floris Schopenhauer. His bourgeois-aristocratic republicanism – he read Rousseau and Voltaire, and had a subscription to the London *Times* – and the Schopenhauers' links over many generations with the free-city traditions of Danzig made him an irreconcilable opponent of Prussian authoritarianism. Yet on one occasion in 1773 he had met Frederick the Great in person. Returning from a long trip abroad, he had stopped in Berlin for a few days. At a parade of troops the King noticed him among the spectators. His elegant and proud figure attracted attention. The King invited him to an audience, in the course of which he suggested to the Danzig merchant that he should settle in Prussia, since – as he allowed it to be understood – Danzig's freedom no longer had much of a future. 'Voilà les calamités de la ville de Dansic,' said the King, mockingly pointing to a map in the corner of the chamber. Heinrich Floris, however, did not take up the offer. Whatever he was he wanted to owe to himself and not to the favour of power.

This story was told in Danzig, along with others which came to the ears of the by then marriageable Johanna. Such as this one: during the blockade of Danzig in 1783 Schopenhauer's grandfather had to accept the billeting of a Prussian general at his country estate outside the city. In order to show his gratitude for the admittedly enforced hospitality given him, the general offered to his host's son, who was Heinrich Floris Schopenhauer, the free importation of forage for his horses. Heinrich Floris, the owner of a choice stud, had a curt reply sent to him: 'I thank the Prussian general for his goodwill. For the moment, however, my stable is adequately supplied, and when my stock is consumed I shall have my horses put down.'

The rigid republican, who was regarded in Danzig as the very personification of the city's will to self-determination, was still a bachelor at the age of forty, but did not wish to confine his love to horses. He looked for a wife and found her in Johanna Trosiener, who did not then suspect her questionable good fortune. She met the well-known magnate with reserved respect, and was thunderstruck when one day, as was then the custom, he asked her parents for her hand in marriage. The Trosieners felt flattered as, unlike the

Schopenhauers, they did not belong to the city's patricians. What was discussed one fine Sunday morning, half outspokenly and half embarrassedly, was a brilliant match. Johanna was aware of it; what she did not realize so clearly was the delicate political aspect of this offer of marriage. For Johanna's father, Christian Heinrich Trosiener, was not by any means imbued with the staunch Danzig patriotism so convincingly displayed by Heinrich Floris. Christian Heinrich Trosiener, also a cosmopolitan though a less affluent merchant, belonged to the city's corporative middle class, the so-called 'Third Estate', which at times fiercely opposed the patrician city government and which, in pursuit of its own corporate interests, at times lost sight of the external independence of the city.

This intra-city opposition, which was as sharply delineated socially upwards as it was downwards, had in the mid-eighteenth century even appealed for the King of Poland's help against the patrician governors, with the result that certain of the middle class's economic interests (restrictions on the immigration of foreign merchants, maintenance of compulsory guilds) had been satisfied, while the sovereign rights of the city in the sphere of harbour and military administration had been lost. The constitutional reform of 1761 gave members of the Third Estate access to the city council. Thus Christian Heinrich Trosiener, a leading light of the opposition, soon became a councillor. During the Prussian blockade of Danzig these middle-class figures, and hence also Johanna's father, were regarded as unreliable characters, suspected of pro-Russian sentiments. Even fifty years later in her memoirs, Johanna was vague on this delicate issue. On the day in her childhood when 'the Prussians came' the bookkeeper had behaved with unusual arrogance in her parents' house: 'Herr M. . . . said a lot more, my mother started to quarrel with him about it . . . I had the impression that he had said something about my father which she would not admit . . . I should have loved to discover why my mother got so angry when Herr M. . . . said my father wore his coat on both shoulders; how else was he to wear it?' Christian Heinrich Trosiener did in fact 'wear his coat on both shoulders', because in the 1780s he became the leader of a movement calling for an arrangement with Prussia. On 24 January 1788, supported by the social club 'Bourgeois Resource', he proposed the motion: 'If our continued existence depends solely on . . . trade with our neighbours, the subjects of Prussia, then we must endeavour to reach them, and if there is no roundabout road leading us there . . . then we must choose the direct one and – no matter how, at first sight, this may outrage the sentiments of a republican – try to become subjects of a King under whose sceptre our closest neighbours are better off than we are.'

Johanna's father did not survive this unsuccessful attempt politically. He had to resign his seat on the council, he liquidated his business and in 1789 retired, as a tenant, to the city domain of Stutthof. Later, following Christian Trosiener's death in 1797, the family became impoverished and had to be supported by the Schopenhauers.

Thus, while Christian Heinrich Trosiener in Danzig was attempting to do a deal with the Prussians, Heinrich Floris Schopenhauer with his Johanna, *née* Trosiener, was in England in order to establish where, if 'the Prussians came', he might best retire to.

Exactly when Johanna discovered that she was pregnant remains unclear in her autobiography. At the outset of the journey, when she was already pregnant, she certainly did not realize it. Given the often total ignorance in which middle-class women then bore their first children, it may be assumed that the father was the first to notice his wife's pregnancy and that, anxious to have his hoped-for son born as an 'Englishman', let her undergo the hardship of the crossing from Calais to Dover without informing her of her state. When her pregnancy became obvious even to Johanna a conflict arose between the couple. Johanna writes: 'That my husband should wish to ensure for our hoped-for son this very important privilege, especially important for a merchant [British nationality], when the occasion so perfectly offered itself to that end, and that he did everything to persuade me to await my confinement in London was very natural; but no woman, at any rate, will blame me for the frank admission that for this once I found it immensely difficult to yield to his wish. Only after a very hard struggle with myself, a struggle I underwent alone, did I succeed in overcoming my inner reluctance, my anxious longing for the calming presence and beneficent care of my mother at that rapidly approaching hour. Thus I finally submitted with reasonably good grace to the will of my husband, to which, as far as I am myself concerned, I was unable to oppose anything rational; initially with a heavy heart but then, through external causes, with a greatly relieved one.' These and the following passages (which will be quoted) from Johanna Schopenhauer's memoirs, written in 1837, must be read very attentively, because they hint, however decently veiled (this she had learned from her ideal, Goethe), at the drama of her marriage, which was to have a lasting effect on Arthur's life.

Heinrich Floris's plans had been 'rational', she wrote, and even 'natural'. There was nothing to be said against them. And yet, they were not in line with her own intentions and wishes. She wanted to give birth to her child in the house of her own mother. These sentences of Johanna's still contain a faint echo of outrage at the fact that she not only had to yield to her husband's will but even, under the pressure of male decision, had to admit that her own wishes were neither natural nor rational. Her only remaining pride rests in the fact that she 'underwent alone' the 'hard struggles' in which she submitted to her husband. But even here the bitterness is not to be missed: no one helped me, I had to overcome my grief alone. The man dragged me, in order to cope with his anxiety, half-way across Europe.

Johanna probably submitted to her husband in that manner which still holds resentment – against the subjecting power and against one's own act of submission: 'Thus I finally submitted with reasonably good grace to the will of my husband . . .' Having survived this struggle, she encountered, surprisingly, the good fortune in London of being surrounded by a considerable number of pleasant people who showed concern towards her. For the first time she experienced what she would later attach great importance to – finding herself the centre of social interest: 'From all sides they came towards me with comforting . . . reassurances and, surrounded everywhere by loving friends, I now looked towards the future with calm.' Here we see Johanna Schopenhauer using her social talent to bridge life's abysses. In London, in the late autumn of 1787, she succeeded in this for the first time. To her this was an exciting self-discovery.

But then came the gloomy days of November. London was immersed in fog. The lamps were alight all day long. Now we, and Johanna also (who normally praised her husband's 'fearless openness'), encounter a very different Heinrich Floris Schopenhauer and can understand what Arthur, many years later, recorded in his secret diary *Eis Eauton*: 'I have inherited from my father that fear which I myself am cursing . . . and fighting with all the willpower I possess' (P IV, 2, 120). This fear now surfaced: 'And now,' Johanna wrote, 'my husband suddenly fell victim to that same anxious worry about me of which I had only just freed myself.'

On this point Johanna is inaccurate. This was not the same fear. She had been afraid of having to face the adventure of giving birth in alien surroundings, away from her own mother. But what was Heinrich Floris afraid of? It could not have been anxiety over Johanna, because she had meanwhile found in London the 'motherly assurance' of men and women friends, and therefore now wanted to stay. Fear for the unborn child can also be ruled out, since it would not be staying in London but the exhausting journey that was dangerous to the unborn child, and of course also to Johanna.

The hints by which Johanna tried to explain her husband's action are obscure: 'My quiet compliance with his will had made a far deeper impression on his mind than at first he wished to show me; the great sympathy that I encountered everywhere aroused in him anxieties about some danger connected with my staying in London, and this eventually led him to the decision to abandon all plans for our yet unborn child.'

What 'anxieties' did the 'great sympathy' which Johanna encountered from all sides arouse? Should this 'great sympathy' not have dispelled all anxieties? There was in the father's life some dark and vague source of fear which later made him hurl himself to his death from the attic of his house in Hamburg. In London that fear seemed to surface in a fairly definite form: as jealousy. Heinrich Floris Schopenhauer evidently could not easily accept the fact that his wife's sociable magnetism displaced him from his favourite spot at the centre of events.

Arthur Schopenhauer, who was able to enter into his father's emotional make-up but not into that of his mother, many years later hinted, in his recollections of his father's death, that he was probably entirely justified in his jealous anxieties: 'As my own father was sick, and miserably tied to his invalid's chair, he would have been abandoned had not an old servant performed for him a so-called service of love. My mother gave parties while he was perishing in solitude, and amused herself while he was suffering bitter agonies' (C, 152).

That her husband had tormented her with jealousy Johanna expressly denies in her memoirs; she also points out that she gave him no reason for it. Even so there are strange allusions in her autobiography: 'My husband was unable to embitter my life by direct utterances of little jealousies . . . He never mentioned the great disparity in our ages, yet when he saw me, in youthful company gaily flitting about with my own kind, I certainly noticed that he was not overjoyed at being reminded of it. The French novels which he had himself put in my hands had taught me that, during his stay of many years in that country, he must have had many an experience that was not apt to elevate my sex in his eyes. I felt, even though I did not tell myself so in explicit words, that the present and future happiness of the two of us depended on his continuing satisfaction with me . . . And even if at times a slight sense of malaise or irritation befell me, one glance at the wonderful scenery around me would dispel it.'

Yet while enjoying this 'wonderful scenery' (the Oliva country house near Danzig) Johanna imposed severe restrictions on herself in order not to give her husband cause for suspicion: 'I never paid any visits in the neighbourhood while my husband was away, I used the carriage at my disposal only for short pleasure drives from which I returned without having called anywhere, outside the extensive range of my garden I chose for my longer walks only paths remote from the highway, as well as meadows, fields and forests; thus I was advised for my own good by a certain inner voice, which I have all my life been ready to follow, as on the rare occasions when I acted against it I invariably found cause to regret it bitterly.'

All this suggests an exceedingly precarious balance between husband and wife, a balance maintained only with an effort. There could certainly be no question of love. Johanna admits this quite openly in her memoirs: 'I no more pretended ardent love to him than he demanded it.' Why, one wonders, did the eighteen-year-old Johanna Trosiener immediately accept the, to her, surprising offer of marriage without even, as she proudly records, taking the time for reflection allowed to her?

She had been, she writes, entirely attuned to resignation once 'the tender divine flower of first love' had been crushed by fate. 'I believed myself to have finished with life – an illusion to which, in one's early youth and after the first painful experience, one so easily and readily surrenders.'

Johanna here hints in outline at an inner history which in her novels, written many years later, she frequently develops to the end – novels which Goethe praised but which less well-disposed contemporary critics referred to as 'the tepid waters of the Schopenhauer novels of resignation'.

These novels are peopled by women who in their youth were violently but unhappily in love, who then kept their vanished lovers enshrined in their hearts while, urged on by reason or sometimes intrigue, they enter into a marriage in which the husbands do not as a rule cut a good figure. Sometimes they are even positive figures of darkness. These women faithfully preserve the sacred image of their first love by not bearing any children to the men who are the beneficiaries of that realistic decision (as in the novel *Gabriele*) or, if they do so nevertheless, then the child is at times – on the model of Goethe's *Elective Affinities* – the personification of an imaginary act of adultery. Fortunately, Johanna Schopenhauer herself in her further life was not as resigned as the heroines of her novels.

A realization which she never admitted to herself in her own case is carefully applied to other women of her acquaintance: 'Splendour, rank and title exercise an all too seductive power over a young, pampered, unsuspecting girl's heart; they lure the inexperienced girl into tying a marriage knot of the kind that is so often being tied today; a false step for which they must suffer the hardest punishment for the rest of their lives, as indeed nowadays rarely fails to happen.' No doubt to Johanna the attractions of marriage to Heinrich Floris Schopenhauer were of a similar nature. But her only references in this context are to her parents: 'My parents, all my relations, were bound to see my alliance to such an important man, as Heinrich Floris Schopenhauer was in our city, as a very fortunate event.'

Yet this marriage did not become a 'fortunate event' for Johanna until after her husband's death. Then her inherited fortune enabled her to lead in Weimar that independent existence which released all those talents lying dormant in her. But we are still in London, prior to Arthur's birth.

Towards the end of November 1787 the Schopenhauers set out. Heinrich Floris, in order to make up a little for subjecting his wife to the exertions of the return journey, showed himself most considerate, almost as though to dispel a guilty conscience. At Dover, for instance, he had the pregnant woman hoisted on board in an easy chair. It was night. Additional lights were called for. To test the soundness of the ropes, the sailors, rewarded with generous tips, had first to haul up Heinrich Floris. The scene aroused Johanna's mockery.

Considering the exertions involved in a coach ride across late-autumnal Germany, on muddy and stony roads, this display of loving care during embarkation seems downright ridiculous. The carriage got stuck in the mud, and on one occasion actually toppled over. There was little protection against wind, rain or cold. Some of the nightfalls were made in emergency quarters, by the open fireplace of a Westphalian peasant cottage. Johanna occasionally suffered from the shivers and was close to fainting. In her womb Arthur was being thoroughly shaken up and tortured even before coming into this world. It is not hard to imagine the bitterness that Johanna, who had been so loath to part from her London friends, had to bite back at her husband's anxious and simultaneously domineering obstinacy. The hasty return journey became a heavy mortgage on the couple's marriage. Arthur's birth, nine weeks after their return to Danzig, on 22 February 1788, was not under a lucky star.

'Like all young mothers,' Johanna writes, 'I too played with my new doll.' With her child as a toy, Johanna henceforth had to combat a sense of boredom and solitude which began to engulf her. Heinrich Floris sent his wife and child to their Oliva country house for the whole of the summer. There, in pleasant surroundings – in her memoirs she describes the 'magnificent garden laid out in terraces, full of flowers and fruit, the fountain, the large pond with a colourfully painted gondola' – Johanna spent each week alone with her child. At weekends Heinrich Floris would occasionally bring visitors with him. But on Monday everything fell silent again – unbearably silent to Johanna.

Meanwhile the mentor of her girlhood years, Dr Jameson, the pastor of the English community who used to visit her at Oliva during the week, had disappeared from her life. In 1789 Jameson returned to his home in Scotland. She writes: 'Jameson could not bear, without personal involvement, to see the gradual decline of the place he had known in the flower of its prosperity; he felt as though he were standing by the bedside of one dying a lingering death.' Danzig's economic decline in the stranglehold of Prussia induced several families from the upper middle-class circle of the Schopenhauers to leave the city. They too left 'many a gap in the ups and downs of life'. Johanna felt encapsulated in 'a semblance of life by which the deep-down gnawing ruin was veiled from the superficial casual glance'.

Once a year, usually in May, Johanna was allowed to visit her parents in the municipal domain of Stutthof. There she felt refreshed by the sight of the busy rural life. But even there, despite all the energetic bustle, the signs of decline could not be overlooked. Anyway, her father, Christian Heinrich Trosiener, had retired to the domain as a tenant since his pro-Prussian initiative had proved a political failure and his commercial enterprises had run into the sand.

Only the sight of the ceaseless motion of the sea near Oliva brought comfort to Johanna. 'In the light of evening, as well as of morning, churned up by gales in its deepest depths, glistening in the bright sunlight, or momentarily darkened . . . by shadows flitting across its surface, the eternally moving sea provided me, in the changing daylight hours, with a spectacle that never fatigued me.'

Distant places were beckoning, and Johanna felt constricted, nailed down by a child whose charm as a toy was diminishing and who less and less compensated her for her sense of renunciation of life. Between a father whom he experienced almost exclusively at weekends, and a mother who was longing to get away from a life that bound her to a growing child, there was unfolding in Arthur a core of experience which was subsequently to give rise to his philosophy.

At the age of twenty Arthur was to record this reflection in his diary: 'Deep down in man there is a confident belief that something other than himself is aware of him just as he is of himself; the alternative, vividly imagined alongside the immeasurable, is a terrifying thought' (P 1, 8). It is this very thought that Arthur would think through to its end, because he had to learn very early to do without that confident belief.

Arthur never knew the relaxed ease and comfort of primal confidence. Nevertheless, any traits of cowering, intimidation, or unsureness are lacking in his character. There was no denying it: he was the son of a patrician merchant who was not lacking in self-assurance, realism or openness to the world. Even his father's piety was proud, devoid of bigotry: God is with the successful. His father coped with his depression by acting resolutely. This he taught to his son, as well as that certain hardness with which one accepts one's duties in life. 'Good posture at the stand-up writing desk is equally necessary as in ordinary life,' his father wrote to him on 23 October 1804, in one of his last letters, 'for if, in the dining rooms, one catches sight of someone stooping, one takes him for a disguised cobbler or tailor.'

Courage, pride and sobriety were what Arthur learned from his father. His cool, brusque self-assurance was his inheritance.

Arthur's strongly developed self-awareness, however, could not unfold warmly because Johanna had to force herself to maternal love. To her, her son was the personification of her own renunciation. Johanna wanted to lead her own life. And her maternal duties reminded her every day that she did not have such a life. With Arthur's birth the trap, for the time being, sprang shut on her.

He who has not received primary love, maternal love, will very often lack love of what is primary, love of his own being alive. He who lacks fundamental affirmation of life, but not proud self-assurance, will be predisposed, as Arthur was, to casting at all living things that alienating glance from which philosophy springs: astonishment that there is such a thing as life. Only a person who does not feel unquestioning (because sympathy-supported) unity with all that lives can regard as alien something which, after all, belongs to him – his body, his breath, his will. A strange alienation filled even the young Arthur with astonishment and indeed with dismay at the will to live, a will we cannot detach ourselves from because we are made wholly of its substance. Astonishment does not necessarily mean dismay. If Arthur was dismayed then it was because from the outset there was in him a disposition which did not allow him to perceive life as warmth. He experienced it differently: it was a cold current which passed through him and on which he himself drifted. The nearest – life's pulsating reality – was to him, simultaneously, the most distant and the most strange, so distant and so strange that it became a mystery to him, *the* philosophical mystery. He would subsequently make this corporeal reality, which he called the 'will', the core of his philosophy. Basing himself on the (to him) estranging experience of his own being alive, he would endeavour to solve the mystery of what Kant had moved into the furthest distance, the ominous 'thing in itself' – the world as it is, regardless of how we imagine it. Schopenhauer would make this most distant thing once more the closest. The 'thing in itself' – that is, we ourselves in our inwardly experienced corporeality. The 'thing in itself' is the will, which lives even before it comprehends itself. The world is the universe of the will, and individual will is always the throbbing heart of that universe. We are always, from the start, what the whole is. The whole, however, is savagery, struggle, unrest. Above all, there is no sense in it, no intent. This is how Schopenhauer viewed it.

The child, who was at any rate not 'intended' by his mother, was familiar from an early age with a world which did not appear to be based on any 'higher intention' or 'higher purpose', but instead was set in motion by some strangely dark activity at its core.

On his walks with his mother in Danzig young Arthur was also able to gain a different, topographical, impression of how the vital centre of the world – and Danzig to the child was the world – was at the same time the mysterious and dangerous heart of darkness.

At the centre of the city, near the parental house, was the *Speicherinsel*, the warehouse island, washed all round by the Mottlau. There the city's entire transportable mercantile wealth was stored: grain, skins, textiles, spices. This was the working soul of the city. At dusk the gates of the island were closed. Anyone then venturing there would be torn to pieces by the bloodhounds released at night from their kennels.

Amidst these frightening surroundings young Arthur also gained an impression of the magic of music which resists the abysmal forces. On one occasion, his mother told him, a well-known cellist, intoxicated with wine, found in himself the temerity to face up to the beasts at night. No sooner had he passed through the gate of the warehouse complex than the pack of dogs rushed towards him. But he pressed himself against the wall and drew his bow across the strings of his instrument. The dogs halted, and as, more boldly, he played his sarabandes, polonaises and minuets, the bloodhounds peacefully crouched around him, listening. That was the power of music, which Schopenhauer was later to claim simultaneously expressed and appeased the torturing and dangerous restlessness of everything alive.

Danzig's warehouse island appears to have been the first arena in which Schopenhauer watched that mysterious clash between the will to live and music.

CHAPTER TWO

LIFE AND LE HAVRE

What Heinrich Floris Schopenhauer had feared for a long time, and what had made him explore the possibility of moving to England, actually occurred in the spring of 1793: Prussia and Russia agreed on further annexations of Polish sovereign territory. The cities of Danzig and Thorn (Polish Toruń), until then free cities under Polish protection, were adjudicated to the King of Prussia. General Raumer – the man who had wished to show Heinrich Floris Schopenhauer a favour and who had been so brusquely rejected – was now put in charge of implementing the city's annexation and the liquidation of its independence, which had grown up over the centuries. The Schopenhauers did not stay to await the entry of the Prussian troops. Immediately after the unanimous resolution by the council and the citizenry, on 11 March 1793, to place the city under the sovereignty of the King of Prussia, the family left. It was more of a flight than a move. Heinrich Floris Schopenhauer had every reason to be fearful, for his affront to the Prussian general had not been forgotten.

Along with the Schopenhauers other patrician families fled the city, families which had likewise exposed themselves as 'anti-Prussian'. The middle class, on the other hand, held a different opinion: incorporation into Prussia promised economic prosperity. At the bottom of the social scale, among the journeymen, the daily labourers and shipping hands, there was open rebellion. Simple city soldiers disarmed their officers, who were ready to surrender, and turned the cannons against the approaching Prussian troops. They had every reason to fear that, following the surrender of the city, they would be enlisted in the Prussian army which was just then fighting against revolutionary France. Unrest and fighting continued until April 1793. Several houses were destroyed by shelling and fire, there was looting, and some people lost their lives. But while all this was happening the Schopenhauers were safely in Hamburg.

Why the Schopenhauers did not in the end move to England we do not know. But why Hamburg?

For Heinrich Floris Schopenhauer, as a maritime merchant, a seaport was the only possible consideration. In Hamburg he had good business contacts.

Moreover, this powerful Hanseatic city seemed to hold out the best promise of independence from Prussia. Heinrich Floris Schopenhauer was to die before Hamburg, too, lost its republican freedom – not to Prussia but to Napoleon's France.

At the time of the Schopenhauers' arrival in the spring of 1793, the city was experiencing an unparalleled economic boom. Throughout the eighteenth century Hamburg was an important entrepôt for French and Dutch colonial products and for English industrial manufactures. In the English trade Hamburg had eliminated all its European competitors, from the time when Charles II in 1663 had granted the ships of the Hanseatic city the privilege of entering English ports. It was through Hamburg that the products of the European hinterland were exported: grain from Mecklenburg, southern Russia and Poland, shipbuilding timber from the forests of Saxony, Russian saltpetre, manufactured goods, glassware and ceramics, coarse textiles and woodwork articles. Important also was the intermediary trade in tar, Russian skins, furs, and blubber from the Scandinavian countries. Spices, tea, coffee, tobacco, textiles and precious metals were imported from the Netherlands, France and England. In Hamburg these goods were stockpiled in continental Europe's biggest warehouses. The number of ships whose home port was Hamburg doubled between 1788 and 1799. In 1795 over 2000 ships called at Hamburg – a European record.

The Abbé Sieyès in a memorandum prepared for Napoleon in 1798 called Hamburg the 'most important part of the globe'. That no doubt was a slight exaggeration, but the Hamburgers were pleased to hear it and did not stint with self-praise: 'Hamburg's flag flew in the Red Sea, on the Ganges and in China, it flew in the waters of Mexico and Peru, in North America, in the Dutch and French possessions in the East and West Indies. It was respected in all parts of the world, and foreign nations did not envy us the fact that our ships brought us the riches of both Indies, for this was done also for the promotion of their own advantage.' This is how the merchant Johann E. F. Westphalen in 1806 described the tremendous development of trade in the last decade of the eighteenth century, and there is an elegiac note in the account because in 1806, at the time of the Continental Blockade, the old glory was over. But until Napoleon incorporated the city in his sphere of rule Hamburg profited from the wars and the territorial reorganization of revolutionary France. The conquest of Holland by the French (1795) resulted in an exodus of French and Dutch firms to Hamburg. The uncertain military situation closed the Rhine as a trade route and diverted the entire traffic from West Germany and Switzerland down the Elbe. As a port for imported American merchandise on the European continent, as well as for the Dutch East Indies and Levant trade, Hamburg replaced Amsterdam and Antwerp.

Along with trade and shipping, money transactions also increased. Hamburg became the principal financial market of the continent. Trades and crafts in the city flourished. The number of inhabitants rose dramatically, and by the turn of the century reached 130,000.

Heinrich Floris Schopenhauer, in spite of having lost a tenth of his wealth by fleeing from Danzig, was soon able to re-establish himself commercially. Trade with England and France, which flourished especially in Hamburg, had, after all, been his speciality back in Danzig.

The Schopenhauers first settled in the Old City, at Neuer Weg 76. As the Schopenhauer business, favoured by the general economic boom, prospered once more, the family, at Easter 1796, moved to a far more impressive house on Neuer Wandrahm 92. This was the area where the great Hamburg merchant houses were to be found – Jenisch, Godeffroy, Westphalen, Sieveking. The house comprised, as was the custom then, both residential and business quarters. In the rear buildings and in the middle block were the storage and stockrooms, the counting-house and the storage cellars. The back of the building adjoined a canal. Freight barges could moor there. Around a spacious inner courtyard ran a carved wooden gallery, and the forecourts were paved with marble slabs. In the front building were the living quarters – ten rooms, four 'cabinets', four lesser chambers, as well as a great ballroom with expensive stucco work, wooden panelling and elaborately worked window glass. In this ballroom, where well over a hundred people could assemble, the Schopenhauers gave their evening parties – 'far above their station', as Adele, Arthur's sister, later insisted.

Maintaining such a splendid establishment, the Schopenhauers were certainly entitled to regard themselves as belonging to the Hamburg élite. Yet these spacious surroundings engendered no sense of home in young Arthur. Nor did any later memories take him back to this Hamburg residence.

Hamburg proved to be the right place not only for business but also for the bourgeois-aristocratic republicanism of the Schopenhauers. In 1712, following civil-war-like disturbances, Hamburg gave itself a new constitution which established a balance of power between the patricians and the middle bourgeoisie. The patrician councillors and the Convention of the old-established resident bourgeoisie shared executive and legislative power in the city. Naturally, one had to own a certain amount of wealth in order to participate in the city's political life. However, the income level had been lowered. More important was the fact that the constitution, on the lines of the English Habeas Corpus Act, guaranteed the citizens' personal freedom. The bourgeoisie was proud of this political system. 'The Constitution is neither wholly aristocratic, nor wholly democratic, nor wholly representational, but all three together,' a contemporary wrote in 1800. 'The once so active factional spirit has been confined within its bounds by the Constitution, and instead there reigns tranquillity, security and freedom to an extent possibly unequalled by any other state.'

'Tranquillity, security and freedom' were what Heinrich Floris Schopenhauer had sought, and what he had now found in Hamburg. What mattered to him most was 'freedom' from Prussia. And, to begin with, there was no lack of that in Hamburg. True, Frederick the Great had cast covetous eyes on the prosperous trade metropolis, but Britain, France and the Netherlands, motivated by their own free-trade interests, supported the city's independence. Prussia, therefore, had to content itself with requesting expert opinions on trade matters from Hamburg's experienced merchants. But these were not in line with Prussia's mercantilist economic policy. 'Freedom must be the slogan,' the Hamburg Commercial Deputation wrote, and Berlin replied that the opinions were cleverly worded but useless.

The French Revolution – at the outbreak of which Heinrich Floris Schopenhauer had hurried from his Danzig counting-house to his wife at their Oliva country seat to bring her the joyous news – also had its ardent champions in Hamburg. These included even Georg Heinrich Sieveking, the most influential councillor, known as 'Hamburg's Rothschild'. His initial enthusiasm was regarded by some of his fellow citizens as un-Hanseatic. Sieveking defended himself in a pamphlet entitled *To my Fellow Citizens*. It was at the Sieveking country estate that Klopstock, on the occasion of a garden party, for the first time recited his odes to the French Revolution. The *Hamburgische Correspondent* and *Hamburgische Neue Zeitung*, then the best newspapers in Germany, were renowned for their detailed reporting from Paris. But in hailing the French Revolution the Hamburgers most of all admired themselves. In 1790 they celebrated not only the anniversary of the storming of the Bastille but also the jubilee of the Commercial Deputation, and they sang: 'Thrice happy our native town / whom peace and freedom above prouder nations / have lent such high renown!' When the French Revolution entered upon its Jacobin phase, the Hamburgers distanced themselves, though trade relations, of course, were not severed. The Hanseatic citizens felt superior to the excesses, the childhood diseases of the struggle for freedom. 'Hamburg may not brag about its Habeas Corpus Act, and in the assemblies of our legislators there is no splendid tablet inscribed with the Rights of Man; but then neither is the former suspended nor the latter veiled,' the *Hamburgische Correspondent* observed, and in a reader's letter to the editor it was said: 'Is it not splendid that we stand so close to the ideal of political bliss without vertigo? That we are free and equal without Robespierre and the Sansculottes? That we respect ancient peaceful custom where others mar sensible innovations with revolutionary atrocities. . . . It is surely strange that what in France is now called new and paradoxical has, in our city, become ancient political orthodoxy.'

Hamburg's 'orthodoxy', however, had no wish to affront anyone; one had to reinsure oneself. Thus, while trade transactions flourished with revolutionary France and while schoolchildren were made to recite Klopstock's revolutionary odes, aristocratic émigrés were at the same time given asylum, complete with their motley entourages.

Until then, Hamburg had been the home of Anglomania; now, charmed by the elegance and the flair of the distinguished French refugees, the city turned Francophile as well. Johanna Schopenhauer, though in fact sympathizing with the French Revolution, was proud to receive at her social evenings such distinguished émigrés as, for instance, the Baron de Staël-Holstein, the husband of the famous Madame.

The émigrés and their followers loosened the stiff customs of bourgeois propriety. There was more dancing, more gambling and more drinking. The trade of prostitution also experienced a boom, and naturally there were rumours current in Hamburg of the 'French lust disease' – a term then used for syphilis – and this rumour was spread even from the pulpit of St Michael's church.

A French colonel, who had deserted from the colours and who proved to be better at cooking than at fighting, opened an out-of-town restaurant at the Elbhöhe, which very soon became the meeting point of the *jeunesse dorée*. 'What is earning this place the highest applause,' a contemporary wrote, 'is unquestionably the manner of the fare served to our German gourmets, because French culinary art has here made an all-out effort to satisfy tongue and palate to the full.' The French café also established itself in Hamburg. In 1794 the French theatre opened. Hamburgers made the acquaintance of revues and vaudevilles, and young men were entranced with the actresses. Madame Chevalier was the star of the stage. Frau Reimarus, the daughter-in-law of the author of *Wolfenbüttler Fragmente*, remarked a little irritably: 'Madame Chevalier turns the heads of our young people and has hit on just the right moment when a few young merchants have money to squander.' These did not yet include Arthur, who was only twelve at the time; but his mother was pleased to number the fashionable angel from Paris among her guests. Soon, however, the French émigrés had spent their fortunes. Some had to change their style: they turned dancing masters, fencing masters, or gave French lessons. It was in these roles chiefly that Arthur came into contact with them.

But the French touch of a lighter lifestyle was no more than an intermezzo in Hamburg. Heine, who lived there a decade after Arthur Schopenhauer, recorded this with regret. Very soon, too soon for Heine, everything returned to propriety and formality. 'The sky was fiercely blue and darkening hastily,' Heine wrote in his *Schnabelewopski*, 'it was Sunday, five o'clock, universal feeding time, and the carriages were rolling, ladies and gentlemen were alighting from them, with a frozen smile on their hungry lips . . .' Too soon also the business sense of the Hamburgers discarded its elegant wrapping and exhibited itself naked and bare. 'And as I watched the passing people more closely,' Heine wrote, 'it seemed to me that they were themselves nothing other than numbers, than Arabic numerals; here a crooked-legged Two was walking alongside a fatal Three, its pregnant and big-bosomed consort; behind them came Mr Four on crutches . . .' This was the mental attitude, the assessment of gain and loss, and the calculation of profit, that had made

Hamburg so great as a trading city and had allowed it to remain rather insignificant as a place of culture. That was why Johanna, years later, would look back with estrangement from the often too playful artistic sociability in Weimar to her Hamburg experiences: 'If such a senator or burgomeister saw me gluing snippets of paper together with Meyer, while Goethe and others were standing by and eagerly dispensing advice, he would feel truly Christian pity for us poor childish souls.'

It was also typical of the spirit of the city that its most important cultural institution was the 'Hamburg Society for the Promotion of Manufactures, the Arts and Useful Crafts'. Anybody who was anybody, and who had the necessary income, was a member of that society. The infiltration of an 'unworthy person' instantly became the talk of the city's 'better circles' – important enough for a schoolfriend to report on it to Arthur Schopenhauer who, while on his European tour in 1803–4, was far away in the south of France. The 'arts', which also figured in the programme of the society, one of whose founders was Lessing's friend Reimarus, were placed under the tutelage of utility. True, grants were made to impecunious painters, subsidies paid to the theatre, and concerts were staged – but most of the finance went to projects for improving the cultivation of fodder crops, the organization of fruit-tree growing competitions, and the support of research programmes for 'the extermination of the sea-worm that does such damage to ships'. A swimming bath was established as well as a public library, swimming instruction and pregnancy advice were provided – an extensive programme of improvements whose excessive practicality put the fine arts in the shade.

This gave rise to complaints even at the time. In the *Essay of a Portraiture of Hamburg Customs*, written in 1811 by Johann Anton Fahrenkrüger, a locally well-known theologian and scholar, we read: 'Scholarship, learning and the arts were looked at askance, unless they made a noise and adapted themselves to the service of the mundane. The scholar's pleasure in his learning as such, divorced from the crude advantages that might spring from it, are not comprehended by the Hamburger. Exercises in thought, purely for the broadening of the mind and for the correction of general ideas, cannot gain his acclaim. This is given only to endeavours which bring advantage to him, his native city, to the trades . . . The value of a man and of things is set by the merchant. This is the Hamburger to perfection.' The high art of utilitarianism was of overwhelming effectiveness in Hamburg and did not stop at anything. Respectable and artistically attractive buildings were mercilessly pulled down. Restoration of the ancient cathedral cost too much money: in 1805 it was pulled down. Medieval monastic buildings shared the same fate. Some of Hamburg's magnificent town gates and fortifications were levelled to the ground. The church of Mary Magdalene disappeared, as did the English House with its famous Renaissance façade. Even the picture gallery of the city hall was unable to resist the spirit of utilitarianism. Its stock was squandered at throw-away prices, including paintings by Rubens and Rembrandt.

Lessing must have been possessed by the devil when – a lifetime before Arthur Schopenhauer – he tried to create a new dramatic art in, of all places, Hamburg.

In 1766 a handful of merchants – predominantly speculators and bankrupts – had got together to finance an enterprise which they grandly named 'German National Theatre'. They offered Lessing a salary of 800 Reich thalers annually, and he arrived to become everything: artistic director, reviewer, author, producer. The theatre periodical, his finest project, was the subsequently famous *Hamburgische Dramaturgie*. It was intended, as Lessing wrote in the announcement, 'to be a record of all plays to be staged, and to accompany each step which the arts of both the poet and the actor will take here'. First, the actors objected to Lessing accompanying their steps. Then the public was outraged by the lessons to which this screwball, who dropped in on them from Berlin, dared to treat them. Lessing was bold enough to challenge the gallery and the pit at the same time. 'The gallery,' he wrote, 'is of course a great devotee of anything noisy and blustering, and it will rarely omit to respond to good lungs with loud hands. The German pit, too, still has much the same taste . . .' Very soon Lessing had to lower his sights and limit himself to providing analyses of the plays and to writing eulogies of Shakespeare. But the repertoire was determined by Hamburg taste. Even so, the enterprise went bankrupt after barely one year, much to the delight of the bourgeois Lutheran authorities, whose relations with the theatre were described by a contemporary as follows: 'If a troupe of comedians reports with good testimonials the Senate will permit their performance; yet I am assured that the severe Sermon Office and the sensible City Authority are both pleased when they depart again . . .'

Lessing departed two years after his euphoric start. 'I am withdrawing my hand from this plough with just as much pleasure as I laid it on it,' he wrote in a disgruntled retrospect. 'The sweet dream of founding a national theatre here in Hamburg has vanished again; and from what I have seen of this place it will probably be the last place where such a dream will come true.'

That Hamburg was a bad place for artistic dreams is proved also by the fate of the Hamburg Opera – as a permanent institution, the first in Germany. Young George Frederick Handel served his apprenticeship there at the last desk of the second violins. A mere half century after its foundation in 1678 the Opera started to go to seed. The Hamburg public got tired of Italian arias and called for a local diet. Thus even Low German singing was heard from the stage. The expensively acquired Italian stars of the opera turned into maidservants, marshland farmers, great merchants with huge watch-chains and pastors with paunches. The songs, according to a contemporary, were 'downright pickled-herring stuff about a dear paramour, about three and four lovers, a lot more of the same'. The real opera lovers resigned. 'What stands in the way of acceptance of opera,' one of them observed, 'is the nature of the inhabitants; to put it briefly: operas are for kings and princes, rather than for merchants and tradesmen!'

In Schopenhauer's day no one any longer mourned the decline of the opera; instead Hamburgers took delight in the newly imported French musical theatre. And in the field of drama the director, producer and actor Friedrich Ludwig Schröder proved a success: he understood, better than Lessing, how to serve the public at the same time as serving art. Goethe, in *Wilhelm Meisters Lehrjahre*, set a monument to that virtuoso of compromise in the character of the theatrical manager Serlo.

Anything wild, eccentric or brash had a difficult time in Hamburg. This was the experience of the young geniuses of Storm and Stress, and – a generation later – of Romanticism. The poet princes of Hamburg were a different breed. There was, for instance, Barthold Hinrich Brockes, lawyer, councillor, merchant – and also poet. To the Hamburgers he was the personification of the city's good sense. In his verses a sober contentment in life acquired poetic splendour; no one was better able to clothe bare utility in such amiable verses. The poems of his *Irdisches Vergnügen in Gott* (*Earthly Delight in God*), running to several volumes, are a continuous song of praise for a world that God has established for 'the use and advantage' of mankind. These heavenly excursions of happiness in nature and a successful balance sheet were bound to please in Hamburg. Brockes gave a living demonstration to his fellow citizens of how one could at the same time be a poet and remain a Hamburger: 'The production of his spiritual poems he made his regular Sunday task,' one of these fellow citizens recorded with admiration.

In Schopenhauer's day Brockes had been dead for half a century but the spirit of his poetry was still alive. In Matthias Claudius, particularly in his *Wandsbeker Bote*, it lived on to the end of the eighteenth century. In Claudius's work, admittedly, the comfortable 'earthly delight in God' is deepened and internalized into pietistic mysticism – a trait which Arthur Schopenhauer would later find very attractive.

The third poetical celebrity of the Hamburgers was Klopstock. Already famous, he settled there in 1770. And because he was already famous, the Hamburgers revered him also. 'Admiration, well-nigh adoration, was shown to him wherever he appeared,' the merchant magnate Caspar Voght recorded without envy. Klopstock was being fêted, but he was not being read much. His marked emotional grand manner was alien to the Hamburgers, but when this poet of the *Messias* died in 1803 he was buried with princely honours at the Ottensen cemetery under the 'Klopstock lime tree', with all the city's bells pealing and senators, scholars, merchants and diplomats, as well as an immense multitude (said to have numbered not much short of ten thousand), accompanying his coffin.

Arthur Schopenhauer's parents knew Klopstock personally; whether they made his acquaintance at one of their social gatherings in their own house or on some other occasion is uncertain. But once a person was accepted into Hamburg's upper circles he could not fail to come across this comfortable velvet-capped, pipe-smoking elderly gentleman. Klopstock was handed around everywhere, as an ornament to any drawing room. He would be found at the Sievekings, at the Voghts, and at the Bartels.

Johanna Schopenhauer enjoyed this intense socal life in Hamburg to the full. She not only wanted to be invited but she pursued the ambitious aim of having her own house become a centre of the best society. Her autobiography comes to an end before her years in Hamburg, but the extant drafts suggest that her social ambitions did not remain unfulfilled. The list of her Hamburg acquaintances included illustrious names: Klopstock; Wilhelm Tischbein, the painter and Goethe's companion on his Italian journey; Dr Reimarus, the son of Lessing's friend and author of the *Wolfenbüttler Fragmente*; Baron de Staël-Holstein, the Swedish diplomat and husband of Madame de Staël; Madame Chevalier of the French Theatre; Count Reinhard, a polyglot French diplomat from Swabia; Professor Meissner, the famous author of innumerable lubricious novels in the *galant* style; Canon Lorenz Meyer, a Maecenas of the arts well known in the city and a member of the Board of the 'Patriotic Society'.

In her elegant house on the Neuer Wandrahm Johanna Schopenhauer endeavoured to live by the slogan coined by Hannchen Sieveking, the wife of the 'Hamburg Rothschild': 'There is nothing better than the experience of a crowd of people feeling at one with each other, and together taking pleasure in life and enjoying it properly.'

Young Arthur took no part in that enjoyment. Schopenhauer's recollections of his early years in Hamburg speak almost exclusively of loneliness and fear. Amidst the comings and goings of guests in that open house the young boy, looked after by a nursemaid and servants, appears to have felt lonely: 'even as a child of six my parents, returning from a walk one evening, found me in deep despair because suddenly I thought I had been abandoned by them forever' (PIv, 2, 121). Middle-class fathers only took an interest in their sons once they entered upon the 'age of education', and that was at about eight years. Only then, in turn, did the fathers begin to exist for their children. Then the hidden god would step out from the wings and utter his fate-determining decrees. Those of Heinrich Floris Schopenhauer did not lack decisiveness. 'Concerning myself,' Arthur Schopenhauer reported in his curriculum vitae drawn up for Berlin University, 'he [the father] had determined that I was to become a successful merchant and at the same time a man of the world and with elegant manners' (CL, 648).

In the summer of 1797, following Adele's birth, Arthur's father thought the time had come for the first lesson in commercial worldliness. He took his son via Paris to Le Havre, where Arthur was to spend two years in the care of the family of a business partner. With the Grégoires de Blésimaire Arthur was to learn French, develop his social graces, and generally, as his father was fond of putting it, 'read in the book of the world'.

In the Grégoires' home Arthur was to spend 'by far the happiest part' (CL, 649) of his childhood. That, at least, was what he felt in retrospect. Yet we know very little of those two years. Arthur's early letters have not survived, but the charm of life far from his parental home, in that 'friendly town situated at the Seine estuary and on the seacoast' (CL, 649) must have greatly captivated him. This can be seen from the reaction of others. Anthime, the son of his host family and the same age as Arthur, wrote to him a few years later, on 7 September 1805: 'You regret that the time you spent in Le Havre is gone.' When Arthur on his grand tour of Europe with his parents in 1803 visited Le Havre again, he noted in his travel diary: 'Throughout that time I had thought a lot of them all, of the places in and around the town, where I was happy, I had dreamed of them a lot, but I had no one to whom I could speak of it, and in consequence it had all become almost like a mere image of my fantasy. And so, naturally, it was an absolutely wonderful feeling to be at the same spot again and to be surrounded by the same objects; I could scarcely persuade myself that I was truly in Le Havre. In a strange way all kinds of things and faces, that I had not thought of during the whole time of my absence, came back to my mind, and I recognized everybody. Soon I felt as though I had not been away at all' (TD, 95).

Not only the ebb and flow of the sea, but the tides of world history were also felt in this town. The fantasy of the ten-year-old was highly active. The sea was a familiar thing to the boy from Hamburg, as were the smell of tar and seaweed, the wind, the rocking ships' masts in the harbour, the screech of the seagulls. But unlike Hamburg, whose neutrality at first kept the turbulence of the Napoleonic age at bay, Le Havre was fully exposed to it.

Arthur's father had used a moment of political tranquillity for the journey to Le Havre. The First Coalition War of the old European powers against revolutionary France ended in 1797. Prussia gave up its claims to the left bank of the Rhine and got out of the war before it ended. In consequence, the entire north of Germany became neutral.

This meant that travel was possible, but one's journey led into uncertainty, into a very un-Hanseatic adventure. France was still ruled by the Directorate, but, favoured by the chaotic conditions in the country, Napoleon's rise was beginning. According to a secret report by the Minister of Police, chaos and civil war were raging in forty-five out of eighty-six *départements*. Men subject to military call-up forcibly resisted the recruitment authorities. Prisons were being stormed, policemen murdered, tax collectors robbed. Marauding gangs roamed the country, some on their own account, others paid by royalists. To Alexis de Tocqueville, France during those years was 'nothing but turbulent servitude'. The nation, he wrote, was 'trembling, as it were, before the movement of its own shadow'. In Le Havre, too, there were popular disturbances when priests who refused to forswear the kingdom and take an oath to the Republic were herded together from the surrounding country and locked up in the town hall cellars. The pious Normans would not accept that passively: royalist songs were sung in the churches and at night they released the incarcerated priests. Near Le Havre a notorious gang of bandits was operating; one day they even had the temerity to burst into the merchant quarter of Basse-Ville. When they vanished again many of the town's wealthy inhabitants were a little poorer. The Grégoires, however, seem to have suffered nothing worse than a fright. Banditry and piracy in the neighbourhood of Le Havre enjoyed an undreamed-of boom as the state itself took over the management of that trade. In 1797 the Navy Minister leased French men-of-war to suitably experienced adventurers who, operating as privileged freebooters, were to seize British merchant ships and share their booty with the state. To avoid the suspicion of state participation, these ships operated not from the big naval bases of Brest, Lorient or Rochefort, but from Le Havre. However, this project did not prove to be outstandingly successful because, of the 70,000 French prisoners of war counted in Britain in 1801, most belonged to the crews of such privateer ships. At the beginning of 1798 Le Havre for a short period even found itself at the focus of 'official' military operations. General Bonaparte, a year before his *coup d'état*, urged a resumption of the war against Britain. He assumed command of an invasion army numbering 150,000 men, inspected the Norman coast, and instructed the shipyards of Le Havre to build a large number of troop transports armed with cannon. Work began in the town, but suddenly the orders were cancelled. It was said that Bonaparte wanted to march to Hamburg in order to strike at British trade with central Europe there. The Grégoires may have informed young Arthur that this terrifyingly fascinating general, whom anyone could have recently encountered in the port of Le Havre, was now going to visit his parents. But everything remained quiet until the sensational news was received that Napoleon had landed in Egypt. Anthime and Arthur looked for this distant region on their map and studied reproductions of the pyramids.

Not only the pyramids but all the events unrolling in and around Le Havre must have been a kind of picture-book world for Arthur – near but not dangerously near, real and yet fantastic at the same time. Life in the Grégoires' home was well-protected and hedged around, and the dangers passed over the boy's head as lightly as the clouds in the Normandy sky. Arthur was fully accepted into the Grégoire family. He was educated along with Anthime and soon mastered the French language so well that on his return he had almost forgotten German. 'My good father's joy knew no bounds,' Arthur Schopenhauer reported in his curriculum vitae, 'as he heard me chatting away as though I were a Frenchman; on the other hand I had forgotten my mother tongue to such an extent that I could only with the greatest difficulty make myself understood in it' (CL, 649).

With the Grégoires Arthur found something akin to parental love; writing subsequently about Monsieur Grégoire he said: 'A kindly, good and meek man, he treated me just like his second son' (CL, 649). He even believed that the Grégoires showed more understanding of his positive features and his oddities than did his parents. Madame Grégoire wrote to the boy after his return to Hamburg: 'You will soon become an interesting man; preserve all your sensitive heart . . . We often talk about you.'

Evidently, in his letters home, Arthur must have raved a little about the love he was being shown in the Grégoire home, because Johanna Schopenhauer found it necessary in her answering letters to point out to her son his father's loving care and almost to defend it. 'Your father permits you to buy the ivory flute for one *louis-d'or*,' she wrote, 'I hope you will now see how good he is to you.' This demonstrative goodness, however, is immediately followed by a reminder: 'He expects you, on the other hand, to devote yourself thoroughly to the multiplication tables. That surely is the least you can do to show him how willingly you do everything he wishes.'

His parents had enjoined Arthur to write regularly – that, too, was part of a bourgeois educational programme. Arthur sweetened this duty for himself by enclosing with his mail for his parents letters to his Hamburg playmate Gottfried Jänisch. He must have described his French bliss in the most glowing colours also to his friend, for Gottfried on 21 February 1799 wrote back rather sadly: 'I understand . . . that you spent your winter very cheerfully. I did not; for I had a kind of ulcer on my throat which caused me a lot of suffering.' Arthur's consoling words to his friend no longer reached him. On 8 April Johanna Schopenhauer informed her son: 'For you too, dear Arthur, I have news of a loss which will certainly sadden you, because your good friend Gottfried became very sick again, 14 days he was laid up . . . he hardly recovered consciousness . . . For 8 now he has been happier than any of us, for he died, and your letter, my dear boy, arrived two days after his death. Thus you had to lose your dearest playmate.' Arthur soon forgot about the friend who died so young. But during New Year's night 1830–1 Gottfried was to appear to him in a dream: a tall, slim lanky man, standing among a group of people in a strange country, and welcoming him. Schopenhauer awoke in terror and shortly afterwards felt the urge to leave Berlin at the outbreak of cholera in 1831. He regarded Gottfried's return in a dream as a warning of death.

In Le Havre, however, in the spring of 1799 the news of Gottfried's death depressed Arthur less than his parents' call to him to return to Hamburg. His parents were worried because all indications were that the whole of Europe would once more become a theatre of war. Britain had succeeded in winning over Austria, Russia and Naples for an alliance against France. There was fighting again in Italy and in Switzerland. The overland route to Hamburg seemed too unsafe. It was thought wiser to go by sea. Arthur was so proud of having accomplished the adventure of this unaccompanied voyage that even in his academic curriculum vitae, drafted in 1819, he mentions it: 'After a stay of more than two years before completing my twelfth year I returned to Hamburg, alone, by ship' (CL, 649).

During this rather dangerous return voyage – after all, there were British and French warships cruising about the North Sea, as well as privateer pirates

– young Arthur seems to have possessed sufficient sangfroid to make scurrilous observations. Because Anthime, replying to a letter written shortly after Arthur's return, wrote: 'You made me laugh with your account of the lady with the moustache. You should have made a portrait of her, as Cook did on his voyages . . . The little pilot in his short coat must have looked very funny, especially his head.'

After his most enjoyable two years' reading in the 'book of life' there now began the less enjoyable lessons which his father had planned for him. In the summer of 1799, immediately upon his return to Hamburg, Arthur was placed in the private educational institution of Johann Heinrich Christian Runge. There, for four years, he spent twenty-six hours each week. The Runge institute was an enterprise specifically designed to train future merchants and was highly regarded. The sons of Hamburg's best families received their education there.

The boys learned 'whatever is useful to a merchant and becoming to an educated person' (CL, 649), as Schopenhauer put it in his curriculum. Regarded as useful and proper in this sense were especially geography, history and religious instruction. Latin, for instance, was only taught *pro forma*, to satisfy the appearance of education.

In later life Schopenhauer commended Dr Runge. This 'excellent man' was regarded in Hamburg as an outstanding educationalist – which was quite an achievement since the eagerness for improvement that was rampant in the city had produced a downright crushing number of outstanding educationists: Johann Bernhard Basedow, the future founder of the famous educational institution in Dessau, the Philanthropinum, was first a schoolmaster at the Altona grammar school. And Joachim Heinrich Campe, the co-founder of juvenile literature, discovered his pedagogical gifts in Hamburg. Runge himself was actually a theologian, having completed his studies in Halle, the stronghold of pietism. He came from Hamburg and in 1790 returned to the city in the hope of a pastor's living. When he failed to obtain this he opened his private school, which soon became successful because of the good relations he maintained with Hamburg's upper crust. In conformity with the spirit of the city, his pietism soon turned more worldly and pragmatic. A novel and attractive feature of Runge's establishment was that he, the first man to do so in Hamburg, aimed at collaboration between school and parental home, and actually achieved it. Enlightenment, and more particularly Basedow's writings, had somewhat lessened the black school practice of penal ritual and mechanical learning by rote. Runge wished to be regarded as a friend by his pupils and he was a frequent visitor in the homes of their prosperous parents – though not without an eye to his own advantage. His pamphlet published in 1800, *Pedagogical Domestic Table for Parents for the Dutiful Education of their Children*, became the pedagogical bible of enlightened Hamburg. This schoolmaster, whose persuasive method so impressed Schopenhauer, died of tetanus in 1811, at the age of only forty-two.

The diaries of Lorenz Meyer, a schoolfriend of Arthur's, provide an idea of the method and content of teaching. The masters delivered their lectures, and the pupils busily took them down. Afterwards questions were allowed. At times there were regular debates, because these were self-assured pupils, fully conscious of their social prestige, who, when all was said and done, regarded their masters as poor have-nots – a fact which frequently led to disciplinary problems. Only Runge himself was accepted, and he often had to stand up for his harassed colleagues. 'Thereupon Herr Runge gave us a little speech,' Lorenz Meyer noted in his diary on 16 January 1802, 'reprimanding us for the contempt we had shown to Herr Hauptmann; he hoped, for the sake of the love we bore him, that we would behave in Herr Hauptmann's lessons.'

At Runge's institute the pupils were taught how to calculate in different currencies (mathematics), they were acquainted with transport routes and trade centres, and with the yields of the soil and of industrial activities (geography); they learned modern foreign languages to the extent needed for writing a business letter. The astonishing thing, however, was that religious instruction claimed the lion's share of teaching periods. But this was 'religion' without mysticism, without devoutness, and also without theological dogmatism; not a doctrine of revelation, nor one of awakening, but a deistically acceptable moral doctrine. Runge must have been a captivating lecturer, because Schopenhauer in later years fondly remembered those lessons. Lorenz Meyer, too, noted the individual themes in his diary – which he failed to do with regard to other subjects. One issue discussed, for instance, was white lies, 'that these were not allowed . . . because one might equally well talk of white theft . . . and thus excuse the worst vices by invoking necessity'. Fortunately Runge's young wards experienced little necessity, so that this source of vice was not too frequent. Matters were worse with arrogance. That was why Runge in another lesson spoke of 'the manner in which one showed consideration for others, that young men in counting-houses frequently infringed this rule by boasting . . .' Close to real life for these affluent pupils was also his warning against the vice 'of how I might misguide others into trouble. For instance, if I invited someone to some pleasure which his purse did not permit.' 'Condescension' was commended and 'garrulousness' condemned, and there was talk of 'how in one's business transactions one could also be useful to others'. One day the lesson was about friendship and neighbourly love – a bad day for moral instruction, for in the afternoon of that day a soldier was seen running the gauntlet. Needless to say, the pupils ran over to watch.

The casuistry of morality, therefore, seemed to be interesting but not too gripping; reasonable but not inspiring; clear but without mysteries; optimistic without a trace of tragedy. The pupils were taught to utter a comfortable yes to life. During Runge's lessons Schopenhauer did not yet raise any objections to this. Or did he? On 20 November 1802 Lorenz Meyer noted in his diary: 'Herr Runge was angry with Schopenhauer.'

The school was situated at Katharinenkirchhof number 44, a good residential neighbourhood. Every weekday, except Wednesday and Saturday afternoons, the pupils attended there from 9 am to 12 noon, and from 3 to 5 pm. If it rained they would be collected by carriage, or else a servant would come running up with an umbrella. The pupils were already young gentlemen. Occasionally they had fistfights – Lorenz Meyer mentioned Arthur in this connection a few times – and they played blind man's bluff, but in the evenings they would go to balls and soirées and flirt with the daughters of good families. These evening entertainments, in particular, were noted in Lorenz Meyer's diary with a bookkeeper's exactitude: 'In the evening I attended a ball at the Böhls. I had a very good time, but would have had an even better one if I had danced more. I danced the first écossaise with Doris, the 2nd and 3rd with Malchen Böhl. The 1st française with Marianne, 2nd with B. Flohr . . . towards 2 o'clock at night we returned home. Actually I danced the 2nd écossaise with Madame Schopenhauer. Mme Böhl saddled me with her.' Lorenz Meyer, who here so unchivalrously records his dancing-floor amusement with Arthur's mother, was exactly fifteen. He, like others of Arthur's schoolfriends, found their future wives at such parties. Arthur did not, although he, too, passionately indulged in dancing. He must have given his friend Anthime in Le Havre some account of it, because Anthime replied that Arthur should get rid of his belly, it detracted from charm. On one occasion he also called him a 'charming lady-killer'.

Not a week passed without a party in the grand style. 'In the evening I was at the Schröders at the "Baumhaus",' Lorenz Meyer recorded; 'I had a very good time, there must have been 150 to 200 people present. They had 12 musicians, including kettle-drums and trumpets.'

Arthur was moving among his own kind, with kettle-drums and trumpets. What a few years later he would call his 'better consciousness' was still locked up, or he was keeping it locked up in these surroundings. Even so there emerges a certain respect from the extant youthful letters of his two schoolfriends Lorenz Meyer and Karl Godeffroy: Godeffroy and Meyer were jealous of each other whenever one of them received a longer letter from Arthur than the other. And they suffered being called to order by Arthur: 'Lorenz Meyer, to whom I spoke recently,' Karl Godeffroy wrote to Arthur on 26 December 1803, while Arthur was away on a journey, 'told me that you have written a very offensive letter to him, of course I have not read the letter but I know my Arthur well enough to know that he would not deliberately offend his friends.' Karl Godeffroy, in particular, often voiced the fear in his letters that he might bore his friend, who could write so fascinatingly, with his own news. In point of fact, Karl Godeffroy's and Lorenz Meyer's letters are rather dull. This casts an interesting light on the kind of friendship linking those three. It was not a sentimental alliance of hearts such as young men maintained in that age of romantic sincerity.

We do not know what Arthur wrote to his friends; Karl Godeffroy and

Lorenz Meyer at any rate mention swindlers who made off after issuing fraudulent bills of exchange, evening dance entertainments that went wrong, pistol firing on Sunday afternoons, new members of the 'Patriotic Society' – and time and again their boredom. No romantic falling in love, no adolescent world-weariness, no proud youthful disdain of the adult world, no mockery of 'philistines', no foolishness.

It was a superficial friendship, but Arthur at that time found none that would go deeper. When he left Hamburg in 1807, Karl Godeffroy and Lorenz Meyer vanished from his life. Both of them made careers for themselves: Godeffroy went into the diplomatic service and became Ambassador of the Hanseatic cities first in St Petersburg and later in Berlin. A man of great wealth, he lived in grand style socially, and in his old age wrote a book on *The Theory of Poverty or Underendowment, a Contribution to the Doctrine of the Distribution of Wealth*. As chance had it, half a century after their joint years at school one of the first and most eager followers of Schopenhauer, Julius Frauenstädt, was engaged as a tutor in the Godeffroy household. Lorenz Meyer succeeded to the parental business, guided it to success, increased his wealth, dabbled in Hamburg politics, married a rich daughter of the city, became a senator, and died at a ripe old age.

That was the kind of life his father had also planned for Arthur Schopenhauer. But even at the time of his friendship with Karl Godeffroy and Lorenz Meyer, Arthur was harbouring doubts as to whether this was the life he himself wanted.

CHAPTER THREE

THE MOUNTAINS AND
THE COUNTING-HOUSE

While Arthur Schopenhauer was attending the Runge Institute, fighting with classmates and going to houseballs and dances, and while his mother was giving parties and his father pursuing his business deals, the political thunderclouds gathered over Hamburg. The danger was underrated, because Hamburgers believed their political neutrality would protect them. They had such confident faith in their future that, in a demonstrative gesture of peaceableness, they even demolished the outer bastions of their city fortifications and allowed a landscape gardener to convert the ramparts into promenades and flower gardens.

Hamburg believed in a balance of power. The former guarantor power, the Holy Roman Empire of the German Nation, was only a shadow of its former self and offered no protection against the covetous Prussians. But Prussia was being kept in check by France. And Britain was confronting a no less covetous Napoleonic France. Britain, it was believed in Hamburg, would never permit the city, an important trading partner, to lose its freedom. Of course, some delicate diplomatic balancing would be necessary, assurances of goodwill would have to be sent out in all directions, to Paris, to Berlin, to London. And business was just then flourishing – another reason for feeling secure. Friendship with Britain was being cultivated most particularly – that was a tradition. Hamburgers regarded themselves as docile pupils of British democracy and of the English way of life. Among the Hamburg bourgeoisie English fashions reigned; just as in the British Isles, afternoon tea was customary. English literature established itself on the Continent by way of Hamburg. Laurence Sterne's *Tristram Shandy* was a great success there. The victorious advance of Richardson's uplifting novels likewise began in Hamburg. The British Consul was the most important supporter of the Hamburg Opera, and the journal *Moralisches Wochenblatt*, though a sworn enemy of that entertainment, was inspired by English moralist journals; the Hamburgers' umbrellas and their bowler hats – their 'stock-exchange helmets' – were likewise English.

Anglomania was so conspicuous that Johann Gottfried von Herder, the poet and scholar, on a visit to the city, gained the impression 'that they [the

34

Hamburgers] next to God Almighty acknowledged no more gracious being than an English lord, no more delicate creature than a lady, and no other angel than an English miss'.

Thus, when Admiral Lord Nelson and Lady Hamilton made a short stop in the Hanseatic city the Hamburgers treated this event like the arrival of a pair of divinities. The *Altonaischer Mercurius* reported on 23 October 1800: 'Yesterday the famous Lord Nelson arrived in the city ... with Minister Hamilton and his consort. In the evening Lord Nelson attended the French theatre here and was received by the public with the most lively applause.' That applause seems surprising because the English naval hero, who had lost his right eye and an arm in his battles, had recently performed some not very glorious actions in Naples, whence he had just come. He had defended the Neapolitan royal house against a republican rebellion, and in doing so had lacked neither cunning nor brutality. He had ordered the leaders of the Republicans, who had been guaranteed safe conduct out, to be hanged from the yardarms of the ship flying his admiral's pennant – not exactly a recommendation in a city like Hamburg, which took pride in its republican traditions. Lady Hamilton, too, was a delicate issue, for this former kitchen-maid, whose beauty and intelligence had assisted her rise into the English nobility, was simultaneously the wife of the British Minister and the mistress of the admiral, whose daughter she bore the following year. Not even that shocked the normally straitlaced Hamburgers – British credit outweighed it all. Even Johanna Schopenhauer forgot her republican loyalties and proudly recorded her meeting with the illustrious pair; and the aged Klopstock, who not so long before had sung of French liberty, was carried away into writing an ode to the beautiful lady and her war-damaged lover; *Die Unschuldigen* (*The Innocents*) was the title of his poem. The Hamburg newspapers printed it on their front pages.

The temporary political tranquillity around Hamburg was rudely terminated in 1801 by the entry of Danish troops. Denmark was acting as France's ally. The official explanation was that the North Sea coast had to be protected against a British attack, but in actual fact Denmark, profiting from the international situation, was hoping to seize the wealthy city – for whose possession she had vainly fought throughout several centuries – as a valuable pledge in the forthcoming political reorganization of Europe. But Hamburg's faith in a balance of power in Europe was once more to be confirmed. Prussia adopted a menacing attitude to Denmark, as did Britain. Admiral Nelson had an opportunity to reward the Hamburgers for their hospitality; by shelling Copenhagen he put an end to Hamburg's brief Danish occupation.

Although peace was once more restored, it remained under threat from then on. This was bound to have economic consequences. Business declined markedly, and many merchant houses had to close down. The boom was over, and a hard struggle for survival began between firms. Any merchant who was not giving up altogether should just then have remained at his post.

But Heinrich Floris Schopenhauer was planning a grand European pleasure trip. We do not know much about his frame of mind, but certain things seem to emerge from his travel plans: he was no longer a merchant body and soul, and, aware of his increasing years, he believed he had to provide some incentive for his wife, who was twenty years younger, to remain with him.

His son Arthur was adding to Heinrich Floris Schopenhauer's worries, now pestering him to be allowed to change over to the Gymnasium, the grammar school. And that could only mean that he did not wish to become a merchant, that he wanted to break out of the family tradition which had become a nightmare to him. He had no wish to be apprenticed to the *Comptoir*. What a merchant's training was like in those days can be learned from the apprenticeship contract of Arthur's boyhood friend Lorenz Meyer, which was carefully copied and attached to his diary. According to the contract Meyer was to remain in his firm for seven years as *Bursche* (apprentice), and then for three more years as *Handlungsdiener* (business servant). He had to live at his patron's house, he was 'not to stay outside it during the night hours, and, to the best of his ability, was to promote his patrons' honour, credit and advantage, without using any of it to his own profit'. Only after seven years would the apprentice receive a salary. Meanwhile he would be clothed by his parents and fed by his employer. If an apprentice was in breach of his contract his parents would have to pay a penalty.

That was the kind of thing Arthur had to expect if, in line with his father's wishes, he should, after leaving the Runge institute at the age of fifteen, become apprenticed to the well-respected merchant magnate and city senator Martin Johann Jenisch.

Among the Runge pupils – all of them boys destined for a merchant's career – revolt against the prospect of becoming 'galley slaves' was quite usual. To Arthur's other schoolmate, Karl Godeffroy, apprenticeship was likewise a 'horror' which he would rather not think about. But Arthur's refusal was more specific, more emphatic, because he knew what he wanted: he wanted to be a scholar, to learn Latin, Greek, literature, philosophy. Scholarship, in which he had already browsed a little, attracted him. Runge, a man of pedagogical sensibility, supported the boy's wishes and tried to influence his father along those lines. At school Arthur shone by his application, and at home he worked his way through his father's library. He even got hold of the treasures in the locked cabinet. There his father kept the *galant* novels, such as the *Amorous Adventures of the Chevalier de Faublas*, a six-volume morocco-bound work by Jean-Baptiste Louvet de Couvray. Arthur devoured these rococo copulation fantasies in bed at night, until he was caught by his father. But the less sensual, and more sensible, literature by the great Frenchmen Voltaire and Rousseau was by then also familiar to him. Altogether he read anything he could lay his hands on, especially *belles-lettres*. Even his mother, who was certainly not averse to belletristic literature, warned her son against excess: 'I would altogether prefer you,' she wrote from Scotland on 4 August 1803 during their grand tour, while Arthur was remaining in Wimbledon for a few weeks, 'to put aside all those authors completely for a while . . . you will find it intolerable if you get accustomed so early in life to spending all your hours with the arts. You are now fifteen, and you have already read and studied the best German, French, and in part also English writers.'

His father was not at all in agreement with Arthur's wishes. But surprisingly soon, in 1802, he seemed, at least for the time being, to have capitulated. That year he was negotiating with the Hamburg Cathedral Chapter with a view to buying a benefice for his son. 'Because his fatherly love,' Arthur subsequently wrote in his academic curriculum vitae, 'was concerned mainly with my wellbeing, and because in his mind scholarship was inseparably linked with impecuniosity, he believed that he had to ensure, above all else, that this menacing danger was averted in good time. He therefore decided to make me a Hamburg Canon, and began to concern himself with the conditions necessary for this' (CL, 649).

By yielding, his father also renounced the realization of his own plans in life. The family tradition was about to be broken. There would be no successor to take over his business. In his son he would lose his own future. The readiness with which he accepted all that was a reflection of his resignation – the same resignation revealed by the loosening of ties with his business: at a difficult moment he was prepared to leave his business to its own devices while he went on a long journey.

Negotiations with the Cathedral Chapter dragged on. The purchase price of a benefice was very high, approximately 20,000 *Reichsthaler*, possibly too high for the Schopenhauers. After all, there was Adele, his daughter, to be provided for.

Arthur's parents originally intended to start on their journey in 1802, but times were still too uncertain and they postponed their departure. They would wait for peace. In March 1802 Britain and France came to an agreement – a very temporary agreement. For Hamburg, however, things seemed to look up. By the Reich Deputation Decision of February 1803 France guaranteed the freedom of the Hanseatic cities. One would, of course, have to have been rather naive to trust in such guarantees at that time. Heinrich Floris Schopenhauer was not naive, but he wanted to get away; Johanna was pressing him and he himself now wished to shed the burdens of business. The date of departure was therefore fixed for the beginning of May 1803. A few days later war was to break out anew, with disastrous consequences for Hamburg.

No final decision had yet been made about Arthur. Then his father had a strikingly sensible idea. He exposed his son to the challenge of freedom and personal responsibility. He set up a dividing of the roads: let his son choose between two careers. Arthur could either stay in Hamburg and immediately enter the Latin grammar school, go on to the university and so forth, or he could accompany his parents on their pleasure trip through Europe, which was planned to take several years, but on their return he would have to be apprenticed to the merchant magnate Jenisch.

His father was forcing Arthur into the school of either/or existentialism. Arthur was placed at the point from which he would have to 'launch' himself. He believed he knew what he wanted, and he had now to make his own decision. And only his decision would reveal to him what he really wanted. It is always more comfortable to do one thing and imagine that one would really have preferred the other. One can then hold others responsible for one's own mistakes or for what one has lacked the strength to do. Freedom of choice confronts us with ourselves. When we make a choice we must also assume responsibility. In making a choice we can no longer evade ourselves. After we have made our choice we know who we are.

Every decision assumes one thing and excludes the other. Strictly speaking, a decision excludes a whole universe of other alternatives. A 'yes' arms itself with nothing but 'no's in order to assert itself. 'Because,' Arthur Schopenhauer would later teach in his *Metaphysik der Sitten* (*Metaphysics of Mores*), 'just as our physical path on the earth is always only a line and never a surface, so in our lives, whenever we wish to grasp and possess one thing, we have to leave countless others behind to our right and to our left, renouncing them. If we cannot decide, and instead, like children at a fair, reach for everything that tempts us in passing, then this is a mistaken endeavour to transform the line of our path into a surface: we zigzag about, wander like a will-o'-the-wisp, and attain nothing. He who would be everything cannot be anything' (LMM, 103).

His father's terrible choice of alternatives ensured that Arthur could have the one thing only by painfully forgoing the other. To choose a scholar's career meant forgoing the grand tour; to enjoy the grand tour now meant selling out his future to a merchant's life.

With this arrangement however, Arthur's father had done more than just attach a price to each possible decision. Without realizing it he had set in motion an interplay of meanings that was to leave an ineradicable pattern in Arthur. The decision-making situation he created made the boy realize this: to become a scholar means to forgo present pleasure. He who wishes to learn must be able to sublimate. He who wants to travel with his mind must leave his body at home. Future happiness as a scholar is bought with the unhappiness of sensual renunciation. If a person has within himself the stuff that makes a scholar, then he also has the strength for renunciation. He can let others depart and stay at home in the secure knowledge of future excursions of a different kind.

And the other way round: if a person cannot deny himself the present pleasure of a journey, then he is not cut out for renunciation or for postponement, then he lacks the strength for the sublime pleasures of the mind. Such a person can do nothing but seize and utilize an opportunity, such a person can become a merchant but not a scholar. To come to know the world means denying one's mind. To cultivate the mind means renouncing the world. The frightening aspect of the arrangement set up by Arthur's father was that he had severed both kinds of mobility – that of the mind and that of the body – into mutually exclusive alternatives. In conceiving this interplay of meanings he was certainly unaware of its far-reaching consequences. But all games, once they involve the players, turn into drama, with victors on one side and vanquished on the other.

Arthur would have had in him the stuff not for a scholar but for a stay-at-home had he decided *against* the journey. Yet by deciding *in favour* of the journey he would nevertheless disgrace himself. That was the diabolical aspect of the situation: in the given circumstances he was bound to see the journey as a betrayal of his ambitions. And he would not be able to conceal from himself that he was betraying them because his wish to become a scholar was evidently not yet as strong as he had assumed it to be before being forced to face that set of alternatives. He would go on the tour, but his self-assurance would suffer. Moreover, he would travel with a sense of having sold his soul for the discovery of the world. Just that: tour the world with giant strides and let the devil take me afterwards – the devil in the shape of the merchant magnate Jenisch in Hamburg.

It would be impossible to overestimate the hidden effects of this drama. Schopenhauer's hostility to history – which distinguishes him from all his philosophical contemporaries – has its roots here. The pact with the devil made the future appear to him as doom, as menace, as a black hole. Anyone thinking historically must be able, however secretly, to expect something from the future. There is no historical thought without the promise of a future. But the journey through Europe was like exercise hour in a prison yard. A few circuits – and back into the dungeon.

Yet Arthur's theoretical curiosity was stronger than any betrayal. Fortunately one cannot escape from oneself in the long run; at the most one makes detours, admittedly with the risk of dying before arriving. Man, Schopenhauer wrote in his *Metaphysics of Mores*, will 'make all kinds of attempts, he will do violence to his character in detail, but on the whole he will have to yield to it' (LMM, 103).

With his future business apprenticeship Arthur would 'do violence' to his theoretical curiosity, yet it would not allow itself to be diverted. For the time being he would take it along with him; it would be his secret journeying companion.

What was the nature of that theoretical curiosity?

It was not world-embracing but brittle. It had no wish to fuse with whatever it touched, but instead tried to keep aloof from it. It was a curiosity of separation rather than of union, an enjoyment of the solitary rather than the universal. A secret metaphysics of separatism was at work in the young man – the mark of injuries in a child deprived of love. But they were injuries which pride had overgrown. And that pride was also part of his inheritance. Arthur inherited it from his father as well as from his environment. He had a well-developed sense of the vertical: it catapulted him upwards. Only thus could the horizontal be tolerated, from the bird's-eye view. That was why Arthur would throughout his life enjoy climbing mountains, most of all at sunrise. Those were moments of ecstasy. He would record them in his travel diary. Below, everything would still be in darkness, asleep, yet he would already be in the sun, in an intimate meeting with the central heavenly body, of which nothing was suspected yet down in the valley. Here, from his height, he would also find pleasure in the universal. He was Dionysus not from below, outwards, but from above, downwards.

From the top downwards – but always keeping a distance. Arthur Schopenhauer could become inflamed by the crystal-clear coldness of an early morning in the mountains; the sharp contours flattered his senses. This is reflected in his language. It does not flow – it strides, with a firm step, clear, positive, but with little wooing appeal. It keeps its distance. And that was the position he wanted for himself: if not loved, then at least not touched. Protected by coldness and sharpness. Even the boy radiated some kind of untouchability: his schoolmates were aware of it and occasionally complained about it. His mother, too, repeatedly urged him to be a little more forthcoming towards his fellow men. 'Little though I care for stiff . . . etiquette,' she wrote to her fifteen-year-old son, 'I like even less a rough, only self-pleasing, nature and action . . . You have more than a slight inclination that way.' His father, too, in his last letter of 20 November 1804, exhorted him: 'I would wish that you learned to make yourself agreeable to people.'

Arthur was never to learn it. His theoretical curiosity was his organ of alienation. The reciprocal action of that gesture by which he kept the world at arm's length brought him closer to himself. This kind of self-love was bound to become the dark spring of universal hostility. How a man can survive something like that without turning to stone, and how a philosophical genius can actually arise from it – that we shall see before long.

The boy in the carriage, at any rate, was accompanied by a far from benevolent curiosity. He looked around sharply, he observed accurately, but he did not allow himself to be overwhelmed. He was collecting evidence; he obviously intended, with the experiences he was seeking and making, to open proceedings – proceedings against the world in which he was travelling. And it should not be overlooked that he was viewing it in the light of a future that would incarcerate him, that appeared to him as a prison yard.

At the time of his grand tour, needless to say, Arthur was passing through the *Weltschmerz* of puberty. But his *Weltschmerz*, immersed in the most sober observation, was unparalleled. Arthur was travelling on the trail of Voltaire's Candide, to whom the world also seemed to be something that had best be avoided. Arthur had found the novel in his father's bookcase.

Subsequently Arthur Schopenhauer, in summarizing his tour, resorted to nobler comparisons. He had experienced the same as Buddha, he noted in his *Cholerabuch* (*Cholera Book*) in 1832: 'In my seventeenth year, without any learned school education, I was gripped by the *misery of life* as Buddha was in his youth when he saw sickness, old age, pain and death. The truth that spoke out from the world loudly and clearly soon overcame also the Jewish dogmas impressed on me, and my conclusion was that this world could not be the work of an all-loving Being, but rather that of a devil, who had brought creatures into existence in order to delight in the sight of their sufferings' (P IV, i, 96). In his curriculum vitae, the *Lebenslauf*, he characterized the journey with less elaborate self-stylization. There he wrote: 'During those very years of awakening virility, when the human mind is most open to impressions of all kinds . . . my mind was not, as usually happens, filled . . . with empty words and reports of things, having in this manner the original acuteness of reason dulled and wearied; but instead it was nurtured and truly instructed by the observation of things. . . . I am particularly pleased that this course of education accustomed me from an early age not to content myself with the mere name of things but to have a decided preference for the observation and investigation of the things themselves, as well as preferring the knowledge growing from the observation to the bombast of words, wherefore I was subsequently never in danger of taking words for things' (CL, 650).

As for Arthur's thoughts not after but during his journey, these are recorded in his travel diaries. He filled three copybooks, in a tidy hand, as demanded by his father. And his mother now wanted to educate her son a little on literary lines. He was to learn to translate into language whatever he saw or experienced. He was to practice judgement, selection and arrangement. In consequence, his travel diary is not an intimate record. Arthur put down only what was also suitable for parental eyes. Arthur's notes are thoroughly formulated, there is nothing hurried about them. His mother was later able to use them for her own travel books.

Travel was at that time considered an unrepeatable experience in one's life. Impressions of foreign lands and strange people were regarded as jewels. The travel diary, which every self-respecting traveller kept, was the box which contained these once-in-a-lifetime jewels. Once a person had such a collection, provided he was sufficiently self-assured and proud of his experiences, he would take it to a publisher, who would be ready enough to print the records of such civilized vagabondage because the great public, leading mostly stationary lives, enjoyed reading them. It was by way of travel authorship that Arthur's mother approached the literary Olympus. But her son was still free from such ambitions.

On 3 May 1803 the Schopenhauers set out, in their own carriage and with their own servant. Adele, then six years old, was handed over to relations along with her nursemaid. The route was carefully laid down in every detail. Throughout Europe there were business partners or friends of friends where one might cast anchor – in Bremen, Amsterdam, Rotterdam, London, Paris, Bordeaux, Zurich and Vienna. Letters of introduction opened doors and established new contacts. Thus the journey became an excursion into Europe's best society, where everybody more or less knew everybody else, or knew somebody who knew somebody else. Before setting out they had informed themselves on the sights worth seeing: there were appropriate handbooks in existence. In Bremen, for example, their first stop, the Schopenhauers hastened to the famous *Bleikeller*, where they admired undecomposed corpses with their skins dried out like parchment. To recover from such impressions they would go to the theatre in the evening or get themselves invited to some local party. In Westphalia the Schopenhauers' carriage got stuck, for the first time, in a deep morass. The sky was grey and rain was ceaselessly falling. 'Black heath,' Arthur noted. The food was inedible. The Schopenhauers resorted to their travel provender: French pâté and wine. The villages were dirty. Beggars mobbed the carriage. In Holland they could breathe freely again. Here the roads were paved with cobblestones. The houses were neat and clean. Altogether everything was tidy and the people were quiet and reserved. An evening at a village inn: 'There was no singing or cheering, no squabbling or cursing as certainly happens elsewhere in village inns; but they sat there like genuine Dutch peasants and drank coffee. The whole scene was just as one so often finds it in Dutch paintings' (TD, 22). The family sat about for a while and then retired to their sleeping quarters. Arthur could not sleep; he picked up his flute. 'We had been there scarcely an hour when suddenly eight peasants entered our room, undressed without further ado, climbed into three beds standing there, and fell asleep to the sound of my flute, and out of gratitude subsequently accompanied me with their snoring' (TD, 22). In Ammersfoort the Schopenhauers were told that war between Britain and France was once more in full swing. Would it be at all possible to cross over to England? Rumour had it that the passage from Calais was suspended. On 11 May they arrived in Amsterdam. 'Amsterdam far surpassed my expectations. The streets are very wide, and hence the crowds are not as unpleasant as usually in great trading cities. . . . The houses do not look modern, but they look new, for they still all have the steep gables in the old manner of building; yet they appear perpetually new because they are forever washed and frequently refaced and painted, like everything else that one sees here' (TD, 29). In a porcelain shop Arthur had his first encounter with his personal saint. In the shop-window he discovered Buddha figures 'which make one laugh even at out-of-humour moments, as they nod at one with such a friendly smile' (TD, 25). The old City Hall was visited – for Arthur a first opportunity to reflect on the sublime. In these rooms man became insignificantly puny. Voices were lost. The eye could not grasp the entire magnificence. It was a human achievement transcending human proportions, the monumentalism of remembrance in stone and the vanity of bustling flesh. Arthur stood before the portrait of a Dutch admiral: 'Next to the picture lay the symbols of his life's story: his sword, his beaker, the chain of honour which he wore, and finally the bullet that made all these useless to him' (TD, 27).

This sceptically laconic distance, which refuses to be involved in rituals of meaning and thus keeps an eye out for involuntary comedy, comes into its own especially on religious occasions. Writing about a Jewish religious service in Amsterdam, Arthur noted: 'While the rabbi, with head thrown back and mouth opened enormously wide, was making an eternally long *roulade*, the whole congregation were talking as if at the corn exchange. As soon as the priest had finished they all sang the same verse after him, from their Hebrew books, and concluded it with the *roulade*, whereby two little boys standing next to me almost made me lose my countenance because at the wide-mouthed *roulade*, with their heads flung back, they always seemed to be yelling at me, giving me fright more than once' (TD, 27). This is not a case of malicious anti-Semitism, for Arthur treated Protestant community singing with the same disrespect. He mentions a visit to a Protestant church, 'where the strident singing of the multitude made my ears ache, and an individual bleating with mouth wide open repeatedly made me laugh' (TD, 34). These are the super-acute observations of an uninvolved spectator. His skill in keeping his eyes open without allowing himself to be involved proved useful also in encounters with so-called persons of importance.

A successful balance sheet for such journeys demanded some proximity to the powerful of this world; brief glimpses into the workshops of world history were part of the sightseeing programme. In London the Schopenhauers managed to gain access to the drawing room of the royal palace. There they witnessed the antechamber scene: a rendezvous of the nobility. Arthur remarked in his diary: 'They looked like peasant wenches in disguise' (TD, 44). In Windsor Park they observed the royal couple taking a walk. The two looked to Arthur like perfectly common philistines: 'The King is a very handsome old man. The Queen is ugly without any bearing' (TD, 58). In Vienna he watched the Austrian imperial couple driving out from the *Hofburg*: 'The Emperor stepped out, leading the Empress, and sat down next to her, taking the reins himself. Both wore exceedingly modest clothes. He is a gaunt man, whose markedly stupid face would lead one to guess a tailor rather than an emperor. She is not pretty, but looks cleverer' (TD, 258).

Napoleon in Paris was a different matter. Here even Arthur could not remain cool. On one occasion he saw him at the *Théatre des Français*. The audience clapped frenetically, Napoleon made a few bows and took his seat. Arthur did not cast another glance at the stage. After all, the demoniac chief actor of contemporary world theatre was sitting in the dark corner of a box: 'He wore a perfectly simple uniform' (TD, 81). Later he saw Napoleon once more at a review of troops: 'It was a splendid spectacle. I could make out the person of the First Consul very well, but I was too far away to distinguish his features. He rides a magnificent grey, and by his side is his ever faithful Mameluk' (TD, 108).

Schopenhauer nevertheless retained his scepticism with regard to the heroes of historical action. His gaze seemed to undress them. He asked: What remains of their thunderous presence? A field of ruins, and then everything rots. The things that endure, he believed, are created only by the great minds. The gallery of statues in Westminster Abbey inspired this reflection: 'The kings left their crowns and sceptres behind here, and the heroes their weapons ... yet the great spirits among them all, whose splendour flowed out of themselves, who did not receive it from outward things, they take their greatness across with them, *they* take with them everything they had here' (TD, 51).

For the time being, however, the 'kings' and the 'heroes' were causing considerable mischief. When the Schopenhauers arrived at Calais on 24 May 1803, the war which had recently flared up again very nearly prevented their crossing to England. They just managed to catch the last boat. Other travellers were not so lucky. Arthur reported: 'Three boats were rowing towards us for all they were worth. They were the passengers from the French packet-boat which was unable to leave because just as we had left the news of the war reached Calais. These unfortunate passengers could not even take their luggage with them, the women and children had to climb up, with fear and difficulty, the side of our ever rolling ship; I noticed how each of them had to give two guineas to the sailors who had rowed them here, moreover they had to pay for the passage aboard our and, I presume, also aboard the French packet-boat' (TD, 35).

After a happy landing in England the next destination, of course, was London. A continental European arriving in London in the evening could not help believing that a great festivity was taking place, for the town appeared to be a sea of lights. Arthur, too, needed to understand first of all that such illumination was the everyday norm. Yet in spite of the streetlights one had to watch out for thieves. Pickpockets abounded among the crowds. In the city a hectic life pulsated; the impression was that some 'dangerous general rebellion was setting the inhabitants in motion', Johanna Schopenhauer recorded in her travel account. Arthur actually ventured out alone into these throngs. His impressions surpassed his expectations. He felt he was travelling into the future.

To avoid drowning in this chaos, one resorted to the firm ground of tested visiting and sightseeing programmes. The choice was more than ample: there was Fitz-James, the famous ventriloquist, and a pantomime troupe just back from St Petersburg. A visit was paid to a hospital for disabled sailors: this was full of naval heroes in slippers. The world's largest furniture store had to be inspected. Every week there was an execution to attend. There were several big theatres. At Covent Garden the famous Cook reeled out on stage. The producer stepped up to the footlights: 'Mr Cook is taken ill'; the pit roared: 'No, no, he is drunk!' At the Haymarket Theatre a spectator in the gallery started to sing during a performance. There was a great deal of jeering, then he was left to carry on. When he had finished the stage business continued. English liberty. Shakespeare was performed with hornpipe interludes. The prompters were too loud. The King's birthday: thousands of carriages swarming about the entrance to the palace. The roar of the guns made one's ears ache. In the end, Arthur was glad to get to quiet Wimbledon, to the boarding school of the Reverend Lancaster. There, while his parents were travelling on to Scotland, he was to learn English. His parents had chosen this school because that old sea-dog Nelson had had his nephew educated there. That was an absolute recommendation. Arthur had to pay the price. School started and ended with prayers. Devotion was all-embracing. Prayers were said for all members of the royal family, for the pregnant and for nursing mothers, for the yet unborn and recently departed serene heads. Treatment of the pupils was mathematically just, a penal ritual of mechanical precision. There was a scale of flogging. The food was such as to make one want to give up eating altogether, and early in the morning the boys were chased into the bathing pool. Towels were in short supply. On Sundays one religious service followed another. First the students had to keep the reverend gentleman company as he rehearsed his sermon. Then they were allowed to hear that sermon once more in chapel. In the evening there was a third service, one virtually without end. It was too cold to sleep.

From Wimbledon Arthur wrote to his school friend Lorenz Meyer. He must have raved a good deal, for Meyer replied: 'I am sorry that your stay in England has induced you to hate the entire *nation*.'

His parents, to whom Arthur complained bitterly about the 'infamous bigotry' in that country, showed only limited understanding. Arthur had concluded his letter to Scotland with the sigh: 'If only Truth with her torch could burn through this Egyptian darkness in England' (CL, 1). His mother's reply began with some mild stylistic criticism: 'How can you expect Truth to do such a thing? Darkness can be . . . lightened, but surely . . . it cannot burn,' and then went on: 'You certainly are getting a generous helping of our dear Christianity . . . but I must nevertheless laugh at you a little, do you not remember the frequent struggle I . . . had with you when on Sundays and feast days you positively would not do anything useful because they were "days of rest" for you? And now you are getting more than your fill of Sunday rest.' Arthur made no friends in Wimbledon. Whenever possible he withdrew, played his flute, sketched, read, walked, and felt relieved when after three months, towards the end of September, he was allowed to return to London, where his parents had meanwhile arrived.

The Schopenhauers stayed on in London for more than a month. Eventually Arthur got bored there too. In November 1803 the family crossed back to the Continent. It was a stormy crossing, and Arthur was sick.

At the end of November the Schopenhauers arrived in Paris. Arthur was still blinded by London and did not feel that he was in the capital of the nineteenth century. Everything he saw and encountered – the promenades, the elegant townhouses and gardens, life in the streets – he compared with London. The English metropolis seemed to him more of a great city. Once one left the great Parisian boulevards behind in the evening, everything was immediately dark and dirty. Unpaved paths, gloomy façades without ornaments. And the ubiquitous milling crowds were absent. The small quarter of the Cité was surrounded by provincial life. The Schopenhauers were shown around by Louis-Sébastien Mercier, the famous author of the *Tableau de Paris*: no one could be better informed on the city. Mercier's passion was the archaeology of the recent past. He guided the Schopenhauers along the tracks of the Revolution: this was where the guillotine stood, over there the Bastille; here the Welfare Committee held its meetings, here Robespierre slept; this was the brothel patronized by Danton. Whole days were spent at the Louvre, which was overflowing with the art treasures Napoleon had looted from all over Europe. Egypt was the great fashion of the moment: it was not so long since Napoleon had returned from the Pyramids. In the great opera house *The Magic Flute* was performed with Egyptian décor. Some elegant gentlemen had taken to wearing red fezzes. The *dernier cri* had always been particularly shrill in Paris. But work was proceeding also for eternity: the Panthéon was nearing completion. Jean-Jacques Rousseau was the first to find a resting place there.

Arthur, on his own for a week, made a detour to Le Havre to visit the Grégoires and his boyhood friend Anthime. His travel diary records no details. The meeting with Anthime was something to be kept from the eyes of his parents.

At the end of January 1804 the Schopenhauers left Paris in the direction of Bordeaux. It was a journey into the past. They crossed an older France, where the Revolution had left fewer traces. It rained continuously. The roads were sodden. Often father and son had to help move stones out of the way. On one occasion a wheel broke. They had to walk for miles to get help. There was interminable waiting at the staging posts. There was a shortage of horses. In the region of Tours the travellers were persistently pestered by an 'unbearably importunate lot of women . . . who were selling knives' (TD, 116). Knives evidently were plentiful but foodstuffs were scarce. Provisions were stolen from the carriage. Between Poitiers and Angoulême marauding gangs were reported to be roaming the countryside. Locals warned against certain routes, but one could not be sure that this itself was not a trap. They passed picturesque villages, with houses clinging to the rocks: 'It seems as though the rock wanted to give birth to the house,' Arthur recorded (TP, 117). On 5 February, finally, the Schopenhauers safely reached Bordeaux, 'the most beautiful town in France' (TD, 122), as Arthur noted in his diary.

Two years earlier another stranger had reacted in the same way – Friedrich Hölderlin. He had arrived in Bordeaux on 28 January 1802 to take up the position of tutor in the house of the wine merchant and Hamburg Consul-General Daniel Christoph Meyer. This Meyer was an uncle of Arthur's schoolmate Lorenz Meyer. The Schopenhauers thus lodged in a house which Hölderlin had left in obscure circumstances two years earlier. Researchers to this day are still puzzled as to why, after a stay of only three months, Hölderlin took such precipitate leave of the Meyer household, a household in which he, like the Schopenhauers after him, had been very happy. 'I live almost too magnificently,' Hölderlin wrote to his mother, and ' "You will be happy here," said my Consul when welcoming me. I believe that he is right.' Whether it was some compromising love affair, or the news from Frankfurt that Susette Gontard was dying, or fits of insanity, that were the cause of Hölderlin's disappearance, we do not know. It is possible that the Schopenhauers, who were received with similar cordiality as Hölderlin was before them, were told the reason by the Meyers. But as Hölderlin at that time was still far from being a famous literary figure Arthur Schopenhauer made no mention of it.

The Schopenhauers stayed in Bordeaux for nearly two months. They witnessed the final days of the carnival, the milling of masked figures on the boulevards, the yelling, the fools' bells, whistling, drumming – and none of this quietened down even at night. The town was brimming over with southern *joie de vivre*, with the shedding of inhibitions, with violence and with obscenity. The carnival was the great equalizer. Common people swamped the better circles, where the Schopenhauers were on visiting terms. At the evening balls, Arthur observed, an aura of garlic would hang about. Even the theatre smelled like market stalls. In the evenings, when it got cooler, a spicy rosemary fire was lit in the fireplaces. The carnival was over and a thirty-day jubilee began, commemorating the restoration of religion. Catholic southern France heaved a sigh of relief; it was no longer necessary to sacrifice to the severe, undistinguished god of reason. The first procession since the Revolution turned into an intoxicating festivity. The whole town seemed to be on the move. Monstrances were carried about like trophies of victory. The smell of incense filled the streets; dragoons, pupils of the cadet school in full uniform, chanting canons, an army of priests, red, white, black, with silver crucifixes, had turned up. In front moved the purple of the high dignitaries, surrounded by awe-struck children; from the trees hung Chinese lanterns; windows and doors were decorated with greenery and branches. Sacred chants, shouts from the marketplace, the din of the musicians – the pious festival seemed to be a continuation of the carnival. Arthur enjoyed losing himself in this unaccustomed tumult of sensual metaphysics. And then spring erupted. Mild air, warm wind, opening buds, clouds in the sky like ornaments. Springtime in Bordeaux – in Hölderlin's words:

> But on holidays
> the brown women walk in that place
> on a silken floor,
> in the month of March,

when day and night are equal,
and over slow highways,
heavy with golden dreams,
lulling breezes travel.

Three days after the joyous fires of the equinox the Schopenhauers left Bordeaux 'in brilliant spring weather' (TD, 129), as Arthur recorded.

They travelled via Langon, Agen, Montauban to Toulouse, 'the most charming region in the world' (TD, 130). Plum trees in blossom, abandoned castles, ruined fortresses, ravaged monasteries along the road – the traces of most recent history. At St Feriol, at the basin of the Languedoc Canal, Arthur experienced the opening of the underground sluice-gate: 'It was as though destruction was falling upon worlds, I cannot compare that terrifying thunder and roar, that horrible howl, to anything else' (TD, 131). Schopenhauer subsequently clarified the impressions received there in his aesthetics lecture on the theory of the sublime. 'Of this frightful noise,' he expounded, 'it is impossible to form an idea, it is much louder than the Rhine Falls because it is in an enclosed space: to produce, no matter how, a sound that was still audible would be quite impossible: one feels as though one were totally and utterly annihilated by the monstrous din: but because, neverthe-less, one stands secure and unhurt, and because the whole thing takes place in the perception, the sense of the sublime arises in the highest degree' (LMA, 107).

Time and again he was fascinated by this aspect: the individual's eclipse before the almighty power of nature – and also by the no less overwhelming dimension of time. In Nîmes they visited the well-preserved ancient arena. Into those piles of stone visitors nearly two thousand years before had scratched their names, and perhaps even declarations of love. 'These traces,' Arthur noted in his diary, 'soon lead one's thoughts to the thousands of long-decomposed humans' (TD, 140). In Bordeaux it was the milling throng of the carnival, on the Languedoc Canal the roar of the volume of water, and in Nîmes the stony silence of time in which the significance of the individual seemed extinguished.

Marseilles was a ten-day stop for the Schopenhauers. Arthur roamed about the port. Several times he stood in front of the so-called 'Speaking House' – so called because from its balcony negotiations concerning preventive quaran-tine were conducted with the couriers of arriving ships. This was a regulation introduced after the last plague epidemic, a hundred years earlier. The inside of the house was filled with the smell of vinegar: every letter arriving from the quarantined section of the port would here be dipped in hot vinegar as a disinfectant. Fear of the Black Death was still haunting sunny Marseilles – a noteworthy circumstance for Arthur's passion for 'pondering on human misery', as his mother disapprovingly observed.

On the way to Toulon they visited the notorious fortress where Louis XIV kept for many years a state prisoner in detention – the mysterious, unidentified Man in the Iron Mask. For Arthur this was a mental preparation for the impressions he would gain in the great arsenal of Toulon, the quarters of the galley slaves. Visitors were admitted there as if to a zoo: the convicts were chained up but could be viewed. Anyone was bound to be seized with horror. Arthur's mother reflected in her travel account on what might happen if the slaves were to break out one day: 'a neighbourhood full of horror'. Arthur reacted differently. His imagination was stimulated not by fear for the intact world outside but by dismay at the pitiable world inside. 'They [the galley slaves] are divided into three classes,' he wrote in his diary on 8 April 1804; 'the first is made up of those who have committed only minor crimes and are here for a short time, deserters, soldiers guilty of insubordination, etc.: they only have an iron ring around one of their feet and walk about freely, i.e. within the arsenal, for no *forçat* is allowed into the city. The second category consists of major criminals: they work in twos, chained together by their feet with heavy chains. The third category, the most serious criminals, are forged to the benches of the galley which they do not leave at all: these are employed on such work as they can perform sitting down. The fate of these unfortunates seems to me far more terrible than a death sentence. The galleys, which I have seen from the outside, seem to be the dirtiest, the most revolting place of sojourn imaginable. The galleys no longer put out to sea; they are old condemned ships. The beds of the *forçats* are the benches to which they are chained. Their food is only water and bread, and I do not understand how, without more substantive nourishment and consumed by grief, they do not succumb to their heavy labour; for during their slavery they are treated entirely like beasts of burden: it is terrible to think that the life of these miserable galley slaves, if that is not an exaggerated word, is totally devoid of joy: and for those whose sufferings have no end even after twenty-five years, also totally devoid of hope: can one imagine a more terrible sensation than that of one of those wretches, chained to a bench in the dark galley, from which nothing but death can sever him! – For some perhaps his sufferings are made worse by the inseparable company of the one chained to him by the same chain. And when finally the moment arrives which he has longed for with desperate sighs for ten or twelve years: the end of his slavery: what is to become of him? He returns to a world for which he has been dead for ten years: what prospects he might have had when he was ten years younger have vanished; no one wants to take in anyone coming from the galley: and ten years of punishment have not purged him of a moment's crime. He is bound to become a criminal for a second time and to end up on the gallows – I had a shock when I heard that there were six thousand galley slaves here. The faces of these men might provide appropriate material for physiognomical reflections' (TD, 155).

Arthur Schopenhauer attached more than mere physiognomical reflections to these impressions. The arsenal of Toulon left in him a supply of garish images, to which he was to refer back later in elucidating, in his *Metaphysics of the Will*, the fettering of individual existence and reason to the anonymous will to live: we are all galley slaves of the will that passes through us. Before all reason we are chained to a blind urge of self-assertion. The chain from which we are dangling simultaneously links us to our fellow men. Any movement we make ultimately causes pain to another being.

In Toulon, Arthur experienced that captivity from outside, as a kind of spectacle approached by an observer. But if captivity is universal, where then is the point of the observer? Where is there an outside? How can the universal become a spectacle? To this question Arthur Schopenhauer would subsequently give a very delicate answer, an answer formulated in the language of subject philosophy, of Buddhism, of Pietist mysticism and of Platonism: there is a transcendental immanence, there is a super-earthly height without a heaven, there is divine ecstasy without God: the ecstasy of pure cognition is possible; the will can turn against itself; it burns in itself and becomes all eye: it no longer *is*, it only *sees*.

Still on his tour young Arthur Schopenhauer found occasion to experience the first models of such metaphysics of height. These were experiences of height in the literal sense.

Three times on his journey Arthur climbed a mountain: first the Chapeau near Chamonix, then Mount Pilatus, and finally the Schneekoppe in the Bohemian Giant Mountains. Each time he wrote an extensive report in his diary. The entries are high flights stylistically as well. Whereas normally he recorded his experiences with what could be a good deal of dutiful pedantry, these accounts of his climbs vibrate with the sense of an overwhelming experience, lending the report vigour and splendour.

First the ascent of the Chapeau. His way led him past an extensive glacier massif known as the *Mer de glace*. It was furrowed by rifts and crevasses, and at times masses of ice hurtled thunderously into the abyss. 'This spectacle, the sight of the huge masses of ice, the booming crashes, the roaring torrents, the rocks all round with waterfalls, up above the floating summits and snow-capped mountains, all this bears an indescribably wonderful imprint, one sees the enormity of nature, it is no longer everyday nature here, it has stepped out of its bounds, one feels one is closer to it' (TD, 186).

This was an ennobling, a proud proximity; up there like and like were joined, down below were everyday things. Whoever climbs a mountain seeks nature at its best, but also at its most merciless, when anything human is rejected. 'In striking contrast to this sublime grand view was the laughing valley far below!' (TD, 186). Up there, where Arthur stood, there was nothing to laugh about. Man is eclipsed, nature can step out of its 'bounds'. Whoever stands up to it passes the test of heroic solitude.

All this, of course, is still half play-acting; there was no real danger about this mountain tour. The height reached was considerable only to a lowlander. But realism is of no importance here. Arthur Schopenhauer experienced the mountain as meaning. Scenery gave him an experience, and his experience chose a *definite* scenery: that of height.

Three weeks later, on 3 June 1804, he climbed Mount Pilatus with a guide. 'I felt dizzy as I cast a glance at the crowded space I had before me. . . . I find that such a panorama from a high mountain enormously contributes to the broadening of concepts. It is so utterly different from any other view that it is impossible, without having seen it, to gain a clear idea of it. All small objects disappear, only what is big retains its shape. Everything blends; one sees not a multitude of small separate objects but one big colourful radiant picture, on which the eye lingers with pleasure' (TD, 219).

Arthur sees what is flattering to him. What is small disappears, blends, swarms. One is no longer part of it. What is big retains its shape. And he who views what is big and is removed from the swarm, is great himself. One is no longer tied to 'separate objects', one is now only an 'eye' resting on a 'colourful radiant picture'. Later, Schopenhauer would call this distant-view enjoyment the 'world eye'.

Finally, on 30 July 1804 – the journey was nearing its end – came the ascent of the Schneekoppe. It was a two-day excursion. At the foot of the peak Arthur and his guide spent the night at a chalet: 'We entered a room full of carousing servants. . . . It was unbearable; their animalic warmth . . . gave off a glowing heat' (TD, 265). The 'animalic warmth' of humans crowding together – later Arthur Schopenhauer would find for this the image of porcupines huddling together against cold and fear.

Having torn himself away from the spiky proximity of humans, Arthur reached the peak of the mountain at sunrise. 'Like a transparent ball and much less radiant than when one views it from below, the sun floated up and cast its first rays on us, mirrored itself first in our delighted glances, below us in the whole of Germany it was still night; and as it rose higher we watched the night creeping back lower and eventually yielding also down below' (TD, 266).

He was already in the light while down below darkness still reigned. 'One sees the world in chaos below one.' On top, however, all is of incisive clarity. And when the sun finally lights up the valley, it does not discover there smiling, delightful plains but offers to the gaze 'the eternal repetition and the eternal alternation of mountains and valleys, forests and meadows and towns and villages' (TD, 266).

Why then undergo the hardships of descent? Eventually, however, it grew too cold at the top. In the chalet on the mountainside was a book in which hikers could leave their names for posterity. Arthur's entry has been found there:

> Who can climb
> And remain silent?
>
> Arthur Schopenhauer from Hamburg.

CHAPTER FOUR

A FATHER'S GHOST

After the ecstasies of height came the hardships of the plain. The lowlands were beckoning. At the end of the journey lay the menace of the *Comptoir*, where the devil was waiting for the globetrotter's soul, first in the shape of the merchant magnate Kabrun in Danzig (September 1804 to December 1804), and then in that of Senator Jenisch in Hamburg.

The final weeks of the tour were already overshadowed by these gloomy prospects. This emerges from the style of Arthur's notes in his travel diary. With the exception of the account of his climb in the Giant Mountains the entries seem cursory, listless, mechanical. The final entry of 25 August 1804 reads: 'In coelo quies. Tout finis ici bas – Calm reigns in heaven. Down here all is ending.'

From Berlin his father returned to Hamburg, while Arthur and his mother travelled to Danzig. Johanna wished to visit her relations; Arthur was to be confirmed at his place of birth and to acquire his first commercial knowledge in Kabrun's firm.

The worldwide horizon had shrunk to the scale of ledgers and bills of exchange. Where could one turn for the adventures of the mind, where direct the curiosity of the eyes in those narrow rooms with their dry-as-dust atmosphere? Under this yoke it would be easy to ruin one's posture. His father, however, having forced him into that yoke, did not want a crippled son. In faulty German he reproved him: 'I will therefore rely on my request to make sure that you do not acquire a round back, which looks ghastly. Good posture at the stand-up writing desk is equally necessary as in ordinary life; for if, in the dining rooms, one catches sight of someone stooping, one takes him for a disguised cobbler or tailor.' And again, in his last letter on 20 November 1804, the father urged his son: 'And with reference to walking and sitting upright. I advise you to request everyone you are with to give you a blow whenever you are caught oblivious of this great matter. This is what children of princes have done, not minding the pain for a short time, rather than appear as oafs all their lives.'

His father, probably suspecting that his son's stooping attitude had something to do with the grief he had caused him by articling him as a trainee merchant, advised riding and dancing as a compensation. Arthur did not have to be told twice and evidently overindulged in these pleasures, for his father reproved him: 'Dancing and riding do not make a livelihood for a merchant whose letters have to be read and must therefore be well written. Now and again I find that the capital letters in your hand are still veritable monstrosities.'

His irritation was making Arthur unsociable. That, too, was criticized by his father: 'I wish you learned to make yourself agreeable to people; for thus you would quite easily induce Herr Kabrun to talk more at table.'

His father in Hamburg, of course, was only able to criticize Arthur's behaviour because his mother in her (non-extant) letters was complaining about him. Altogether the clique of relations in Danzig was not sparing in criticism of Arthur. Aunt 'Julchen', his mother's sister, urged him in almost identical terms: 'You should therefore accept people as they are. And not be too severe. You would gain by making yourself more agreeable to others and you would certainly be much more cheerful yourself.' In mid-December 1804 Arthur changed his slave-driver. Mother and son returned to Hamburg, where Arthur continued his period of apprenticeship with Senator Jenisch.

In an ironical turn of events, just as the son was forcing himself into his father's world, the father himself began to drift away from it. The first symptoms of his mental and physical decline appeared. The carping and brusque manner of his last letters to his son may have been aspects of this condition.

Instances were now occurring of his father's loss of memory. A friend of the family, who had shown Heinrich Floris Schopenhauer many a kindness during his stay in London, visited him towards the end of 1804, to be received with: 'I don't know you! Lots of people come here and say I am so-and-so – I don't wish to know about you.' An assistant ran after the startled caller to apologize for his employer.

In the winter of 1804 Heinrich Floris fell ill with jaundice. Wearily he spent his days in an armchair. He was also plagued by business worries. His trade was being affected by the Continental Blockade. His long absence during his European tour had likewise not benefited his business. Suspiciously he would rummage among his account books and balance sheets. The old spirit of enterprise, which had helped him to succeed in Danzig, was gone. His friends in Hamburg were shocked to see this once impressive man age so rapidly. The journey evidently had taken its toll of his reserves of strength. He was tired – and this must have pained him doubly as he observed his wife's vivacity. Several times during their journey she had complained in her letters of her husband's ponderousness. The gap between their ages was making itself felt more strongly now – and there was no sentiment of love to cushion this strain. 'As you know,' Johanna had written to Arthur in Wimbledon in 1803, 'your father is not fond of meeting new people, and thus I have not had much company except my own.' And in another letter: 'You know very well how your father is fond of worrying when there is no cause to worry. . . . I am busy staying at home because I do not know where to go, and meanwhile I declaim the popular verb, je m'ennuie, tu t'ennuies, etc.' That was what Johanna wrote from Scotland; back in Hamburg she knew 'where to go' and how to fight her boredom. Forty-five years later Arthur Schopenhauer was to blame her harshly for it. 'I know what women are like. They regard marriage solely as an institution to provide for them. As my own father was sick, and miserably tied to his invalid's chair, he would have been abandoned had not an old servant performed for him a so-called service of love. My dear mother gave parties while he was perishing in solitude, and amused herself while he was suffering bitter agonies. That is women's love for you' (C, 152).

This was written from the perspective of his later estrangement from his mother, and it is surely an unfair judgement. After all, what else was Johanna doing but refusing to sacrifice her own *joie de vivre*? She did not wish to be swallowed up in the depressive morass in which her husband was in danger of drowning. She was trying to bring life, diversion and activity into her home. She was doing it to please herself, but she was hoping at the same time to provide comfort and support for her husband.

Arthur was probably watching his mother's demeanour with such disapproval because he was envious; after all, unlike his mother, he was sacrificing his own life to his father's wishes. This might have been something to be proud of, but such pride was undermined by self-doubt: did not the compliance with which he set out on a life he knew was wrong for him also reveal weakness? Arthur, who did not rebel against his father's world, opted for the contrivances of a double existence. He resorted to secrecy. He would hide, in his business office, the books to which he devoted himself in unsupervised moments. When the famous phrenologist Gall was giving some lectures in Hamburg about his cranial theory, Arthur used a white lie to get time off to attend the lectures. 'There never was . . . a person less dedicated to business than myself,' he concluded later (CL, 651); his double life, moreover, had made him 'unadaptable and troublesome to others'. Others, under a similar compulsion to lead a double life, might become gamblers and masters at managing their lives, such as E. T. A. Hoffmann. Not so Arthur Schopenhauer. He internalized his father's weighty authority. He felt any momentary breakout from his 'wrong way of life' as a deception and a treason against his father. His secret thoughts, fantasies and literary experiences were accompanied by remorse.

On the morning of 20 April 1805 Heinrich Floris Schopenhauer was found dead in the Fleet behind the warehouse section of his residence. The sick man would have had no reason to visit the warehouse loft from which he had tumbled down. Numerous indications suggested suicide. But that was unacceptable. The official notice sent out by his widow Johanna Schopenhauer limited itself to the phrase: 'I hereby discharge my sad duty of informing my relations and friends of the death of my husband . . . caused by an unfortunate accident, and request them to desist from any condolences which would only increase my sorrow.' Arthur, too, in his curriculum drafted fifteen years later, remained similarly vague: 'My beloved father, that best of fathers was abruptly snatched from me by a sudden accidental and bloody death' (CL, 651). The subject of the cause of death remained taboo for a long time even between mother and son. But when their ties finally broke in 1819, this delicate event erupted between them with wounding violence. In a letter Arthur evidently accused his mother of being responsible for his father's suicide. His sister Adele recorded in her diary: 'She [their mother] found the letter, read it unprepared, and a horrible scene followed. She talked of my father – I learned the dreadfulness that I had suspected, she was beside herself.' Adele was so shattered that she wanted to jump from the window herself, but at the last moment thought better of it.

To outsiders Arthur Schopenhauer would all his life be very vague about his father's death. Only *vis-à-vis* his young admirer Robert von Hornstein, in 1855, does he seem to have been less circumlocutory. 'He blamed his mother for his father's suicide,' Hornstein noted in his memoirs.

Heinrich Floris Schopenhauer's death – there can be no doubt about it – ultimately meant liberation not only for Johanna but also for Arthur, even though he never admitted it. His letters to his friend Anthime in Le Havre, who had likewise lost his father the year before, abound with expressions of grief. Anthime consoled him and cautiously advised him to moderate himself a little. On 15 May 1805 he wrote: 'On such cruel occasions courage is needed; but one should also try to bear one's misfortune patiently by reflecting that there are others even more unfortunate than oneself.' Four months later, when Arthur evidently was still inconsolable, Anthime wrote: 'It is my wish that your grief might have moderated, now that you have paid nature its due of the mourning that every good son owes to the memory of a venerable father, and that you might have begun to face your grief more philosophically.'

Arthur's mourning for his father conceals a subtle mixture of emotions. Had he loved his father? He certainly was convinced of it, even though he confessed later: 'Admittedly during my upbringing I had to suffer a good deal from my father's hardness' (C, 131). The hardest thing his father had been able to inflict on him was forcing him into a commercial apprenticeship. Arthur might have hated him for that. Had his father lived on, it is unlikely that Arthur would have embarked on a career as a philosopher. Even his dead father was powerful enough to prevent him from doing so for the time being. Arthur stayed on at Jenisch's office, more desperate than ever. Sorrow over his father's death and despair at his continuing power blended into each other. In his curriculum vitae, written in 1819, this is formulated as follows: 'Although, in a manner of speaking, I was my own master, and although my mother was not standing in my way, I continued to hold my position with my merchant patron, partly because my excessive grief had broken the energy of my spirit, partly because I would have had a guilty conscience were I to rescind my father's decisions so soon after his death' (CL, 651).

His mother was not only 'not standing in his way' but indirectly even encouraging her son to plan his life anew, quite simply by drastically changing her own lifestyle. She demonstrated a freer spirit than her son: four months after Heinrich Floris Schopenhauer's death she sold the impressive house on the Neuer Wandrahm and started on the liquidation of the business. It was a fateful decision, which relieved Arthur of a heavy burden. Arthur's continued apprenticeship for the hated career of merchant made sense only if it led to his succession to the parental business, to the continuation of the family tradition. Once the firm was no longer in existence, Arthur could consider himself released from his bond. By freeing herself of her past, Arthur's mother also removed his chains, or at least the external ones; internally Arthur remained under the spell of his father's world.

Johanna, on the other hand, acted – move by move, with great energy, as though she were reborn. She rented a new apartment at the other end of the city – a provisional solution because she intended to leave Hamburg as soon as the firm was liquidated. In May 1806 she travelled to Weimar in order to look for a new place to live. Why Weimar? Johanna wished to be close to the serene heads of cultural life. She wanted to test her social talents on Mount Olympus. She was swept along by an unparalleled élan: after a mere ten days she wrote to her dejected son in Hamburg: 'Existence here appears to me to be very agreeable and not at all expensive, with little trouble and even less expense it will be easier for me to assemble around my tea table, at least once a week, the leading minds in Weimar, and perhaps in Germany, and generally lead a very pleasant life.'

Johanna was about to conquer a new world, while Arthur was still deeply stuck in the old one, into which his father had thrust him.

'Through this pain my sadness deepened to such an extent that it was scarcely distinguishable from real melancholia,' Schopenhauer wrote in retrospect about the time after his father's death (CL, 651).

The anatomy of that melancholia was complex. At its core was an irreconcilable rift between the internal and the external world. Externally Arthur was fulfilling the duties imposed on him by his father. He might be able to preserve his inner life, if only he were allowed to despise his father's world in which he was obliged to act. For that, however, he would have to be able to rise above his father. Kant, whom Arthur had not then read, passed this judgement on melancholia: 'Melancholic withdrawal from the noise of the world, out of justified weariness, is noble.' Arthur's inner withdrawal from the 'noise' of his paternal world may have been melancholic, but he would not have perceived it as being 'noble' because – at least for the time being – he could not admit to himself that his world-weariness was 'justified'. He could not defiantly insist that what separated him from the external world of business was a reality of a higher order. It would have been presumption towards his father, a lack of filial piety. In this situation he must have regarded as very attractive a mental attitude which combined internalization, scepticism *vis-à-vis* the world and filial devotion. Arthur was reading Matthias Claudius, whose interpretation of self and the world had the advantage of reflecting the painful dualism between the internal and external world in a manner which had been expressly approved by his father. For Heinrich Floris Schopenhauer had himself given Arthur the little book which he was to treasure to the end of his life and in which he was to read frequently; this was the brief essay *An meinen Sohn* (*To My Son*), published in 1799. Claudius had not shrunk from conveying his intimate injunctions to his son by way of the open market. Soul guidance among sensitive persons was then a public affair. Heinrich Floris Schopenhauer gratefully seized the opportunity to try to influence his son, even though with a borrowed voice. And, after his father's death, the son read the little book like a legacy. 'The time is slowly approaching,' he read in Claudius, 'when I must go the way from which one does not walk back. I cannot take thee with me; I leave thee behind in a world where good advice is not superfluous.' Claudius can advise only those who consider themselves strangers in a reality that imposes external duties on them. Hence Arthur might feel that he was being addressed. 'Man is not at home here,' Claudius writes. If one feels a stranger in the world, then it is not because there is an inner treasure with which one might exalt oneself. The internal, which by its own right opposes itself to the external, is presumptuous. We are all sinners, and such dualism is the sin of vanity. We are strangers in this world, according to Claudius, because we are not of this world, and because we are called to higher things. But this is not our own merit but a gift of grace received by sentiment. By a devout heart we are relieved of the crushing burden of earthly bustle. Such devoutness, however, is left behind in lowland skirmishing. It is not for us to look down upon this world; instead we must pay it the necessary tribute.

The sometimes twisted and tormented overcoming of the world by early Pietism is softened by Matthias Claudius to an attitude of retarded cooperation at an inner distance: possess as though one does not possess; one must not try to escape the world but equally one must not pin one's heart to it. This 'lad of innocence', as Herder once called Matthias Claudius, occasionally speaks with almost the same scepticism as the elegant French moralists who were subsequently to inspire Schopenhauer. 'Be honest towards everybody, but be slow to trust yourself,' we read there; or 'Mistrust gesticulation and disport yourself just as the spirit moves you'; or 'Do not say everything that you know, but always know what you say'; or 'Do not attach yourself to any Great one.' A compromise has to to be made with reality, a compromise which protects one against its presumption. Outside, one performs the inevitable commitments with the greatest caution, but internally one remains a participant of another world, where the 'noise of the street' falls silent. This well-concealed inner world thus becomes an 'enduring wall on which the shadows pass by'. That seems acceptable: Arthur's misery in the counting-house a mere shadow play? This strategy of derealization of life's hardships strips the disease of dualism of anything rebellious. The inner transcendence of the world, which Claudius offers, enjoys divine blessing, as well as – more important to Arthur at the moment – that of his recently dead father.

Arthur was bound to wish for an interpretation of his life's reality that would help him to eliminate the dualism he experienced between the internal and the external, between duty and inclination. He would certainly seek such an interpretation so long as, for whatever reason, he did not succeed in moulding for himself a homogenous life, and in implementing it. The scepticism based on religious-sentimental internalization, as offered by Matthias Claudius, might well be such an interpretation. In it, however, the dualism is totally occupied by the paternal world: not only the reality principle but also whatever opposes it is coded entirely paternally. The internally experienced, received, God that Claudius speaks about is, though paternal, still held as a mental reservation *vis-à-vis* Arthur's father's world. Cooperation is a duty to his father, and the slowing-down of such cooperation by an internalized religious reservation is the kind of aloof distance conceded to Arthur by his father. With Matthias Claudius, in consequence, Arthur remained in thrall to his father.

Lacking the strength to change his life (even though his mother was setting him a living example of just that), Arthur at that time was questing for an inner transcendence of the world. In Matthias Claudius he had found a method of derealizing the burdens of his life, but it could be effective only if one really believed in the God of one's fathers. 'Whatever you can see,' Matthias Claudius wrote, 'see it, and use thine eyes, and concerning the invisible and eternal hold to God's word.'

Arthur had been using his eyes – especially on his grand tour – and what he had seen had by no means convinced him of the existence of an ordering, just, loving God. The mountain peaks had intoxicated him not because he was nearer to God there but because he was further removed from the human throng. He was seeking not humble love of God but world-overflying sovereignty.

In retrospect Arthur Schopenhauer asserted that his belief in God had collapsed even at the time when he was reading Matthias Claudius as a bequest from his father: 'As a young man I was always very melancholic, and on one occasion, I was perhaps eighteen years old then, I reflected, even at that early age: This world is supposed to have been made by a God? No, much rather by a devil' (C, 131).

This was the ancient theodicy problem, which Arthur Schopenhauer claimed had disturbed him as an eighteen-year-old, the problem which Leibniz believed he had formulated with acute precision and solved: Is the existence of evil and of a multitude of wrongs in the world not proof against the existence of an all-powerful loving God?

The fact that such questions were even posed betrays the influence of a way of thinking that made recognition of a divine Being dependent on rational or empirical justifications. Thus Leibniz resorted to his mathematical world model for his 'solution' of the problem: each element is in itself incomplete, yet perfectible, i.e. within the framework of a sensible combination of the elements it becomes a perfect functional context. Evil in the world is what, in a clockwork mechanism, is achieved by the retaining and therefore tensioning spring. Without resistance no progress. Without shadow no light. Voltaire and others, for instance, were unable, with the best will in the world, to discover any 'sense' in the Lisbon earthquake which buried several thousand human beings. They radicalized the rational discourse and introduced strict method into empirical experience, with the result that the God presented as the architect and helmsman of the world found himself in increasing straits. There was no holding the drama of secularization. Was it replayed once more, at an accelerated rate, in young Arthur Schopenhauer, who was just then reading Matthias Claudius? Or did Schopenhauer attempt, in retrospect, to raise his mind to the level of the great epoch-making problems of the Western spirit?

We do, in fact, even in very early notes (about 1807), find subtle discussions of the theodicy problem. 'Either everything is perfect, the Greatest as much as the Smallest . . . then every pain, every error, every fear . . . would have to be the immediate, only right corrective . . .; or else – and who could stop at this assumption in view of this world? – there are only two possible alternatives: we have to postulate – unless we assume everything to be directed to an evil purpose – the existence, alongside the good will, of an evil power which compels the former into detours, or we have to ascribe that power to chance, which means ascribing to the guiding Will imperfection in its dispositions or in its power' (P 1, 9).

Without having yet studied Leibniz, Schopenhauer rejected his theorem of the 'best of all possible worlds'. That was possible only because the spirit of the age had by then written off the great Leibniz as old hat and allowed an under-age apprentice merchant to dismiss him.

Equally, however, Schopenhauer rejected the demonology that had been mobilized against Leibniz, the inverted God who arranged everything for the worst. It is hardly surprising that, tormented by the dualism of his own situation, he favoured the dualist solution in his reflection of the theodicy: there is an antagonism between a good and an evil world will and the good is victorious only by roundabout routes, or else there is an antagonism between good will and chance – a variant of the first alternative, as 'chance' is the evil element without features or shape, the negation of order.

Even in their historical beginnings the theodicean reflections were an attempt to offset, by cool reasoning, the pain at the disappearance of an ardent religious sentiment. The emotional background of the theodicy discourses was anxiety. Reason was to re-supply what one was about to lose.

Many regarded this as a wrong road even then. Pascal, for instance, found an intimidated internal world behind the façade of ostentatious reason, which believed it could summon God or bow him out of the world. Pascal declared that God was not to be found in rational discourse; he pleaded for a radical separation of faith and knowledge: the two, he argued, were of disparate origin and did not relate to any common territory. Anyone mixing the two worlds, Pascal said, was perverting both of them, muddying knowledge and confusing the 'order of the heart', the real bastion of faith; in other words, knowledge puffed itself up because the strength for religious experience was waning.

But Pascal was himself drifting in the current of secularization: his faith was a faith in faith, a will to faith, stemming from the misery of existential homelessness in an environment of rationalism and empiricism.

The deduction of a God from the construct of a world model, or, the other way about, the denial of his existence by means of such models, could not touch upon the core of the religious problem of life. This was true also of young Arthur Schopenhauer. His dethronement of God by a dualist construction (God has to fight with evil or with chance) did not correspond to his real sentiment. He would have liked to believe in a God who surrounded the individual with his attention and carried him along, which was why Matthias Claudius's childlike faith represented to him not only a paternal prison but also an allurement.

But the naivety of the parental faith was gone; Schopenhauer himself discovered in the emotional background of the theodicy discourse no longer faith, but only a will to faith. 'Deep down in man lies a trust,' he wrote, 'that something apart from him is as aware of him as he is himself; the alternative, vividly imagined alongside infinity, is a terrifying thought' (P I, 8). He did not have to imagine the 'alternative', he had experienced it himself, though not at first as exalted metaphysical solitude but as the solitude of an unloved child. 'Even as a child of six,' we read in Schopenhauer's later intimate memoir *Eis Eauton*, 'my parents, returning from a walk one evening, found me in deep despair because suddenly I thought I had been abandoned by them for ever' (P IV, 2, 121).

In a poem dating from that period, when Schopenhauer was engaged in his theodicean reflections, reading Matthias Claudius and pondering the will to faith, the two intermingle: the 'small' fear of the abandoned child and the 'great' fear of metaphysical homelessness.

> In the middle of a stormy night
> I woke in great fear,
> Heard the storm, the howling outside
> Through yards and halls and towers;
> . . .
> But no gleam, no faint glow

Could pierce the deep night.
As though it could not yield to any sun,
It lay solid and impenetrable,
So I believed day would never dawn:
Then very great fear gripped me,
I felt so anxious, so alone and abandoned.

[P I, 5]

This limping poem was written by Arthur Schopenhauer at about the time that the *Nachtwachen des Bonaventura* (*The Nocturnal Vigils of Bonaventura*) appeared, a work which, initially unnoticed, revealed the nihilistic undercurrent of the Romantic movement and simultaneously parodied it. The fears, but also the promises, of the night enjoyed a boom. The fearful visions of night were those in which darkness stood for an absence of meaning and orientation. Needless to say, night also dominated Jean Paul's nightmarish sequence *Speech by the Dead Christ from the World's Edifice that there is no God*, and the whole of Hölderlin's poetical work revolved around the 'night of the gods'.

'The night is silent and almost terrible,' we read in *Bonaventura*, 'and cold death stands in it, like an invisible ghost which holds on to the overcome life. Now and then a frozen raven falls from the church roof . . .'

In the past night could be successfully faced with the torches of the old faith or of the new reason. When Schopenhauer wrote his night poem a mere ten years had passed since the Romantic eruption began by facing the nocturnal element not only with anxiety but with enthusiastic ravings. A new source of light had been discovered: music and poetry, which offered reconciliation with night because they themselves radiated a peculiar darkness.

The news of this 'discovery' also reached Arthur Schopenhauer. Because, to cope with his misery, he was reading not only Matthias Claudius but also, for instance, the writings of Wilhelm Heinrich Wackenroder, published by Ludwig Tieck in 1797 and 1799.

Wackenroder was the comet of the Romantic religion of art. He spread a magic brilliance, a nocturnal splendour, but was soon extinguished. By the time Tieck published his writings Wackenroder, having died at the age of twenty-six, had long been dead. Wackenroder and the Romantic movement had proceeded from a similar problem as young Arthur Schopenhauer did ten years later: the young generation, dropped out from the old faith, unsatisfied by reason, and encouraged by the historic turning point of the French Revolution to indulge in the boldest flights of imagination, was painfully aware of the unsatisfactory nature of a normality it experienced as the crushing inheritance of its partly rational and partly pious, or perhaps simply unimaginative and uncourageous, fathers. These young escapees from the humdrum mill of bourgeois everyday life were seeking a refuge, and they found the new God of art. Wackenroder, too, was such a seeker of refuge. His father, Secret War Counsellor and Juridical Burgomeister in Berlin, was a respectable civil servant and hoped to make his son into just such another. The son, along with his friend Tieck, indulged in fantasies about art, but nevertheless got stuck in the dualism. He was not carved out to be a good-for-nothing. A contemporary said of him: 'As if dimly suspecting that this inner world required an external counterweight unless he was to be totally lost in it, he clung anxiously to certain forms of order. Once they had become a routine, he never abandoned them again. Anyone seeing him at such moments might think him sober or indeed pedantic. His father's bourgeois nature then appeared to be dominant. . . . Music, above all else, seemed to pervade his entire being. Some electrical substance had accumulated here, waiting only for the right kind of touch in order to blind by its shower of sparks.'

Young Schopenhauer likewise clung anxiously to 'certain forms of order' and enjoyed dwelling under the shower of sparks of Romantic artistic and musical fantasies. The most famous, very soon even 'classic', parable of Romantic yearning for salvation was the story *Ein wunderbares morgenländisches Märchen von einem nackten Heiligen* (*A Wondrous Oriental Fairy-Tale of a Naked Saint*). Well into the late part of his life Schopenhauer was to draw on the imagery of this text. The saint in the story incessantly hears 'the wheel of Time spinning with a roar' and is thus obliged to perform the violent movements of a man 'endeavouring to turn an enormous wheel'. One summer's night he finds his salvation through the song of a pair of lovers: 'With the first note of the music and the song the roaring wheel of Time had vanished for the naked saint.' Music, poetry and love, the heavenly powers of the new generation, offered salvation from the 'wheels' of a prosaic daily routine, from the 'monotonous, rhythmical roar' of empty Time. In Schopenhauer's philosophy we shall subsequently encounter the 'wheel of the Will', to which we are bound and by which we are driven round, and there is also the sudden arrest of this motion by immersion in works of art.

At the time when he read the Romantics young Arthur Schopenhauer noted in his diary: 'Take away from life the few moments of religion, art and pure love, and what is left but a series of trivial thoughts?' (P 1, 10).

Religion here still figures as a power of salvation, but in its Romantic conjunction with 'art' and 'love' it is a different religion from that of the fathers. Matthias Claudius, for instance, always vehemently objected to art and religion being mentioned in the same breath. That was why he opposed the Romantic movement as a modern veneration of idols. And from his point of view ('keep to the Word of God') the worthy fellow was right. For the Romantic religion was a religion not of humility and belief in revelation, but one of self-empowering, of the numerous facets of an unleashed imagination. One has to understand the inner dynamics of Romantic religiosity if one wishes to understand how and why Arthur embraced it.

If, like Schopenhauer, one is stuck in one's father's earthly life, then it is most important that one should at least get over the fatherly concept of the Beyond (Matthias Claudius). Romantic religion and art religion (especially Wackenroder's metaphysics of music) were young Schopenhauer's trailblazers in this respect. By allowing himself to be swept along some distance by this current he emancipated himself to some degree from his father's religion. From a paternally legitimate transcendence he drifted into a paternally illegitimate one. In doing so he copied as an individual the destinies of an epochal spiritual movement, one which, in view of its irretrievability, is being called here the wild years of philosophy.

They had begun with the Kantian revolution, with the demagification of traditional metaphysics, the erosion of traditional faith, with the pragmatic empowering of the subject and with the diversion of curiosity from the 'world in itself' to the production patterns of a 'world for myself'. The old 'order of things' (Foucault) broke up with Kant and gave birth to that modernity whose magic we may have lost but which we have still not overcome.

Not until later would Schopenhauer advance to the caesura associated with Kant's name; but even then he was totally enveloped by the atmosphere of that upheaval: in his encounter with Romanticism he had already come up against one aspect of its epoch-making effect. In a manner of speaking, the second or third act of the great drama was already being enacted when Schopenhauer decided to participate. That is not without significance: moving backwards, via Romanticism, he would arrive at Kant, and having arrived there he would perform a revision of the action which his successors had laid against Kant. In doing so. he was being driven forward, with the thrust of Buddhist and mystical esotericism, beyond Fichte, Hegel and Marx, right into a transcendence without a heaven, into a radically completed 'analysis of finiteness' (Foucault), which, however, accomplished the trick of not surrendering its metaphysics.

Meanwhile, however, during his final two years in Hamburg, Schopenhauer shared in the infinite flights of Romanticism. The infinity of Romantic art, however, lacked the opportunity for 'objective' revelation, in which Matthias Claudius and Arthur's father had believed. Romantic infinity was subjective through and through, an infinity to which one surrendered by creating it, or which one at least accepted in the belief that one might create it. There was altogether nothing that one could not create with the aid of an unleashed imagination: that was the conviction of the Romantic spirit of the age.

By peering into their own mystery the Romantics believed they could touch upon the mystery of the world. The world would sing if one found the magic formula within oneself. One could not descend deeply enough. Such descents were the true upsurges. The trapdoor led to the centre of a magnetic field of force. At that point reeling reason learned how to dance. At the point where the ineffable begins within us, we are most intimate with the world. Here the

Romantic scepticism towards language begins. To Wackenroder it is the 'grave of the heart's inner raging'. In language the ineffable easily becomes unutterable. Language cannot follow the flow of emotions. It has to replace the richness of the simultaneous by the thin thread of the consecutive. To Novalis, indeed, the modern fall from grace began with Luther's translation of the Bible. It inaugurated, he argued, the age of the tyranny of the letter. Imagination and inner meaning had been put under tutelage and had forgotten how to soar. Novalis, like Wackenroder, praised 'holy music'. In it everything was still able to move, with it one could acquire the metaphysics of floating. Wackenroder, still on a small scale, speculated about individual salvation through music. Novalis went for the whole, and with his 'holy music' hoped to save Europe from its hostilities and platitudes. The self-assurance of Beethoven, who regarded General Bonaparte as an equal and the Emperor Napoleon as a defector, moved entirely at the height of such ambitions. Not only Wagner, but Beethoven before him, regarded himself as a kind of founder of a religion. To him music was 'mediation of the divine and a higher revelation than all wisdom and philosophy'. Later on, in dealing with Schopenhauer's philosophy of music, we shall return to this exalted Romantic intoxication with music.

Access to the ineffable within us, and hence to the mystery of the world – in the view of the Romantic spirit – is enjoyed primarily through music and religion. They are equally primordial. Even half a century earlier this would have been regarded as a blasphemous statement. But secularization and the liberation of a self-empowered subject had shattered the old heaven, to which music had looked up and from which religion received its revelations. Now the two – music and religion – were products of our imagination which, arising from the ineffable, represented a divine force, a divinity from below. The contemporary philosopher Jacobi, who disliked the whole movement, very shrewdly laid bare the simple alternative: 'God is outside me, a living Being existing on its own, or else I am God.' The Romantics opted for their own divinity. Schleiermacher declared: 'Not he has religion who believes in some holy scripture, but he who needs no holy scripture or might well produce such scripture himself.'

This extravagant religion, pouring forth from the individual's sensitivity, fascinated Schopenhauer because it represented not a paternal body of revelations and moral norms but a pattern of experiences of self and the world that could be aesthetically enjoyed. In the boarding-house of the insurance broker Willinck, where he was lodging after his mother's move to Weimar, he surrendered to Romantic, heaven-ascending moods – admittedly at a time when their spokesmen were about to begin their 'salto mortale into the abyss of divine mercy' (Friedrich Schlegel). The trend was now reverting to the ecclesiastical faith from which Schopenhauer wished to break free. In Wackenroder he read: 'One must with courageous arm reach through the pile of rubble into which our life is being crumbled, in order to hold on powerfully to art, to the great and enduring that extends beyond everything into eternity, which offers us its radiant hand down from heaven, so that in bold attitude we float above the wild abyss, between heaven and earth!' To his mother in Weimar Schopenhauer wrote: 'How did the heavenly seed-grain find room on our hard soil, on which need and want fight for every little corner? Surely we are banished from the primal spirit and not meant to rise up to it. . . . And yet a merciful angel has prayed for the heavenly flower to be granted to us, and it stands proud and tall in its full glory, rooted in this soil of misery. The pulse of divine music has not ceased to throb throughout the centuries of barbarism and a direct echo of the eternal has remained for us in it, comprehensible to every sense and rising even above vice and virtue' (CL, 2).

The symbiosis of art and religion was, initially, of advantage to both. Religion as art emancipated itself from dogma and became a revelation of the heart, and art as religion lent these 'revelations' a celestial consecration. The religion of art made it possible 'in bold attitude to float above the wild abyss, between heaven and earth'. And Schopenhauer, mauled by the commercial world, was hoping that it might help him in his attempt 'with soft light step / to wander through this desert earthly life, / so that the foot be never caught in the dust . . .' (P I, 2).

In his father's faith transcendence was a solid, reliable asset. The Romantic religion of art, on the other hand, even as it saw itself, was more like a risky enterprise. In his novel *William Lovell*, which young Schopenhauer read several times, the youthful Tieck wrote: 'If such a being ever feels the strength of its wings flagging . . . then it lets itself drop blindly, its wings are snapped, and in all eternity it has to *crawl*.'

The vibrations of Romantic enthusiasm stem from an undercurrent of fear – fear of sobering up, of the end of the sleepwalker's sure step. In its most merciless moments Romanticism realizes that the scope of resonance of its celestial music is frighteningly empty. 'Music is almost an image of our life to me,' Wackenroder wrote, 'a touchingly brief joy which springs from nothingness and passes into nothingness – which emerges and vanishes, no one knows why: a small cheerful green island, with sunshine, with singing and music – that floats on the dark, unfathomable ocean.'

Those who, after the great twilight of the gods, wished to create their own gods by their own effort were faced with the following dilemma: they were to believe in what they had themselves created, and they were to experience that creation as something received. They wanted to extract from Creating that *unio mystica* which would permit only a Letting Be. They wished to admire the great play from in front of the footlights while, at the same time, standing in the wings. They were producers wishing to enchant themselves. The Romantic religion of art wanted the impossible: it hoped to produce naivety through sophistication, with the result that the place of the old substances was taken by the mirror cabinet of duplication: the emotion of emotion, the faith in faith, the idea of the idea. According to one's mood this produced either the enjoyment of an infinitely variegated Something – or the agony of Nothing. Jean Paul observed: 'If every I is its own father and creator, why then cannot it also be its own garrotting angel?'

Those were the extraordinarily delicate upward currents on which Schopenhauer allowed himself to be carried. He remained familiar with the fear of falling. But what forces, exactly, were those which he feared might cause him to crash to the ground?

It was the sensuality which erupted during the late puberty of the young man that prevented him from weightless flight. Sexual desire – that is, his body – caused him to crash. This was his garrotting angel, to whom, at the time of his Romantic flights, he dedicated a significant poem: 'O lust, o hell, / O senses, o love, / Not to be assuaged / From heights of heaven / You dragged me / And flung me down / Into the dust of this earth: / Here I lie in fetters' (P I, 1).

'Lust' and 'love' – what did they mean to young Arthur Schopenhauer?

To begin with: after his father's death and his mother's departure the young man, not yet twenty, lived without family supervision. Meanwhile Anthime, to put an end to his 'boredom' in Le Havre and to complete his training as a merchant, had arrived in Hamburg. He wished to be near his friend, he wrote. A lot has been made of the 'dissipations' in which the two young men allegedly indulged; they were the usual pattern in bourgeois circles.

At weekends Anthime would come to Hamburg from Aumühle, where he lodged. He wanted to 'experience something', and Arthur was to be his guide. The two, mutually encouraging each other, picked up actresses and chorus girls, and if they were unsuccessful with them they would console themselves in the 'embraces of an industrious whore', as Anthime wrote in one of his letters. Arthur was occasionally irritated by Anthime's posturing as a lady-killer, his replies were ironical or grumpy, and Anthime took offence. Then the two were once more reconciled. Arthur supplied Anthime with lubricious literature and seemed to have made the right choice, for Anthime thanked him with the remark that he felt 'these days in the mood for amorous thoughts'.

Both of them were in the mood for 'amorous thoughts', even though Arthur's mood was always sceptically muted. On a Sunday excursion to Trittau in Holstein, while the two of them were stretched out in the shade of a tree in a summer meadow, Arthur spoilt his friend's erotically enterprising spirit by arguing that 'life is so short, questionable and evanescent that it is not worth the trouble of major effort' (C, 15).

Arthur, admittedly, had not found a love affair which would have been worth a major effort. His problem was that his bodily desires humiliated his mind, they triumphed over him but not over the women. That was what he could not forgive them – neither his bodily desires nor the women. 'And as for women,' Arthur Schopenhauer admitted in a conversation many years later,

'I was very fond of them – if only they would have had me' (C, 239). Because they did not want to have him they had to become for him obscure objects of desire, and that was why he experienced the entanglements of the physical as a threat. 'Lust, hell, senses, love' – all these were the same to him, a 'fetter of weakness' that caused the failure of any 'striving upwards'. Because it earned him only defeats, or only all-too-easy victories, he experienced his sexuality as a humiliation, and because Anthime was an accomplice of its tentative first steps he soon became estranged from him. Anthime, the erotically more successful, was totally unable to copy Arthur's intention 'not to be too firmly enclosed in his body'.

Thus Schopenhauer spent his days in the counting-house of Senator Jenisch and his evenings at the boarding-house of his insurance broker, and now and again along with Anthime he reluctantly pursued lust. For Arthur this was an external world of the worst kind. He did not change his situation in the external world but instead dreamed of 'blissful spiritual hours of intimacy': 'Why must the few noble people, whom chance has not so firmly enclosed in their bodies as the legion of the others – why must these individuals be separated by a thousand obstacles so that their voices cannot reach each other, cannot recognize each other and cannot indulge in a blissful spiritual hour of intimacy? Why must such a person . . . sense a similar being at most in a work of art . . . and why must longing then increase his torment, while he thirsts in solitude where, like sand in the Sahara, only the countless herd of shallow semi-animals encounter his gaze?' This life in the Sahara continued for a while, until the summer of 1807. By then Johanna could no longer bear the Jeremiads from Hamburg. She took the initiative towards Arthur's liberation. He had been unable to free himself by his own strength. His mother helped him to be born again, she carried him out of his father's world. He ought to have been boundlessly grateful to her for doing so. But perhaps it was precisely that which he could never forgive her – being in her debt.

CHAPTER FIVE

WEIMAR

For nearly a year Arthur lived in Hamburg on his own. Under civil law and the law of inheritance he was still a minor. But his mother, ever since her move to Weimar, had been treating him as an adult. In her letters she very conspicuously struck a new note. She spoke to him not like a mother but like an older woman friend or an elder sister. On the day of her departure she was anxious to avoid a farewell ceremony. All that Arthur found on the morning of 21 September 1806 was a letter his mother had written during the night: 'You left a moment ago, I can still smell the aroma of your cigar, and I realize that I shall not see you for a long time. We spent the evening together very cheerfully; let that be our goodbye. Farewell, my good, dear Arthur, when you receive these lines I shall presumably no longer be here; but even if I am, do not come to see me, I cannot bear farewells. After all, we can see one another again when we wish to; I hope it will not be too long before reason, too, permits us to do so. Farewell, this was the first time I ever deceived you; I have ordered the horses for half past six, I hope you will not be pained by my deception of you; I did so for my own sake; for I know how weak I am at such moments, and how much any violent emotion affects me.'

The important features about this letter are the nuances, for instance the mention of the cigar smoke on their last evening spent together. She wished to remember Arthur not as a son but as a man. Shrewdly she avoided the sentimental goodbyes: she did not feel like them. She was full of joyous expectation of her new life. 'I did so for my own sake' – with this logic Johanna freed herself from the conventions of maternal duties.

She was perfectly well aware that the pattern of her new life offended against bourgeois tradition. It filled her with proud self-assurance: she was not going to have her life impoverished by anxious considerations. She was, as she wrote to Arthur on one occasion, 'too determined, too inclined, to choose what may appear the more wonderful between two roads, as I did in determining my place of residence, when, instead of moving to my native city, to friends and relations, as almost any other woman in my place would have done, I chose Weimar, which was almost entirely strange to me' (28 April 1807).

After her husband's death she had no intention of displaying any piety
vis-à-vis her clique of relatives; she was happy to have escaped them. In a
letter to Arthur she had this to say about the squabbles among her Danzig
relations: 'Thank God I was sensible enough to withdraw from all similar
family affairs, I can watch the mischief from afar, and I realize each day more
clearly how much all that petty ado would destroy my own well-being' (30
January 1807). Johanna was so totally immersed in her new 'well-being' in
Weimar that in her numerous letters to Arthur at the time she wrote almost
exclusively about herself and her new environment without – certainly
initially – reacting to Arthur's equally numerous letters, which she later
destroyed. There was nothing like an epistolary dialogue. Johanna's intention, as she somewhat apologetically wrote several times, was to let Arthur
participate in her world; with a coy reference to her maternal role she
remarked: 'I always want to have something to report to you; after all, it was
always my custom to bring my children home some bonbons from society' (8
December 1806). She did not display any particular curiosity about Arthur's
life in Hamburg, but she made use of the fact that Arthur was living there by
giving him little commissions. Arthur was allowed to perform delivery
services for her: a letter from the Dowager Duchess was to be conveyed to
Rostock; the circle of Goethe's friends needed embroidery patterns and
pastels; his mother's admirer Fernow wanted a book that was unobtainable
in Weimar; and his mother needed a straw hat. Arthur was to wrap
everything up well, but put the hat on himself first, 'not forgetting,' as
Johanna wrote, 'that my head is as big as yours, the hat must fit you,
otherwise I cannot wear it' (10 March 1807). On this occasion alone the
common big-headedness proved an advantage. When he had seen to
everything Arthur was highly commended: 'Dear friend Arthur . . . I made a
present of one crayon each to Goethe, Fernow and Meyer, and they were all
very grateful.' Arthur caught a corner of the prophet's cloak; Goethe sent his
regards and thanks for a consignment of pastels. A little warmth of the solar
splendour was thus enjoyed by Arthur as he performed his messenger services
for fabulous Weimar.

Anyone maintaining even the most tenuous links with the world of the
spirit was bound then to enter Weimar trembling in awe. The two levels of
culture were more brilliantly occupied there than anywhere else in Germany.
Residing on the elegant level were Herder, Schiller, Wieland and of course
Goethe; the basement was bustling with the popular figures: August von
Kotzebue, Stephan Schütze and Vulpius. Small wonder that even such a
disrespectful contemporary as Jean Paul on his first visit to the small princely
residence in Thuringia exclaimed: 'At last . . . I have pushed open the gates of
heaven and am standing right inside Weimar.' A few weeks later, however, he
complained in a letter to his brother: 'You have no idea of the shoving and
quarrelling and elbowing that is going on here for a tiny space beside the
throne.'

Those not dazzled by the literary splendour of Weimar first noticed with irritation on arrival that, no matter from which direction they came, they had to turn off the well-surfaced main road. All the important traffic routes bypassed Weimar. This was true of the west–east road from Frankfurt-on-Main via Erfurt to Leipzig as well as of the north–south link from Eisleben via Rudolstadt to Nuremberg. The secret capital city of German culture was, from the transport point of view, off the map. The final stretch of road into Weimar was in a deplorable state. Goethe, since 1779 Director of Highway Construction, tried in vain to change this state of affairs. Eventually he gave up and travelled to Italy. The roads around Weimar continued to be dangerous. When Goethe was travelling to Frankfurt in the summer of 1816 his carriage overturned a few miles outside Weimar. The bruised Secret Councillor scrambled out from underneath the vehicle and henceforward abandoned the idea of any major journey.

The streets of the town were in better condition. Here Goethe, who also held the office of Court Councillor for Urban Pavement Construction, had worked to better advantage. The principal streets, footpaths and squares were paved. The inhabitants of Weimar were so proud of this that travellers and strangers were immediately made to pay a pavement tax. There was a decree for this showpiece of Weimar's urban culture to be treated with care: there was a speed limit, carriages had to keep to a trot, and smoking tobacco in the street was forbidden.

'Upon his entry into this town the pilgrim disciple of the arts, the enthusiastic friend of the Muses, is preceded by a sorceress,' we read in a contemporary travel account; 'to him Weimar appears magnificent, as the beautiful temple of the Muses. . . . But this is in no way due . . . to the style of building, the houses, the streets or the ornaments; this is the *physical* while the other is the *poetical* Weimar which the new arrival beholds in his mind's eye.'

As for the *physical* Weimar, matters – as confirmed by numerous contemporary reports – were far from perfect. A certain Wölfling, visiting Weimar in 1796, reported: 'You get the best view of the town from the mountains beyond the hills. But you may view it whichever way you choose, it still remains a mediocre place, whose streets do not, either in cleanliness or in design, or in the architecture of the houses, equal the cheerful or airy aspect of Gotha. The houses are for the most part skimpily built, and everything here has the mean appearance of an impecunious country town. One does not have to move far from the main streets to find oneself in corners and holes to further confirm that impression. There is not a single spot that would lend the town the appearance of anything like a ruler's residence.'

About 1800 the population of Weimar was approximately 7500. And in spite of its cultural prominence there was no appreciable growth. In proportion to the overall population growth at the time Weimar actually lagged behind. During the period between Goethe's arrival (1775) and the turn of the century a mere twenty new houses had been built. The old nucleus of the town was full of nooks and corners, with the houses – about seven hundred at the turn of the century – huddling around the Jakobskirche, the church of St James. In 1760 a start had been made on the levelling of the fortifications, which gave the town more space and air at its periphery. The ancient town gates were pulled down, though the gate tax for the movement of merchandise continued to be levied. On the cleared ground new parks, gardens and avenues were laid out, and living quarters built for farming citizens. Weimar, even so, had not lost the character of a country town, though it was no longer as marked as at the time of Goethe's arrival. Then pigs roamed the streets, cattle grazed in the churchyard, and ducal hygienic decrees such as the following were customary: 'The excrement in the town is caused by dung carts. Whoever has no gateway should cart the dung out into the smaller streets, except on market days, and not leave it lying at the appointed places over Sundays or holy days.' About the middle of the eighteenth century nearly half the population of Weimar consisted of peasants; by the turn of the century they accounted for only some 10 per cent. However, many of the small artisans, carters, innkeepers, and even some of the court employees still owned minute agricultural plots. The numerous dung heaps outside the houses therefore continued to be part of the aspect of the town, and in summer attracted swarms of midges and flies, which was why the upper crust would flee to the nearby watering-places.

The 'upper crust' was grouped around the ducal court. There was no independent upper middle class in Weimar. Trades and crafts were numerous and varied, but limited to the lower middle class. Of the 485 trade enterprises listed in 1820, 280 had no and 117 only one journeyman assistant. The sixty-two shoemakers, forty-three tailors, twenty-three butchers, twenty-two joiners, twenty bakers, twenty linen weavers, twelve blacksmiths, eleven locksmiths, ten coopers and ten saddlers were strictly organized in guilds and regulated competition among each other in such a way that no one was able to expand to any great extent. The age of industrialization had scarcely brushed Weimar. That, at least, Goethe was hoping to change during his poetically unproductive period. As the building of the new palace was only making very slow progress, he demanded in 1797 that the Commission for the Construction of the Palace establish a 'Central Joinery Workshop' with the argument that '. . . unless at least part of this is manufactured in a factory, and with all the advantages offered by machines and by several people working together, the end will not even move within sight.' Goethe's colleague in office Voigt, on the other hand, believed that 'some consideration should be given to the guilds. . . . As is well known, the joinery trade here is already involved in tiresome quarrels about journeymen, which greatly limits its activity. There would be even more squabbling if a non-guild joinery products factory were to be set up.' Weimar did not wish to have a proletariat.

The only major 'industrial' entrepreneur in Weimar was Friedrich Johann Justin Bertuch, a qualified lawyer, a dilettante of the arts, merchant, publisher and Keeper of the Ducal Privy Purse. Bertuch – significantly for the artistic little town – started off with a factory for artificial flowers, in which Christiane Vulpius, Goethe's mistress and subsequently his wife, worked at one time. He founded a publishing house and published several periodicals, including the famous *Jenaische Allgemeine Literatur-Zeitung* and the *Journal des Luxus und der Moden*. In 1791 he concentrated all his publishing and arts-and-crafts enterprises in a *Landes-Industrie-Comptoir*. Needless to say this was not 'industry' in the modern sense of the word; even his contemporaries noticed the false label: 'Although the *Industriecomptoir* of Herr Bertuch has for some time brought the term "industry" into currency in Weimar, that term is about all that exists here of industry.'

In Weimar's near neighbourhood, on the other hand, the modern age had, however tentatively, arrived. At Apolda there was a factory for the production of stockings. One loom manufactured approximately ten stockings a week. Not a spectacular balance sheet. A water-hose factory earned itself a better reputation: it was the first in Germany.

About 1820 some 26 per cent of the earning population were directly or indirectly dependent on the ducal court: administrative and police officials, court employees, members of the court orchestra and of the theatre, ministers of religion, teachers, physicians, apothecaries, lawyers – all regarded themselves as rather superior and drew a line between themselves and the craftsmen and day-labourers, though these in turn too were largely dependent on orders from the court. However subtle the social pecking order may have been, the outsider entering the famous town with high expectations saw it in the cold light of day shrink into a philistine backwoods dump. Wölfling wrote: 'Among . . . the people who inhabit the town by far the greatest number are a race of small-town philistines, displaying neither the refinement of a princely residence nor any particular affluence.' An Englishman, used to very different things, noted: 'In vain would one seek in Weimar for the cheerful bustle or the noisy sensual pleasures of a capital city; there are too few here who love leisure, also too few prosperous people to indulge in unnecessary distractions. Without the need for a police, let alone a secret police, the small size of the town and the accustomed lifestyle places everyone under the special supervision of the court. . . . A man concerned mainly with pleasure might easily regard Weimar as a sad place. The morning is devoted to business, and even the few select ones who have nothing to do would be ashamed to be counted idlers. . . . At six o'clock everyone hurries to the theatre, which one might call a reunion of a big family. . . . At approximately nine o'clock the performance ends, and it may be assumed that by ten o'clock every householder is fast asleep or at least spends the night quietly within his four walls.'

Anyone wishing to attend some place of entertainment other than the coffee house would be disappointed in Weimar. Wölfling reported: 'You visit the coffee house, and you see an empty room, where the host rubs his hands in boredom and with his compliments nearly drives you into the furthest corner because you have made him so happy by giving him your custom. In the evening, however, you will at best find there a club of clerks, scribes, etc., which nearly chokes you with its tobacco smoke.'

Public life in Weimar flared up whenever the town was free, at its periodical markets, to revert uninhibitedly to its rural origins. The autumnal onion market was a great popular festivity. Houses were decorated with greenery. Wine flowed generously, and there was even dancing in the streets. There was a harvest thanksgiving atmosphere about, and a smell of leeks and celery everywhere. Twice a year, with similar festivities, a big timber market was held, which attracted even the rich shipbuilders from Holland. A pig market was held every month outside St James's church, much to the annoyance of Chief Consistory Councillor Herder, who lived nearby.

Between these periodic resurgences of rustic gaiety Weimar, seen from close up, was a 'snail's shell world', as Schiller observed with disappointment on his arrival. The aristocratic clique with its class pride wished to keep to themselves, and so did the petit-bourgeois circles. Until 1848 the balcony in the Weimar theatre was divided into a bourgeois and an aristocratic section. Goethe, too, occasionally experienced the arrogance of the aristocracy. The circle of the sixteen most serene families, who considered themselves the cream of society, had still not reconciled themselves to Goethe's love life. Christiane Vulpius, the former worker from Bertuch's flower manufactory, was regarded as simply 'impossible'. At a ball an aristocratic Chief Forester boorishly addressed Secret Councillor Goethe: 'Send your wench home! I've got her drunk!' That time he sent Christiane home,' but generally he refused to be put out. The actress Karoline Jagemann, the subsequent mistress of the Duke and an enemy of Goethe, noted in her memoirs: 'When I arrived from Mannheim the affair was publicly established, and the fact that the Vulpius woman was living with Goethe was something unheard-of for the small town. He was the first and only one to dare show unabashed contempt for public opinion, and this was felt to be the more offensive as it was seen as an abuse of the privilege that the Duke's friendship accorded him in many a respect.' Goethe aggravated the affront by producing a son, August, by Christiane and actually legitimizing him. Of course Goethe continued to keep up relations with the court; his official duties made this necessary. He also had his listening post within the closest circle of the nobility – Frau von Stein. But whenever possible he avoided purely aristocratic parties; at his own home on the Frauenplan he attempted a social mix, even though only within the stricture of stiff etiquette. The host, when all was said and done, was the Secret Councillor rather than the poet of the *Walpurgisnacht*.

Among petit-bourgeois circles there was a lack of self-assurance. They kept themselves to themselves, and attached a lot of importance to distinctions which, if one behaved oneself and was eager to show obedience, might rain down from the sky of high society. In Weimar, more than anywhere else, a title mania and 'councillor mischief' were rampant. 'What struck me most particularly,' a visitor to Weimar reported, 'was that everyone invariably spoke of *Court Councillor* Wieland, *Secret Councillor* Goethe, *Vice-President* Herder. They were never referred to without a title. . . . In the whole of society there was probably, with the exception of myself, not a single untitled person, even among the few merchants.'

Johanna Schopenhauer adjusted to this and hurriedly dug up the Polish Court Councillor title of her husband (which he himself had never used). In Weimar she was then referred to only as *Hofrätin* Schopenhauer. Rückert, who had also been immediately struck by that title mania, had an explanation: 'A bourgeois, as in any princely residence, is here oppressed and held down by the aristocracy. . . . This gives rise in his heart to a reverence for those small honours that he has to show without having them recipro- cated. . . . To his jealous eye something appears as an honour that in fact is mere ceremony, and hardly deserving of mention among people of common sense.'

Squeezed between these two blocks lived Weimar's world of the spirit – another snail's shell of its own. Rückert remarked: 'Between the two [the petit-bourgeois and the aristocrats] stand the *scholar* and the *artist* as the innocent party, who however is of little interest to either because he does not fit into their circles, avoiding the one and despising the other, and, close to them and apart from them at the same time, lives among them as though on an inaccessible island.'

Yet even this world of the spirit was divided by rifts. Battlefield standards were planted everywhere, and the various loyal followers rallied around them: Wieland and Goethe, leaders of factions, avoided each other; likewise Herder and Goethe. The old friendship between the two broke up one day when Herder, commenting on Goethe's play *Die natürliche Tochter* (*The Natural Daughter*) cattily remarked: 'I prefer your natural son to your natural daughter.' The Dowager Duchess Amalia's 'court of the Muses' was in opposition to the circles around Goethe. Kotzebue, anxious to be loved by everyone, plotted intrigues and fell out with everyone.

Schiller in one of his last letters to Wilhelm von Humboldt complained of the 'unfortunate standstill' of Weimar life. He was surprised that Goethe could have endured it for so long. 'If it were at all feasible, I would leave,' Schiller wrote two years before Johanna Schopenhauer arrived in Weimar with high expectations on 28 September 1806.

She had scarcely been in the town for three weeks when she wrote to Arthur: 'My existence here will be agreeable, people have come to know me better in ten days than otherwise in ten years.' After a few days Johanna Schopenhauer felt 'more at home than I ever did in Hamburg'.

She had come from Hamburg with letters of introduction: one from the painter Wilhelm Tischbein, Goethe's travel companion on his Italian journey. Another was to the Lord of the Bedchamber Dr Ridel, formerly tutor to the Weimar hereditary prince. Ridel was a native of Hamburg, where Johanna had made his acquaintance; his wife was born a Buff, the sister of that famous Charlotte Buff from Wetzlar, the model for Lotte in *The Sorrows of Young Werther*.

Useful as such introductions might be, one could not put down roots with them alone. The same was true of the social prestige surrounding the widow of a Hanseatic merchant magnate and Polish court councillor. Such prestige excited curiosity and opened all possible doors – but one could not be accepted as something like a native on the grounds of that prestige alone. Johanna's good fortune sprang from the misfortune of the war which had begun a few days prior to her departure from Hamburg and found its dramatic climax just a few miles from Weimar, in the battles of Jena and Auerstädt. Weimar did not remain unaffected. 'Goethe said to me today,' Johanna wrote to Arthur on 19 October 1806, 'that the baptism of fire had made me into a Weimarian.' What had happened?

The years following the French Revolution and especially those at the beginning of the Napoleonic regime had been so charged with warlike events that people had become used to them; the critical aggravation of relations between Prussia and France did not therefore necessarily seem an obstacle to a removal from Hamburg to Weimar. Besides, why should not the Duchy of Saxony-Weimar, as Hamburg had so far done, succeed in keeping out of the war? On her journey through Prussia Johanna had already been held up by military transports. On her arrival in Weimar she very quickly realized that one could not feel safe in the Duchy. But she allowed herself to be infected by the general confident belief that Weimar would not be affected. 'Here everyone is of good cheer,' she wrote to Arthur on 29 September 1806, 'the army will soon advance, what will happen then is of course still in the dark, but everything is going well, the war of course is inevitable but meanwhile all is full of courage and life.'

For ten years Prussia had succeeded in keeping out of the European wars; she had preserved her 'neutrality' – on Napoleon's side. To make quite sure Prussia would not join the Austrian–British–Russian Alliance, Napoleon at the beginning of 1806 was urging her to join an alliance against Britain. The King of Prussia, Frederick William III, however, wanted to reinsure himself. Behind the back of his new ally Napoleon, he concluded a treaty with the Tsar. Napoleon, who would really have preferred to enlist Prussia as a junior partner rather than to have to defeat her, responded to this escapade with a threatening deployment of his troops in Thuringia. Prussia mobilized in her turn and, in the form of an ultimatum, demanded the withdrawal of the French troops. Napoleon was not going to stand for such impertinence and set his troops in motion, at the very moment when Johanna arrived in Weimar. Prussia, though totally unprepared, could not pull back. Though a mere three months earlier the ally of Napoleon, Prussia on 9 October 1806 declared war on France. One of the few rulers who joined in this reckless enterprise against Napoleon was Duke Carl August of Saxony-Weimar. Goethe had urgently advised against it. 'Although the world was on fire at all its ends and corners, and although on land and on the sea cities and navies were turned to ruins, yet central Germany, northern Germany, still enjoyed a certain hectic peace, during which we indulged in a doubtful security.' Goethe wished for things to stay that way – but who would listen to him?

On 18 October and during the following days, when the storms had passed, Johanna wrote a monster of a letter – twenty sheets of quarto – in which she described the events of the preceding days with great clarity and in detail. The letter, in fact, was a circular: Arthur was to pass it on to her friends in Hamburg and her relations in Danzig. Later she even demanded it back from Arthur for her memoirs. This letter provides us with a fairly accurate picture of what went on in Weimar during those days. In the first week of October the Prussian and Saxon troops were being concentrated around Weimar. A vast camp was set up between Erfurt and Ettersberge, close to Weimar; over 100,000 troops were encamped there. The officers were billeted in Weimar. The Prussian royal couple and the Duke of Brunswick arrived in the town. The French guns could already be heard in the distance. 'Every heart beat with impatience at all this.' Among the generals was Field Marshal von Kalckreuth, whom Johanna had met at a soirée in Hamburg. As Johanna was considering fleeing from threatened Weimar with her daughter Adele, she hoped that the aged officer, who had smashed the Mainz Republic in 1792 and now entertained tender feelings for her, Johanna, might help her. Before riding off into battle with drums and trumpets – a battle eventually lost largely because of his wrong decisions – he found time for a cordial embrace, though even he was unable to provide her with horses for an escape. He could take Johanna and Adele with him, but her servants would have to stay behind. Johanna did not wish to leave her loyal domestics in danger. 'Then the drum beat for the third time and he tore himself away. My heart ached to see the handsome old man leave like this.'

The date was 13 October 1806. Still sounding out the possibilities of escape Johanna called on Fräulein von Göchhausen, the lady-in-waiting of the Dowager Duchess. On the palace stairs she encountered the Dowager Duchess and was presented to her. So this acquaintance was also accomplished. In the general bustle of departure Johanna was even allowed to talk to Anna Amalia for half an hour; about to leave Weimar herself, she would take Johanna and Adele along with her, but she was unable to provide horses for her. Johanna remained in Weimar. She would not regret it, for in the vacated houses the French soldiery was to rampage worst of all.

The noise of the departing troops continued that day until dusk. Then silence fell – a frightening, pregnant silence. Nevertheless, or just because of it, there was a performance at the theatre. The play was the light-hearted

Singspiel Fanchon. Johanna sent Adele to see it with the housemaid Sophie.

The following morning towards nine o'clock the thunder of the guns could be heard approaching. Johanna sewed her jewellery into her corset, the fine damask napery was hidden under woodpiles, other valuables were buried in the cellar. The housemaid Sophie had a kind of girdle containing 100 *louis-d'or* strapped round her body. Wine was brought up from the cellar, so it should be at hand for placating any looters. Johanna made all these preparations because she distrusted the reports of victories which were coming in. After all, she had never had a high opinion of the Prussians.

At midday, suddenly, there was terrible shouting in the streets: 'The French are here.' First of all, however, Prussian soldiers, bedraggled, dirty and wounded came racing through the streets of Weimar. 'Now the cannon were booming, the floor shook, the windows rattled, oh God, how close to us was death, we no longer heard a single crash but the penetrating whistling and hissing and rattling of the bullets and howitzers which flew over our house and fifty paces further on struck a building or the ground without causing any damage. God's angel was hovering above us, my heart was suddenly filled with calm and joy, I took my Adele on my lap and sat down with her on the sofa. I hoped one bullet would kill both of us, at least neither would lament the other. Never had the thought of death been more present to me, never had it been less frightening.'

There was banging on the door. French hussars demanded to be let in. They still behaved in quite an orderly fashion, allowing themselves to be fed with chicken and wine, and to be shown to sleeping quarters. After the hussars, however, the notorious 'spoon guards', the scum of the Napoleonic army, burst into the town. Napoleon, in order to punish Weimar for its support of Prussia, had given his troops permission to loot. Two women burst into Johanna's house; they had only just escaped being raped by pillaging soldiers. Several members of Weimar society who were in bad straits sought refuge with Johanna. Trembling with fear and yet giving one another encouragement they sat together, sipping hot bouillon and drinking wine. A single candle burned in the room, the windows were curtained, for any light penetrating outside might attract disaster. That was the hour of the great community's birth. 'Necessity extinguishes all petty interests and teaches us how closely we are related to one another,' Johanna wrote. Under the scourge of fear this otherwise so stiff and formal society developed a strange sense of ease. Those who might otherwise be rivals now drew together. Strangeness and remoteness vanished like ghosts. The common danger allowed everyone to drop their masks of self-importance.

Late at night there was more hammering on the doors; these were the 'spoon guards'. 'Just imagine those horrible faces, their bloodied sabres drawn, the grubby white blood-spattered tunics they wear on those occasions, their wild laughter and talk, their hands stained with blood.' Nine-year-old Adele walked into the room. The little girl, who 'quite sweetly talked to them, asking them to leave, because she could not sleep', placated the soldiers: they moved off again, having supplied themselves with food. Johanna had the most improbable luck: her house, one of few in Weimar, was spared looting and wrecking again on the following day.

That night, from 14 to 15 October, Weimar's suburb burned. The French would not permit the fires to be put out. Only the total absence of any wind saved the town from being razed to the ground. The night was lit up brightly by the fires. People fled to the nearby woods. The next day the worst was over, and wild rumours were flying around of how this person or that had fared. Outside the front door of the cultured 'Art-Meyer' a gunpowder cart stood all night long. At the house of Herder's widow they had torn up all the manuscripts he had left behind. The Ridels were crouching on a chest of drawers – the only thing that had remained intact. Later they also discovered a silver tea urn. The Kühns had dug themselves into a hole in their garden. The Town Purse Administrator, an elderly hypochondriacal man, had kept vigil by his treasure chest. It was looted, however, and the ledgers, the mainstay of his life, had been torn up. Goethe told Johanna that he had 'never seen a greater picture of misery than that man in an empty room, surrounded by his torn and scattered papers, himself sitting on the floor, cold and as if turned to stone. . . . He looked like some King Lear, except that Lear was mad and here the world was mad.'

A conversation with the Duchess, who alone had stayed behind, and the genuflection of a Weimar shoemaker, eventually induced Napoleon to put an end to the savage activity.

Now the dead and wounded were carried in. At the Comedy Theatre the corpses were piling up. Makeshift hospitals were established. 'I could tell you things,' Johanna wrote to Arthur, 'that would make your hair stand on end; but I will not do so, for I know how fond you are of brooding on human misery, but you do not yet know it, my son: all that we two have seen together is nothing compared with this abyss of suffering.'

Johanna helped where she could. She sent linen for bandages, visited the wounded, poured wine, tea, and madeira, and made bouillon. Her example, she proudly reported, was followed by others, even by Goethe who opened up his wine cellar. There was no accommodation left for the wounded, and one therefore welcomed the early death of those who anyway had no chance of surviving. In this manner room was made: 'death is helping frightfully.' There was a danger of epidemics. Fortunately the military hospitals were cleared in time: 'I am glad now when I hear that 4500 are moved on with their shattered limbs, I who only a few weeks ago would on no account let the boy who broke his arm outside our house leave without help!' These were years of apprenticeship for her heart.

The storm had passed. But the manner in which they had comforted one another in danger was too valuable to surrender in a hurry. Goethe approached Johanna, who both by luck and by her care and attention had won sudden fame in Weimar, and said to her: 'Now that winter approaches more gloomily than usual, we too must move closer together in order to brighten the dreary days for one another.'

That was the moment when Johanna Schopenhauer's subsequently famous tea party was born.

Goethe had paid his first call on Johanna shortly before the evil days, on 12 October. 'A stranger was announced to me; I stepped into the anteroom and saw a handsome serious man in black clothes, bowing low with much etiquette and saying to me: "Permit me to present to you the Secret Councillor Goethe." I looked about the room to see where Goethe was, for after the stiff description that had been given to me of him I could not recognize him in this person.'

After the 'baptism of fire' Goethe became a regular visitor at Johanna Schopenhauer's soirées, and naturally he acted as a magnet. But there was yet another reason why Goethe – at least during the first few years – was so frequently found in Johanna Schopenhauer's drawing room.

The ground under his feet had been shaking for Goethe, too, during those bad days. Until then he had always succeeded in creating around himself a homogeneous space, a world which, through the emanation of his personality, became his own. Anything alien, disturbing or irritating he either managed to keep out or to absorb into his own world. 'Yet in the so-called enjoyment of his full life nothing must disturb him,' Henriette von Knebel wrote in a letter of 1802. The battle of Weimar, the looting, the catastrophe of the Weimar state – all these were a 'disturbance' inflicted on him by another Prometheus, Napoleon, a disturbance against which his own Prometheanism – 'Still you must leave / my earth intact . . . Here I sit, forming men / In my image' – could no longer prevail. 'One would like to be outside, but there is no Outside,' he remarked in a conversation with Stephan Schütze at the time.

But Goethe had in fact been lucky. Christiane's courageous behaviour had averted the worst. There had been grotesque scenes. The 'spoon guards' had broken in, they had drunk wine, made a great uproar and called for the master of the house. Goethe's secretary Riemer reports: 'Although already undressed and wearing only his wide nightgown – otherwise jocularly called by him his prophet's cloak – he descended the stairs towards them and inquired what they wanted from him. . . . His dignified figure, commanding respect, and his spiritual mien seemed to impress even them.' But it was not to last long. Late at night they burst into his bedroom with drawn bayonets. Goethe was petrified, Christiane raised a lot of noise and even tangled with them, other people who had taken refuge in Goethe's house rushed in, and so the marauders eventually withdrew again. It was Christiane who commanded and organized the defence of the house on the Frauenplan. The barricading of the kitchen and the cellar against the wild pillaging soldiery was her work. Goethe noted in his diary: 'Fires, rapine, a frightful night . . . Preservation of our house through steadfastness and luck.' The luck was

Goethe's, the steadfastness was displayed by Christiane. Heinrich Voss, the tutor of Goethe's son August, reports that Goethe had been 'an object of most sincere sympathy in those sad days . . . I have seen him shed tears. Who, he exclaimed, will take my house and home so that I can go far away.' His position, linked as it was to the court, was in fact in jeopardy, as the fate of the whole Duchy hung by a silken thread. Napoleon was considering breaking it up completely and amalgamating it with the states of the Rhenish League. 'I set my affairs at nothing' is the opening of a poem written by Goethe at the time. Christiane, with whom he had by then been living for eighteen years, gave him support. So Goethe had the court preacher called; very quietly a marriage service was held in the court chapel, with his secretary Riemer and his son August acting as witnesses. Goethe had their wedding rings engraved 14 October, the day of the battle of Jena. To Johanna Schopenhauer he said that 'in peacetime one may well bypass the laws, but in days such as ours one must respect them.'

Weimar was piqued, the journals scoffed. In the newspaper of Goethe's publisher Cotta one could read: 'Amidst the thundering cannonade of the battle Goethe is married to his housekeeper of many years, Demoiselle Vulpius, and thus she alone scored a hit while so many thousand shells were duds.'

A woman visitor to Weimar noted with surprise that Goethe was 'making a point of honouring his wife also publicly and admitting his affection for her'. Goethe, therefore, greatly appreciated the fact that Johanna Schopenhauer was the first, and to begin with also the only, person in Weimar society to receive the 'newlyweds'. She herself wrote to Arthur: 'That same evening he called on me and presented his wife to me, I received her as though I did not know who she had been before, I think if Goethe gives her his name then we can surely give her a cup of tea. I saw clearly how my demeanour pleased him, there were a few other ladies at my house, who at first were formal and stiff but subsequently followed my lead, Goethe stayed for nearly two hours and was more loquacious and friendly than I had seen him for years. He has not brought her to anyone in person except myself, as a stranger and a person from a big city he trusted me to accept the woman as she must be accepted. She was in fact very embarrassed but I soon helped her over it, in my position and with the respect and love I have acquired here in a short time I can make social life very much easier for her. Goethe desires it and he has confidence in me, and I shall certainly earn it, tomorrow I shall return her call.'

Johanna Schopenhauer's acceptance of the Vulpius woman was to have beneficial results for her. Goethe repaid her by frequent visits, other prominent figures were attracted as a result, and Johanna's success was achieved. On 28 November, two months after her arrival, she wrote to Arthur: 'The circle that assembles around me on Sundays and Thursdays probably has no equal anywhere in Germany, if only I could bring you here by magic one day!'

But how serious was she really about that 'magic'? Johanna realized full well that her present well-being, her 'second spiritual spring' as Adele was to describe it later, was due to her having freed herself of her past, of her marriage to Heinrich Floris Schopenhauer. In the new living space she had conquered for herself there was no room for Arthur, the man who was his father's son and who, though complaining, was following in his father's footsteps. In other respects, too, Arthur invariably reminded her of his father – his brooding manner, his brusqueness, his criticizing everything and everybody. When Arthur moved to Weimar towards the end of 1807 Johanna would have to defend her territory, anxiously yet self-assuredly, against her son's encroachments.

To begin with she refused to let Arthur's lamentations over the misfortune of his merchant's existence, or his pessimistic reflections on life generally, concern her. Eventually, in the spring of 1807, when she reacted to them, she wrote: 'That you have been dissatisfied with your whole existence I have known for a long time, but I did not worry about it much. You know to what causes I ascribed your displeasure, added to which I know only too well how little of youth's cheerful spirit you enjoyed, how much of a disposition towards melancholy brooding you have inherited as a sad legacy from your father. This has often worried me but I could not change it, and so I had to content myself and hope that time, which changes so much, might perhaps change you too in this respect.'

But Johanna was flexible enough at least to consider a fundamental change in Arthur's situation. To her the career predetermined for him by his father was less of a taboo than it was for Arthur himself, who might complain but made no effort to change the situation. In a letter of 10 March 1807, interspersed with cheerful chatter about her social life, Arthur read: 'I often wish you were here, and when Fernow and Schütze tell me how late they started their studies, and when I see what the two have become, many a project flies through my head, but of course both brought school knowledge and painfully self-acquired knowledge to the Academy, which you, given the elegant education you received and in our position had to receive, lack. Both of them, born in very limited mediocrity at a small place, were able to do without many a pleasure without even desiring it, the kind of pleasure that you are bound to think indispensable, at least in the future, so you will probably have to stay with the career which you have chosen. Here, where no one is rich, everything is seen differently. Over there everyone strives for money; here no one gives it a thought, one merely wants to live.'

The reflections broke off: Arthur was to stick to his path. He was probably not cut out for another. Over there, in Hamburg, the elegant, sophisticated world of money which Arthur had chosen, here in Weimar a modest, restricted outward life with the joys of the spirit. Over there was having, here was being. Arthur's love of being was not strong enough to make him forgo having. That was how his mother saw it. That Arthur believed he had to keep the promise he had made to his father – an idea on which he was fixed – never entered his mother's mind. That kind of attachment to the dead was alien to her. On the contrary, she was not sparing with posthumous criticism of her husband's authoritarian decisions. 'When everything for you was still possible, my voice did not count,' she wrote, still offended. Between the lines she was suggesting: you do not owe your misery to me, but to your father whom you venerate so much. At the end of her letter of 10 March 1807 Johanna described an encounter she had with Wieland, which triggered off a lot in Arthur: 'He spoke a great deal of himself, of his youth, of his talent. "No one," he said, "knew me or understood me . . ." Then he related . . . that he was not really born to be a poet, that only circumstances . . . had led him to be one, that he had missed his career, he should have studied philosophy.'

This letter and especially Wieland's confession seem to have once more stirred up Arthur's whole despair about his career which he knew to be a mistake, for in response to her letter his mother received a 'long serious letter which deserves a serious answer, and which,' Johanna wrote, 'has cost me some thought and some worry whether and how I could help.'

Johanna gave herself two weeks for reflection, then she showed Arthur's letter to the palaeologist Fernow, with whom she had in the meantime become friendly and whose judgement she respected. On 28 April she wrote a very long letter which , along with Fernow's opinion, was to mark a turning point in Arthur's life.

The letter reveals the self-denial it must have cost Johanna to write it. She was distressed by Arthur's 'indecision' and by his assumption that she should take responsibility for her by then adult son. No one, she assured him repeatedly, could relieve him of that responsibility; he should listen to his own inner voice. She advised the future metaphysicist of will to explore his own will and then to follow it; 'with tears in my eyes I implore you, do not deceive yourself, deal with yourself seriously and honestly, your life's well-being is at stake.' Johanna appealed to his courage to free himself, to his will for happiness. Could a mother better respect her son's sovereign right to his life?

The question of the correct road of Arthur's life stirred up in Johanna bitter thoughts and memories. More clearly than ever before she spoke to her son of her marriage as a period in her life that had been a mistake: 'I know what it means to live a life that contradicts our inmost nature, and if possible I wish . . . to save you that misery.'

Once more she put the alternative before her son's eyes: on the one hand a merchant's career, with the 'hope of becoming rich and perhaps respected, and living in a big city', on the other that of a scholar, 'a moderately busy life, quiet and without splendour, perhaps unknown, lit up only by the striving and accomplishment of something better'. Johanna could not know how accurately these words would apply to Arthur's future life.

If Arthur were to decide against being a merchant, she advised him to opt for a 'daily-bread discipline', 'so that you have a definite objective towards which you work, because only a firm purpose ensures happiness'.

In any event, Johanna wished to smooth both roads for her son. 'When you have come to a decision let me know,' she wrote, 'but you must make your decision yourself, I do not wish to and will not advise you.'

Nor could Fernow advise him by his expert opinion, but he declared at once that, provided only Arthur had the resolute will, it was by no means too late to switch to a new course of study. Fernow added some very shrewd remarks about the fundamental problem of planning one's life, about the difficulty of finding oneself – observations which were later to appear almost verbatim in Schopenhauer's 'Aphorismen zur Lebensweisheit' ('Aphorisms on Practical Wisdom'). Fernow wrote: 'But such a decision, which is decisive for one's whole life, must therefore be preceded by the most serious and severe examination of oneself, or else the urge should have been so strong and decided from the outset that one might absolutely surrender to it as to every true natural instinct; this last course, needless to say, is the safest and best, for it proves the inner calling. Without this it is, admittedly, very ill-advised from mere dissatisfaction with one occupation to hurl oneself into another that may attract us by its outward charms but of which we do not know whether sooner or later it may not likewise excite our boredom or dissatisfaction. In that case not only is precious time irretrievably lost, but as a result of such a deception one turns mistrustful even of oneself, and loses the courage and strength to create a new plan for one's life and to follow it.'

This encouragement finally gave Arthur the strength to make his decision. 'When I had read this essay,' Arthur Schopenhauer confessed in his old age, 'I shed a flood of tears' (C, 382). He immediately gave notice of termination of his apprenticeship with Jenisch; he was going to study, he was casting off his father's world. But it was his mother who had given him the freedom which he had not seized for himself.

CHAPTER SIX

THE OUTSIDER

Arthur replied by return to the liberating letter from his mother. Johanna was convinced by the prompt resolution of her normally rather hesitant son. 'That you have so quickly come to a decision, against your wont, would disquiet me in anyone else, I should fear rashness; with you it reassures me, I regard it as the power of the natural instinct that drives you' (14 May 1807). But now he should display perseverance, concentrate his strength, renounce the splendid prosperity of a future merchant magnate; any remorse now would be too late. 'You can be happy only if you do not waver now,' Johanna wrote. He had now also incurred an obligation towards her, because she did not want to have to blame herself later 'that I did not strive to meet your wishes'. Johanna, as she had promised, cleared the road for her son; she wrote a letter to Arthur's patron, another to his landlord, she organized his move, and she prepared quarters for her son in nearby Gotha.

Gotha's '*Gymnasium illustre*' enjoyed a high reputation; it was regarded almost as a university. Friedrich Jacobs, for instance, its classics master, was well known in the literary and in the scholarly world. He had gained fame mainly by his translations of Demosthenes' speeches. One of these, the *Oration against Alien Oppressors*, was circulating in liberal-minded circles. Jacobs also followed an idiosyncratic interpretation of Christianity, which he called a 'religion of liberty and equality'. He was well liked in Romantic circles, where Arnim and Brentano were his friends. He corresponded with Jean Paul. He also maintained contact with Johanna's close friend Fernow. In fact it had been Fernow who suggested the Gotha grammar school.

Johanna Schopenhauer arranged board and lodgings for Arthur at the house of Karl Gotthold Lenz, a professor at the *Gymnasium* and brother of the headmaster of the Weimar school. She settled Arthur's admission to the school and engaged teachers for private tuition. All this his mother organized promptly; she kept the initiative. Arthur's wishes, as far as accommodation, school and teachers were concerned, were not consulted. The possibility that he might catch up on his grammar-school education in Weimar was not even considered by Johanna. Arthur, delighted at the new turn in his life, appeared to have unresistingly approved of his mother's arrangements.

Parting from Hamburg, towards the end of May 1807, was not painful. There was no one there to whom he was especially attached – except for Anthime Grégoire, who had lodged with him at the Willinck boarding house for the past few months. But even his relationship with Anthime was fed mainly by the past, by memories of the happy years of his youth in Le Havre. And that kind of friendship is even better cultivated at a distance, when dreams and backward-looking expectations remain untouched, unused, unrealized, and hence beautiful. Their present togetherness was – to Arthur at least – disappointing in the long run. True, Anthime did not follow his commercial career with any passion either, but cultural or philosophical interests were equally alien to him. Unlike Arthur, he felt no inclination to break out of his tradition-prescribed commercial career. His brief visits to the world of the spirit were made for the sake of his friend. He dutifully followed the reading programme (Goethe, Schiller, Jean Paul, Tieck) dictated to him by Arthur. Ten years later he would write to his friend: 'I live like a real businessman, and had I not learned something in the past I would probably be the most ignorant creature on earth.'

Only as a lady-killer did Anthime feel his friend's equal, or even his superior. And only in this respect did Arthur feel challenged by his friend. As late as his stay in Dresden, between 1814 and 1818, Arthur seems to have felt the need to boast to Anthime of his love affairs: on 1 June 1817 Anthime, replying to a letter from Arthur, wrote: 'As an old practitioner I confess to you that I am unconvinced that the faithfulness of your belle will be of long duration. Meanwhile make the most of your illusion.'

On Arthur's departure the friendship between the two faded rather rapidly. Anthime, too, left Hamburg at the end of 1807 and returned to France. One more meeting was planned *en route*, at Erfurt, but Anthime at the last moment cried off: he wished to save his purse for Paris. That seemed more important to him, and Arthur for his part evidently did not grieve over the cancelled meeting. Infrequent letters continued to be exchanged until 1817. Anthime was running his business in Le Havre with success, albeit 'without deriving much pleasure from it', as he wrote on one occasion. He was pursuing the 'joys of life . . . horses, carriages, servants . . .' Almost twenty years later, on 17 September 1836, Anthime got in touch once more. He had seen a mention in a newspaper of Johanna Schopenhauer's novel *Die Tante* (*The Aunt*) and been reminded of his old friend. Via his sister Adele, Anthime's letter reached Arthur, who responded with an extensive account of his life. Soon, however, the newly revived correspondence focused on financial matters, evidently the only subject now linking the two men. Arthur requested Anthime's advice on whether he should invest his money with a Paris life assurance company. When Anthime offered to manage part of the Schopenhauer fortune Arthur at once became mistrustful. On the back of Anthime's letter he noted Baltasar Graciáni's Rule 144: 'Make one's entry with another's affair in order to leave with one's own.'

The relationship broke off again. In 1845, nearly forty years after their parting in Hamburg, there was a final meeting. Anthime, twice widowed in the meantime, visited Arthur Schopenhauer in Frankfurt – for Arthur a disappointing reunion. To others he described the friend of his youth as an 'unbearable old man' and drew the conclusion that 'the older one grows the more one diverges. In the end one is quite alone' (C, 264).

Arthur Schopenhauer emerged from his personal crisis at the moment when the worst ever economic and political crisis began for the city of Hamburg. Perhaps his life as a merchant would have come to an end anyway. Following the French occupation of the city on 19 November 1806 and the intensification of the Continental Blockade against Britain, Hamburg's wholesale trade was almost totally wrecked at one blow. Within a few weeks over 180 merchant houses suspended payments. Three hundred sea-going vessels were laid up in port. High taxes, compulsory loans and requisitioning wiped out the fortunes of even the affluent. It was this grave crisis that induced Anthime to return to France prematurely. But economic bankruptcy was only the first of the sufferings still in store for the city. During the War of Liberation of 1813–14, Hamburg became the theatre for the fiercely fought final engagements. The suburbs were destroyed by fire, and the city itself trembled under the French threat that it would be turned to ashes sooner than be surrendered to the Russian–Prussian troops. Epidemics spread. Anyone unable to lay in stores for the siege was expelled. Death and hardship reigned in the city. All this Arthur Schopenhauer was spared: he was leaving a sinking ship when he set out for Gotha at the end of May 1807.

Gotha, like Weimar, was a small princely residence. It cowered beneath the massive Friedenstein Castle, in the metaphorical sense as well. The old town numbered 1297 houses. Life there unfolded within an area only 1200 paces wide. Everything huddled closely together: the churches, a barracks, a prison, several clubs where billiards were played and newspapers read, an orphanage, a theatre, beer saloons and inns. The adjacent Castle Park was open to the public on certain days. In it reigned the charm and gracefulness of the rococo. 'Vive la joie' – 'Long live joy' – was inscribed on one of the Trianons. Gotha court life was renowned for its relaxed style. In the eighteenth century the leading figures of hedonistic-materialistic Enlightenment, d'Allembert and Helvetius, were members of the round table of the castle; a few years later the Duchess adorned her drawing room with the busts of the Paris revolutionaries, and the small court orchestra played the march of the sans-culottes.

In the town below all this was seen as mere extravagance. There, preference was given to the strict spirit of Pietism, and the upper bourgeoisie allowed itself to be passed through the moral purification filter of the Masonic lodges. The town was proud of its grammar school. Its pupils came from far and wide. There were booksellers in town, as well as a lending library whose use, however, was not permitted to unmarried women. Gotha was renowned for its grilling sausages; Arthur had to send some to his mother. On summer evenings the school choir sang in the park. On the birthdays and service anniversaries of senior officials small processions were staged in academic garb: black gowns and tricorn hats. The bulk of the population – artisans, shopkeepers, farming citizens, court employees – lived their small-town lives as anywhere else: in awe of the greater and lesser gods, jealously guarding the often minute differences in social rank among them, anxious for their accustomed security, spiteful against anything that did not conform to their mould. A few weeks after his arrival Arthur, with condescending amusement, nailed this small world in a poem about the 'Gotha Philistines':

> They snoop, they listen, they watch
>> Everything that happens,
>> What everyone is up to, what everyone does,
>> What everyone says, aloud or softly,
>> Nothing escapes them.
> Their eyes peer through windows,
>> Their ears listen at doors,
>> Nothing must happen unobserved,
>> The cat must not climb on the roof
>> Without them knowing about it.
> A man's spirit, ideas, or worth
>> Do not make them prick up their ears:
>> But how much he consumes each year,
>> Whether he justly belongs
>> To the town's dignitaries,
> Whether he must be saluted first,
>> Whether he is 'Herr von' and gracious,
>> Whether Councillor or mere Secretary,
>> Whether a Lutheran or Roman Christian,
>> Married or single.
> How big his house, how fine his coat,
>> Is thoroughly considered,
>> Yet: Can he be of use to us?
>> Counts more than any other
>> Great or small consideration.
> Another question is what does he think of us,
>> How does he speak of us?
>> One makes inquiries of Hinz and Kunz,
>> One weighs one's words with Loth and Unz,
>> Examines all their features.

(P 1, 3)

Arthur, buoyed up by upper-middle-class pride and carried along by the élan of a new start, refused to be drawn down into this petty world. Zealously he flung himself into his studies. Professor Jacobs praised his German essays. Headmaster Doering praised his progress in the classical languages. It seems that in his letters to Anthime and to his mother Arthur was not sparing with hymns of self-praise, for Anthime replied: 'Your enormous progress does not astonish me, as I also know your *enormous* abilities and consider you capable of learning anything you wish' (4 September 1807). His mother was rather reserved in her reactions: 'That you are doing well in your studies is no more than I expected,' she wrote on 29 July 1807. He should not let Doering's praise go to his head, because Doering, as was known even in Weimar, had the 'weakness . . . of blowing his pupil's trumpet mightily'. Nor should he allow the success of his German essays to lead him into entangling himself prematurely with 'the fair sciences': 'the applause which one gains with them is too pleasant not to surrender to them entirely, and yet, if one wishes to rise above the universal dilettantism that is now practised by every hairdresser's apprentice and to achieve something worth while in them, one must first engage in serious and thorough studies.'

His progress at school was not the only thing that Arthur boasted of to his friend and to his mother. Proudly he reported on his pleasures, which he was seeking and finding in aristocratic circles. This might impress Anthime. 'I envy you,' he wrote back, 'especially for your beautiful party in the Thuringian Forest, and how unbending was Monsieur to be dancing with princesses' (4 September 1807). His mother, on the other hand, was far from delighted with the social conquests he reported from Gotha. 'I do not much like the idea,' she wrote, 'of your attaching yourself to no one but *Comtesses* and *Barons*. Is there really no one of our class that might interest you? The views and prospects of those people who, unlike yourself, are not born to make money and who therefore think themselves better, are different from ours; moreover, contact with them leads to greater expense and distorts our point of view. Like it or not, you belong to the bourgeois world, stay in it, and remember that you assured me that you wished to renounce all glamour if you could only live for the sciences, and that this would bring you greater honour than a chase after tinsel and glitter' (12 August 1807).

Johanna's objections to Arthur's movement in aristocratic circles was motivated not only by bourgeois pride but also by the painful subject of money, which was later totally to destroy relations between mother and son. Johanna enjoined Arthur to be more frugal – and not without good reason, for Arthur was in fact living in grand style. Within five weeks, for instance, he spent over 160 *Reichstaler*, the monthly salary of a senior civil servant. On an excursion to Liebenstein with his aristocratic friends he spent 10 *Reichstaler* in a single day – the monthly earnings of a small craftsman. *Hofrätin* Ludecus, Arthur's mother informed him, had lived in the same place for the same money for nearly a week. Arthur hired riding horses, was fond of eating elegantly, and was anxious, as his mother suspected, 'to present himself as a rich freely-spending Hamburger'. According to the law of inheritance Arthur was not yet of age. His share of the family fortune was administered by his mother. The money she sent him regularly was therefore money due to him. Why then her appeals to economy, and why her pecuniary supervision which Arthur found so irksome?

Johanna was concerned, not without justification, that Arthur's scholarly ambitions, while satisfying him, would not feed him and that, in consequence, he would have to husband his share of the family fortune if he wished to preserve his independence. His fortune would also have to maintain a whole family, for she did not doubt, at least for the time being, that Arthur would found a family. She was hoping, moreover, that Arthur would 'beautify' her old age; she was hoping, she wrote, 'to spend my last days in your house with your children, as befits an old grandmother'. And finally she expected her son to look after his younger sister Adele, 'if I die before she is provided for'. Arthur's fortune would only be sufficient for all these bourgeois obligations if he now, during his school and university days, spent it carefully – living well but dispensing with Hamburg 'elegance'.

Johanna felt the more entitled to supervise her son's monetary affairs as Arthur for his part invariably assumed the right to criticize her economic management. The frequency with which Johanna reports on her 'cheap' entertainments, acquisitions, journeys, etc., is striking; the way she emphasizes the inexpensive life in Weimar or the modest means by which she maintained her *salon*: she offered her guests only tea with bread and butter, and they were satisfied. 'Once you see . . . the life we lead here you will regard all this [spending money] as philistinism and feel ashamed of it,' she wrote. There is always, in these passages, an undertone of having to justify her lifestyle to her son. 'I always . . . have a lot of visitors, who cost me nothing,' she pointed out, or, 'Myself, I shrink from all unnecessary expense.'

Arthur's mistrust of his mother's economic management sprang from his fear that by her lavish domestic style she might spend part of the family fortune even before the share-out. Having decided in favour of a scholar's career he kept an anxious eye on their joint fortune, because he too realized that he might have to depend on his inheritance in the future. Altogether his mother's *joie de vivre* after his father's death seemed sinister to him. He was afraid she might marry again. Johanna had to reassure him: her close friend Fernow was over forty years old, ailing, not a handsome man, and moreover married already. On another occasion she wrote: 'I have no shortage of admirers, but do not let it worry you' (23 March 1807). None of this was to the taste of Arthur, who would have liked the role of his father's representative *vis-à-vis* his mother and who would have had no objection to seeing her lead a quiet, retiring life, piously devoted to the memory of the deceased and dedicated exclusively to caring for her children.

So far his mother was displaying care for her son, and he was courting her approval. But mistrust was growing. It first showed in money matters. While the geographical distance between them was great, the mother's letters were particularly cordial and the son felt encouraged to pour out his grief-laden heart to her. The move to Gotha brought them closer together, and mutual irritation increased. The moment of truth arrived when Arthur, after a mere five months, had to leave Gotha and was about to encroach on his mother's preserves in Weimar.

At school Arthur very soon became a 'kind of celebrity', as his mother put it. His academic progress was conspicuous, he attended only those subjects which were taught in German, and in these, as he had little leeway to make up, he shone especially. He was older than his classmates, his man-of-the-world manner set him apart from them, his lifestyle was totally unlike that of a young man at school. His classmates admired him, listened to his oracular pronouncements, allowed him to pay for them, imitated him, and crowded around him – as, for instance, did Carl John, who was to become Goethe's secretary and later a Prussian censorship official (whom Varnhagen called a 'butcher of thought'), or Ernst Lewald, subsequently a famous philologist in Heidelberg.

His sense of intellectual and social superiority – also to some of his teachers – encouraged Arthur into 'dangerous pranks'. In one poem, which he recited to a circle of friends, he lampooned a Gotha schoolmaster who had pilloried the bullying of younger pupils by their elders. Otherwise, this Christian Ferdinand Schulze was a meek man with the inevitable vanities of a small-town notable. The poem read:

> The pulpit's ornament, the master's desk's delight,
> The town's storyteller and the lodge's spokesman,
> A perfect Christian, perfect Jew and pagan,
> Carrying books in the morning, a fan in the evening,
> The master of all seven liberal arts,
> The man who can do everything and knows everything,
> The flower and crown of all great spirits,
> Who has thousands of friends – and drops their names.

> [P I, 4]

It was the 'friends' of this 'master's desk's delight' who brought disaster upon Arthur. The teaching body got wind of the lampoon. They had no sense of humour, and headmaster Doering, out of collegial solidarity, cancelled Arthur's private tuition. Arthur, as he reported in his curriculum vitae, could have stayed on at the *Gymnasium*, but his pride was hurt by Doering's punitive measure. Losing the good will of persons in authority had a chilling effect. He was unable, as he might do later, to stand up to it and face it out. He wrote to his mother that he wished to leave Gotha. Johanna was alarmed, for Arthur had allowed it to be understood that he would like to come to Weimar.

This situation represented a challenge to Johanna. If Arthur should come to Weimar her own happiness would be at stake. She had to face a whole series of questions: How did she feel about Arthur? Did she want to have him close to her? What were her wishes, what did she expect of life? What moral duties did she have, and how did these 'duties' relate to what really went on inside her?

As for the immediate cause – Arthur's silly prank on the schoolmasters – she did not attach much importance to that. But she blamed Arthur for having lacked the sovereign detachment which would have accepted a fool as being a fool. In consequence he had now become the victim of foolish wrath. Anyone attracting the wrath of fools was a fool himself. And what had led him into his foolishness was his 'super-cleverness', his self-righteousness and his arrogance. Johanna, irritated but yet striving for precision, drew a somewhat unflattering portrait of her son, one that left little to be desired in explicitness. Johanna did not rail but, unsentimentally, held a merciless mirror up to Arthur: 'You are not an evil person. You are not without a mind or education. You have everything that might make you an ornament of human society. I am acquainted with your disposition and I know that few are better, but you are nevertheless irritating and unbearable, and I consider it most difficult to live with you. All your good qualities are darkened by your super-cleverness and rendered useless to the world, merely because you cannot control your rage at wanting to know everything better, of finding fault everywhere except in yourself, of wanting to improve and master everything. Thereby you embitter the people around you – no one wishes to be improved or illuminated in such a forcible manner, least of all by such an insignificant individual as you still are, no one can tolerate being criticized by you, who display so many weaknesses yourself, least of all in that derogatory manner of yours which, in oracular tones, proclaims this is so and so, without even suspecting the possibility of contradiction. If you were less like you are, you would only be ridiculous, but thus you are most annoying. People generally are not evil unless you provoke them; you might have quietly lived and studied in Gotha as thousands of others, and the universal law would have permitted you all personal freedom if you had calmly followed your road and let others calmly follow theirs, but you did not want that, and so you are expelled ... such an ambulant literary journal as you would like to be is a boring hateful thing because one cannot skip pages or fling the whole rubbishy thing behind the stove, as one can with the printed ones.'

Johanna was here indirectly formulating the sceptical maxims of her life: you live in a society, you cannot escape from it, you have to come to terms with it, and you can come to terms with it provided you let everyone go his own way and make sure you are not prevented from going yours. Hence – and there is already a hint to that effect in these passages – she was determined not to let her son prevent her from going her own way. The Gotha incident disturbed her because it revealed Arthur's character, a character from which she feared encroachments on her living space. After all, Arthur had already, on his few visits to Weimar, provided samples of his bad-tempered mania for criticizing. Prior to one of these visits his mother had for that reason enjoined Arthur to 'bring with you good humour and leave your argumentative spirit behind so that I need not argue every evening over fine literature or the emperor's beard'. Now, however, it was no longer a case of an isolated visit but of her son's possible removal to Weimar. To begin with she stalled Arthur: she needed time to consider, and there was also the risk that her recent displeasure at Arthur's foolishness in Gotha might lead to 'violent scenes'. If meanwhile Arthur's stay in Gotha was purgatory to him, then this would do him no harm. If he had to act like that, let him face the music afterwards.

A month later, by the end of November 1807, Johanna had made her decision: she recommended to Arthur the *Gymnasium* in nearby Altenburg but would, at a pinch, agree to his move to Weimar. In that case, however, certain rules would have to be observed, to prevent them clashing with each other and 'impairing the freedom of both'.

More outspokenly than ever before Johanna discussed her relationship with her son: 'I think it wisest to tell you straight out what I desire and how I feel about matters, so that we understand one another from the outset. That I am very fond of you you will not doubt, I have proved it to you and will prove it to you as long as I live. It is necessary for my happiness to know that you are happy, but not to be a witness of it. I have always told you that you are very difficult to live with . . . I will not conceal from you that, so long as you are as you are, I would rather make any sacrifice than decide in favour of living together. I am not blind to your good points; besides, that which repels me from you lies not in your . . . inmost being but in your manner, in your exterior, your views, your judgements, your habits. In short I cannot agree with you in anything that concerns the external world; moreover, your ill humour depresses me and upsets my serenity without helping you in the least. Look, dear Arthur, you were visiting me only for a few days, and each time there were violent scenes, about nothing and again about nothing, and each time I only breathed freely again when you had gone, because your presence, your complaints about inevitable things, your scowling face, the bizarre judgements uttered by you like oracular pronouncements not permitting any kind of objection, oppressed me, and even more so the everlasting struggle inside me, by which I forcibly stifled everything I would have liked to object to, in order not to provide an occasion for renewed quarrelling. I now live very calmly, for many years I have had not a single unpleasant moment that I did not owe to you, I am tranquil in myself, no one contradicts me, I contradict no one, not a loud word is heard in my household, everything runs its monotonous course, as I run mine, nowhere could you tell who commands and who obeys, everyone quietly goes about his own business, and life glides along I do not know how. This is my truest existence, and it must remain so if the tranquillity and happiness of what years are left to me mean anything to you. When you grow older, dear Arthur, and see many things more brightly, we shall also be in better harmony with one another.'

In Weimar Johanna, encouraged by her great model Goethe, had acquired a relaxed attitude ('life glides along') which she now felt was threatened by Arthur and which, rather less relaxedly, she would now have to defend. Let things take their course, let oneself and others be, hold back with judgements, interference and commands – that was Weimar's Taoism, in which Johanna had then found her inner peace. In fact, this was also what Arthur was longing for, but he, so fond of climbing mountains, was meanwhile only able to find it at sublime spots, from which one might 'observe with greatest calm and without participation, even though that part of us which belongs to the corporeal world is being torn this way or that' (P I, 8). This sublimity he found in music, in literature, and even on his first excursions into philosophy. Yet 'participation' in the bustle while at the same time preserving calm, in other words a relaxed participation – that he was not capable of. In one of the few extant fragments of letters written to his mother at that time we read: 'It is incomprehensible how, when the eternal soul was banished into the body, it was torn from its former *sublime apathy*, drawn down into the pettiness of the earthly and so scattered through the body and the corporeal world that it forgot its former condition and participated in what from its former point of view was an infinitely small earthly existence, and so established itself in the latter that it limited its whole existence to it and filled it with it' (CL, 2).

He allowed himself to be drawn down into the 'pettiness' of the 'earthly' more than he would have liked. Curiosity, pride, the desires of his young body, thirst for experience – all these entangled him. True, he had learned to keep his distance, but it was a militant distance. At the age of nineteen he realized himself not in letting himself be but in active delimitation. He had to criticize, to judge, to condemn – only thus could he maintain his sphere. He was too old and not yet old enough to let himself go; an ever alert mistrust kept him tense. He could not just go along with things: he lacked the basic confidence to do that. He found silence difficult; he had to join in, he could not simply accept what was to him strange and heterogeneous. When his mother, remarking on his occasional visits to Weimar, called him an 'ambulant literary journal' and complained of his literary quarrelsomeness, it is easy to imagine what this argumentative young man was after: Arthur, of course, had discovered the Romantics in Hamburg, such as Wackenroder, Tieck . . . and their 'extravagances' were not greatly appreciated in Goethe's Weimar and hence neither in Johanna Schopenhauer's *salon*. Arthur, on the other hand, is certain to have fought for his cause, for the tender empiricism of the Romantics, against his mother whom, as the son of a father with conventional views on women, he did not take seriously intellectually and in whose opinions he probably only heard an echo of Weimar's appeals for moderation. His mother, however, had not only absorbed new opinions in Weimar but found a new rhythm of life, her 'truest existence', as she put it. Did Arthur understand that? We cannot tell: his mother could not tell either and therefore, to defend her living space, did not rely on Arthur's understanding but laid down a new, exceedingly precise, ritual of relations that would, at least outwardly, ensure mutual tolerance. 'Mark now on what footing I wish to be together with you: you are at home in your lodgings, in mine you are a guest, rather as I was in my parents' house after my marriage, a welcome, dear guest who is always cordially received but who does not interfere in any domestic arrangements; these, as well as Adele's education and health, or my domestic staff are none of your concern at all. I have managed these so far without you, I shall continue to do so without tolerating any objection, because this makes me angry and is of no help. Every day you will come at one o'clock and stay until three, then I shall not see you again all day long, except on my social days which you may attend if you wish, also eating at my house those two evenings, provided you will abstain from tiresome arguing, which makes me angry, as well as from any lamentation about the stupid world and human misery, because this always gives me a bad night and ugly dreams, and I like to sleep well. During the midday hours you can tell me everything that I have to know about you, the rest of the time you must look after yourself. I cannot provide your entertainment at the expense of mine. Besides, this would not work; I have been used too long to being on my own, I cannot break the habit now and so I ask you do not speak against it. I am not departing from this plan on any account, as for your supper I shall send it to you every evening by my cook, as for your tea you should have that in the house, I shall give you the necessary crockery for it, also a caddy of tea if you wish. . . . Three times a week there is the theatre, twice parties, you can find enough relaxation, also you will surely soon find some young acquaintances, suppose I were not here? Enough, now you know my wishes, I hope you will act precisely in accordance with them and not repay me for my motherly care and love, and for my quick agreement to your wishes, by grieving me by opposition, which would not help you but make everything even worse.'

Arthur arrived in Weimar on 23 December 1807; he had accepted his mother's terms. He moved into a small apartment in the house of a hatter. He prepared himself for the university by private study; he also received tuition from Franz Ludwig Passow, a grammar-school teacher only a few years older than himself. Arthur immersed himself in his work. By the end of his time in Weimar he would have complete mastery of the classical languages and be familiar with the major works of ancient literature. He would enter Göttingen University in the proud knowledge of his superiority: his fellow students and even some of his professors would not be his equals. And yet he would not be happy during those two years. In Gotha he had been the central figure; in Weimar he was an outsider. Julius Frauenstädt reported in 1863: 'Schopenhauer also told me that vis-à-vis his mother and her circle he had always felt a stranger and lonely, and that in Weimar, too, people had been dissatisfied with him' (C, 130).

Unlike Johanna, who was willing and able to regulate her relations with her son in an unequivocal manner, Arthur was full of unadmitted ambivalences. Towards his mother he displayed a will to independence and self-sufficiency, but subliminally he also expected his mother to make a comfortable home for him. Johanna had sensed this expectation and had therefore, prior to his arrival, written to him very clearly. 'Of all the reasons which led you to choose Weimar I can see only the one that you wanted to be here. You are no more at home in Weimar than you were anywhere else, whether you will be so in time we shall see. I am letting you be, as I have always done.' Arthur evidently felt that the freedom granted him by his mother demanded too much of him. But his pride stopped him from acknowledging this. He became an eyewitness of his mother's social successes, but without actually participating in them. The result was envy. Even a lifetime later its echoes were heard in Arthur Schopenhauer's conversation. Frauenstädt recorded: 'With even slighter respect he spoke of his mother, of whom he told me what a glamorous life she had led, and how she had been surrounded in Weimar by aesthetes' (C, 130). But they had not only been 'aesthetes': Goethe himself was a frequent guest at Johanna's house and in those two years he never once addressed Arthur. That was hurtful, especially as, according to unanimous contemporary reports, Goethe showed himself more relaxed, more obliging and more human at Johanna's house than anywhere else. Arthur had to be content with being a mere spectator whenever that natural phenomenon Goethe made his appearance.

Goethe would usually arrive towards seven in the evening, with a hand lantern. For his return home he had occasionally to be helped out with a fresh taper. He liked chatting to Sophie, Johanna's housemaid. He would also go to the nursery to see Adele, who was then ten years old; she produced her toys for him and he would make the puppets dance on their strings. Whenever Goethe entered the room, Johanna recounted, he was 'always a little silent and in a way embarrassed . . . until he had taken a good look to see who was present, and then he would always sit down close to me, a little way back, so that he could support himself on the backrest of my chair. I would then first start a conversation with him, then he would come to life and be indescribably charming. He is the most perfect creature I know, also in his appearance, a tall fine figure, holding himself very straight, very carefully dressed, always in black or in very dark blue, his hair rather tastefully done and powdered, as befits his age, and a very magnificent face with two clear brown eyes, mild and piercing at the same time, and when he speaks he turns incredibly handsome.'

He did not 'oppress' anyone by his greatness, Johanna thought; indeed, his presence encouraged everyone's naturalness. This, however, was not as others saw it. Stephan Schütze reported: 'One would feel quite alarmed when he entered the company in bad humour and strode up and down. When he was silent one did not know who should speak next.' For such an event Johanna had a little table with painting things all prepared. There the ill-humoured Goethe would sit down and lighten his mood by sketching and watercolour painting. Afterwards people would be fighting for the sheets, unless Johanna had first safely put them away. But even in good humour Goethe might seem despotic. On one of Johanna's evenings Goethe had brought along some Scottish ballads and, according to Schütze, offered 'to recite one of considerable length himself, but in such a manner that the refrain which recurred in each verse should always be spoken by the women in chorus. The bombastic recital began, the ladies kept themselves ready and entered at the right moment, the first verse was successfully accomplished, but as the same words recurred for the second and third time Frau Professor Reinbek was overcome by involuntary laughter; Goethe stopped, lowered the book and turned on them all the fiery eyes of a thundering Jove: "Then I will not read!" he said quite curtly. There was a good deal of alarm; but Johanna Schopenhauer pleaded, again pledged obedience and vouched for the others. So in God's name a fresh start was made – and indeed! to see all the ladies move their chins in simultaneous rhythm upon command had about it such a comic aspect that it required the full authority of a Goethe to keep the whole company in the commanded solemn seriousness.'

Goethe himself, admittedly, missed the involuntary comedy he had caused. In his *Tages- und Jahreshefte* (*Daily and Yearly Notebooks*) he recorded the event in these words: 'Hilla, Lilla, a Scottish ballad, was welcome to us also in the taste of a litany; the text was read in an audible voice, and the company repeated the bell-ring of the refrain in chorus.'

When Goethe was relating something or reading aloud a firework of metamorphoses took place. In mime and in intonation he turned into the person he spoke of, nothing would keep him in his chair, he gesticulated and became so loud that *Hofrätin* Ludecus, who lived above Johanna, knocked on her floor.

Goethe would talk about everyday matters, he could lament for a full hour about a *pâté de foie gras* which had been intended for guests in the evening but which, in a sudden fit of hunger, he had consumed on his own at lunchtime. In social conversation he would avoid controversies; altogether, as he frequently remarked, he found the critical manner of the younger generation most distasteful. If anyone wished to hear firm opinions or judgements from him, he would sometimes mock them by turning his initial observation into its opposite at the end of a speech. He was often heard in Johanna's *salon* to utter his dictum: 'When the people believe I am still in Weimar I have long been in Erfurt.' Arthur would have scored badly with Goethe with his critical forays and his taste for pronouncements. But in Goethe's presence Arthur still restrained himself – though this was to change during his later sojourn in Weimar.

When Goethe was in a good mood he would approve anything, even the shallow romances of Lafontaine or the tearjerkers of Kotzebue (which he frequently staged at the Weimar theatre). To the ladies in Johanna's drawing room he lectured that all that mattered was the art of enjoyment, and he was fond of suggestive remarks. From Goethe everybody would accept anything, including even Arthur, who never missed a soirée at his mother's if Goethe had promised to attend. Arthur Schopenhauer, therefore, was frequently present at the evening parties when Johanna sat behind the tea urn and in her circumspect manner kept the conversation going. Some of the illustrious visitors, who were attracted to the house by Goethe's presence, have recorded the evenings at *Hofrätin* Schopenhauer's house in their memoirs or in letters. None of them, however, took any notice of Arthur. This is true of Bettina and Clemens Brentano, of Achim von Arnim, and of the Humboldts. They all visited Johanna at the time. Only Zacharias Werner, then a comet in the theatrical sky, seems during his stay in Weimar to have also maintained contact with Arthur. Werner's diaries contain brief references to this fact, and Arthur Schopenhauer in his later years still boasted of his acquaintance with that curious man.

Zacharias Werner was at the pinnacle of his fame when Goethe brought him back with him from Jena to Weimar at Christmas 1808. His Luther play *Weihe der Kraft* (*Consecration of Power*) had been a great success on the Berlin stage in 1806. Arthur had read it in Hamburg, fascinated by the monstrosity of its action and by the drama of its language.

Werner was born in Königsberg, where he grew up in the same house as E. T. A. Hoffmann, who was his junior by eight years. His hysterical mother saw Christ reincarnated in her boy. Zacharias had no objection to that, and later switched to become a poet-god. When Schiller died he rejoiced: 'What a post has now fallen vacant!' Others too, such as Iffland and Madame de Staël, credited Werner with becoming Schiller's successor. Goethe initially scoffed at *Weihe der Kraft*, calling it 'strong incense', but when Zacharias Werner manufactured pretty little sonnets to Minnchen Herzlieb in Jena, Goethe, too, was affected and took the 'minnesinger' with him to Weimar. Their relationship, however, remained extremely ironical. Following the Weimar performance of Werner's play *Wandra*, Goethe at a banquet crowned the author with a laurel wreath which until then had adorned a pig's head. In Weimar Werner soon became a figure associated with scandal. On one occasion, when he was late for an evening party, a servant girl was sent to his home. She came running back, screaming that Werner had tried to rape her. In later years Werner became religious again: ordained a Catholic priest in 1814, he settled in Vienna as a penitential preacher, a kind of flagellant for the better classes.

Arthur had come to know Werner during his time in Gotha and had felt flattered by the illustrious acquaintance. Now in Weimar he let Werner fill him with enthusiasm for the theatre.

Frequent visits to the theatre were entirely usual in Weimar, which had little else to offer by way of entertainment. Arthur was no exception, but to him the theatre meant more than an evening's pleasure. It is interesting to note how Arthur's early philosophical reflections were triggered mainly by the theatre, particularly by tragedy. Sophocles, for instance, suggested to him a Platonism of misery: just suppose, he reflected, that our real misery was not real at all but merely an 'image' of 'real evil present in eternity' (P 1, 9). We do not project real necessity into the heavens, but, the other way about, we project the evil of the heavens into our reality and by doing so make everything worse still. Was immediate real evil then an illusion? Was the courageous gaze into metaphysical evil a relief from present evil? Arthur, subtenant of a hatter and outsider in the drawing room of the *Hofrätin* Schopenhauer, with a view to attaining impertubability, considered the strategy of derealizing real evil by way of metaphysical out-bidding. Arthur was to refine that strategy in the future – but it was hardly suitable as a lecture at Johanna's evening parties.

Johanna's social successes aroused envious hostility in some quarters. It was probably more by chance than by intention that Arthur found himself among them. There was, for instance, Passow. Arthur's mother had engaged him as a private tutor. This ambitious young philologist – whom Goethe had brought from Halle to the Weimar *Gymnasium* in the summer of 1807 – in an excess of zeal tried to outdo Goethe's 'diatribes' against the new literature by also criticizing Schiller. Goethe, out of loyalty for his dead friend, thereupon allowed it to be understood that, at parties which he attended, he did not wish to see Passow. Johanna was faced with the embarrassing task of disinviting her son's tutor. Passow, needless to say, was deeply offended. Unable to vent his anger against Goethe, he vented it against Johanna. He wrote to an acquaintance: 'You are probably aware that the bustling and garrulous Madame Schopenhauer holds certain exhibition tea parties every winter, which are exceedingly boring ... but to which all the educated and the would-be educated are rushing because Goethe has frequently been seen there.'

It is not difficult to imagine what Arthur was told about his mother by Passow, whom he regarded as an expert in his field and at whose house he even lodged for a time. Passow was a resentful man. He barricaded himself in classical antiquity and from there fired his invectives against the so-called 'aesthetes'. In company he would always remain silent, but his silence was felt to be arrogant, with something sinister lurking in it. Even Goethe was disconcerted by it, so that, as Riemer recorded, 'that which would have come out humorous and witty now issued dry and monosyllabic'.

The people seen in Johanna's drawing room were described by Passow as 'the common bipeds'. Along with philological information, Arthur also adopted this expression from his ill-tempered schoolmaster. Arthur Schopenhauer, of course, was to extend his own craving for admiration to a monstrous degree.

Another Weimar celebrity whom he saw regularly, and whose relations with Johanna Schopenhauer were likewise strained, was Johannes Daniel Falk.

Falk was a writer, promoted to Legation Councillor after 1806, though previously he had been an opponent of Napoleon. He established an orphanage in Weimar and, as a forerunner of the Domestic Mission, did much beneficial work. His passion and at the same time his weakness, however, was his excessive social ambition. His contemporaries' judgements on him are not very flattering. Riemer called him an 'intolerable chatterbox' whose verbal flow stopped only when someone superior to him appeared on the horizon, when he would instantly flutter over to him. Otherwise, as Riemer put it, 'it was impossible to insert a pin into his flow of words'. Johanna, too, ridiculed the pretensions of this man with whom, as he also came from Danzig, she had made contact before anyone else in Weimar. In a letter to Arthur she wrote this about him: 'His elegant pretensions are in fact as unbearable as they are unwise, because they become an irritation to everybody, and eventually all bourgeois doors will be closed to him, for which he is unlikely to find compensation at the courts.' Falk for his part had nothing good to say about Johanna, for the *Hofrätin* from Danzig had upset the Weimar pecking order. In his book *Goethe aus dem näheren persönlichen Umgange dargestellt* (*Goethe Presented from Close Personal Acquaintance*) he carefully avoided, in reproducing the numerous conversations he had with Goethe at Johanna's house, any mention of the place of these encounters.

With Falk, therefore, Arthur was in frequent contact; in September 1808 he travelled with him to the Rulers' Congress in Erfurt. Goethe had been summoned there: Napoleon wished to meet him and speak to him. Falk, Arthur and a few others constituted the comet's tail. The old and new dynasties, summoned by their Protector, here had a glamorous rendezvous. Arthur, however, was not greatly impressed. To Falk he engaged in 'scandalous comment on the court ladies . . . who before the comedy declared the oppressor of nations to be a monster, and *after* it the most charming man on earth' (C, 21).

Arthur's stay in Weimar was drawing to a close. Passow confirmed to him the great progress he had made in his studies: in the autumn of 1809 he would be able to enrol at the university. On 22 February 1809 Arthur celebrated his twenty-first birthday; he was now of age. His mother handed his inheritance over to him – just under 20,000 *Reichstaler*, which could yield nearly 1000 *Reichstaler* annually. That was enough for a fairly comfortable life. But his finest birthday present was participation in the grand *Redoute* of that year. What made this festive masked ball at the City Hall – organized by Goethe and Falk – so attractive to Arthur was the fact that taking part in it was Karoline Jagemann, Weimar's dramatic and operatic star, the mistress of the Duke and Goethe's adversary. Arthur was all aflame for this woman, about whose beauty the whole of Germany was raving. At the masked procession he would be close to her. She represented Thekla, he a fisherman. Thekla, however, took no notice of the fisherman. She was wearing all the jewellery the Duke had given her. Her entire attention was focused on the Duchess: how

CHAPTER SEVEN

BETWEEN PLATO AND KANT

Why in fact Göttingen? Jena was nearer – but Arthur, after two years in Weimar, may have wished to establish a greater distance between himself and his mother's world. Besides, Jena was no longer the dazzling centre of modern erudition it had been at the end of the century, when Fichte, Schelling, the Schlegel brothers and Schiller were living and teaching there.

Jena had been a fireworks display, but Göttingen was the fixed star among the German universities. Founded in 1734 by King George II of England, it soon earned a high reputation for scholarship. Here the spirit of the new age did not first have to struggle out of a theological embrace. The natural sciences, a form of speculative empirical pursuit, here set the tone from the outset. Albrecht von Haller was the leader of this philosophical trend in Göttingen about the middle of the eighteenth century. He taught medicine, botany and surgery, wrote didactic political novels of an aristocratic-republican nature, and founded the Anatomical Theatre, a panopticon of exposed slices of the body. This active enlightener was also responsible for the establishment of a botanical garden and a maternity hospital. Haller earned lasting acclaim in the field of physiology. He used all his influence to make Göttingen the stronghold of 'modern' science. The famous satirist and author of aphorisms, George Christoph Lichtenberg, taught physics and mathematics at the Georgia Augusta University; Carl Friedrich Gauss was director of the Göttingen astronomical observatory and also taught mathematics. Yet another scientific celebrity was the anatomist and anthropologist Johann Friedrich Blumenbach. Arthur Schopenhauer actually attended the lectures of this patriarch of the good old days. It was the scientific reputation of Göttingen's university which induced August Wilhelm Schlegel to advise all those who wished to devote themselves to philosophical and speculative pursuits to start by laying the solid foundations of empirical studies in Göttingen. Schlegel called the Georgia Augusta University a 'centre of German scholarship', where it was possible 'to keep abreast of all new scientific knowledge of the century'. To be up-to-date with the knowledge of the day was also the desire of Arthur, a latecomer but the more ambitious for that. Moreover, Göttingen was up-to-date in another respect: there was something smart and elegant about the university. It was a favourite place for the aristocracy and upper bourgeoisie to send their sons because, alongside the natural sciences, the university also promoted the English-inspired political sciences. Anyone passing the examinations of Ludwig Schlözer or Johann Stephan Pütter had a senior civil-service career open to him. All this probably also nurtured student arrogance. The city administration tried to reduce the number of cattle in the town because the students felt disturbed by the sight of the cows. The artisan lads, on the other hand, got on well with the cows but not with the students. There were frequent clashes, invariably triggered off by 'right of the pavement', who had to yield to whom in the street. Clashes escalated into riots and retaliatory raids on apprentices' hostels and the premises of student associations. When the young gentlemen, in spite of their epees, were worsted by the young artisans (a student manual of the day called them 'lumps of flesh without sense, wit or reason') there were occasional 'exoduses'. The students left the city, and the citizens, worried about their lucrative source of income, had to beg the gentlemen to return. Satisfaction would be demanded by the students. And so the apprentices were punished, and the most gifted among them even composed poems of apology. To celebrate the students' return the innkeepers granted them the freedom of their taverns. They could be noisy all night long.

That the students in Göttingen were particularly prone to excess is confirmed by Heinrich Heine. 'Some people even claim,' Heine says in his *Harzreise* (*Journey through the Harz Mountains*), 'that the city was built at the time of the Migration of Nations. Every German tribe then left there an unbound copy of its members, and from them are descended all those Vandals, Frisians, Swabians, Teutons, Saxons, Thuringians, etc., who to this day march down Weenderstrasse in Göttingen, in hordes, distinguished by the colour of their caps and pipe tassels, and who, on the bloody battlegrounds of the Rasenmühle, the Ritschenkrug and Bovden, eternally fight one another, their customs and practices still the same as at the time of the Migration of Nations.'

Arthur Schopenhauer felt attracted to the nobler part of this local mixture of rioting and blasé disdain, of elegance and pugnaciousness. He remained aloof from rowdiness and riots, his pistol remained suspended over his bed. His pugnaciousness was confined to debating, though he practised this in a rather rude manner in the small circle of his acquaintances. His fellow student Karl Josias von Bunsen, Prussia's future representative at the Holy See, reports: 'His debating is rough and spiky, his tone is as sulky as his brow, his disputation when he is heated and his paradoxical argument are terrible.'

As a city Göttingen had little that was of particular charm. Heine thought it most beautiful when 'viewed with one's back'. He says: 'The city of Göttingen, famous for its sausages and university, belongs to the King of Hanover, and comprises 999 hearths, diverse churches, a maternity hospital, an observatory, a prison, a library and a Ratskeller, where the beer is excellent.'

In that city Arthur Schopenhauer was to spend two years. Little is known about the outward aspects of his life there. From the second semester onward he lodged with Professor Schrader, at the latter's official residence in the botanical garden. The rhythm of Schopenhauer's life, which he maintained into his old age, was developed in Göttingen. The early hours of the morning were used for demanding intellectual work; his relaxation was playing the flute. In the afternoons he would go for long walks; in the evenings he would visit the theatre or attend parties. The people he saw were Friedrich Osann and Ernst Arnold Lewald, both of them acquaintances from his time in Gotha; also Carl Julius von Bunsen and William Backhouse Astor, the son of Johann Jakob Astor, an enormously rich fur dealer who had emigrated to America. He also met Karl Lachmann, later to become a famous classical philologist, as well as Karl Witte, the boy prodigy who entered the university at the tender age of ten. These were not close personal friendships, and they ceased when Arthur left Göttingen. After that there were only more or less casual encounters.

Within that circle Arthur was the undisputed centre: here, unlike at his mother's house, his 'oracular pronouncements' were listened to; here his 'argumentative spirit' was not restricted; here he was always right. But perhaps it was just because of this that he did not attach any great importance to these acquaintances. In his curriculum vitae, written in 1819, he observes: 'During my two years in Göttingen I pursued my scholarly studies with the persistent application that I was by then accustomed to, and contact with the other students could not in any way detain me or lure me away from them because my more mature age, my richer experience and my totally different nature at all times led me into isolation and solitude' (CL, 653).

That application was first of all concentrated on the sciences. He had enrolled for medicine. Was he, by doing so, meeting his mother's wishes that he should choose a course leading to a 'livelihood'?

From his earliest notes we know what Schopenhauer's philosophical inclinations were. The study of medicine in those days certainly did not call for an abandonment of those inclinations. Kant himself had viewed medicine as a discipline adjacent to philosophy: the empirical method applied to the human body should teach the speculating mind what it had better abstain from doing. The fundamental cosmic forces of repulsion and attraction, Kant argued, could be studied also on the body; the dietetics of the mind, i.e. practical philosophy, and those of the body were close interlinked. By this approach Kant invested medicine with philosophical dignity. And the scientist and medical man Blumenbach, whose lectures on natural history, mineralogy and comparative anatomy Arthur attended, was pursuing his métier in the halo of that dignity. Blumenbach, seeing himself as a *physicus*, not only accepted the claims of traditional metaphysics but actually believed his science to be competent to provide answers to the so-called 'ultimate questions'. Blumenbach's physics tried also to satisfy metaphysical curiosity:

he attributed the 'germ of life' to chemical compounds; he opposed man's centralist arrogance with reflections on fossil prehistory; he was the first to draw conclusions, from fossils, about the huge time spans of geological history; he taught humility, not so much before God as in the face of empirical nature; he disrespectfully called man 'the most perfect of domestic animals'. Arthur Schopenhauer studied physiology with Blumenbach; subsequently he would describe that branch of knowledge as the 'peak of all natural science'. It was in Blumenbach's physiology that Schopenhauer first met the concept of the 'creative urge'.

By this Blumenbach understood a kind of 'organic life potency', which evaded mechanistic concepts. Kant had commended the creative urge theory, Schelling had called it a 'bold step outside mechanistic natural philosophy', and Goethe too had approved: the mystery of a thing, he observed, was well kept in a mysterious concept.

In Blumenbach, therefore, the firm ground of fact was thoroughly undercut by natural philosophy. Schopenhauer's philosophical inclinations did not have to hide here. Blumenbach's teachings and the private reading of Schelling's *Weltseele* (*World Soul*) were not yet such worlds apart as natural philosophy would subsequently be from the exact natural sciences. Not until his third semester, however, did Schopenhauer turn exclusively to philosophy. In his *Lebenslauf* he says: 'But when I had gained some reasonable knowledge of myself, and also of philosophy . . . I changed my resolution, gave up medicine and devoted myself exclusively to philosophy.' What was that 'knowledge of himself' that led him to devote himself 'exclusively' to philosophy?

In Hamburg he had indulged in his philosophical and aesthetic inclinations as escapism from the career prescribed for him by his father. Cutting short his apprenticeship as a merchant was the first practical step against his father. Now the world of the spirit was no longer something to counterbalance the duties imposed on him by his father. He had changed sides, he had dared to break out of his father's world – but he was still being pursued by his father's shadow. This shadow lent Arthur's break-out a paternal diversion: in the world of the spirit he was now less keen on escapism than on the solid, the exact. Hence his shift towards science, hence also his zeal in studying the ancient languages and the 'classics'. With a merchant's conscientiousness he endeavoured first of all to accumulate the basic capital of education before venturing on risky enterprises. Only after three semesters did he permit himself to break out for good. Only by deciding in favour of philosophy did he accomplish a radical turning-away from bourgeois considerations of purpose and usefulness.

In a conversation with the aged Wieland in Weimar on the occasion of a visit there, Schopenhauer gave clear and, at the same time, curt expression to that emancipation of his philosophical passion from the aims of bourgeois life. Wieland had warned him against such 'unpractical studies' as philosophy. Arthur replied: 'Life is an unpleasant business; I have resolved to spend it reflecting upon it' (C, 22).

Although Wieland himself tended to incline towards a philosophy of happiness, allowing to scepticism no more than a certain muting of his surfeit of vitality, he was nevertheless deeply impressed by the determination displayed by Arthur Schopenhauer. 'Indeed, it now seems to me,' the old gentleman answered, 'that you have acted correctly. . . . I now understand your nature, young man; stick to philosophy' (C, 22). Life was an unpleasant business; he would like to reflect on it, undisturbed, without being diverted by its complications – that was Arthur's programme. Again, and still, he longed for the experience of high mountains. At the end of his time in Göttingen, during a journey through the Harz in 1811, he noted: 'Philosophy is a high-altitude Alpine road; it can be reached only by a steep path over sharp stones and prickly thorns. It is lonely and ever more deserted the higher you climb, and whoever takes it must be immune to terror, he must leave everything behind him and confidently clear his own way in the cold snow. Often he will suddenly stand over an abyss, seeing the green valley below. Vertigo draws him powerfully down; but he must hold on, even if he has to glue the soles of his feet to the rock with his own blood. But in exchange he will soon see the world below him: its sandy deserts and swamps vanish, its unevennesses are smoothed out, its discordant notes fail to reach his heights, its curvature is revealed. He himself always stands in pure cool Alpine air and sees the sun when down below black night still lingers' (P 1, 14).

Towards what light was Schopenhauer striving, what sun had risen for him in the philosophical sky? His first teacher of philosophy, the sceptical Kantian Gottlob Ernst Schulze, pointed out to him two stars – Plato and Kant. Schulze was a knowledgeable and shrewd man who knew how to reconcile antagonisms sceptically. In Plato one might still find the old, self-assured metaphysics; in Kant one encountered at every step a reservation about metaphysical frontier crossings.

Plato and Kant – these were the two poles between which the philosophical spirit of the age was moving, going beyond Kant and aiming at a renewed metaphysics that would construct the whole – God and the world – according to laws which had just, with Kant's help, been discovered within the subject, within the individual.

Kant, that blend of rococo and Pietism, had set the ancient and respectable truths – immortality of the soul, the existence of God, the beginning and the end of the world – to balance on the frivolous point of a needle: they were valid and yet they were not valid. The problems of metaphysics could not be solved, Kant taught, and if they had to be raised time and again then it was best not to take too seriously whatever answer was given at the moment. If it was found possible to live with an answer, then it should be seen as valid in the sense of 'as if'. That was Kant's rococo-like eye-winking epicureanism.

In this frivolous balance of the 'as if' the truths were unable to survive for long; they were bound to crash down and once more become serious. Fichte, Schelling, Hegel – they would not tolerate the 'as if'; they would once more philosophize with a renewed self-assurance of the absolute. But that new absolute – to that extent Kant remained effective – would belong to the subject.

Even before Arthur Schopenhauer learned to appreciate Kant properly he had understood his refinement and frivolity in dealing with the so-called ultimate questions. 'Epicurus is the Kant of practical philosophy, just as Kant is the Epicurus of speculative philosophy' (P 1, 12), reads a marginal gloss made by Schopenhauer in 1810.

Epicurus, as is well known, had put aside the existence of the gods; he had separated practical morality from heavenly obligations and promises, and instead had placed the pursuit of happiness upon earth and the avoidance of pain and sorrow at the centre of a pragmatic practical wisdom. He had conceded to absolute values no more than an 'as if' validity. Whenever they could play a part in serving happiness they might be used; in that case they were life-supporting fictions which attained reality only to the extent that they contributed to the realization of happiness.

By describing Kant as the Epicurus of speculative philosophy Schopenhauer proved that he had already understood some of Kant's philosophy. The unknowability of the 'thing in itself' does in fact play a similar part with Kant as the gods did with Epicurus: the ancient optimistic philosopher also preferred to leave it aside.

Kant was the great caesura at the end of the eighteenth century. After his appearance nothing in Western thought was ever the same as before – and he knew it. 'Until now,' he wrote, 'it was assumed that all our cognition must be based on the objects. . . . Let us try to see . . . if we do not manage better by assuming that the objects must behave in accordance with our cognition. . . . This is much the same as the first idea of Copernicus, who, when the explanation of the motion of the heavens failed to work properly by assuming that the entire hosts of stars revolved around the spectator, examined whether it might not work better if he allowed the spectator to revolve and instead left the stars in peace.'

Kant had begun his investigations in the style of the old metaphysics, by seeking the *a priori* elements of thought, i.e. the certainties inherent in thought *prior to* all experience (*physis*) and which therefore, in the traditional manner, might form the basis of a meta-physics. Kant discovered such certainties prior to all experience, but these, as he showed, were valid only *for* experience and could no longer form the basis of any metaphysics. That was the big bang: the *a priori* had crashed down from heaven. Instead of vertical anchoring it now permitted only horizontal orientation.

It is necessary to look back to Descartes in order properly to assess the new leap of modernization and secularization performed by Kant.

Descartes had first caused reason to raise her proud head and deprived the *revealed* God of much of his power. It was necessary to support him. Descartes, from the self-reflection of reason, proved that there must be a God just as there was a world. Kant, from his self-reflection of reason, demonstrated why there must be the fiction of God. That is the gulf which divides the two. In Descartes God had been demoted to a reason-based being; in Kant he had shrunk further, and dramatically, into a 'regulative' idea.

What Descartes had started to do, even before Kant, was make the self-reflection of reason the beginning as well as the end of the search for ultimate metaphysical certainty. The spirit of the new age is first active in Descartes, because naturally – in spite of his pretence – he did not doubt the existence of the world but only the existence of God. That was why, from his famous 'Cogito ergo sum', he derived not so much a proof of the world (a proof totally unnecessary) as a proof of God. However, with his rationally proved God Descartes found himself on dangerous ground, because his examinations set free the sovereign spirit of analysis which ultimately would dissolve even the most powerful synthesis, which is God. That, however, was not to be Descartes' work but that of his successors.

Descartes himself, that Prometheus of modernity, of 'disintegrating' analysis and of monstrous mathematical constructs, spent twenty years in his Dutch exile, sitting by the fireside, gazing out of the window, where winter, spring, summer, autumn and once more winter took their turn. He observed the genre scenes of life outside: people with tall hats on the snow-covered streets, the seagulls on the garden wall, children playing after a summer shower, the blue of the sky reflected in the puddles, market days in autumn, giggling servant girls under his window, at nightfall the crackling fire in the fireplace. Descartes indulged in such meditations amidst this peaceful life, meditations of tranquillity, of passivity, of letting be. Meditations which, so strangely, unleashed a fury of action and domination. But, as usual, all was calm in the eye of the storm.

Cartesianism, that universe of rationality, springs from the Archimedean point of retreat, of tranquillity. Descartes' rational certainties, regardless of all the talk of 'mathesis', of order or of 'deductions', are tied into the infinity of meditation. That is why it is foolish to identify Descartes' 'Cogito' with modern rationality's emaciated concept of reason. Descartes' meditations were truly a dialogue with God. Descartes believed: the reason by which I can recognize God makes me God's property. It is not I who appropriate God by dint of my reason, but the other way about: God appropriates me in my reason. However, the relation is balanced on a knife-edge: the slightest movement would change everything. A reason-based God becomes divine reason.

Descartes' *'mathesis universalis'*, further outbid by Spinoza likewise reflecting in meditative tranquillity, along with the experience-hungry forays of English empiricism (Locke, Hume), had mobilized a rational activity of work and world as well as the self-assertion of the senses, though initially without relegating proud reason into metaphysical homelessness.

Montaigne's and Pascal's sceptical or spiritual reservations were unable to halt the triumphant advance of reason. In Leibniz and subsequently in Christian Wolf the whole, God and the world, are once more magnificently united. Unproblematically, whether inductively or deductively, intertraffic proceeds between heaven and the best of all possible worlds. Everything is a continuum, nature performs no leaps, and any transitions are covered by the 'perceptions petites' (the unconscious perceptions) and by calculus. Just that: Leibniz taught his century to calculate with the infinite, supported by the genius of that musical mathematical wizard Johann Sebastian Bach, who raised 'mathesis universalis' to a musical devotion before God.

In the style of traditional metaphysics Kant searched for the *a priori* elements of thought, and his search proved more successful than anybody else's. He produced a whole apparatus of *a priori* elements: the perceptional forms of space and time, a complex mechanism of categories of reason, a veritable crushing mill of 'apperception' that grinds down the matter of experience to what we are eventually capable of perceiving and conceptually comprehending. All these he saw as *a priori* features, that is, equipment with which we are fitted even before the matter of experience enters into us. These *a priori* features, however, as Kant proved, no longer link us to heaven. They exist *prior to* experience, i.e. this side of experience and not beyond; they do not refer to things transcendent, they are merely transcendental. They are the conditions, the pure form, of any possible experience. They are uninteresting metaphysically; they are of interest only for cognition theory. If we focus on them we transcend experience in the direction of the conditions that make it possible, i.e. horizontally, not vertically. The 'transcendental' in Kant is, in a sense, the opposite of the 'transcendent', as transcendental analysis consists in the demonstration that, and why, we can have no knowledge of the transcendent. There is no road from the transcendental to the transcendent. To give an example: our reason arranges the matter of our experience in accordance with causality principles. Contrary to the sensualist David Hume, who derived causality as a presumption of probability from experience, i.e. *a posteriori*, Kant demonstrated that we have not acquired causality from experience but that we approach experience with it, i.e. that we apply it *a priori* to the matter of our experience. Hence causality, according to Kant, is not a schema of the external world but a schema of our mind, one that we superimpose on the external world. This *a priori* causality, however, exists only in the sphere of our experience. To try to use the causality principle to derive a God as a prime mover means to transgress the realm of all possible experience, and hence to make incorrect use of a category of reason. This Kantian demonstration burst the neatly crafted chains of argument of the rational proof of the existence of God, which had been valid for more than two centuries. Kant destroyed traditional metaphysics and became the godfather of modern cognition theory. He disciplined the thought process and acutely demonstrated to it on what occasions, and tempted by what inducements, it came off the rails and found itself roaming in bliss-promising fields where it had no business to be. Kant moved the joy of speculation, in which he had himself indulged in his early writings on the origin of the world, into the vicinity of shady dealers anxious to succeed by overdrawing their accounts. He had presumably been tempted by the fantastic forays of the Swedish theosopher Swedenborg (1688–1772) into marking out the territory. He would, Kant wrote, wait patiently 'until the gentlemen have ceased dreaming' in order, thereafter, to lead them with his bone-dry reflections into the secret workshop of their mirages. In his dispute with the highly popular 'seer of spirits' Swedenborg he realized the urgency of an enterprise concerned 'not so much with objects as with the manner of knowing such objects'. He wished to confront the delirium of initiation into the transcendent by the cool reason of the transcendental. Another occasional essay from the time when Kant was working on his great *Critique of Pure Reason* bears the revealing title *Essay on the Sickness of the Head*. It deals with another metaphysician, likewise blown off course, the so-called 'goat prophet' Jan Komarnicki, who was then haunting Königsberg. Barefoot, clad in animal skins, surrounded by fourteen cows, twenty sheep and forty-six goats, he engaged in prophecies about God and the world.

Kant made quite sure the miraculous was downgraded to the curious. His epoch-making work, his *Critique of Pure Reason*, grew out of that intention.

Arthur Schopenhauer, who had started reading Kant while in Göttingen, initially viewed the Königsberg philosopher merely as the spoilsport of metaphysics, to whose promises he was, for the moment, still wide open. A marginal gloss by Schopenhauer, from 1810, reads: 'One man tells a lie: another, who knows the truth, says this is all lies, the truth is as follows. A third, who does *not* know the truth but has an acute mind, shows up contradictions and impossible assertions in the lie and says: that's why it is all lies. The lie is life, the acute-minded one is Kant alone, truth has been served up by many, e.g. Plato' (P I, 13).

Kant, of course, did a lot more than merely post notices with prohibitions, than merely supervise the orderly business of reason and prevent, or unmask, arrogations of competence ('all lies'). And that something 'extra' lit a spark among his contemporaries, even though Arthur Schopenhauer, then engrossed mainly in Plato, had not yet noticed it or did not wish to notice it.

Kant's construction of his rococo-style music box of our perception and cognition faculties, with its four different kinds of judgement, to which tentacles are attached, each with three categories, thus, in the case of quality judgement, the categories 'reality, negation, limitation', etc. (indeed Kant intended to instal an even more delicate clockwork, or at least he threatened to do so when he said that he could, at will, 'paint in full the family tree of pure reason') – that whole apparatus is anything but a 'tree'; to ensure its functioning, for grinding down the matter of experience and reassembling it afresh, it requires live energy. The determination of that energy is a key part of

Kantian philosophy. He called it – and this must nowadays come as a surprise to anyone regarding Kant only as the engineer of reason – 'productive imagination'. 'That this imagination,' he wrote, 'is a necessary ingredient of perception itself has presumably not as yet occurred to any psychologist.'

The enthronement of imagination was not the work of 'Storm and Stress' alone. Kant himself had seen to it and, remembering his public appearances, he no doubt was the most effective king-maker. Admittedly he had received a hot tip: that was when he was reading Rousseau's *Émile* and, engrossed, actually missed one of his regular walks.

Under the heading *Credo of a Savoyard Vicar* Rousseau had inserted into the fourth book of his educational novel *Émile* (1762) a philosophical essay in which he pretended to be trying to 'establish' some (to him evident) mooring points in the ocean of opinions. Rousseau opposed the cognitional concept of the English sensualists. These, according to Rousseau, comprehended the cognizant, percipient person merely as a passive medium in which the sensory impressions were somehow recorded. By contrast, Rousseau developed his exceedingly fertile ideas on spontaneity, i.e. on the active side of cognition and perception. With great virtuosity Rousseau, from an analysis of the capacity of judgement, derived the performance of the ego.

A purely sensory being, Rousseau demonstrated, could not possibly comprehend the identity of an object simultaneously seen and touched. To him, what was seen and what was touched would fall apart into two separate 'objects'. Only the 'ego' could unite them. The unity of the ego therefore ensured the unity of external objects.

Rousseau went further. He compared the 'sensation of self' and the 'perception' of the external world, and arrived at the conclusion that an individual could 'have' a sensation only if he entered into the sensation of self; and since perceptions brought home what existed outside, while at the same time existing only in the medium of the sensation of self, it followed that without a sensation of self there was no existence. Or the other way about: the sensation of self produced existence. Sensation of self, however, was nothing other than the certainty of *I am*. At this point Rousseau simultaneously turned against Descartes by reversing his classic statement 'I think, therefore I am'. 'I am, therefore I think,' proclaimed Rousseau. Thoughts do not think themselves. Although the logic between two ideas may call for the most cogent connection, for that connection to come into being I must *want* to make it. There is no line between two points unless I draw that line.

To Descartes, the will was the source of error; 'pure' thought was thought thinking itself without an impulse of volition. Rousseau demonstrated that even the most elementary act of thought could take place only as the result of an existing and hence willing ego.

This fundamental activism discovered by Rousseau, which first sets perception and cognition in motion, is what Kant called the 'power of imagination'. He also discovered considerably more difficult concepts about this fundamental performance of the ego. Undaunted by verbal monstrosities he speaks of the 'transcendental synthesis of apperception' or more simply of 'pure awareness of self', calling it the 'highest point to which all use of the intellect, even the whole of logic, and after it transcendental philosophy, must be attached'.

It may seem strange to us today to observe the effort of analytical intellect with which something so seemingly obvious as 'I am' was then being dragged out from the hopeless confusions of thought. Indeed it *should* seem strange to us if we genuinely wish to understand how awareness of self had to struggle out into the light of day during its birth as a philosophical concept, and if we wish to understand the euphoria which accompanied that birth. For this is something that is, as a rule, overlooked in usual critiques of reason – the joy, the intensity, the vitality which accompanied the discovery of the world-creating ego. That simple thing was so difficult, long paths had to be traversed before man came face to face with himself. The euphoria of the encounter can be understood only if one realizes the kind of concealment of self that existed in the pre-modern era. Thought, belief, perception, as Foucault taught, had different polarities then. Thinking disappeared in what was thought, perception in what was perceived, volition in what was willed, and belief in what was believed. A gale of disappearing had conjured the subject into his creations and held him there. And now the stage was turning, now the producer was emerging from his creations, saying: Behold, I made all this!

At the first moment this happened – at the time of Rousseau and Kant – this was perceived as a new dawn justifying the boldest hopes.

The man who discovers himself to be the producer in the theatre where he had until then felt himself to be a spectator, suddenly finds himself showered by heaven with all the riches he had lavishly surrendered to it in the past. And what he holds in his hands are all things he has made himself. For a while this will delight him, but soon it will disappoint him. As, among the old riches of metaphysics, he discovers what he has himself made they lose their magic, their promise. They turn colourless and trivial. The solution will be: if one really is the maker, then one should make as much as possible; one's future would be one of hectic accumulation. Truths will exist solely in order to be 'materialized'. This gives rise to the secularized religion of progress and growth. Eventually the time will come when one feels surrounded by *what one has made* and longs for *what has grown*, a time when the 'appropriation' of one's 'property' becomes a problem. Suddenly there will be talk of 'alienation' within a world one has made oneself: the things made now engulf man. Imagination will discover a new utopia: the controllability of what one has made. Wherever these utopias lose their power a new kind of anxiety will spread: anxiety about the history one has made oneself.

Needless to say, none of this was thought through or foreseen when it began. The predominant mood was the euphoria of conquest. That, at least, was how Kant celebrated the process of self-justification and self-reassurance in a sea of forlornness and uncertainty. 'The land of the pure intellect . . . is an island, enclosed by nature itself within unalterable boundaries. It is the land of truth . . . surrounded by a vast and stormy ocean.'

Kant consolidated; he created a base from which the gigantic unknown might be viewed with some calm. That 'unknown' he called by the rather quaint name of 'the thing in itself'.

That 'thing in itself' is the unknown in a far more radical manner than anything that is merely 'not yet' known can be unknown. The 'thing in itself' is the name of that unknown which, paradoxically, we first created by making something known to us; it is the shadow we cast. We can comprehend anything only as what it is *for* us. What the things 'in themselves' are, independently of the 'organs' with which we imagine them, must always evade us. Being is 'being imagined'. With the 'thing in itself' a novel transcendence appeared on the horizon; not a transcendence of the old Beyond, but a transcendence that was no more, but also no less, than the forever invisible reverse side of all imagination before us.

Kant himself was very relaxed about leaving the cognition-theory 'thing in itself' outside ourselves to look after itself. Admittedly he was at first also troubled by curiosity as to what the world beyond our imagination really was, but he controlled that curiosity with an acute analysis of the contradictions ('antinomies') of our reason.

'It is the peculiar fate of human reason,' Kant began the preface to his *Critique of Pure Reason*, 'that it is troubled by questions which it cannot reject, for they are posed by the nature of reason itself, but which it cannot answer either, for they surpass all capacity of human reason.' This contradiction cannot be resolved, it has to be suffered; this can be done the more easily as our intellect enables us to manage quite well in an ultimately unknown world. If we entrust ourselves to experience and knowledge we may have no absolute truth, but we know enough to assert ourselves in the world. Today we would say: although our forms of experience and knowledge do not provide us with absolute cognition, they do provide us with adaptation rituals to the real world.

Kant's 'thing in itself' was set to have a strange career.

Kant left behind him a well-appointed house for rational cognition, except that the 'thing in itself' was like a hole letting in a draught.

Kant's successors would not be able to be as relaxed as the wise bachelor from Königsberg about letting the 'thing in itself' look after itself. They would want to seize it at any price. A tumultuous curiosity would wish to penetrate right into the presumed heart of things – whether Fichte's 'ego' or Schelling's 'natural subject' or Hegel's 'objective spirit' or Feuerbach's 'body' or Marx's 'proletariat'. They would all want to shake the world out of its slumber, and if there was no magic formula they would invent one; and if there was no ultimate truth to be discovered then that truth would be 'made' – or, more accurately, the history man had made himself would be expected to produce truth. The trail of blood in most recent history is the signature of that truth. Truth would be pursued like an enemy. 'There is something we lack,' Büchner's Danton exclaims; 'I have no name for it – but we will not tear it out of each other's guts, why should we break open our bodies for it? Leave us alone, we are miserable alchemists!'

Young Arthur Schopenhauer likewise refused to content himself with Kant's relaxed scepticism. He too wanted to penetrate into the heart of things. He tried to balance Kant's critique with Plato, whom he believed to be not only a doorkeeper but an apostle of truth. Kant merely taught table manners and knew a few recipes; Plato, on the other hand, served up the meal. In a marginal gloss of 1810 Schopenhauer had this to say about Kant: 'It is perhaps the best description of Kant's shortcomings if one says: he did not know what contemplation is' (P I, 13).

To Schopenhauer, as we know from his Hamburg period, 'contemplation' was the kind of knowledge that was possible on sublime mountain peaks and held out a promise of escape from the constraints of usefulness, a bourgeois career, and generally the rat-race of self-assertion. The 'truth' which Schopenhauer was seeking was to him, primarily, not a body of correct judgements but a mode of existence. One did not *have* truth, but one stood *in* truth. What mattered was not utility but the happiness of cognition. A secularized kind of Pietist 'conversion', the rebirth of the child of the world as a child of God – all these are included in what Schopenhauer understood by 'contemplation', in what he found lacking in Kant. He was looking for – it is impossible to put it differently – a beatifying inspiration. That was a need which Schopenhauer could not initially satisfy with Kant. He was unable to see him as the engineer of reason; to him Kant embodied what was sound in philosophy, the soundness which Arthur left behind him in civil life when he gave up the commercial career his father had mapped out for him. In the fatherless world of philosophy Kant was the only one who, in a sense, enjoyed the father's approbation, but no more than that. At the end of his student years, and especially during his time in Berlin, Arthur Schopenhauer would rediscover Kant, and he would then find in him that dimension of existentially inspired philosophizing that he was still searching for in vain. He would then understand the Kant who has not so far been mentioned – the great theoretician of human freedom.

Kant had approached that mystery of freedom in a manner which, at least as much as his theory of cognition, was to be of epoch-making importance. As a theoretician of freedom Kant was the Sartre of the early nineteenth century.

Kant had come close to the secret of freedom not only in his *Critique of Practical Reason* but already in his principal cognition-theory work, the famous 'antinomies', chapters which Arthur Schopenhauer was to describe as downright 'inspired'.

Let us recall: Kant understood the 'thing in itself' as the reverse side of all our imaginations. In the frivolous and sceptical manner already described he left the 'thing in itself' outside us to its own devices. Yet with unparalleled boldness, though with complete consistency, Kant transferred this reverse side also into ourselves.

We too are an imagination to ourselves, but in addition we are a 'thing in itself'. We reflect, but at the same time we are the back of the mirror. We are an eye, and that is why the world is an eye world, but the eye cannot see itself. Thus the once exalted transcendence is transformed into the blind spot of our existence, into the 'darkness of the experienced moment' (Bloch). We act now, and we shall afterwards always be able to find a necessity, a causality, for our action; at the moment of acting, however, we are 'undetermined', we experience ourselves as beings not linked in a chain of causalities but as the beginning, as it were out of nothing, of a new chain of causalities. At every moment the universe of necessary being is torn apart. Kant illustrates this with a trivial example: 'If I now rise from a chair . . . entirely freely, and without the necessarily determining influence of natural causes, then a new series begins with this event, complete with its natural consequences into infinity. Afterwards, having risen, I am, in respect of that event, the prey of causal explanations; then the necessity will become visible, but only because the event of rising is over. Every instant confronts me with a choice, hands me over to freedom.'

'Necessity', 'causality' – these are the categories of our imagining intellect, and therefore of the world as it appears, as it appears to us. I myself am a phenomenon to myself in so far as I contemplate myself, as I reflect on my actions. Simultaneously, however, I experience myself in freedom. Man lives in two worlds. On the one hand he is, in Kantian terminology, a 'phenomenon', an element of the sensory world which exists according to its laws; on the other he is a 'noumenon', a 'thing in itself' – without necessity, without causality, a something that exists before I can comprehend and explain it, and which is infinitely more than, and different from, what I can comprehend.

Here lies the secret centre of gravity of the whole of Kantian philosophy. Kant himself admitted it in a letter when he confessed that it had been the problem of freedom – 'Man is free and, on the other hand, there is no freedom, everything is necessity in accordance with natural laws' – which had roused him from his 'dogmatic slumbers' and induced him to develop the critique of reason.

When Kant defines the event of freedom as invariably an 'unconditional' beginning of a causal chain, then this is again a reflection of Rousseau. Rousseau, dealing with the question of whether a beginning of the world was even thinkable, had boldly answered that such a beginning was thinkable because we ourselves were able to make a fresh start at any time: 'You will ask me,' we read in Émile, 'how I can know that there is movement out of its own impetus; to this I reply to you that I know it because I feel it. I wish to move my arm, and so I move it, without that movement having any other immediate cause than my will.'

Rousseau therefore had established 'will' as the force of freedom. Kant, however, chose a significantly different road. To him 'necessity' is the central concept of freedom. He is led to this conclusion by an involved argument, though ultimately by a simple idea: the 'will' is the nature within us. What nature within us wills, that is therefore natural necessity and not freedom. We are free only if we demonstrate the strength to break the chains which bind us as natural creatures. Freedom is triumph over our urge-driven nature. As natural beings we belong to the realm of phenomena, but we step beyond the phenomenal world with its necessities when we hear the voice of our conscience; when we transcend ourselves as natural creatures; when we do something to which we are compelled not by any necessity but by the voice of our conscience. We act 'unconditionally' when, in a fundamental action, we have decided in favour of a particular 'necessity'. And if that 'necessity' has the power to produce a 'will', then the 'thing in itself' triumphs within us, the 'thing in itself' that we, as moral beings, have always been.

Such action Kant calls 'moral'. Moral is something that receives its laws not from the world of phenomena; we are moral if we surpass ourselves as natural creatures. Our morality conveys us to the silent heart of the world.

At this point the moralized 'thing in itself' enters into the inheritance of the old metaphysics. 'Thing in itself', 'freedom' and 'moral law' are drawn together into a 'practical reason' which makes up for the now empty heavens outside by a heaven of morality in man's head. Theoretical and practical reason find themselves in a surprising constellation. The categories of theoretical reason, according to Kant, can function only if used as the conditions of possible experience. For practical reason, things are the other way about: practical reason is valid only if it opposes the rules of practical moral experience (personal profit, self-assertion, pursuit of happiness, etc.). If practical reason were to demand only what experience teaches and what nature compels us to do, then it could not stem from 'freedom' or from the 'thing in itself' which is beyond experience. But that is precisely what it should do. Hence to Kant the force of freedom is not Rousseau's 'will' (which is too nature-bound for Kant) but 'necessity', which is strong enough to produce volition autonomously, i.e. out of itself.

Practical reason, stemming from the mystery of the 'thing in itself', has thus, according to Kant, the power to cause actions which are performed solely because they are reasonable; that force does not require any supporting impulses of inclination or fear. Indeed it must reject such impulses: 'there are,' Kant wrote, 'some sympathetically attuned souls which . . . find an inward pleasure in spreading joy around them, and who can take delight in the contentment of others, in so far as that is their work. But I maintain that this kind of action . . . no matter how kind it may be, nevertheless has no true moral value.'

That was too much even for that passionate follower of Kant, Friedrich Schiller. He composed this epigram:

Gladly I serve my friends,
but alas I do so with pleasure,
and often therefore it irks me that I am not virtuous.
There is no other way: you must try to despise them
and with distaste you must do what duty commands you.

The imperatives of Kant's practical reason hold out no promise of reward; their implementation cannot be used as a means for the pursuit of other purposes. It is pure duty for its own sake. It stands at the top of all conceivable purpose chains. We hear the call of duty in our internal moral law.

It was as if the old dethroned metaphysics, driven out from the vast spaces of the universe, had rallied its remaining strength and settled in the consciences of the now secularized subjects, pricking them a good deal.

That is what Kantian morality must seem to us if we view it from the point of view of the fate of metaphysics. Seen differently, from the angle of the material world we live in, it reveals equally astonishing features. Certainly the kind of rigorous direction of the self, as visualized by Kant, was hopelessly ahead of his day's culture of conscience, even though it was derived from it.

Kant's period, unquestionably, was a boom period for conscience. Moreover, it had its own prehistory. There had been several phases in the development of Western civilization when the force upholding a certain system of coexistence was driven inside the individual in the form of conscience.

Prior to the modern age, force, individually practised, was various and ubiquitous. The power of the state was exerted on an ambulant basis and could not therefore be everywhere at the same time. Mostly it was present in an absent form, just like heaven and hell. Yet the latter's promises and threats gave rise to important rules of behaviour. One felt enveloped by them, even sheltered, yet they remained 'outside', one could communicate with them through the institutions of the Church and its rituals. The business arrangements of the trade in indulgences, for instance, represented a major relief, stemming as they did from a spirit of concordat between God and the Devil, i.e. 'between spirit and matter, whereby the autocracy of the spirit is proclaimed in theory, while matter is enabled to enjoy all its annulling rights in practice . . . You may yield to the tender inclinations of your heart and embrace a pretty girl, but you must confess that this was a shameful sin, and for that sin you must do penance' (Heinrich Heine). St Peter's Cathedral, therefore, built as it was with indulgence money, might therefore be seen, according to Heine, as a 'monument to the pleasures of the flesh', just as was that pyramid built by an Egyptian daughter of joy with the money earned by prostitution.

Luther was the great spoilsport; but he was only able to be that because the age was calling for a new God, for an intimate, internalized God. And it called for it because the emerging bourgeois society, based on the division of labour, needed and produced individuals who could control themselves, who could 'stand up for themselves', who did not need to be compelled from outside but could compel themselves. The chains of action in which the individual was enmeshed grew longer and more opaque. The finely spun social web was transformed into an action-inhibiting grid in the mind.

Kant was carried by this development, yet he overestimated its success. Although the total seizure of power by the conscience had become conceivable as a long-term objective in the eighteenth century, it did not yet come about. Kant's categorical imperative, in which he summed up the murmuring of the conscience in a precise apodictic statement: 'Act only according to a maxim which, at the same time, you would wish to become a general law' – that imperative is a postulate raised to the power of two: it expresses the demand that the conscience should make such demands. It is not directly evident, and as a demanded demand it instantly became the victim of casuistic sniping. The Königsberg philosopher was, for instance, being persuaded that any thief might regard himself justified by the categorical imperative: I steal, and my maxim is, let property be abolished; I want others to do likewise, hence there will be no property and ultimately no thieves either. Hence I as a thief bring about the abolition of thieving.

It has to be admitted that the social history of the conscience had not yet reached a point where one might rely on its evident demands and findings for regulating social relationships. People, though possibly slowed down by internal controls, continued to run off course. What Kant had outlined was a utopia. Just as, according to Adam Smith, bourgeois society stabilized itself and advanced by means of the market and by the market-conforming actions of individuals, without the need for state intervention, so it was supposed that bourgeois society could also balance itself ethically, without state tutelage, as a kind of self-supporting system of spiritual welfare. With his categorical imperative Kant sought to provide a formula by which the moral ecological environment of bourgeois society would prosper.

The further history of the alliance between bourgeois society and the world of morality is well known. It is based on the motto: Confidence is good, verification is better. The call for an internalization of conscience has dramatically diminished in our century: there has been encouragement by the state to unscrupulous action on the greatest possible scale, while the web of control from above has become even finer, and a newly discovered psychological underground has given rise to a whole culture of excuses and unconcern – so that little is left for the conscience to do, with the result that it wastes away once more to its pre-modern-age level, practising its trade in indulgences in the form of court fines and medical certificates.

When considering Kant's rigorous ethical demands we should not overlook the fact that they spring from a need to compensate for the subliminal frivolity of the 'as if'. Belief in God is to be replaced by belief in one's own moral strength. And conversely, moral strength is to operate as absolutely 'as if' God were watching over it. 'It is wise,' Kant wrote, 'to act as though . . . another life were unalterable.' This admitted fictionalism raises the otherwise very serious discourses of the Königsberg philosopher into a strange state of suspension. From this state even sentences like the following may venture to be uttered: 'It may sound questionable, but it is not reprehensible to state that every individual makes a God for himself.' A gentle irony, which the young Schopenhauer sensed as epicureanism, overlies all Kant's thoughts on the so-called 'ultimate' questions. 'Here,' Kant wrote, 'even the serious sage must admit his ignorance. Here reason extinguishes her torch and we remain in darkness. Imagination alone can roam about in that darkness and create phantoms.'

Arthur Schopenhauer did not wish to rely on imagination, certainly not on his own. Plato lit for him the torch which Kant had denied him. Time and again he read the parable of the cave from the *Republic*: We are in a dark dungeon. Behind us burns a fire, even further behind lies an exit into the open. We are chained up, we cannot turn our heads, we gaze at the wall facing us. There we follow the shadow play of the objects which are carried past the fire behind us. If we were able to turn we should see the real objects and the fire; if we were actually free and stepped out of the dungeon we should be in the sun, and only then would we be within the truth. This is Platonism: a cognition which simultaneously signifies another being. What matters is not seeing the objects more clearly but being in the sun. It is even conceivable that, with a surfeit of brightness, we might not see anything at all. Like comes to like, or: through cognition we become similar to what we have recognized. The most perfect way of seeing the sun is for us to become the sun ourselves. The Platonic 'idea', this quintessence of unchanging, perfect being, relieved of all becoming – that can be known only by appropriation: you must change your life. No critique, no dialectic, no logic – what is offered here is the eroticism of truth. 'Phantoms'? Surely not if they transform you.

Arthur Schopenhauer, at any rate, sought in his reading of Plato that exalted relaxation which he normally experienced only on mountains. With Plato he felt elevated, here he found what, a few months later in his Berlin notes, he was for the first time to call the 'better consciousness'.

At the very end of his stay in Göttingen, some time in the summer of 1811, he first tried to connect Plato, whom he loved, with Kant, from whom, against his own will, he was unable to struggle free. He made Kant's ethics ring in the Platonic manner. 'One consolation there is, one sure hope, and this we experience from our *moral sense*. When it speaks to us so clearly, when within ourselves we feel such a powerful motivation for the greatest sacrifice, running totally counter to our seeming advantage: then we vividly realize that ours is a different advantage, in accordance with which we should act against all worldly motivations; . . . that the voice which we hear in the dark comes from a bright place' (P I, 14). This is still a very tentative, a very cautious formulation. What fascinated him was not dry moral duty but that force of freedom invoked by Kant, the force of freedom which burst the chains of everyday reason, of mere self-assertion and self-preservation. Translated into Plato's parable of the cave this was the way into the open, into the sun, to participation in being.

Subsequently Arthur Schopenhauer would give another name to this happening out of freedom: the renunciation of the will.

CHAPTER EIGHT

FICHTE AND THE EGO

In the summer of 1811, after four semesters in Göttingen, Arthur Schopenhauer decided to move to the newly founded Berlin University.

'In 1811 I transferred to Berlin,' he recorded later, 'in the expectation of meeting a genuine philosopher and great spirit in Fichte' (CL, 654).

In addition to Fichte there were other scholars in Berlin whose famous names attracted him: Schleiermacher, who interested him less as a religious philosopher than as the translator and exegetist of Plato; the zoologist Martin Hinrich Lichtenstein, a leading scientist in his field, whose acquaintance Arthur had made in his mother's salon; and Friedrich August Wolf, the most important Greek scholar of his day, whom even Goethe used to consult whenever he needed expert advice. Eventually something like friendship developed between Wolf and Goethe.

Pestered by Johanna, Goethe composed for Arthur a rather lukewarm letter of introduction to Wolf: 'As one should not miss any opportunity that offers itself for breaking a long silence, I should not, revered friend, like to deny a letter of introduction to you to a young man who is going to Berlin. His name is Schopenhauer, his mother is Frau *Hofrat* Schopenhauer, who has been living here for a number of years. He studied in Göttingen for some time and, as I know from others rather than from my own knowledge, he has been serious about it. He seems to have changed his studies and occupations a few times. How much he has achieved, and in what discipline, you will readily judge for yourself if, out of friendship to me, you will give him a moment of your time and, in so far as he deserves it, give him permission to see you again.'

Goethe agreed to perform this half-hearted courtesy only because – as he later quite openly confessed to Johanna – he expected Arthur to stop over in Weimar on his journey from Göttingen to Berlin so he, Goethe, could get him to take back with him a few books he had borrowed from Wolf. Arthur, however, travelled through the Harz mountains. The dubious recommendation was hardly worth a detour through Weimar.

Arthur Schopenhauer knew Berlin. He had visited the city with his parents on two occasions, in 1800 and 1804. All he remembered of his first visit were the frequent military march-pasts and some theatrical performances. He had witnessed the King of Prussia fall off his horse when an 'unfortunate stray hare ran through the dense crowd of spectators' which began to mill about, and he had witnessed the famous Iffland being booed on the stage and thereupon stepping in front of the curtain to declare that 'it was impossible for him to go on acting because he was not used to such disapproval'. On his second visit Berlin was the final stop of his great European tour, the end of the moratorium granted him by his father before setting out on his apprenticeship as a merchant. He had then not noted anything of importance in his travel diary. 'At noon today we finally reached Berlin,' he wrote, and below: 'Everything comes to an end in this world' (TD, 279).

Now, in the late summer of 1811, Berlin to Arthur Schopenhauer was no longer a trap snapping shut but a door opening promisingly, the gateway, as he hoped, to the most sublime philosophy. This time he expected the Prussian metropolis to provide exalted spiritual viewing points. First, however, he had to descend from the real heights of the Harz (he wrote a poem there: 'He lies down on the mountain's flank, / he rests there quietly, he rests there long / In deep and blissful pleasure' – PP II, 654–5) down into the flat country, and he entered a city which, on dry windy days, seemed like a colonial frontier town hurriedly set up on the sandy soil of the Brandenburg Marches. 'The fine dust,' we read in a contemporary travel account of 1806, 'then swirls through all the streets in small clouds. If the wind is a little stronger one finds oneself transferred to the sandy deserts of Africa. A column of dust as high as a house then sweeps across the wide squares. At the *Schlossfreiheit* I was on one occasion faced by such a monster coming from the *Schlossplatz*. In the distance it was already turning all objects dark. It swirled along the houses, and I am not exaggerating when I maintain that I could not see any person within three paces. All the stalls standing in the open squares are then buried in sand, and the small merchants and fruit vendors have to toil a long while to bring their precious wares back to the light of day from under the grit which covered them in an instant.'

The sand-carrying winds also worried Arthur: he kept his windows closed and complained about the unclean air which made him ill. His memories of Berlin were even worse. Four decades later he wrote to Frauenstädt: 'A lot of suicides in Berlin? Better believe it; it's a physically and morally damnable dump' (CL, 338).

The sandstorms could make one forget that Berlin at that time was beginning to develop into a European metropolis. The city had approximately 200,000 inhabitants and was still growing. The street scene was a swarm of original characters – not yet fashionable but no longer provincial. 'In Berlin a man can walk about in a fool's cap with bells, and no one will take any notice of him,' a contemporary wrote. On the wide promenades, which Berlin had had since the nineties of the preceding century, one might admire 'a living fashion journal of the whole period'.

Altogether, everything in Berlin gave the impression of hasty novelty, as if conceived on the drawing board, without any history. Buildings were going up everywhere, the 'old Franconian' living quarters were disappearing, and on the outskirts the first tenement blocks were going up, accurately drawn up in straight lines as if for military manoeuvres. The uncontrolled growth of something organically developed was lacking; the making of things, and things made, predominated. One had to know other cities in order to realize the peculiar modernity of Berlin. Madame de Staël wrote: 'Berlin is a modern city with wide, straight streets and regular architecture. As it is for the most part newly built there are few traces of an earlier age. . . . Berlin, this entirely modern city . . . does not produce any solemn, serious effect, it bears neither the stamp of the country's history nor that of the character of its inhabitants.'

Just as new was the university to which Arthur Schopenhauer was now moving – it had been going only a year when he arrived. Numerous ambitions had led to the foundation of the university.

Following Prussia's disastrous defeat at the hands of Napoleon in 1806, and the resultant loss of the ancient university of Halle, the Prussian reformers, anxious to renew the state from the top, had aimed at a new education of the mind. Wilhelm von Humboldt had been won over to the idea of a university to be founded in Berlin, one which, in the words of the king, would 'compensate the state through spiritual strength for what it has lost in physical strength'. Humboldt, to begin with, was allowed to implement his high-flown ideas of a humanist education which would go beyond a mere preparation for the exercise of a profession. Special importance was therefore attached to the *Studia humaniora*, i.e. to philological, philosophical and theological disciplines. Leading figures in these fields were to be brought to Berlin. And this was accomplished by Fichte, Schleiermacher and Wolf. Fichte was elected Rector a few weeks before Arthur's arrival.

Fichte had not been anxious to be appointed to this post; he had suspected that his innovatory zeal would be hard put to prevail over the forces of tradition and custom in academic life. No sooner had he assumed office than he found himself at the centre of an argument. He regarded the traditional customs of duelling, affairs of honour, compulsory drinking, the insularity of regional students' associations, the boasting display of medals and decorations as immoral and undignified survivals of the old order. He began his term as Rector with a vigorous appeal to the students. 'On the Only Possible Disturbance of Academic Freedom' was the title of his inflammatory address. It was no use. The newly founded university refused to be that new. Within a few weeks he had to deal with the first disturbances. Medical students and pupils of the Army Health Institute attacked each other. The battle in the hall was continued out of doors. The army had to intervene. On another occasion a student struck a Jewish fellow student in public with a hunting crop, having in vain tried to provoke into a duel. Brogi, the victim, complained to the Rector. The case was heard by the Court of Honour, which punished not only the striker but also the person struck. Fichte protested; he saw it as a punishment for Brogi's refusal to fight a duel. A short time later Brogi once more was the victim. This wretched Jewish student, a bit of a swot, seemed positively to attract acts of violence. This time it was the son of the Berlin Secret War Councillor Klaatsch who had struck his victim and sneeringly invited him to complain to the Rector. Brogi did complain, and again he was punished for it by the Court of Honour. Thereupon Fichte requested to be relieved of the office of Rector. In his application for release, dated 14 February 1812, Fichte described the judgement of the Court of Honour (composed of professors and students) as 'a practical introduction of the principle that a student who, rather than fighting a duel, complains to the academic authority, is to be treated as devoid of honour'.

In Fichte's conflict with his colleagues, Schleiermacher was the spokesman of the opposing side. Schleiermacher had found little to criticize in such acts of violence: they were, he argued, no more than rough, naturally vigorous and youthful aspects of student life and tradition. Fichte ultimately saw this difference as the 'conflict between his teaching and a system which, based on fictitious history and natural philosophy, regards as a mere product of nature and history something that should be judged by moral laws'. The excitement about the student disturbances leads us directly to the delicate complications of post-Kantian intellectual life, to Fichte and the Romantic movement.

These were the burning issues of the day: nature versus morality, letting things be or changing them. The question of whether students should be allowed to beat each other up was raised by Fichte, and also by Schleiermacher, to the elevated level of 'great' truths. Arthur Schopenhauer therefore was able to gain insight into the latest convolutions of the spirit of the age not only in the severely 'scholarly' lectures of the Berlin master thinkers but also from the turbulent rowdyism of the students.

Fichte, Schopenhauer reported in retrospect, had drawn him to Berlin, even though he did not particularly love the city. Fichte had started his meteoric rise two decades earlier, and was soon proclaimed to be Kant's legitimate successor; he had also made a name for himself as a political writer defending even the Jacobinism of the French Revolution, and subsequently became the champion of a republican national rebirth of Germany ('Speeches to the German Nation', 1807). As an established philosopher he was past the peak of his fame and influence by the time Schopenhauer attended his lectures.

His career had begun with a drumbeat.

Born in 1762, Johann Gottlieb Fichte, like Kant the son of an artisan, studied theology and jurisprudence and made a modest livelihood as a tutor. One of his pupils wanted to be introduced by him to Kant's philosophy, which all the world was talking about. Fichte thereupon studied the *Critiques*, which until then had deterred him because they were so difficult to understand, and was so fascinated that at once, in the summer of 1791, he travelled to Königsberg to visit the great philosopher. He found a weary old man who treated him with indifference; small wonder, considering that the famous man was beleaguered by an ever increasing number of adoring juveniles. Kant was even pestered by ladies who would ask for moral advice in difficult amorous situations. Fichte, therefore, like the rest of the ladies and gentlemen, was initially sent packing. For thirty-five days he went into a self-imposed confinement and in feverish labour composed a work with which he hoped to introduce himself to the master: *Essay of a Critique of All Revelation.* Kant was so impressed by this that he not only invited the author to luncheon but also found him a publisher. The book appeared anonymously, against Fichte's will, in the spring of 1792. The publisher had been cautious for censorship reasons, but there were also commercial considerations: the work was so much in the spirit of Kantian religious philosophy that the public might be expected to ascribe it to the Königsberg philosopher, especially as some definitive religious pronouncements had been expected from him for some time, and in consequence they might be eager to buy. Which was exactly what happened. *Allgemeine Literatur Zeitung,* a literary review published in Jena, carried this note: 'We consider it our duty to inform the public of the existence of a work of the greatest importance in every respect, just published this Easter: *Essay of a Critique of All Revelation, from Hartung in Königsberg.* Anyone who has read even the slightest of the writings with which the Königsberg philosopher acquired undying merit for mankind, will instantly recognize the distinguished author of this work.' Thereupon Kant, in the same periodical, expressed his thanks for the flattering assumption, pointing out, however, that he was not the 'distinguished author'; that honour belonged to the hitherto totally unknown Fichte. With this announcement Fichte overnight became one of the most famous philosophical writers in Germany.

In this work Fichte carried Kant's subjectivism further into the religious field: our morality, in favour of which we can decide freely, without the threat of punishment or the promise of future reward, is of such nobility, according to Fichte, that it guides behaviour in such a manner as if heavenly revelations existed. We require no faith in order to be moral, but if we are moral then in our minds we partake of the divine; only at the exalted moral level to which we climb unaided do the revelations of religion acquire evidential value. This is a religion *post festum,* an ornament of our autonomy. Religion does not establish morality, but the other way about: morality, the revelations of a sense of duty, make us receptive to the revelations of religion. Religious revelation does not invest morality with validity (e.g. in respect of reward or punishment), but merely lends it additional dignity.

Fichte thus answers a question which had been worrying many of those who professed Kant's philosophy, the question of whether, under the principles of critical philosophy, revelation was still conceivable. Fichte's answer was a clear yes, always provided that revelation was not the foundation of morality but the other way about: morality was the foundation of revelation.

This first work shows very clearly the direction in which, and the starting point from which, Fichte, as a disciple of Kant, intended to continue his master's work. His concern was the doctrine of freedom, the autonomy of the world-creating ego. Fichte combined Kantian criticism with the inspirations of the French Revolution. Kant taught him the transcendental point of view, i.e. the method of first of all viewing the perceiving and comprehending subject in everything perceived and comprehended. Kant also taught him that the classic questions 'What can I know – what shall I do – what may I hope for?' are best answered if one tries to find an answer to a fourth question: 'What is man?' Fichte believed he had found it by deriving from the Kantian statement 'The "I think" must accompany all my conceptions' the concept of an all-powerful ego and thence, with unparalleled boldness, developing from it a complementary concept of the world as a mere product of the 'actions' of that ego. A glance across the Rhine gave him confirmation: history was not a happening but something that was made. There was a rational subject standing behind it, steering it towards a definite destination across the ocean of historical facts – to make the world as moral as reason has always been when, within the ego, it becomes aware of itself. This discovery of the ego as the heart of the world had the effect of a thunderbolt on him, Fichte later reported; again and again he was to demand of his disciples that they should allow themselves to be transformed by this inspiration, as otherwise the totality of his involved philosophy must remain incomprehensible to them.

Kant had proceeded from the 'I think' as from something given; but that, Fichte taught, was wrong. Instead we should watch what was happening within us when we think the 'I think'. That 'I', that ego, was something we only produced by thinking, and simultaneously the productive force was the non-prethinkable ego-ness within ourselves. The thinking ego and the thought ego were both enclosed in the circle of an activism. There was no solid existence to which we could refer; there was only that non-prethinkable activity which, among other things, allowed us to think. The world began with an action, and so did what we call the ego begin with an action. Fichte might say: I give birth to myself as an ego, and therefore I am.

The conclusions which Fichte went on to draw might at first sight seem downright monstrous: 'The source of all reality is the ego,' he declared; hence 'all reality of the non-ego is only a reality transferred from the ego.' The non-ego, i.e. the material world, therefore existed only because the ego, in order to become aware of itself, created its own boundaries. Activity existed only where there was resistance. Hence activity created resistance. Activity, therefore, was activity in a triple sense: (1) it was primary activity; (2) it was activity creating resistance; and (3) it was activity aware of itself as such by encountering (self-created) resistances. This conceptual delirium means that restriction is self-restriction of an infinitely active ego. These constructs, admittedly, must seem monstrous if understood to mean our empirical, psychologically comprehensible ego. In that case mockery would be easy.

Jean Paul wrote: 'Well, if every ego is its own father and creator, why should it not also be its own angel of death?' We shall meet with Schopenhauer's mockery of Fichte's *tour de force* in due course.

Fichte, however, never tired of emphasizing that one must not understand one's ego as one's own ego, indeed not as an empirically unique 'individual' ego at all, but as an 'ego-ness' pulsating, as an active force of self-awareness, below any individual sense of ego. Fichte's ego had to be made so space-embracing (some said: inflated) because Fichte ranged himself on the side of the post-Kantians who rejected the ominous 'thing in itself' as irrelevant and therefore only retained the presenting ego.

Fichte, basing himself on Schopenhauer's Göttingen philosophy teacher Gottlob Ernst Schulze (who had published his critique of Kant under the pseudonym of 'Aenesidemus') and on Maimon, had discovered a faulty derivation of the 'thing in itself' by Kant. He argued like this: The assumption that the world as it appeared to us was concealing a world as it was in itself, and that this world-in-itself as 'material' was ultimately the *cause* of what, by means of our senses and reason, we would transform into the phenomenal world – this, as it were, 'realistic' assumption was itself only made by means of the causality principle, i.e. by means of our intellect. In other words, the causality principle, which was valid only for the phenomenal world, was being applied to a sphere that lay beyond appearance. Thus the 'thing in itself', which was beyond experience and intellect, was derived only with the aid of causation, which, however, applied only to the phenomenal world.

In consequence it was no longer a 'thing in itself' but a 'thing for ourselves'. (Schopenhauer was subsequently to adopt this argument against Kant.)

Kant had located this transphenomenal 'thing in itself' within ourselves, within the mystery of our freedom, which, not being subject to any causality (i.e. to any compulsion), itself produces causalities; a freedom which starts from nothing and maps itself out by realizing itself. Kant had said that in his freedom man participated in what existed beyond all appearances (causalities). And Fichte now was taking Kant a step further in precisely that sense: proceeding from that inward-turned 'thing in itself', from the freedom with which the ego could, of its own, *begin to be* at any moment.

At the same time he did not wish to maintain the world-shaking omnipotence of the empirical, individual ego – indeed he frequently rejected the idea of such transcendental Napoleonism – but he wished to make it clear that the dynamics of the life process of history and nature could be comprehended only if their entirety was thought of in *ego-like* terms. The force which moved nature and history was of the same kind as that experienced in activism, in the spontaneity of our ego. Rousseau's idea was here thought through boldly to the end: I know of the beginning and the movement of the world because I myself can at any moment begin and move. Self-experience leads us into the world as a universe of spontaneity. I am the 'thing in itself' – the revealed secret of the world. This realization was to

Fichte the fiery 'thunderbolt' which heated his philosophy to the end. The 'thunderbolt' came from the tension-laden spiritual atmosphere of the wish for emancipation, an atmosphere carried across from the French Revolution. Fichte's influence, however, did not come from his difficult deductions, which very few understood, but from what could provide ready coin for the new ecstasy of being an 'ego'. Of course Rousseau had prepared the ground for that ecstasy. From him the age learned a defiant opposition of the self against the social milieu and its conventions. Rousseau's *Confessions* then very rapidly became a cult book. That a study of heaven and earth should start by self-observation was welcome news. The first few sentences rang out like fanfares: 'I alone. I read in my heart and I know human beings. I am not made like any of those whom I have seen.'

That was how people wished to be, so non-interchangeable and yet universal, so familiar with the riches of their own hearts. Goethe's Werther was such a person. 'I return into myself and I find a world,' he had exclaimed, and many people echoed his words and tried to live like him.

Fichte had, with a great deal of noise, elevated that ego to a philosophical Mount Olympus; there it now stood like a figure by Caspar David Friedrich, the world spread out before his feet: a splendid prospect. Through Fichte, who had the knack of popularizing his difficult philosophy by captivating rhetoric, the word 'ego' acquired a very particular colouring, comparable only to the wealth of meaning that Nietzsche and Freud subsequently lent to the 'Id'. Fichte popularized became the crown witness for the spirit of subjectivism and unlimited feasibility. The putative power of subjective creating produced euphoria. There you would find Hölderlin, Hegel and Schelling at the end of the century cheerfully sharing a bottle of wine and developing the outlines of a new mythology which would have to be 'created'. Where did one find such a mythology? In oneself, of course. That should not be beyond one's powers: one 'made sense', one created a new society-shaping idea in order to amalgamate the demoralized social entity once more into a magnificent super-ego. Subsequently the account of this euphoric meeting came to be known as 'the oldest system programme of German idealism', a youthfully fresh document, driven by the world-shaking spirit of creation and of the ego, the spirit of the wild years of philosophy.

Those who so emphatically reassured themselves about their egos frequently felt threatened or restricted by a world which, after all, offered considerable resistance to the ego's wish to unfold. Mostly the ego was stepping out from a background of sorrow and pain. The young Hölderlin said in a letter: 'Who can keep his heart within beautiful bounds when the world is pounding him with its fists? The more challenged we are by Nothingness which, like to an abyss, yawns all around us, or even dissipated by the thousandfold Something of society and human activity, which pursues us shapelessly, soullessly and lovelessly, the more passionate and eager and violent must *resistance* become from our side. . . . Neediness and indigence from without turns your heart's abundance to indigence and neediness for you.'

The 'heart's abundance' demanded an outpouring; any holding back would be fatal. At the end of that outpouring stood the Tower in Tübingen, where Hölderlin, whether as a 'noble malingerer' or as a sick man, spent the final decades of his life in seclusion – an ego which had given up appropriating the world to itself.

As with Hölderlin, the sense of ego emerged from darkness also with the young Friedrich Schlegel. To his friend Novalis he wrote: 'I, a refugee, have no house, I was cast out into infinity (the Cain of the universe) and am expected to build myself one out of my own heart and head.'

Unlike Hölderlin, Friedrich Schlegel was determined not to let 'the heart's abundance' degenerate to 'indigence' in the face of a negating reality. He drew the forces of negation, which were obstructing the excess encouraged by the French Revolution, over to his own side and made them the power of 'annihilation'. Anything that negated one, he argued, one must oneself negate. No time for sadness; Hölderlin's elegy for things lost was not for Friedrich Schlegel, who, in his *Conversation on Poetry*, presented himself as someone 'who, with his revolutionary philosophy, has been fond of pursuing annihilation on a large scale'. When Schlegel wrote these lines his 'revolutionary philosophy' was that of Fichte. Jena, where Fichte taught between 1794 and 1799, was for a short time the rallying point for all those who wanted to use their egos 'on a large scale'; August Wilhelm Schlegel taught philosophy in Jena; his house became the centre of the young movement. Fichte was a frequent visitor. Friedrich Schlegel lodged with his brother. Tieck was there. The 'assessor' of the salt works in Weissenfels, Friedrich von Hardenberg, who wrote under the name of Novalis, frequently came over to Jena. Clemens Brentano was studying medicine there. Hölderlin came to hear Fichte. Schelling was called to the university. Henrik Steffens, the future natural philosopher, was a member of this circle and, in retrospect, recorded of these years: 'They had concluded an intimate alliance, and they in fact belonged together. What the French Revolution intended to achieve as an external natural event, and Fichte's philosophy as an inner absolute deed, this alliance wished to develop as pure, wildly playing fantasy.'

Goethe, a frequent visitor to Jena, watched this cheerful bustle with a certain pleasure. To him these were all geniuses, if a trifle eccentric; they stood 'on the brink', he remarked, and they might come to a bad end, which he would regret. But when Friedrich Schlegel told everyone willing to listen to him that Schiller's exaltedness invariably made him fall off his chair with laughter, then one Olympian surely had to support another. Friedrich Schlegel had a strip torn off him and went to Berlin in order to continue his narcissistic, ironical and disrespectful activities there. The journal *Athenäum*, which he founded there, was originally to be called *Herkules*, as a signal that the ego and its 'productive imaginative power' need not fear the Augean stables of the period.

Fichte had encouraged the ego to go for a moral seizure of power; the Romantic circle in Jena, on the other hand, was aiming more at the aesthetic enjoyment of the creative, world-creating ego. 'Productive imagination', which for Kant kept the clockwork of apperception ticking, and for Fichte acted as the midwife for the birth of the moral world, became, for the 'new wild men', the 'principle of divine imagination'. For Schiller, who understood the workings of art but wished to keep it on the long leash of morality, all this went much too far. 'The fantast abandons nature out of sheer arbitrariness,' he wrote, 'in order to yield the more uninhibitedly to the wilfulness of desires and to the inclinations of imagination. . . . Because fantasticality is not an excess of nature, but freedom, and therefore springs from a respectable disposition, one that is infinitely perfectible, it also leads to an infinite fall into bottomless depths and can end only in total ruin.'

This was a lesson the Romantics did not need. Their intellectual virtuosity, by which they had always wanted ironically to surpass themselves, had made them realize the risks of their bold flights. Ludwig Tieck, Friedrich Schlegel, Clemens Brentano – they all had an acute realization of the threatening abysses of their strivings, and they actually derived particular enjoyment from that sensitivity to 'nihilism' (the term was just then emerging). Tieck made the character William Lovell in his novel exclaim: 'Fly with me, Icarus, fraternally we will jubilate into destruction.' If accused of acting 'arbitrarily', they would reply: But how else? Arbitrariness is our best part. Jean Paul, who knew what he was talking about because he too enjoyed indulging in poetic self-elevation and overcoming of the world, took Schiller's side in order not to find himself among the sorcerer's apprentices. In his *Vorschule der Aesthetik* (*Propaedeutics of Aesthetics*, 1804) he wrote: 'It follows from the lawless arbitrariness of the present spirit of the age – which, ego-addicted, prefers to destroy the world and the universe provided this will give them free, empty elbow-room in nothingness . . . that it must speak disparagingly of the imitation and the study of nature.'

In Fichte's circle, disregarding for the moment the master himself, there was no disparaging talk at all about the study of nature. Equipped with Fichte's deductions, according to which the ego, as the force of Becoming, reaches deep down into the foundations of Being, they were ready to gaze also into the interior of nature. Schelling attempted this systematically with his natural philosophy. Novalis, the mining engineer, overflowed with rhapsodic, disjointed, allusive remarks: 'The mysterious road leads inward' or 'The exterior is the interior raised to a mysterious state' or 'We search for the design of the world; we ourselves are that design'. Novalis contrasts the 'outward gaze' at nature, which is bound to discover causality everywhere, with the 'inward gaze', to which 'analogies' reveal themselves. This 'inner' way of thinking ('productive imagination' comes in here), he explained, 'permits us to surmise the external world as a human being; it shows that we can only understand everything in the way that we understand ourselves and those we love, us and you'.

Supporting himself on this process of analogy, Novalis developed magnificent images, for instance his suggestion that nature might only have rigidified into rock when man's searching glance fell upon it. Instead of a heartless analysis of nature, Novalis pleaded for an erotic comprehension of nature. For Novalis, Fichte's ego, which supposedly underlies nature as well, becomes 'you'. And just as everything is possible between lovers, so here too: 'Whatever I wish I can do. Nothing is impossible for human beings.' As our bodies are the part of nature nearest to us, our loving power – Novalis fantasized – should extend to them also. Once one has ended hostility towards one's body there is nothing to hold one back, 'then everyone will be his own physician, able to acquire a complete, assured and exact feeling for his body, then man . . . will perhaps even be able to restore lost limbs, to kill himself by mere volition and only thus acquire true knowledge of the body, the soul, the world, life, death and the spirit world. It may possibly depend on him alone whether a dead person is reanimated. He will compel his senses to produce for him the shape he demands, and he will be able, in the most real sense, to live in his world.'

Anyone submerging his ego as deeply into the non-ego of nature as Novalis must ultimately make the strange discovery that nature no longer appears to him ego-related but, the other way about, his ego appears to him nature-related. He will drown in what he regards as his ego, in the 'dark alluring womb of nature', it will consume his 'poor personality', as Novalis has it in *Die Lehrlinge zu Sais* (*The Apprentices at Sais*). The ego, wanting to find itself and meet itself everywhere, suddenly stands in the dark, suddenly finds itself on the nocturnal side of nature. A shadow realm opens to it within itself. The outlines of an unknown continent, of the unconscious, become visible. This becomes the destination of a new curiosity. Nor could it be otherwise: anyone wishing to feel and comprehend himself so intensively must very soon discover the indefinable and the ambiguous. Internal 'twilight' begins when the curious discover more in the ego than the common coins of 'community spirit'. While scientific expeditions were setting out to explore the jungle beyond the Pacific Ocean, others were getting down to exploring the jungle within ourselves.

Many of those who found themselves too deeply entrapped in their own jungle by the joy of being an ego ultimately overexerted themselves. In reply to Werther's jubilant exclamation, 'I return within myself and find a world,' Clemens Brentano in 1802, by then rather contrite, remarked: 'Whoever directs me to within myself kills me . . .'

The overworked egos were seeking something solid. After all, even the ego comet of Bonaparte had meanwhile consolidated itself by stiff imperial dignity.

August Wilhelm Schlegel found refuge with the corpulent and wealthy Madame de Staël. Friedrich Schlegel was preparing his defection into the bosom of the Catholic Church. Tradition was once more in demand; folk songs and fairy tales were being collected: thank God one did not have to do everything oneself. Solid positions and durable relationships were being sought.

Fichte alone remained what he had always been: his trumpet still heralded the ego's Judgement Day. The crowd of ego disciples had drifted on; with Fichte the moral ego alone remained in all its massive earnestness.

This then was the man whom Arthur Schopenhauer wanted to hear in Berlin – for one thing, because one simply had to have heard Fichte if one wished to be up to date in philosophy, and for another, because Arthur was still searching for a language in which Platonic removal from empirical consciousness might be understood and formulated in a modern way.

Whatever filtered through to Göttingen of Fichte's strict concepts of morality or of his subtle escalations of ego consciousness seemed less promising than his continually repeated declaration that philosophical truth must strike into everyday consciousness with the 'evidence' of a 'thunderbolt'; that truth knew only one blinding instant, one single explosion, but of immense force; that real philosophy, strictly speaking, could consist of but a single idea, which subsequently, solely for the purpose and under the conditions of communication, was spun out into a thread of arguments.

Arthur Schopenhauer, who had been instructed by his father in Pietist aloofness from the world, who had, with Wackenroder and Tieck, tried distancing through art, who was compensating Kant's scepticism with Platonic upsoaring, now felt, as did so many of his contemporaries, torn between the unreasonable demands of earth and the joys of heaven. Yet in one decisive respect Schopenhauer took a totally different road from his contemporaries. They would wish to dull or reconcile their own dichotomy. They would seek that Archimedean point from which life might again become whole. Sophisticated constructions would be thought up, Hegel's and Marx's dialectics would let the irreconcilable work towards its own reconciliation. The old metaphysical forces would be restrained and placed in the service of history.

Not so Arthur Schopenhauer. He was not out for reconciliation; he threw his entire philosophical passion into the project of comprehending the 'duplicity of consciousness'; of comprehending why and to what extent we are, and must be, torn between two worlds; he would separate the two consciousnesses with relentless acuity – the one being the empirical consciousness, and the other one for which Schopenhauer himself had as yet no name; he was searching, probing, occasionally using religious terms, and finally during his Berlin period decided in favour of the name of 'the better consciousness'.

CHAPTER NINE

THE 'BETTER CONSCIOUSNESS'

'But I say,' Schopenhauer noted in his philosophical diary at the beginning of 1813, 'that personality and causality do exist in this temporal, sensory, comprehensible world; indeed they are necessary. But the better consciousness within me lifts me up into a world where neither personality nor causality, nor subject nor object, exist any more' (P 1, 42).

Under the label of 'better consciousness' Schopenhauer now gathered together everything that he had previously experienced as acts or ideals of transcending: Matthias Claudius's 'Man is not domiciled here'; the ecstasy of art, especially music; the experience of high mountains; that inward transcendence which made sensuality and self-preservation seem a mere game; the self-oblivion of engrossed contemplation or, the other way round, the experience of the ego as a mirror reflecting the multifariously appearing world without being part of it; the Platonic 'idea', even though adopted hesitantly as yet; Kant's 'having to' – that riddle of freedom which tears apart the world of necessary being.

He was still searching for a language for these transcendences. It was to be the language of reason, but it was being put to an extreme test because it was supposed to express something it had not found. The 'better consciousness' was, to Schopenhauer, not something produced by reason but something happening to reason, not something made but something admitted: a 'brainwave', not to be summoned deliberately, an inspiration, a pentecostal experience. Empirical elements and 'better consciousness' are divided by a gulf. There is no way across it, only a trans-lation, a carrying across. However, this is so difficult because the 'better consciousness' would have to be carried across into the language of the subject, or, more accurately, that of the subject–object relationship. But that is an impossibility because the experience of the 'better consciousness' relates to a strange eclipse of the ego and hence also to the disappearance of a world calling for action, self-assertion and self-intervention. The world as something concrete disappears. The 'better consciousness' is not a consciousness *of something*, not a thought approaching an object with the intention of seizing it or producing it. It is not a case of something being thought of because one wants something of that something. The 'better consciousness' is not a presence of mind in an affray; it is a kind of wakefulness at rest within itself, not desiring anything, not fearing anything, not hoping for anything. Stripped of ego, and hence unrelatable, the 'better consciousness' has the world before it – admittedly a world which, as it no longer 'acts' upon an ego, ceases, in a certain sense, to be 'actual'. The world becomes an 'arabesque', Schopenhauer noted in his philosophical diary, the 'law of gravity' seems to have been suspended, 'everything else is left, but nevertheless an entirely new course of things has arisen, at every step we are taken by surprise by what is normally impossible, the difficult has become easy, the easy has become difficult, from what seemed nothingness a world is now spilling out and the immense vanishes in nothingness' (P 1, 27).

The difficult course of the world and the order of things appear as 'a game'. 'Man should rise above life,' Schopenhauer wrote, arguing against suicide, 'he should realize that no happenings or incidents, joys or sorrows touch upon his better and inner self, that it is all a game' (P 1, 32).

The transformation of the world and of the ego entangled with it into a 'game' was occasionally described by Arthur Schopenhauer as an 'aesthetic' experience. But this is not a case of Kant's 'disinterested pleasure', because here, while admittedly dealing with a case of 'disinterest', one is not dealing with one of 'pleasure'. The 'better consciousness' is a crack in what to us is everyday and self-evident, an amazed wakefulness, beyond pleasure and pain.

The 'better consciousness' is a state of the beyond. There are no judgemental relations left with regard to the world, hence neither yes nor no. Schopenhauer was later to discover with some satisfaction that the early German mystics (Jakob Böhme, Meister Eckhart, Tauler) and the Indian teachings of wisdom used similar words to encompass that indefinable, incomprehensible nothingness which, at the same time, is everything.

Schopenhauer speaks of a consciousness 'beyond space and time' – another paradoxical expression forced upon us by our language. If at one instant I am totally immersed in attention, then the division between ego and the world is suddenly removed. It makes no difference whether I say: I am outside with the objects, or the objects are within me. What matters is that I no longer experience my attention as a function of my embodied ego. That attention is lifted out of the space–time coordinates, whose intersection is the ego: oblivious of space, time and self. The mystics had called this experience '*Nunc stans*', the standing now. The intensity of that present is without beginning and without end, and it can vanish only because *we* vanish from it. Attention ceases when I am driven back into my subject-being; then all the dichotomies are back again: I and the rest, *this* space, *this* time. Once my empirical ego has repossessed me, I shall firmly anchor that 'instant of attention' in the moorings of my individuality, my time of life, my location, and I shall have lost what had lent that instant its inexchangeability – its nowhere and nowhen. That kind of attention must have ceased if I can ascribe it to a place and to a time. I have once more sunk back into individuation, or surfaced to it, whichever way one looks at it. Undoubtedly the 'better consciousness' is a kind of ecstasy, a crystalline ecstasy of clarity and immobility, a euphoria of the eye which, from a surfeit of being able to see, loses sight of the objects. *This* ecstasy stands at the exact opposite pole from that which has always been associated with the name of Dionysus: the plunge into a flood of desire, carried away by the body, self-dissolution in orgiastic sensuality. Here the body is not abandoned but magnified into the world body. Here, too, an ego disappears by surrendering to the non-ego-like powers of urges: 'And I will not practise caution! / Far from you I'm driven by the wind, / On the river I will sail, / blissfully blinded by the splendour! / . . . / Sail on! I shall not question / where the voyage finds an end!' (Eichendorff).

Dionysus, the patron of these outings – he guards what is alive against the ego – was, according to the myth, torn apart alive and boiled to make broth. Thus for a while he lived in the circulating and secreted fluids of everything that lives: in sperm, in the amniotic fluid, in sweat and in blood; eventually he was once more condensed into a shape, but stricken by madness he would reel about, producing fertility everywhere and therefore loved; he was loved in opposition to the gang of other gods. He was always the coming god, not descending from heaven, but oozing from the ground, dirty, greasy and lecherous, recklessly spinning the wheel of birth and death; whoever encountered him exploded with happiness and lost himself. Dionysus was the 'reeling god', the metaphysics of the body. Metaphysics is the right term, because we are dealing with the breathtaking beyond, to which we are carried by the pleasures of the body. The terrifying moment of sexual intermingling is also a transcendence of the boundary, when space and time disappear for us. As the senses take over consciousness disappears. The ego is here responsible only for *coitus interruptus*, therefore it has to disappear; if it stayed behind, Dionysus, the 'coming god', could not come.

The rather mixed-up sons of pastors and civil servants, Hölderlin, Schelling, Hegel (and later Nietzsche), had, in Schopenhauer's day, been strewing flowers in the path of Dionysus, the coming god. But in actual fact they only wanted to hire him for work: with his spirit a new state, new laws, a new language were to be set up. The Dionysian element, responsible for the kind of happiness one does not wish to survive, was to be spun out into threads for a new network of cultural sociability to be woven from them. They all wanted the no longer risky presence of the 'reeling god'. Arthur Schopenhauer, however, was not in the mood for such conciliatory proceedings; he wanted no compromise: Dionysus frightened him. He wanted him out of the way. Dionysus frightened him because he was seeing him in his nakedness and his wantonness – not a figure to whom one might entrust the mild everyday mystery of 'bread and wine' (Hölderlin).

This is not to say that Arthur Schopenhauer was a follower of Apollo, the official opponent of Dionysus. Apollo stood for accomplished form, for a rounded individuality that dammed up the overspilling non-ego of the urges, collecting it and channelling it to its own mills. True, Arthur Schopenhauer's style, with its calm, measured pace, with its plasticity and clarity was to be Apollonian, but the inspirations of the 'better consciousness', from which ultimately his philosophy stemmed, were also boundary-transcendent, ego-dissolving, and therefore not Apollonian but, to use Hölderlin's term, 'sacredly sober'. It was a bright ecstasy which could not be understood simply as 'post-orgiastic thoughtfulness' (Sloterdijk), as the dying vibrations of after-pleasure at the incorporation of the world into his theory. Such theoretical pleasure might be seen as an attempt to let a reflection of festive Dionysian ecstasy fall into everyday life. Arthur Schopenhauer's 'better consciousness', however, is not a substitute, not a compensation; it is equipped with its own force, a feast day of the spirit, indeed a pentecostal feast of the pouring out of the Holy Spirit. From the heights of such ecstasy Schopenhauer hurled his anti-Dionysian thunderbolts, invectives against the temptations of the body, invectives the more bitter as all illusions about the power of the body are lost. He wrote: 'Laughingly look upon the temptations of your body as you would at the playing of a practical joke planned against you but divulged to you' (P 1, 24). It would be pleasant if from being the 'one ridiculed' one could become the 'one laughing', yet sensuality has its own seriousness and cannot be trifled with: 'Voluptuousness is in fact very serious. Picture the most beautiful, the most charming couple, full of grace attracting and repulsing one another in beautiful love play, desiring and fleeing, a sweet game, a delightful playfulness – Now look at them at the moment of enjoyment of their lust – all playfulness, all that gentle gracefulness is suddenly gone, all of a sudden vanished at the beginning of the *actus*, giving way to deep seriousness. What seriousness is that? – The seriousness of the animalic. Animals do not laugh. The forces of nature act seriously everywhere. . . . This seriousness is the *opposite* pole of the high seriousness of ecstasy, of transportation to a higher world: there is no playfulness there: and none in the animal realm' (P 1, 42). Love play is still civilization, capable of observing sovereign distances. The 'animalic seriousness' of coitus, however, sweeps me down into ego-less nature and makes me the object of its action. I can no longer play, I am played with. 'I am passive,' Schopenhauer wrote. The bright ecstasy of the 'better consciousness' is also a kind of passivity, but it is the passivity of having escaped; here we are dealing with the passivity of being driven. That was not what he wanted: he saw desire as an attempt on his sovereignty. Yet it was at particularly bright moments that the urge rose in him, and he could not conceal from himself that there was a strange complicity between the 'better consciousness' and sexual ecstasy. He began by comparing the two 'focal points' of ego-dissolution, head and genitals: both are hairy. He quoted the observation 'that the greatest discharge of semen and the greatest mental activity occur simultaneously, mostly at the full or the new moon' (P 1, 42). The genitals to him are the 'root' and the brain the 'crown' of the tree. The sap must rise so there should be blossom at the top. Brain and genitals, both of enormous power, reciprocally stimulate each other to an unfolding of that power. 'On the days and at the hours when the urge to *lust* is strongest, not a feeble longing springing from an emptiness and dullness of consciousness, but a burning desire, a violent rut: just then the highest forces of the spirit, indeed the better consciousness, are *ready* for greatest activity, even though *latent* at the instant when consciousness has surrendered to desire and is totally filled with it: yet it only requires a massive effort to reverse the direction, and instead of that tormenting, needy, desperate desire (the realm of the night) the activity of the highest mental powers fills the consciousness, the realm of light' (P 1, 54).

These are astonishing observations: the same set of urges evidently transports us either into the 'light' of the 'better consciousness' or into the 'night' of sexuality; between abdomen and head rages a struggle for that energy which, either downward or upward, makes us burst out of the confines of our ego, a struggle for our (evidently not so meagre) reserves of vitality, whose allocation, following the disappearance of the old god as an ecological conciliation authority, can no longer be determined by anyone with absolute authority.

But why then was Schopenhauer afraid to surrender himself to the explosion of the body, whose power he felt so clearly within himself?

We recall that Arthur, in his late puberty in Hamburg, wrote the following verses in about 1805: 'O voluptuousness, o hell . . . From heights of heaven / You dragged me / And flung me down / Into the dust of this earth: / Here I lie in fetters . . .' (P 1, 1).

Schopenhauer had been unlucky. Up to the moment when he hurled his thunderbolts against sexuality he had not experienced any love affair in which he might have enjoyed sex as something integrating with the whole personality, something that would carry the whole person away as if on a trip. Where he had found sex he had not been in love, and where he had been in love (e.g. with Karoline Jagemann in Weimar) sex had been excluded. This was bound to have had a twofold effect: the unity of a person is torn apart either by the accomplishment of sex or by the lack of it. Sexuality either shrinks to the unplayful 'animalic' seriousness' of a mere function, or as an unassuaged desire it derealizes the all-too-playful arabesques of unrequited pining. Whichever applies, it is a spoilsport: either by precluding the game altogether, or by letting it evaporate into a meaningless performance. In either case its conclusion is, if not sad, then certainly ludicrous. Hence Schopenhauer's grim determination to turn from being the 'one ridiculed' into the 'one laughing'. He intended to look on his sexuality as though it did not belong to him, as if it were a 'practical joke' for which one did not fall.

What Schopenhauer experienced – his clash with his own sexuality – is a piece of his private history, yet it also reflects something of the cultural history of sex.

An age which was just learning to enjoy saying 'I' did not wish, confirmed as it was in autonomy and internalization, to be caught napping by its own 'nature'. One need only recall the absurd circumstances contrived by Rousseau in his amorous novel *La Nouvelle Héloïse* to avoid touching the soft spot of tenderness in love. And the young Romantics' posturing as libertines and lady-killers was ultimately unconvincing: hot air, desire for desire rather than desire itself.

Nevertheless, or perhaps just because of this, a secretive muttering seemed to be spreading about sex. An entirely new curiosity was turning towards it. For many centuries sexuality had occupied its well-known, not at all mysterious place in the metaphysical order of life: this was where our flesh, that flesh in need of salvation, was stirring.

Sex only began to appear abysmal from the perspective of an ego believing itself to be autonomous. Only then did sex become that 'nature' within us which we fear might dissolve our self-glorifying ego. Secularization stripped sex of sinfulness, but instead it made it the bearer of a dangerous mystery. 'Sex,' Foucault wrote, 'has gradually become an object of great suspicion; a universal and alarming sensation which, despite us, crosses our behaviour and our existence; the vulnerable point whence disaster threatens; a piece of night that every one of us carries within him.'

Sexuality was beginning to be suspected of knowing the secret truth about ourselves. Efforts would be made to make it confess. Yet it was to take a whole century before, through Sigmund Freud, the suspicion that our sexuality, and it alone, knew what the real trouble was with us, became a system and presently an epidemic.

That suspicion began to arise in Schopenhauer's day. That was why Arthur Schopenhauer was to direct his inspirations in a double movement against the sexual organs while simultaneously, as part of his general offensive against the self-overestimation of the mind, developing a magnificent metaphysics of the body, based on the 'focal point' of the will in sexuality. As a rule, he taught, we do not stand a chance against our sexuality. As the most garish manifestation of 'will' it is the 'thing in itself' in action, humiliating the poor ego and sweeping it along before it. In his unsatisfactory relationships with women Arthur Schopenhauer very personally experienced sexuality as the humiliation of his supreme autonomy.

He had been unlucky. Quite apart from the circumstances of a historical period there is such a thing as a personal disposition to being unlucky. Sartre has demonstrated, by the example of Flaubert, that a child closeted with his mother, who loves him only out of a sense of duty, is inadequately born into his own body and grows into it inadequately. There remains a vulnerable aloofness and strangeness: the inner warmth which causes the ego sensation, when its awakens, to fuse with the body as a whole, may be lacking in these conditions.

Much the same must have happened to young Arthur. The living element in himself, in his own body, was to him 'the other', not his own; something like a cold current that carried one along but to which one would not wish to abandon oneself. When, eventually, the body got heated after all, the ego would shiver with cold and apply for asylum to the protective authorities of ego-like sovereignty. In Arthur's case his father, Heinrich Floris, was such an authority. He towered above the swollen muddy waters. From him the virtue of proud self-control might be learned, his advice in all circumstances was to keep one's head. And since, at the time when Arthur grew up, there was no longer any erotic tension left between his parents, the cooling process in Arthur was bound to proceed further. And when sexuality inevitably stirred in him it was experienced, as we know from Arthur, as a tempting but at the same time alien force. Arthur's erotic career began with a condemnation of 'lust' rather than with outpourings of romantic infatuation. It was as if, between 'naked' sex and a precociously developed intellect, no gently calming 'soul' had interposed itself for young Arthur, the kind that ensures an acceptable peace treaty between the two centres of vitality. Schopenhauer himself subsequently saw matters in this light when he wrote that, especially at moments of a powerfully soaring intellect, the 'urge towards voluptuousness' would erupt unmitigated and crudely. An intermediate level of a domesticated *modus vivendi*, where mind and sex were traded at half price and thereby approximated one another, does not seem to have existed for him. He lacked what Thomas Mann in his novel *Doctor Faustus* called the 'essentially sentimental level of life'. The novel's Adrian Leverkühn lacked it, and Arthur Schopenhauer likewise showed little interest in it. 'It is a fact,' Thomas Mann wrote, 'that the proudest intellect confronts the animalic, the naked urges, most immediately, and is most pitifully at their mercy.'

Thus, at loggerheads with oneself, one is bound to see woman as an accomplice of the power which threatens self-assertion. Desire draws one to the woman, but she is made to feel, willy-nilly, that she will not be forgiven for having caused the male's grand autonomy to be thus offended. It will, in consequence, be difficult to experience a love affair in which mind and sex jointly, in an unleashing of happiness, sweep aside all antagonisms and dualisms. Such an experience would have the power of transformation. Suddenly nothing would be the same as before. If such an experience is not encountered, then the energy of that fundamental dichotomy grows, and it becomes increasingly improbable for a way to be found out of that dichotomy, simply because the experience of love as such becomes increasingly improbable.

Arthur Schopenhauer, too demanding, too hungry for intensity to content himself with his empirical ego and consolidate himself in it, would therefore yield to transcending the boundary into the supra-sovereign, to the 'bright' ecstasy of the 'better consciousness', while resisting the crossing of the border to the infra-sovereign, the ecstasies of Dionysus. His philosophical reflections, however, were to furnish that underground with the old metaphysical dignity of the concept of substance. This underground, as the 'will', was even declared to be the only substance. Everything is flesh of the flesh of the will. The 'will' is so much 'everything' that it can only be balanced now by 'nothingness', i.e. by the 'better consciousness'.

By transcending the boundaries of the empirical ego, the 'better consciousness' has not only momentarily escaped the working of the will, but has also passed beyond the world-immanent working of reason (causality, personality, space and time concepts). On occasion Arthur Schopenhauer uses religious terms to speak of 'grace' and of the 'peace of God that passeth all understanding'. We are confronted here with a sudden mental state that is raised above all conceivable immanent purposes; it cannot be degraded to a means for anything. From this experience Schopenhauer derives an exceedingly fateful certainty: the modern concatenation of an idea and the realization of that idea has no validity here; realization is no longer the verification of an idea. The 'better consciousness' cannot be realized because it is itself 'real' in a manner which nullifies everything else that is real. This experience made Schopenhauer decide once and for all against all projects of conciliation attempting to eliminate the malaise of reality by working for its improvement. He holds fast to the irreconcilable 'duplicity' between our empirical existence and consciousness on the one hand and the 'better consciousness' on the other. He illustrates this by the example of man's attitude to death: 'An experience that elucidates the *duplicity of our consciousness* is our, at different times different, attitude to death. There are moments when we think of death so intensively that it appears before us in such horrible shape that we cannot understand how, with such a prospect, one can have a quiet minute and not spend one's life in lamenting the necessity of death. At other times we think of death with calm joy, indeed with longing. We are right in both cases. In the first mood we are wholly filled with temporal consciousness, we are nothing but a phenomenon in time; as such, death to us is annihilation, rightly to be feared as the greatest evil. In the other mood our better consciousness is alive, rightly looking forward to the dissolving of the mysterious tie by which it is linked with empirical consciousness into the identity of *one* ego' (P 1, 68).

The fact that there exists an irreconcilable duplicity of consciousness, the possibility of a dual perspective, of dual experience, is so evident to Arthur Schopenhauer that, like Wittgenstein after him, he actually charges philosophy with a negative duty: it should, in discursive language, say what can be said in order to delineate the sphere which is *not* reached by language; it should advance to the frontiers of possible conceptual work, in order to discover that of which *no* concept can exist. It will be the task of philosophy, as Schopenhauer understands it, to ensure that one is not seduced by oneself, by the élan of one's own conceptuality. The unutterable must not become the unknowable.

CHAPTER TEN

PHILOSOPHY AT ARMS

Having come to Berlin in order to attend Fichte's lectures, Schopenhauer had expected from him some inspiration similar to his own. While still in Göttingen he had heard that Fichte invariably claimed that philosophy must start not from an awareness of objects but from 'absolute contemplation', when the ego becomes conscious of itself as freed from all space–time relations and, in a manner of speaking, can observe itself producing all those relations.

Yet after a few weeks Arthur observed in Fichte that self-seduction of conceptual philosophy which he had determined to resist. Fichte, it seemed to him, was out to operate with concepts and to discover what could, at best, be 'translated' into concepts: the 'better consciousness'.

The first Fichte lecture which Schopenhauer attended in the autumn of 1811 was on the 'Facts of Consciousness'.

So long as Fichte was arguing that philosophy stemmed from astonishment he met with Schopenhauer's agreement; he continued to do so when he referred to the 'flash of evidence' as the starting point of that astonishment. But when Fichte derived that 'evidence', tempting as it was to Schopenhauer, from the spiral of empirical self-reflection, Arthur began to bristle. He doubted that reflection of reflection or perception of perception actually achieved a new quality – which was what Fichte was aiming at. To Schopenhauer these were barren duplications. A reflecting or perceiving instance, even if attempting to observe itself, would always remain a reflecting or perceiving instance. That way, according to Schopenhauer, it was impossible to get out of immanence; that was a hopeless course. But Fichte had only just begun his flight. When, in his fifth lecture, he maintained that consciousness enlightened in self-reflection meant the disappearance of being, Schopenhauer, in a mixture of annoyance and puzzlement, wrote in the margin of his notes: 'I have to confess that everything said here is very obscure to me, and that I may have incorrectly understood it' (P II, 37).

He missed the next few lectures because he was ill. Recovered, he heard Fichte explain that 'knowledge is a schematization of perception'. Schopenhauer noted: 'I don't know what this means . . .' (P II, 41). But instead of falling sick again he was gripped by anger: 'In this lecture he . . . said things which made me wish to place a pistol to his chest and say to him: You must now die without mercy, but for your poor soul's sake tell me whether with all that gallimaufry you had anything precise in mind or whether you were merely making fools of us?' (P II, 41). Unperturbed, however, Fichte continued to soar higher. Faced with Fichte's statement, 'The absolute link between vision and seeing is the foundation,' Schopenhauer could think only of the lines from Bürger's poem: 'Be extinguished, extinguished forever, my light, / Away, away to horror and night!' (P II, 44).

Schopenhauer by then was no longer intimidated by the delirium of concepts, and anger had yielded to mockery. He realized that concepts must start tumbling when assigned the false task of, for instance, leading to the 'better consciousness' or, as Fichte put it, to 'absolute contemplation'. When, in a subsequent lecture, Fichte went into laborious contortions in order to get behind the ego, Schopenhauer remarked with laconic brevity: 'There is only One Viewing, the ego: and for that reason it is never the Viewed' (P II, 68).

Schopenhauer's marginal glosses on Fichte's next lecture on 'Theory of Knowledge', in the summer of 1812, are even more cutting: 'Raving nonsense', 'lunatic babbling' (P II, 123). He used the Shakespearean quotation 'Though this be madness, there is method in't' as a heading for his whole set of lecture notes. Schopenhauer began to be amused by that 'madness'. When Fichte said: 'The ego is because it seats itself' he drew a chair in the margin. Fichte taught: 'The ego is not clarified from anything else, but is clear and is absolute clarity itself.' Schopenhauer's comment was: 'As today he only supplied his pure light but no taper, these notes could not be continued' (P II, 193). During the next few lectures – Fichte was speaking about the pure form of visibility – the darkness continued. Schopenhauer's comment: 'As no tapers again provided visibility today, these notes had to be discontinued' (P II, 195). Arthur did not believe in the Irish wisdom: 'If you look into the dark long enough there is always something in it.' He had meanwhile parted with Fichte's philosophy with the oracular remark: 'Here philosophy will sit in the dark for a long time.'

Fichte's philosophy, however, was illuminating whenever practical, and possibly political, morality was at issue. And its finest hour was approaching. Towards the end of 1812 the great patriotic intoxication of the anti-Napoleonic wars of liberation erupted. Prussia, since her defeat at Jena and Auerstädt in 1806 a vassal of the French Empire, had been forced for some time to tread a middle path between compliance vis-à-vis Napoleon and a policy of not permitting Prussian patriotism to run riot while, on the other hand, not outraging it too much. The beginnings of democratic reform of the state system (Stein, Hardenberg) similarly preserved a delicate balance: the subjects were to be involved, up to a point even made to participate, in administration and political rule, but within limits. Any democratic movement which, in the given situation, was bound to turn patriotically German, and, on the other hand, any patriotism escalating into democratic 'impertinence' had to be avoided – both in the class interest of the rulers and out of caution *vis-à-vis* the French Emperor. Although Fichte's *Speeches to the German Nation* of the winter of 1807–8 had been allowed public hearing, the Prussian censors refused permission for the first two speeches to be printed. Foundation of the new university in Berlin, urged with ulterior patriotic motives, had been authorized, but any excessive patriotic pronouncements were forbidden. Anything too 'German' that Schleiermacher had written into its articles of incorporation was deleted, such as the statement that the university was to be a 'nursery of German youth'. The difficulties encountered by the patriotism of Kleist's *Berliner Abendblätter* in dealing with the Prussian authorities are well known.

The government devoted its particular attention to the theatre. Iffland, then director of the National Theatre, was made to include French operettas in his programme; he even had German plays occasionally staged in French. He spent many a night dictating translations to his scribe. Yet the regular German audience would seize any opportunity to vent its patriotism. During Schiller's *Maid of Orleans*, when in the coronation scene the call went up 'Long live the King, Charles the Good!', the last three words were drowned by howling. All that was heard was 'Long live the King!'

The theatre was altogether one of the few arenas where attitudes and views could be collectively reflected. The general rule, however, was fragmentation, individualization, a retreat within the familiar circle. Varnhagen von Ense reported: 'Wherever one looked one saw upheaval, break-up, an uncertain future in every direction; in vain did social and spiritual forces oppose the political ones; they were bound to feel that the bourgeois soil that bore them had been shaken . . .; everyone pursued his momentary advantage as best he could, as the day might provide it.' Anyone seeking firm ground under his feet in that uncertain situation felt himself 'forcibly thrown towards the intellectual life; one was united in the enjoyment of ideas and emotions which aimed to be the opposite of that reality'.

For a while, therefore, Berliners enjoyed the 'intellectual life', and as, after the great famine of 1807–8, material conditions were once more improving, a certain tranquillity reigned – until 1812. That year Napoleon embarked on his most gigantic enterprise, the war against Russia. The dramatic final phase of the Napoleonic age was beginning. Napoleon, hoping to force Britain to her knees with the Continental Blockade, now marched against Russia because that country had defected from the anti-British alliance. Napoleon assembled the largest army Europe had ever seen: the *Grande Armée*, to which all his allies, including and especially Prussia, had to contribute contingents. Considering, however, that Prussia was going to war alongside an ever-victorious Napoleon, there was not, initially, any particular concern in Berlin. 'Here everything is quiet in politics, while, as I am told, outside everything is full of the prospects of war. Here everyone is convinced that

Prussia is France's ally, and that therefore we are not threatened by anything,' the Berlin theologian de Wette said in a letter to Fries, dated 22 February, at the time when the military alliance against Russia was signed. The patriots even entertained high hopes: territorial expansion, restoration of Prussia's glory. . . . The Berlin professor Uhden said in a letter of 3 April 1812: 'Our institutions here are prospering magnificently; the present political circumstances will bring us even greater blessings.'

By the spring of 1812 Napoleon had assembled 500,000 men for his campaign. Berlin experienced the biggest passage of troops in its history. A Europe armed to the teeth was flooding the city. For a while it had to feed that military monster and it groaned under the heavy burdens of billeting. Moreover, high taxes were being exacted to provide barrack accommodation for the troops.

The move to the east began and a suspicious silence fell on the city. Imagination was hard at work. Rumours arrived about Moscow being in flames, about an unprecedented winter as early as late summer. All that had a sinister ring. Some people tried to divert themselves. The historian Niebuhr engrossed himself in the 'innocent study' of his *Römische Geschichte* (*Roman History*) in order, as he put it, to escape the 'smell of corpses' which was wafted to him.

The troops meanwhile were advancing without encountering appreciable resistance. This ghostly campaign ended in the winter of that year with a disastrous collapse: the vastness of the territory, winter, hunger, the demoralizing delaying tactics of the Russian army, the exhausting skirmishes with partisans behind the front – all these caused the main army to disintegrate. Shrunk to a few thousand men it dragged itself back to Europe in December 1812.

After the months of disquieting silence the disastrous news now spread like wildfire. There were stories of cripples without arms and legs, of soldiers killing each other for half-rotten dead horses. On 20 January 1813 the first fugitives arrived in Berlin. The military hospitals filled up with wounded and sick. There was a risk of epidemics. The Berlin professor of fine arts Solger wrote to his friend Raumer: 'It is a gruesome moment, what appears as salvation may bring about the final end. . . . I have no peace left, day and night I am forced to think of what is happening in the world.'

Arthur Schopenhauer, however – presumably he did not have to think of what was 'happening in the world' day and night – wrote in his diary: 'Man should elevate himself above life, he should realize that none of the events and incidents, the joys and sorrows, touch upon his better and internal self, i.e. that the whole is a game' (P 1, 32).

When the *Grande Armée* passed through Berlin in the spring of 1812 Arthur was pondering Fichte's *Wissenschaftslehre* (*Theory of Philosophy*). When news of the fire of Moscow seeped through he did not let it interfere with calm contemplation of the Dresden Gallery of Fine Arts. While the ragged remnants of the army were arriving in Berlin he visited a lunatic at the Charité hospital and wrote him a dedication into his Bible. While a death-dealing world history was washing its jetsam towards Berlin, Arthur Schopenhauer reflected on everyday death: 'Every breath we draw forces back a steadily advancing death, and thus we struggle with death at every second: in larger units of time we struggle against death with every meal, every sleep, every warming, etc. For we have become his prey through our birth, and our entire life is nothing but a postponement of death' (P 1, 75).

Already filled with horror at the everyday aspects of life, he refused to think in historical terms. Those who did so fluctuated between horror and hope. In a letter Solger stated: 'The remnants of the *Grande Armée* are streaming through in the most pitiful state. A great and amazing divine judgement has taken place. . . . It would be difficult to find a similar example in history of such abject misery. Europe's fate must depend on the manner in which this moment is made use of.'

With due caution – after all, letters were being opened at the time – Solger here formulated a hope that was being shared by many: the hope of a Prussian change of sides. Together with Russia and with the active participation of the people, the French yoke was to be shaken off and – if possible – Germany was to be reborn as a nation, maybe even as a democracy. A first step in that direction was taken by General Yorck on 31 December 1812 when, on his own authority, he signed the Tauroggen Convention with the Russians, thereby neutralizing the Prussian army contingent.

The King had disapproved of this step. The Court was still undecided. The anti-Napoleonic public mood could, of course, be useful, but it was also dangerous as it might go beyond purely Prussian aims. The Court preferred siding with the stronger battalions: whether these would be the French or the Russian remained to be seen. As a result there was the curious incident of a proclamation being issued at the end of January 1813, calling on the 'affluent classes' to volunteer for military service – without any indication of the presumed enemy. That month public disorders, commotions and riots broke out in Berlin. Windows were broken at the French headquarters, but Prussian Guards officers also were pelted with stones. There were rumours of a planned storming of the Potsdam palace. Troops, both French and Prussian, took up position.

The great passion of the age now erupted also in Prussia: politics. The political transformations which had taken place since the French Revolution were now being felt with full force in Berlin as well.

Politics had become expansive, absorbing passions, attitudes, hopes and aspirations which until then had had no place among the political public. Under absolutism, politics had been the monopoly of the monarchist state. But the absolute claim to power was not totalitarian, as the scope of politics was limited: dynastic self-preservation and power politics abroad, preservation of peace and skimming off of resources at home. The monarchical summit was absolute because it possessed undivided political power. Society was free from politics in a double sense: it neither, as a rule, sought forms of political expression, nor was it the object of politicization from outside, by the state.

The French Revolution was the crisis of 'old' politics: society crushed the absolute monopoly and took politics back into its own hands. In consequence the scope of politics changed. Politics became the business of the *whole* individual and of the masses. The narrow political concept of latter-day absolutism was now a thing of the past; politics henceforward would be flooded by emotions and ambitions formerly dammed up in the social sphere and within the individual: liberty, equality, fraternity, happiness – all these were now thought to be capable of being produced politically there and then. Politics is feasible life. Politics had become an enterprise in which anything on people's minds could be invested.

One should try to realize the tremendous divide which, at the end of the eighteenth century, is associated with this explosion of politics. Questions about purpose, previously the concern of religion, were now being addressed to politics – a shift towards secularization which transformed the so-called 'ultimate questions' into socio-political ones. Robespierre performed a religious service of political reason, and the prayerbooks of patriotism were circulating in the Prussia of the wars of liberation; one of them indeed had been written by Heinrich von Kleist. Arthur Schopenhauer had not read it.

The development triggered off by the French Revolution was irreversible. The coalition of the traditional powers had initially fought against revolutionary France with the old methods ('Cabinet wars') and had been worsted by the French who were acting from conviction. What had long been maturing culturally, ever since 'Storm and Stress', was now erupting: a political national awareness. Nation, fatherland, liberty – these were now values for which men were ready to die. This shift towards politics may be assessed by comparing the personal announcement of the defeat of 1806 with the royal proclamation of March 1813.

In 1806 it was said: 'The King has lost a battle. Keeping calm is now the prime civic duty.' By contrast, the proclamation of 1813 contained an elaborate justification of past royal policy and thereupon called for unconditional championship of the national cause: 'Yet whatever sacrifices may be demanded of individuals, they do not weigh as heavily as the sacred values for which we make them, for which we must fight and conquer unless we wish to cease to be Prussians and Germans.'

That was the voice of the New Politics. No one translated it better into philosophical language than Fichte.

'The ego is because it seats itself . . .': translated into the new politics this meant: the fundamental rules of life, transgressing the ego, must justify themselves before the essential freedom of the ego. The non-ego of the state is a limitation created by the ego itself and imposed upon itself, and can therefore also be rescinded by the ego. This applies to Napoleon, who is about to exit from world history and after whom the brave patriots now cry blue murder, but it also applies to the state generally, such as that of Prussia. If it encourages activity, the self-application of liberty – even by the boundaries it sets itself – then it is a positive thing; if it acts in a paralysing manner, then it must be revoked by the ego, or, more accurately, by the socialized ego-subjects. 'Society, the proprietor of material forces,' Fichte proclaimed during the turbulent days of March 1813, should reflect upon itself and proceed to the deed of liberation. He himself wanted to become a field preacher at Prussian headquarters; they smiled at him and declined the offer. But the frustrated field preacher had equipped himself against possible disappointment. To State Minister Nicolovius he said: 'If the experiment is successful the gain will be immeasurable; if it fails it has nevertheless been clearly uttered. . . . Withdrawal to the spot where I am now standing, to the world of pure concepts, is always open to me.' But not for long. On 29 January 1814 the brave man died of a nervous fever which the wounded of the war of liberation had brought back.

The war against Napoleon was officially opened, in the proper manner, with a divine service on 28 March 1813. Schleiermacher, against whose patriotism the censors had taken action not so long before, was now free to be exuberant. This was the scene: he up in the pulpit, the public in uniform listening, ready to move off, rifles leaning outside the church, horses grazing behind the sacristy. 'In devout exultation, speaking from the heart, he penetrated into every heart, and the full clear stream of his speech swept everyone along,' a contemporary reports. Schopenhauer kept aloof: he had not trusted Schleiermacher since the day he discovered that the learned gentleman who spoke so eloquently about the medieval scholars had not in fact read even one of them in the original.

The university became deserted. Nearly two-thirds of the students joined the colours. Professors contributed money and got hold of rifles. Niebuhr organized foot drill on his own initiative in his garden and a few colleagues from the faculty joined him. He took delight in the calluses which formed on his hands: 'For while I still had a delicate scholar's skin,' he said in a letter, 'the rifle left a deep cut.' Professor Solger was drifting about, asking whoever he could get hold of whether he should have his wedding before the battle or afterwards. Those professors who wished neither to be drilled in the garden nor to march into battle compensated for this by reading uplifting literature. Böckh said in a letter: 'I cannot now . . . read anything except Greek tragedies and Shakespeare; . . . Goethe and Schiller are not fit to be read at present, they are too weak for our time.'

By the end of April Berlin was in danger of being attacked by Napoleonic troops. On 21 April organization of the *Landsturm* began. Anyone not fit to bear arms was sent to dig fortifications outside the city. Entire university departments were to be seen there at work. But the younger scholars were armed. Solger, having meanwhile decided in favour of marriage, was devoting himself to organizing a widows' support fund. He had sent his young wife to Silesia; unfortunately this was the wrong direction because that was where the enemy was lined up. But then everyone was a little confused. Bettina von Arnim, who stayed behind in Berlin, now an armed camp, has left a lively picture of the scholars' cohort in one of her letters:

> While *Landsturm* and *Landwehr* were being raised an odd kind of life was going on in Berlin. Any day you could see men and children (of fifteen years) of all classes assembled in the open street, swearing to King and country to die for them. . . . It was also a strange sight to find acquaintances and friends running along the street at every hour of the day with all kinds of weapons, some of whom one would not have thought of as soldiers before. Just picture in your mind, for example, Savigny, who at the stroke of three runs down the street like a man possessed carrying a long pike (a very common weapon in the *Landsturm*), the philosopher Fichte with an iron shield and a long dagger, the philologist Wolf with his long nose with a Tyrolean belt full of pistols, knives of all kinds and battle-axes . . . Pistor . . . wearing buck-skin armour. . . . With Arnim's company there was always a band of young females who found that soldiering suited him equally well from the front and from behind.

At the beginning of May the situation became even more alarming. Napoleon was believed to be quite close. Berlin, stripped of regular troops, feared his revenge. Arthur Schopenhauer decided he could not stay in Berlin any longer. He fled in the direction of Weimar. But first he paid his due to the spirit of the age: he donated money for the equipment of one soldier (horse, uniform, etc.). But he did not wish to fight. Patriotism was alien to him; he had no passion to invest in international squabbles. That kind of secularization had passed him by. To his 'better consciousness' the warlike events were 'sound and smoke', an exceedingly foolish game. A few months later, looking back on those weeks, he wrote a letter to the Dean of the philosophical faculty in Jena, where he wanted to take his degree: 'When, in the early summer of this year, the noise of war drove the Muses from Berlin, where I was studying philosophy . . . I, who had sworn allegiance to their colours alone, likewise left the city with their retinue – not so much because, due to a special concatenation of circumstances, I am a stranger everywhere and have no civic duties to discharge anywhere, but because I was most deeply pervaded by the conviction that I was not born to serve mankind with my fist but with my head, and that my fatherland is greater than Germany' (CL, 643). Schopenhauer left Berlin with the intention of writing his philosophical dissertation. Yet he was after more than the acquisition of a university degree: he had seen the intellectual outlines of a great work, and he knew that it would be his life's achievement.

A burning sensation, a captivating inspiration, an unprecedented creative urge were gripping him amidst the turbulence of the war and seething political passions. In a euphoric moment, at the beginning of 1813, he wrote in his diary:

> Under my hands, or rather in my mind, there grows a work, a philosophy that would be ethics and metaphysics in *one*, though they have so far been as wrongly divided as man has into soul and body. The work is growing, gradually and slowly acquiring shape as a child in its mother's womb: I do not know what was created first and what last, just as with the child in its mother's womb: I who am sitting here and whom my friends know do not myself comprehend the growth of the work, just as the mother does not comprehend that of her child in her womb. I look upon it and, like the mother, I say: 'I am blessed with the fruit.' Chance, ruler of this sensory world! Grant that I live and enjoy peace for a few more years! For I love my work as the mother does the child in her womb: when it is mature and born, then you may exercise your right over me and collect the interest of the delay. [P 1, 55]

Arthur Schopenhauer, 'blessed with the fruit', turned his back on the battleground of the great trends of his day in order to give birth to his work in some quiet corner.

BOOK TWO

CHAPTER ELEVEN

THE THINKER WITHOUT A STAGE

Arthur Schopenhauer, *en route* to Rudolstadt via Weimar, stayed at a village inn, where, with his dissertation written there, *Über die vierfache Wurzel des Satzes vom zureichenden Grunde* (*On the Fourfold Root of the Principle of Sufficient Reason*), he embarked on a period in his life that was to last just under five years, during which the whole of his philosophy would emerge 'like a beautiful landscape from the morning mist'. During those five years all his essential theorems would find their definitive formulation; he would complete this phase of his life in the knowledge of having accomplished his life's essential task. After that he would step before the public and would, to his horror, discover that the audience was missing. Without having had his scene he would have to leave the stage. There would be no opportunity for him to become a 'thinker on the stage'. As nobody would be listening to him anyway he would have no need to try to capture attention by surprising ideas. He would not have to excel continually, he would not have to stage a game of self-concealment and self-revelation; he would not ceaselessly slam doors merely to break them down noisily; he would be in no danger of confusing glittering self-staging with truth. As his words would die away unheard, he would not have to take himself at his own word in a self-destructive manner. In short: he would be spared the fate of his most famous disciple, Nietzsche. He would not consume himself in a theatre of transformation, he would not be caught up in the vortex of philosophical masques. To him two faces would be sufficient: one turned inwards and the other turned outwards; one immersed in the heart of the matter, the other gazing sceptically at the course of the world and his own course caught up in it. After some initial disappointment he would attribute the fact that he was receiving no answer from outside to the true value of his philosophy. In consequence his philosophy, looking outwards, would become even fiercer and more inaccessible in its inspirations – in spite of the crystal-clear language in which he would present it.

And yet he would wait for an answer, more so than he was willing to admit to himself. Too proud to seek a public, let alone to curry favour with it, he would nevertheless secretly hope that the public would seek *him*. His self-staging, not wanted by any theatre, was directed inwards: he would see himself as a person whom others would have to discover. What he wished to embody to himself was: the truth that eludes. At the end of his life, when he was actually 'discovered', he would, in retrospect, interpret his prolonged incognito as the long journey to truth.

With regard to himself, Arthur Schopenhauer merely felt that his journey *to* philosophy had been prolonged, but not that *in* philosophy. He had had to break out from a course which was to have taken him elsewhere, and for that reason had to accept some detours. However, once he had gained a foothold in philosophy everything – or so he saw it himself – had moved very rapidly. The inspirations of the 'better consciousness' derived their language from Romantic and Platonic recollections, and in the reflection of empirical consciousness he was following in Kant's footsteps. And when, in 1815, he identified the 'will', as experienced in himself, as Kant's ominous 'thing in itself', the germ of his whole philosophy was ready. All it needed was development. His dissertation was the beginning of that explicatory work. This cognition-theory essay has a secret point of reference, which is nowhere explicitly formulated but which emerges very clearly from his subsequent main work, *The World as Will and Representation*: he wishes to assign its own place to the 'better consciousness' – not mentioned in his dissertation at all – by, radicalizing Kant, defining the limits of empirical consciousness. What mattered to him most was what he did not mention: he became a follower of Kant in his own fashion in order – again in his own fashion – to be able to remain a Platonic.

In his notebook on Fichte Arthur Schopenhauer in 1812 formulated this secret point of reference of his prelude to a critique of knowledge:

Thus the true criticism will separate the better consciousness from empirical consciousness like gold from the ore, presenting it in pure form without any admixture of sensuality or intellect; it will present it in its totality, collecting Everything by which it manifests itself in the consciousness, unifying it into an entity: then it will obtain empirical consciousness in pure form also, and classify it according to its difference: this work will in future be perfected, worked out more accurately and finely, made more readily comprehensible and easier – but it will never be overthrown. Philosophy will exist; the history of philosophy will be concluded. If prolonged peace comes to mankind, if culture advances and if perfection of all mechanics provides leisure – then one day religion can be cast off like the reins of childhood: mankind will stand there, having reached the highest self-awareness, the golden age of philosophy will have arrived, the commandment of the Delphic temple, *gnothi sauton* (= know thyself) will have been fulfilled. [P II, 360]

Once and only once, we encounter here a kind of historical-philosophical superelevation of the duplicity of empirical and 'better' consciousness. What is that empirical consciousness capable of when it becomes aware of its capability? It will provide us with the 'perfection of mechanics', with command over nature, with a sensible arrangement of external conditions of life. But all this is only a world of means, not of ends. The objective lies in 'leisure'. By successfully dealing with matters of practical coping with life, empirical consciousness gives birth to that possible form of existence which it cannot itself attain but for which it can clear the ground: self-knowledge in the medium of the 'better consciousness'. The practical successes of empirical consciousness open up the prospect of a life in truth, undeflected by empirical interests, resting within itself. 'Philosophy will exist,' Schopenhauer wrote. 'The history of philosophy will be concluded' – meaning: the entire history of philosophy so far, representing as it does a history of its unhappy involvement in the struggle for life, will be at an end because experience, duly authorized, will cope on its own with practical problems and philosophy once more will receive its freedom to deal with the truths unconcerned with practical life. The spheres are separated. Both parts – empirical consciousness and the 'better consciousness' – benefit from the separation. That separation is the work of criticism, which encourages and empowers empirical consciousness but simultaneously keeps it out of those regions where it has no business. To Arthur Schopenhauer this criticism is a service of love to the 'better consciousness', which he hopes he will help to victory by illuminating the area in which empirical consciousness is allowed to romp about.

As Arthur Schopenhauer wrote these cheerful sentences in the early summer of 1812, Napoleon was just getting ready for his mighty campaign against Russia. 'If prolonged peace comes to mankind, if culture advances . . .' – this optimism did not stem from the events which were unrolling before Schopenhauer's eyes but from the euphoria of his confident work. The euphoria of a person 'blessed with the fruit' gilds also the prospects of history. For a few brief moments it glows brightly, even though the light is borrowed. History was now reflecting back to Arthur the light that had been kindled within him.

But when that 'history' cut up rough in his immediate neighbourhood and when normally sound people suddenly discovered a delight in cutting and thrusting, Arthur once more found himself thrown back to his inner world, while empirical consciousness outside was reeling in militant folly. While Berlin was arming itself against Napoleon's revenge Arthur fled via Dresden to Weimar, where he made an intermediate stop. After a short while he left his mother's house and withdrew to nearby idyllic Rudolstadt. From June to November 1813 he lodged at an inn, where in total seclusion he composed his dissertation, intoxicated with the happiness of creation, though now and again tormented by doubt. Who, he asked himself, was really right – he by retiring or those 'excited people' outside, on the history-shaping battlefields beyond the pleasant valley? In retrospect he wrote: 'Moreover, I was then again deeply suffering in my humour and dejected, mainly because I found my life placed in an era which demanded rather different gifts from the ones I felt I had within me' (CL, 654). But these were passing moods because, as Schopenhauer continued in his account, 'in my seclusion in Rudolstadt . . . I was fascinated by the ineffable charm of the region. In my whole nature hostile to matters military, I was happy that in that valley, framed on all sides by wooded mountains, not a single soldier was to be seen throughout the whole warlike summer, nor a drum to be heard, and I was lying in deepest solitude, undiverted and undistracted by anything, ceaselessly concerned with the remotest problems and investigations' (CL, 654).

The problems with which Schopenhauer was concerned in his dissertation must have seemed 'remote' not only from the point of view of political passions. Equally 'remote' from the mainstream of topical philosophical thought was his attempt to lay the foundations of a new cognition theory. The philosophical spirit of the age believed it had 'overcome' Kant; Schopenhauer was opposing that spirit, though for the moment modestly rather than demonstratively.

Fichte, Schelling and Hegel had meanwhile, one after another, torn down the barriers which Kant had erected against the metaphysical use of reason. They had once more developed systems embracing God, the world and the ego, and in these systems there was no room for reflection on the limits of possible cognition. The subjective spirit was once more empowered by them to comprehend the Whole from out of itself.

Hegel had rejected Kant's reflection on the possibility of cognition with the dictum that you cannot learn to swim without getting into the water. Arthur Schopenhauer refused to be put off by this. Yet he did not content himself with recalling Kant's cognition-theory results; he simplified and radicalized them. Of Kant's entire complicated machinery of the faculty of cognition, he retained just one principle: the principle of sufficient reason. Our entire conceptual activity (perception and cognition), he argued, operates by means of a mechanism which can be expressed in the sentence: 'Nothing is without a reason for being.'

Schopenhauer's 'simplification' provides a new clarity: the principle of sufficient reason expresses the fact that with regard to anything that can enter into our idea we must always ask for reasons, for a connection; we must ask for it not because the external world compels us to do so but because – and Schopenhauer to this extent remained a follower of Kant – our perceptual and cognitive faculty compels us to do so.

According to the different 'objects' which we may be dealing with Schopenhauer distinguished four kinds of 'asking' for reasons, four kinds of establishing a connection. He called it the 'fourfold root of the principle of sufficient reason' – as the not particularly reader-friendly title of his dissertation put it.

These four kinds are as follows:

With regard to everything that happens in the corporeal world we ask for the reason why it is happening. We therefore ask about a *reason for becoming*. That is the question about causality in the narrow sense.

In the case of all judgements (cognition, concepts) we ask for whatever underlies that judgement. We do not therefore ask why something is as it is but we ask why we maintain that it is so. We therefore ask for the *reason for cognition*.

The third kind of the principle of sufficient reason relates to the realm of pure geometry and arithmetic. Here neither a reason for becoming applies, nor a reason for cognition. The reason why the numeral '1' is followed by the numeral '2', or why any triangle constructed over the diameter of a circle with its apex on the circumference contains a right angle can be demonstrated by the being-so of visual space (geometry) and of directly experienced time (counting, arithmetic). We are dealing here with evidence not amenable to further questioning. To Schopenhauer this is the 'principle of sufficient *reason of being*'.

The fourth kind of the principle of sufficient reason relates to human action: with regard to everything that is done we ask for the motive why it is done. In the second, substantially enlarged, edition of his dissertation Schopenhauer would be using the exceedingly revealing expression: 'causality from within'.

The common feature of these four kinds of asking for reasons is that we are downright unable to have anything 'individual, or detached' in our minds; if and to the extent that something enters our minds (and hence exists for us) it is invariably entangled in a network of reasons. While Leibniz says: 'Nature does not make leaps,' Schopenhauer would say: our mind does not permit anything to make 'leaps'. It would be easy to misunderstand Schopenhauer by thinking that the 'principle of sufficient reason' was being applied only by our reflecting intellect, i.e. consciously. That is the way Kant, at least, understood the principle of causality. Here Schopenhauer is more radical: he claims that even the pre-conscious, purely physiological sensory perception operates with the principle of causality: 'From a change in the eye, ear, or other organ a reason is presumed to exist, and this is placed in the space whence its effect issues, as the substratum of that force.... The category of causality is therefore the real transition point, and in consequence the *condition of all experience*.... It is above all through the category of causality that we recognize an object as *real*, i.e. *acting* upon us. The fact that we are unaware of this conclusion presents no difficulty' (D, 36). When we are seeing there exist, immediately, only the sensory data of retina stimulation, nothing more. We see, feel, hear corporeal objects in space because we interpret the sensory data in our own body as an effect and instinctively search for a cause, which we then project into space. This elementary imagining activity, according to Schopenhauer, is performed by our intellect. It is only through this action of the intellect that the whole visible, sensorily perceptible world enters our imagination. In this sense animals, too, have an 'intellect', because and to the extent that they perceive a world of objects outside themselves.

Schopenhauer was later to call this process 'intellectual visualization', in the following precise meaning: direct visualization is already shot through by the principle of the intellect. Without the intellect there would indeed be states of excitation in our bodies, but no corporeal world outside us, since only the intellect understands the physiological excitation as the effect of an external cause. States within our bodies have to be understood as *effects* in order that a *reality* may exist outside us.

This conception of an unconsciously operating intellect gives rise to far-reaching consequences. If the intellect is so intimately interwoven with sensory visualization, if it reaches down so far into animalic acts of perception without becoming conscious, then the traditional hierarchy of cognitional faculties is reversed. In that case 'matter' is not simply passed on at the base of sensory visualization to our conceptual faculty in order to be given shape there, but the decisive step is already being performed down there at the base: it is not subsequent conceptualization but intellect-pervaded sensory visualization that builds up the multifarious phenomenal world before us. 'An essential difference between Kant's method and the one I follow,' Schopenhauer wrote, 'lies in the fact that he [Kant] proceeds from indirect, reflecting, cognition, while I by contrast proceed from direct, intuitive cognition. . . . He leaps over that entire visual, multifarious, significant world around us and clings to the forms of abstract thought' (WWR I, 609).

In its concatenation with sensory visualization, the intellect, in Schopenhauer's philosophy, undergoes an upward revaluation which at the same time – and herein lies the explosive nature of his thesis – brings with it a relativization of reason that runs counter to the philosophical spirit of his age.

Reason, according to Schopenhauer, does no more and no less than sum up our visual perceptions into concepts ('visualization of visualizations'), preserve them, and perform combinations with these 'concepts' as if with grammalogues. Reason spells out, using the alphabet supplied to it by intelligent perception. Without that basis reason would remain empty; it does not *produce* anything.

This statement should have come as a provocation in an age which expected everything of 'reason': power over nature (Schelling), power over history (Hegel), morality (Fichte) and the power of faith (Jacobi). But this was not the effect the dissertation had: it passed virtually unnoticed. There were three reviews of it, commending it condescendingly. Scarcely more than one hundred copies were sold, the rest was remaindered and, a few years later, pulped.

In its original version the work was unable to attract much attention because it was not yet sufficiently assertive or vigorous enough in drawing the far-reaching conclusions which followed from its propositions; moreover, it barely adumbrated the outlines of Schopenhauer's ultimate aim – to which this publication was no more than a curtain-raiser.

Today Schopenhauer's dissertation is usually read in its second, greatly enlarged, edition of 1847. There the lines of thought are firmly pursued, linking up with his main work; there a challenge is issued to philosophical tradition, and there is no curb on attacks against the philosophical spirit of the age.

In the first version of his dissertation, written in the autumn of 1813, Schopenhauer was partly still covering himself, and partly he was not yet, at that time, entirely clear about what it was all leading to. Schopenhauer was covering himself, for instance, when elucidating the explosive consequences of his critique of the confusion between 'cognitional reason' and 'reason of becoming' (i.e. causality).

In examining cognitional reason we look for a 'visualization' on which we might base cognition, on which it would be 'based'; or else we test the logical accuracy of a statement. When conclusions are correctly drawn from correctly formulated premises they have their 'reason'. The question as to cognitional reason thus comes to rest, comes to its conclusion, with the identification of a reason. Here the principle of causality applies. And that principle does not tolerate any stopping: each identified cause can in turn be understood as the effect of another cause, and so on *ad infinitum*. To the intellect there can be no ultimate cause in the sphere of perceptible objects. 'The causal law,' Schopenhauer wrote in the second edition of his dissertation, 'therefore is not so accommodating as to let itself be used like a hired cab, which we dismiss when we have reached our destination; rather does it resemble the broom brought to life by the sorcerer's apprentice in Goethe's poem, which, when once set in motion, does not leave off running and fetching water' (FR, 42–3).

In dealing with the age-old question – is there a beginning of all things, is there a prime cause of the world? – these two kinds of 'reasons' can now be effectively blended. We ask about the origin of things, i.e. about a prime cause of becoming, but in doing so we have already changed planes, away from reality to objects imaged: it is there that we form the concept of the 'unconditional'. It is now possible to conclude logically and compellingly that this 'unconditional', this 'absolute', cannot itself be conditioned or caused (that would contradict its concept); hence this unconditional must be what conditions everything else without being itself conditioned; hence the unconditional, since not caused but only causing, must be the prime cause. One need only let this 'prime cause' present itself by the name of 'God' and one has before one a proof of God's existence. But what has actually been proved by this line of argument? We have not proved that there is a beginning to the world of becoming, an ultimate cause, but only that it is possible to extract logically from one mental object (the concept of the 'unconditional') another mental object (the concept of 'prime cause'), in other words that the concept of 'prime cause' has its cognitional reason in the concept of the 'unconditional', the 'absolute'.

And now we once more change planes, returning to the world of becoming, but taking along with us into the empirical world the plausibility of our purely logical argumentation, so that we are now able to state: there is an absolute beginning of the world, a prime cause, a God, an absolute spirit, etc.

Schopenhauer's critique of this procedure is only cautiously hinted at in the first edition of his dissertation; thirty years later, however, in the second edition, it is formulated in its entire far-reaching nature and with polemical pointedness. There the procedure is described as 'a trick of legerdemain', and it is there that Schopenhauer first ventured to present the whole of Schelling's and Hegel's philosophy of the absolute as a modernized version of that piece of legerdemain.

In the autumn of 1813, when he was writing his dissertation, Schopenhauer clearly did not yet wish to cross swords with the luminaries in German university posts. To Professor Eichstädt, the Dean of the philosophical faculty in Jena, where Schopenhauer submitted his dissertation for a degree, he wrote in a covering letter: 'I would also request you not to conceal from me anything that might seem to you spiteful in it' (CL, 644). In all that letter contained nothing of Schopenhauer's subsequent aggressive self-assurance: 'Our human weakness,' he wrote, 'is too great for us to be entirely certain even of what we have before our own eyes without the confirmation of someone else's approval; even less therefore may one rely on one's own judgement in matters of philosophy' (CL, 644).

Such modesty is certainly not found in Schopenhauer's private notes at the time. In his manuscript notes he had harsh things to say about philosophical tradition and, above all, about his philosophical contemporaries; there he was not plagued by any self-doubt. His motive for covering himself in his dissertation is therefore likely to have been caution rather than lack of assurance.

He practised the same caution in the formulation of another, equally explosive, aspect of his first venture into publication: in his reassessment of reason. Compared to the rational philosophy of his contemporaries, Schopenhauer's concept of reason contains a clear tendency towards demystification: reason is the ability to create concepts from the matter of intelligent perception; reason remains linked to experience. Reason is not the gift of 'superior' understanding, it is not an organ for transcendental truths. 'I know that this explanation of reason and concepts diverges greatly from all other earlier ones' (D, 50), he wrote in the first version of his dissertation, practising considerable caution. Thirty years later, in the second edition, Arthur Schopenhauer was to highlight and justify that 'divergence' in a furious polemic against his opponents:

Our professors of philosophy have thought fit to do away with the name which had hitherto been given to that faculty of thinking and pondering by means of reflection and conceptions, which distinguishes man from animals . . . [and] decided that this faculty should henceforth be called *Understanding* instead of *Reason* . . . The fact was, they wanted Reason's place and name for a faculty of their own creation and fabrication, or to speak more correctly and honestly, for a completely fictitious faculty . . . a faculty for direct, metaphysical knowledge: that is to say, one which transcends all possible experience, is able to grasp the world of things in themselves and their relations, and is therefore, before all, consciousness of God: that is, it knows God the Lord immediately, construes *a priori* the way in which he has created the universe, or, should this sound too trivial, the way in which he has produced it out of himself, or to a certain degree generated it by some more or less necessary vital process, or again – as the most convenient proceeding, however comical it may appear – simply 'dismissed' it, and left it to get up on its legs by itself and walk away wherever it liked. Nothing less than the impudence of a scribbler of nonsense like Hegel could, it is true, be found to venture upon this last step. Yet it is tomfoolery like this which, largely amplified, has filled hundreds of volumes the last fifty years. . . . *Reason*, to which all this wisdom is falsely and audaciously imputed, is pronounced to be a 'supersensory faculty', or a faculty 'for ideas'; in short, an oracular power lying within us, designed directly for Metaphysics. During the last half-century, however, there has been considerable discrepancy of opinion among the adepts as to the way in which all these supersensory wonders are perceived. According to the most audacious, Reason has a direct intuition of the Absolute, or even *ad libitum* of the Infinite and of its evolutions towards the Finite. Others, somewhat less bold, opine that its mode of receiving this information partakes rather of audition than of vision; since it does not exactly see, but merely *hears*, what is going on in cloud-cuckoo-land . . . and then honestly transmits what it has thus received to the Understanding, to be worked up into textbooks. [FR, 131–3]

All the variants of 'rational philosophy' here castigated – Fichte, Schelling, Hegel, Jacobi – were flourishing at the time Schopenhauer wrote his dissertation. But they are not the ones specifically criticized by Schopenhauer in his first version; it is Kant, the highly-praised Kant, who is mildly reproved: in his practical philosophy of moral reason he had, Schopenhauer suggested, wrongly conceded the existence of a peculiar link with the supersensorily transcendental. Schopenhauer wrote: 'As for . . . reason, it is not, in my judgement, the source of virtue, of sanctity (as postulated . . . by Kant's teaching), but, as the faculty of concepts and, in consequence, of action in accordance with them, it is merely a necessary condition for them. But it, too, is only a tool, because it is equally a condition for the perfect villain' (D, 91).

Why was Schopenhauer in the autumn of 1813 still practising such restraint? Why that caution?

First: the philosophical spirit of the age had not yet offended him; the fate of being ignored still lay ahead. His philosophical critique did not as yet need to escalate into personal bitterness.

Second: although his inherited wealth made it possible for him not to have to live *by* philosophy but *for* it, he had nevertheless set his sights on a university career. He did not wish needlessly to renounce the dignity of academic acclaim for the philosophical road along which he had so confidently set out. He refused to conform, but equally he did not wish just yet to provoke the whole profession. Strictly speaking – and this is the third explanation – he had not yet reached the point at which he could open a frontal attack.

True enough, at the beginning of 1813 he noted in his diary: 'Under my hands, or rather in my mind, there grows a work, a philosophy that would be ethics and metaphysics in *one*' (P 1, 55). In reality, however – as is revealed by a glance at his private notes – the decisive breakthrough had not yet been accomplished at the time he wrote his dissertation, even though he was permeated by a powerful sense of anticipation.

That breakthrough was to take place when the mystery of the will revealed itself to him. The will experienced by his own body, from within, would lead him into the heart of the world such as it is, beyond all objectivizing imagination. . . . Schopenhauer was still feeling his way in that direction. He knew that an exit existed from a kind of philosophizing that was 'merely an application of the theorem of reason' (P 1, 126). He was assured of this by the inspirations of his 'better consciousness', though he was still unable to put them down in discursive language. The short-circuiting flash between Platonic idea, Kant's 'thing in itself' and the inwardly experienced 'will' had not yet happened. In 1815, two years after his dissertation, the moment had come. In his notes we find the laconic sentence: 'The *will* is Kant's *thing in itself*; and the Platonic *idea* is the fully adequate and exhaustive cognition of the thing in itself' (P 1, 291).

In his dissertation Schopenhauer was still moving within Kant's field of transcendental investigation, i.e. an investigation into the possibility of experience. Here he wished to define the frontier which he felt was cutting him off from the discoveries he was after. He wished to show why this was so. He would not discover his 'truth' there, but he would understand why he could not find it there. It was not a wide-ranging search, but more of a covering, flanking enterprise, almost as if he wished to make his hinterland secure before embarking on risky forays. This attitude also marked the style of the whole work: calm demonstration, categorization, ordering. Nowhere is there a hint of the excitement which throbs in his private notes of the same date, where he was approaching the hot zones of his 'better consciousness'. By pedantically and painstakingly digging up the fourfold root of the theorem of sufficient reason Schopenhauer ultimately aims at fixing in their empirical weight just those structures which would vanish like a spook when, before the bright 'flash' of the 'better consciousness', all suddenly loses validity: space, time, causality. The theorem of reason disappears, the real bottom is bottomless, an abyss.

With the discovery of the metaphysics of will he found a language for this new knowledge; it was to lend him that proud assurance which made it possible for him brusquely to turn his back on the whole of philosophical tradition and on his contemporaries. In his dissertation he felt he was on the right road, but he did not yet know exactly where that road would take him. He only knew there would be an awakening. And he did not shrink from hinting at *that* certainty, though with proper restraint. In the penultimate paragraph he gave notice of a 'major work whose content would be to that of the present essay as wakefulness is to dreaming' (D, 91). That is an old topos of philosophy: life as a dream, in thrall to mere appearance; empirical awareness does not by any means guarantee conscious being.

From this perspective the sober, strict dissections of our recognizing, visualizing faculty – presented by Schopenhauer in his dissertation – appear in a strange light: they show how we perceive the world as an 'object', how we, when 'visualizing', have to veil it in a network of reasons. But there is no proof for a feeling that underneath these 'reasons', under these ceaseless questions of 'why', there hides a *what*. There is a suspicion that object-related cognition (even if we ourselves become that 'object') perpetuates a division, a split, and that the principle of reason, as Heidegger once put it, may lead to the reasons but not to the bottom. From this suspicion stems the traditional philosophical distinction between essence and appearance. The great religions, too, are aware of this distinction and on it have based an entire mythology of salvation.

At the end of any awareness of the method of our cognition of a *something* offering itself to us remains an unrest that is directed towards something entirely different, something that wishes to enter into a very different kind of connection with the *something* which is an object to us. It is the pellucid awareness of the method of our imagining that reinforces our consciousness of the fact that the imagined, i.e. objective, being really only reflects to us the structures of our consciousness without revealing itself. This is what Schopenhauer described as the 'dream' from which he wished to awake. In his manuscript notes he relates a parable, subsequently incorporated into his main work, for the dreamlike entanglement with what is already known: 'It is . . . as though I were in the company of persons who are all strangers to me, and each of them presents to me the other as his friend or cousin, while I, each time assuring the introduced person that I was delighted to make his acquaintance, continually have at the tip of my tongue the question: "But how the devil did I get into this company?"' (P I, 208). The unknown becomes known by being presented in its reciprocal relations. One introduces the other. Schopenhauer's dissertation, as it were, analyses the introduction ritual. A few weeks after completing the work Schopenhauer wrote in his diary: 'In their pursuit of the principle of reason (which teases them like a hobgoblin in four different shapes and makes fools of them) they are hoping to find satisfaction in knowledge and happiness in life. And thus they go forward confidently, like someone running towards the horizon on a plain, hoping that eventually he will touch the clouds. They no more attain the essential than a person turning and feeling a sphere from all sides will thereby reach its centre; indeed they are exactly like a squirrel running in a treadmill. . . . If this way of looking upon life seems to us everywhere to resemble a horizontal line, then we can liken the second way of observation to a vertical line which can intersect the former at one point and move away from it' (P I, 153). That change-over to the vertical line is the awakening from the spinning dream. The vertical takes one not into the old Beyond but into the centre of the Here and Now. The diary entry for 1814 ends with sentences which will be echoed powerfully in Schopenhauer's main work: 'They were looking for the Why instead of looking at the What; they were striving for the remote instead of seizing what was close at hand everywhere; they went off outwards in all directions instead of going into themselves, where any riddle can be solved' (P I, 154).

CHAPTER TWELVE

RETURN TO WEIMAR

Schopenhauer needed three months, from mid-June to mid-September 1813, to write his dissertation in the solitude of his Rudolstadt inn. He also found time for some extensive walking. He became footsore and had his boots made more comfortable while gazing out on the sunny landscape. The tumults of history spared the birthplace of the 'fourfold root'. But when Arthur was faced with the problem of sending his dissertation out into the world he had to acquaint himself once more with the squabbles of his day. He made inquiries and was told that Saxony had now become the principal theatre of war: the road from Rudolstadt to Berlin was blocked. Although it was possible for a private person to make the journey it was doubtful whether a manuscript would reach Berlin safely. Schopenhauer therefore decided to apply for a degree *in absentia* in Jena. Even before dispatching his dissertation he sent ten *Friedrichsdor*, the graduation fee, to the Dean of the philosophical faculty in Jena. Two days later he dispatched his manuscript together with a covering letter containing a brief curriculum vitae, a justification of the subject of his work, and a courteous and modest request for comment and criticism if his work called for it. The fact that he went to war not against Napoleon but only against the misinterpretations of the principle of sufficient reason could not, at that patriotically stirring time, be entirely passed over in silence: 'When, in the early summer of this year, the noise of war drove the Muses from Berlin, where I was studying philosophy . . . I, who had sworn allegiance to their colours alone, likewise left the city with their retinue' (CL, 644).

Arthur, as the son of Goethe's friend Johanna Schopenhauer, a lady well known also in Jena, received preferential treatment. Immediately on arrival of the manuscript the Dean, Heinrich Karl Eichstädt, professor of ancient languages and rhetoric, drafted a circular to his faculty colleagues who thereupon a few days later, on 2 October – presumably without having read the dissertation – approved Schopenhauer's doctorate *in absentia*, with the distinction of *magna cum laude*. On 5 October Schopenhauer received his doctor's diploma. Publication of his thesis had been put in hand.

At his own expense – he paid sixty-nine *Reichstaler* for it – the work was published by the *Hof-Buch- und Kunsthandlung* in Rudolstadt. First of all, however, Arthur had to dispel some political misgivings on the part of the firm's proprietor, Friedrich Bertuch. The work, he assured the publisher in a letter, contained 'no direct reference to religion and not the remotest reference to the state or to politics' (CL, 3).

By the end of October he held the first of what would be five hundred copies in his hands. Goethe received a copy, and so did the publisher and bookseller Frommann in Jena, who had made some source material available to him. Other presentation copies went to Friedrich August Wolf, the Greek scholar, and to Friedrich Schleiermacher in Berlin; to Carl Leopold Reinhold, a Kant follower, in Jena and to Gottlob Ernst Schulze, Arthur's philosophy teacher in Göttingen. Yet another, for reasons of filial piety, went to a friend of his late father, Herr Kabrun in Danzig, to whom Arthur had been apprenticed for a short while at the time of his confirmation: the newly graduated doctor of philosophy sent a conciliatory wave to a world from which he had happily escaped.

While Schopenhauer spent October in Rudolstadt waiting for the arrival of the first copies fresh from the press, the war was taking a decisive turn. On 18 October 1813 Napoleon confronted the united forces of Prussia, Russia and Austria in the battle of Leipzig. The coalition was victorious, though with horrendous losses on both sides: over 100,000 men were left on the battlefield dead or maimed. A few months earlier Arthur had commented upon his philosophical intentions to the effect that he would 'reprove . . . all those truly governed by passion', including those 'who stake their lives on the opinion of others or some other rubbish, or lose it in a duel or in some other self-chosen danger'. The patriotic jubilation which followed Napoleon's defeat left him unmoved; instead he was worried at the thought whether, in the foreseeable future, 'there will once more be a philosophical public' (letter to Böttiger, 6 December 1813, CL, 9).

The scattered units of Napoleon's army withdrew towards the north and the west. Cossacks and Austrians began to be seen in the quiet valley of Rudolstadt. The time had come for Arthur to change his refuge. He had not yet decided where to settle for the next few years; he would rather await developments and therefore opted for a provisional solution: on 5 November 1813 he left Rudolstadt to return to Weimar. Into the windowpane of his Rudolstadt inn he scratched the Horatian quotation 'One praises a house that looks out on fields'. Forty years later, Schopenhauer's admirers were to make pilgrimages to the spot in order to read the inscription with their own eyes – a 'sacred relic' (C, 186), as the by then famous philosopher remarked.

Arthur arrived in Weimar with mixed feelings. He 'disliked certain domestic circumstances' (CL, 654) which he had encountered in his mother's house after his flight from Berlin in May 1813 and which had then caused him to continue his journey to Rudolstadt. He felt uneasy at the presence of a new gentleman friend of his mother's.

At the beginning of 1813 the Secret Archival Councillor Georg Friedrich Conrad Ludwig Müller von Gerstenbergk had moved into a few rooms on the first floor, above Johanna Schopenhauer's apartment. He took his meals with Johanna, accompanied her socially, and was frequently present at her soirées. She had made the acquaintance of Gerstenbergk, who was twelve years her junior, in Ronneburg three years earlier, and they had then travelled together to Dresden. That was enough to nurture the rumour that Johanna intended to remarry. Goethe got his wife to keep him *au courant*. In 1810 Christiane reported to him in Karlsbad: 'The Schopenhauer woman is now in Dresden with Müller [von Gerstenbergk]; his brother visited us . . . and from the way he talked I really can conclude nothing other than that she is really going to marry him. In Ronneburg she even lodged at his house, and his first mistress took this so much to heart that she went mad.'

Goethe, who enjoyed being a string-puller on such occasions, was probably involved in bringing the Ronneburg City Syndic to Weimar as a Government Counsellor; Gerstenbergk had certainly addressed himself to Goethe with his request for a transfer.

Gerstenbergk was a career-minded civil servant who, in order to gain standing in Weimar's aristocratic society, had added to his family name (Müller) the name of his ennobled uncle (von Gerstenbergk). He also dabbled in writing stories and poems and sought out philosophical conversations in which he revealed himself as a sensitive character. Though thirty-three years old, he still acted very much the young man: his gently wistful charm was successful with some women, though others regarded him as a rascally 'court-payer'. Husbands, in particular, complained, among them the actor Pius Alexander Wolf: 'I . . . turned a blind eye when he paid court to my wife, and as a meek husband . . . I tolerate him writing her the tenderest letters with regularity.'

Gerstenbergk was certainly not one of the more impressive figures on the Weimar scene. Nevertheless Johanna, without giving annoyance, was able to be seen at his side even at Goethe's house. She did not love the man, whose age was between her own and Arthur's, but she appreciated his devotion. No doubt she was also a little flattered to have the attentions of a man who was such an obvious success with the younger ladies. Following the death in 1809 of the classical scholar Fernow, whom she had loyally nursed to the end, she had been seeking a new soulmate, a relationship more intimate than the customary social contact without, on the other hand, restricting her independence. She no longer entertained any intentions of marriage, as rumour attributed to her. Why should she give up the independence she was enjoying so much? Over the years she had declined several 'good matches': a wealthy Frankfurt merchant had asked for her hand, and so had the Gentleman of the Bedchamber Louis von Stein, a brother of Frau von Stein, no less. In 1807 she had written to Arthur: 'I have no shortage of admirers, but do not let that worry you.'

In Gerstenbergk she found the soulmate she was looking for, and she was sufficiently self-assured to keep up the liaison despite the flurry of rumours. She did not even shirk the appearance of ambiguity: she could afford to act the way she did. After her initial social successes her reputation in Weimar had not only been consolidated but possibly even enhanced.

Meanwhile she had emerged before the public as an author. Earlier, the detailed accounts of the military events of 1806–7 in her letters had been passed around among her relations and acquaintances like literary documents. Even her son Arthur, scarcely inclined to pay her compliments, had commended them. After the death of Fernow, whom she had admired, she wrote his biography, not out of literary ambition but in order to use the book's proceeds to pay off Fernow's outstanding debts to the publisher Cotta. When the book met with a certain interest among the public, and when it was eagerly praised in her narrow Weimar circle, she felt encouraged to further literary adventures. The visitors to her tea parties praised her gifts as a raconteuse whenever she spoke of her extensive travels. It seemed an obvious decision therefore for her to exploit her experiences in book form. In 1813–14 her *Recollections of a Journey in the Years 1803, 1804 and 1805* were published. Flatterers were now describing her as another Madame de Staël. In 1817 she published *A Journey through Southern France*. In 1818 she was to make her debut in the area of *belles-lettres*: a volume of stories in a bibliophile edition, on fine paper, with delicate sentiments. The volume sold well; Johanna had found her métier. After that, one novel followed another. By the end of the twenties Brockhaus was able to publish a twenty-volume edition of her collected works. For a decade Johanna Schopenhauer was the most famous woman writer in Germany.

That point, however, had not yet been reached when she became involved with Gerstenbergk, though she had already taken the first steps. Gerstenbergk for his part tried his hand at literature – another thing they had in common. They would read to one another, encourage one another, suggest improvements, and draw inspiration from each other. In what was probably her most successful novel, *Gabriele*, Johanna included poems by Gerstenbergk. Gerstenbergk published Adele's poems under his name. Gerstenbergk was a member of the Schopenhauer production cooperative.

Gerstenbergk's literary talent and intellectual capacity were limited, but that does not mean that he was the evil person he was later made out to be. He was seeking a place in the sun, and Johanna, in whose house Goethe was a frequent visitor, could ensure it for him. Besides, as was to emerge later, Gerstenbergk was a helpful person: when Johanna lost a large part of her fortune in 1819 he offered financial support to her and Adele. During a prolonged absence he undertook to look after Johanna's household without deriving any advantage for himself.

A delicate situation was to develop long after Arthur Schopenhauer had left Weimar again. Adele had so far looked in vain for a husband, and when

Johanna tried to bring Gerstenbergk and Adele together this led to considerable complications and introduced a woeful chapter in the story of Adele's sufferings. But in the late autumn of 1813, when Schopenhauer arrived in Weimar, there was no talk yet of any such plans; then it was still only a matter of a friendship between Gerstenbergk and his mother – a friendship to which Schopenhauer reacted with bitterness. Why?

He was intolerant – not only in this situation but generally. Anyone, to stand up to his judgement, would have to display outstanding qualities in some respect – intellectually, morally, or artistically. If Arthur could not detect any such qualities in a person then that person to him was 'a mass-produced article', his standard term for people of average cut.

And now, in his mother's house, he had encountered such an average person in a role which struck him as presumptuous: alongside his mother, in the place formerly occupied by his (in recollection glorified) father. Here Arthur reacted quite conventionally: he could not forgive his mother for blossoming in his father's absence, for the fact that indeed she had only found her own life without him. Having only been able to realize his philosophical calling by freeing himself with his mother's help from his father's posthumous power, he now expected his mother to make that pious renunciation of her own life which he himself, fortunately for him, declined to perform. The space which his father had once occupied at his mother's side was to remain empty, or rather, if anyone were to replace his father then it should be he, the son. Johanna understood her son perfectly. That was why, time and again, she had dispelled Arthur's suspicions that she might want to remarry. At the same time, however, she was not prepared to give up her own life for the sake of Arthur. She was too much in love with her own life to take such a step, quite apart from being convinced that her own independence would also benefit her son, by ensuring his freedom also. Yet the son was not as independent as his gruff declarations would lead one to believe. His mother had allowed him to go his own way, yet he did not possess the sovereign assurance to leave his mother be; he had to interfere in her life. Within a few days of his arrival there was a quarrel. In his diary he had called upon himself to be tolerant – unfortunately without success.

He wrote: 'Mark it well, dear soul, once and for all, and be sensible. People are subjective; not objective but utterly subjective . . . examine your love, your friendship, make sure your objective judgements are not, for the most part, concealed subjective ones; ask yourself whether perhaps you do not properly acknowledge the qualities of a person you do not like, etc. – and then be tolerant, it is your damned duty' (P I, 71).

Arthur could not remain tolerant. He puffed himself up into the role of master of the household.

At their joint luncheons he would ignore Gerstenbergk or cross swords with him. The conversation, for instance, would be about the most recent political developments. Gerstenbergk was swimming with the tide, praising the heroism of the patriots; the talk was about Germany's liberation, it had been high time to strike Napoleon down at long last, et cetera. Arthur contradicted and dismissed the whole business as a superior kind of dance-hall brawl. There were unpleasant scenes. Chairs were upset, doors slammed, Johanna found herself in the crossfire.

As communication between mother and son had become so difficult the two, though living under one roof, were continually exchanging letters. In one of them Johanna said: 'You irritate me especially when you rail against those who, caught up in the great period we live in, take up the sword even though nature has not destined them to do so. You should let others live their own lives, just as you are left to live yours, that's what I think.'

At the beginning of January 1814 Arthur had a friend from the university come to join him, Josef Gans, an impecunious Jewish student whom he was supporting financially and who, in turn, eagerly if not in a particularly inspired manner supported him in his arguments. This annoyed Johanna the more as Arthur kept telling her that she was surrounding herself with mediocre people only in order to have herself admired. To her criticism of Arthur's attacks on patriotic passion she therefore added the remark: 'Gans is glad . . . to conceal his inborn cowardice behind you and babbles anything after you without having your mind.'

Gerstenbergk, who had to take a good deal from Arthur while being, as a rule, prevented by Johanna from paying him back in like coin, vented his anger in letters to his friends. 'Over me,' he wrote to Ferdinand Heinke, a light infantry officer adored by Adele, 'the *philosophus* performs his cosmic existence. He has got himself a devoted little Jew from Berlin, who is his friend because he patiently takes his daily dose of objective laxative, the fourfold root. Of you he expects that Kleist's corps has captured Paris solely in order to purge the French with it. The Jew's name is Gans, and with this ominous subjective object a veritable non-ego has joined us at the tea table.'

In order to keep annoyance within bounds Johanna introduced a new regime. Gerstenbergk now had his midday meal alone, and she arranged matters in such a way that she met Gerstenbergk only when Arthur was not about. However, she continued to enjoy Gerstenbergk's company; by limiting his presence she merely traded away the unpleasantness of increased contact with her ever carping, often bad-tempered, know-all son. 'You seem to me too derogatory, too contemptuous of those who are not like yourself, too condemnatory without cause, and at times you sermonize too much for my taste,' she wrote.

This regime remained in force for three months, until mid-April 1814, by which time Johanna had got tired of living with her son and having to restrict her contact with Gerstenbergk. At first she feigned financial reasons: although Arthur was paying board and lodging for himself and his university friend, the money was not enough; on the other hand, she did not wish to raise the charges, she would much rather not be in a situation where she had to accept payment for board. It would therefore be best if Arthur made himself independent. She, at any rate, had 'valid reasons' for wishing to live on her own again. Surely Arthur must understand; after all, he himself had repeatedly suggested that it would be better for both of them to live separately. Arthur should practise what he preached. But, as so often, Arthur did not live in accordance with his better judgement. He felt aggrieved; he felt he was being turned out of the house. He reminded his mother that at the time of his stay in Weimar she had begged him 'with tears' to settle in her apartment. That, of course, was the truth, but Arthur knew perfectly well why his mother had asked him to do so. She reminded him: 'I wanted you . . . to see my way of living more closely and over a longer period, so that you should not walk away with any wrong ideas.' But Arthur was clearly not to be talked out of his 'wrong ideas'. He tortured his mother with his suspicion that Gerstenbergk was really her paramour.

Johanna was tired of having to justify herself to her son. She wanted, as she had some years earlier (1807–9), a separation of their spheres: only thus could they get on with one another, she wrote. But one thing was out of the question for her: she would not break off her friendship with Gerstenbergk for Arthur's sake. 'If I were to sacrifice my friend to you because you two do not get on with each other, I should be doing an injustice to him and to myself.'

She did not ask Arthur to pretend a liking for Gerstenbergk, but she expected him to accept her friendship with him. After all, she was not telling Arthur whom he could or could not meet. She had even admitted the well-nigh unbearable Josef Gans into her house.

In short, Arthur should move out. If he decided to stay in Weimar she would help him to find suitable quarters. Gerstenbergk would move into the back rooms of her apartment which Arthur and Gans had occupied. 'Do not answer this letter, there is no need; when you have decided on your departure tell me, but there is no hurry, I do not have to know it much in advance.' Thus ended the letter which the housemaid carried from the mother's drawing room to Arthur's back room on 10 April 1814.

No doubt it was during these tension-laden weeks of conflict between mother and son that the memorable dialogue took place which Schopenhauer many years later reported to a friend, Wilhelm Gwinner:

Johanna, picking up Arthur's dissertation on *The Fourfold Root*: 'No doubt this is something for pharmacists.'
    Arthur: 'It will still be read when scarcely a copy of your writings can be found in a lumber room.'
    Johanna: 'Of your writings the entire printing will still be in the shops.' [C, 17]

The predictions of both of them, mother and son, were eventually to prove correct.

After Johanna's letter of notice it was another month before relations between mother and son were finally broken off. In the meantime financial difficulties arose. Arthur accused his mother of wrongfully spending his share of the inherited fortune. Money he had made available for the support of his grandmother, he claimed, had been used up by his mother.

It must have been a wild scene. The following day, 17 May 1814, Johanna, still greatly put out, wrote:

> The door which yesterday, after your highly improper behaviour towards your mother, you slammed so noisily is closed forever between you and me. I am tired of bearing your behaviour any longer, I am leaving for the country and I shall not return home until I know that you are gone. I owe this to my health, for another scene like yesterday's would bring on a stroke that might prove fatal. You do not know what a mother's heart is like, the more tenderly it loves the more painfully it feels every blow from a once loved hand. Not Müller [von Gerstenbergk], this I declare before God in whom I believe, but you yourself have torn yourself away from me; your mistrust, your criticism of my life, of my choice of friends, your desultory behaviour towards me, your contempt for my sex, your clearly expressed reluctance to contribute to my contentment, your greed, your moods which you allowed free rein in my presence without respect for me, this and a lot more that makes you seem vicious to me, all this divides us. . . . If your father, who, a few hours before he met his death, enjoined you to honour me, never to cause me annoyance, were alive, what would he say if he saw your behaviour? If I were dead and you had to deal with your father, would you dare to schoolmaster him? Or try to control his life, his friendships? Am I then less than he? Did he do more for you than I did? Or suffered more? Loved you more than I did? . . . My duty towards you is at an end, go your way, I have nothing more to do with you. . . . Leave your address here, but do not write to me, I shall henceforth neither read nor answer any letter from you. . . . So this is the end. . . . You have hurt me too much. Live and be as happy as you can be.

A few days later Arthur Schopenhauer left Weimar. He was not to see his mother again, and there would be some very vicious letters yet.

Why this outburst of hatred, anger and contempt? Did it perhaps come from despair? He had shown brusqueness towards his mother all those months, and Johanna, certainly not fighting for her son's love but seeking a quiet, comfortable coexistence with him, was reacting to the face that Arthur had shown her. Yet that face was a mask. Arthur was practising a double bluff. His outward behaviour and his secret hopes conflicted with each other. Ultimately it was not his mother but he himself who fell victim to that self-staged play-acting. His mother caught him in the trap he himself had set. In voicing her wish that they should separate she could refer to Arthur's own statements: 'You have often told me on other occasions, and with justice, that we are two people, and that is how it must be,' she wrote. Yet Arthur, as it now emerged, did not wish to be taken at his word. He would prefer to stay at his mother's house and offered her a larger sum for board and lodging. Just picture it: at first he gives himself airs, he does not want to move in with his mother, he gets her to implore him 'with tears'. Next, he takes up lodgings in her house, and then his mother cannot stand it any longer. She wants her son out of her house, but now he does not want to leave and offers her money. This is both an insult and a desperate plea to be allowed to stay. His mother cannot hear the plea because Arthur is ashamed of it and hides it under the proud, insulting brusqueness of a business ritual. Everything to him becomes a struggle in which there are only victors and vanquished. The noise of battle must drown the whimpering of the unloved child. That is why he eventually attacks his mother with such boundless and insulting energy. Simultaneously, however, he writes in his diary: 'we follow the darkness, the grim urge to want to live, we go deeper and deeper into vice and sin, into death and nothingness – until gradually life's anger turns against itself, until we realize what road we have chosen, what kind of world we have wanted, until torment, dismay and horror make us come to, until we go into ourselves, until the better realization is born out of pain' (P I, 158).

The 'better realization' is something we are familiar with: his 'better consciousness'. But where was Arthur's relaxed assurance in life that was supposed to let the 'better consciousness' act, where was the peace that was higher than all reason or self-assertion? Why could he not let his mother do as she pleased, even if Gerstenbergk did not appeal to him? Where were his inspirations which, in sudden moments, would free him from all constraints of animosity – was their force sufficient only for the writing of philosophical works in a spirit of contemplation, and was it insufficient to practise that irony of life that would resolve all distortions and tensions in the spirit of the 'as if'? Schopenhauer wrote in his diary: 'Only he is truly happy who, *in life, does not want life,* i.e. who does not strive for its chattels. For he makes his burden light. Picture a burden loosely supported by struts, and beneath it a man standing stooped. If he straightens up, if he pushes towards it, he bears the whole burden; if he withdraws from it, into himself, he bears nothing and he feels light' (P I, 102).

Arthur did not, during those bad weeks, embody any of the above: he was fighting like a man gone berserk, lashing about him, and looking into himself so little that he failed to observe the deep ambivalence in his relationship with his mother. And this was not the only thing he failed to observe. There was also the suffering his scenes were causing his sister Adele.

His sister, his junior by nine years, was a stranger to him. For many years they had not seen one another, or only for brief periods. The age difference alone had precluded contact between equals. Meanwhile, however, Adele had grown into a young woman of seventeen, who was present at her mother's soirées and was invited by Weimar's best families. Goethe enjoyed talking to her; she was the active organizer of a female 'Club of the Muses', where the daughters of a few aristocratic families assembled to make music, crochet, read and paint. 'Witty' Adele was almost a celebrity in Weimar. Prince Pückler-Muskau made her acquaintance in 1812 and reported back to his fiancée: 'Adele is one of those females who are bound to leave you entirely cold or to arouse deep unchanging interest. . . . I like her exterior, her interior is a beautiful creation of nature.'

Pückler-Muskau's judgement was not shared by anyone else. As a rule people admired Adele's cleverness, decorum, sensibility, artistic talent, delicacy of feeling, and fantasy – in short, the soul of the young woman, while deploring her outward appearance. Strangers were enjoined not to be scared off by it. Even her mother wrote to her friend Karl von Holtei along those lines. The sculptor Rauch, who met Adele in her mother's drawing room, called her 'terrifyingly ugly', and Levin Schucking painted a downright monstrous picture of the by then aged woman: 'From Adele's cradle . . . the graces had absented themselves to a positively outrageous distance. The tall bony figure supported a head of unusual ugliness . . .; it was round as an apple, it would have been of the Tartar type if in its peculiar originality it had not mocked any type. But out of this head shone a grave pair of loyal woman's eyes and no one could make her acquaintance without soon feeling himself attracted to her by a character of rare, undemanding competence and an education of quite exceptional thoroughness and astonishing scope.'

Some men did not like Adele's cleverness. Ernst von der Malsburg, the translator of Calderon, described Adele in a letter to Tieck as 'appallingly rattling and displaying her intellect' and never wearying of pulling 'all the bells and organ stops of her genius'. The famous lawyer Anselm von Feuerbach, who made the acquaintance of the Schopenhauer ladies in Karlsbad, called the eighteen-year-old Adele simply a 'goose' who chattered too much.

The discord between her inner and outer self, which caused such a dissonance mainly among the men around her, inevitably affected Adele's view of herself. Her ugliness caused her grievous suffering. She was a sensitive person, in need of being loved, and she felt cut off by her own body from the world of embodied love. Her diaries, written shortly after Arthur's departure from Weimar, are full of eloquent laments. She had the misfortune of having the beautiful Ottilie von Pogwisch, later the wife of August von Goethe, as a friend. Ottilie, like Adele, was in love with love. The inseparable young girls raved jointly about the young men who were paying court to them, while – at least in an erotic respect – being interested only in Ottilie. Adele, sadly, was sought out only by young men who wanted to pour out their hearts; with Adele the young lovers could weep when Ottilie proved coy, or else let their joy brim over if Ottilie returned their sentiments. For a while Adele found it flattering to be sought out as a confidante, but in the long run this could not satisfy her. In connection with one of those, to her invariably unhappy, affairs she wrote in her diary: 'Who could have been happier than myself, who could have loved better or, I say this without presumption, make another happier by love? And yet – it is over . . .'

She was surrounded by love, she wrote on another occasion, but no one loved her the way she wanted to be loved. She felt used but not wanted. Small wonder, therefore, that her intimate friendship with the romantically so successful Ottilie was gradually tinged with a certain resentment: 'Every vacuous Englishman occupies [with Ottilie] that share of thoughts that otherwise turned towards me,' she complained, forgetting that not so long before she had herself had hopes of one of those 'vacuous Englishmen'. When Charles Sterling, mockingly called the 'demoniac youth' by Goethe, left Weimar, Adele lamented to her diary: 'As the voice of an angel dies away who proclaimed God to us, so his presence now dies away in my life . . . to my existence he is only linked through Ottilie.'

What Adele criticized in her friend Ottilie – that she contented herself with 'seeking nothing else, thinking nothing else, breathing nothing else but love' – now applied to herself and represented the real tragedy of her life. The wish to be loved by a man, body and soul, was at the core of all the sentiments, thoughts and reflections which Adele confided to her diary. Of course her mother as well as conventional considerations were urging her to look out for a good match – but the degree to which this obsessive desire displaced all her much-praised intelligence and accomplishments is nevertheless remarkable. She attentively searched all around her for signs of affection, her hopes lurking ready to pounce, ready to seize upon any friendly glance or friendly word. Adele's black moods and depressions invariably stemmed from such disappointed hopes.

She wrote a little poetry, she cut out silhouettes, she read, she sang, she acted. She was good at many things and was commended for it. Her talent was confirmed. But everything remained just polite and casual; it failed to fulfil her. These were preliminaries, substitute activities for an unlived life: 'My days flow along in an uncertain twilight, joy, pain, worries, jests; as though on a journey they unroll past me, with nowhere a firm hold, nowhere a calm sense of existence and activity.'

In such a depressive mood she began to suspect her own sensitivity: were these not secondhand emotions, she asked herself, copied feelings, sorrows and joys merely shared, without that powerful urge that could spring only from personal involvement in life? Life as she desired it was passing her by, it was outside, with other people, with her mother, with Ottilie – or else in the theatre, where, poeticized, it took on dramatic form. Disappointment with life was the mainspring of Adele's passion for the theatre. She enjoyed acting on the Weimar amateur stage. Goethe commended her in the role of Iphigenia. At social gatherings she was often asked to recite. For the personification of powerful emotions she here had the security of a ready text, while in life she lacked that support; there she lacked what touched her, here she lost herself by abandoning herself. Adele spoke well and fast, almost breathlessly. Speech had to compensate for the lack of other contact, other closeness. Adele breathed rarefied air; hence her liking for delicate filigree-like cut-out silhouettes, which likewise could only be handled with great care and were best shown off under glass. Adele's basic mood was elegiac. Events scarcely had time to develop, almost instantly they became recollections; yet in recollection they were resuscitated to a life that they had lacked in reality.

A few weeks before her brother's arrival in Weimar such an event took place, one that Adele was to dwell on for a whole decade.

In the spring of 1813, following a minor engagement between Prussian and French troops, Ottilie and Adele had made a fateful find. On a walk in the park just outside the town they found a wounded light infantry officer from Lützow's corps. Weimar at that time was still on Napoleon's side; hence what the two young ladies discovered on that spring morning was in fact the wicked enemy. But that was not how Ottilie and Adele saw it: Ottilie, from an aristocratic, if impoverished, Prussian family, had a warm romantic feeling for the brave men who were fighting for the liberation of Prussia; Adele, the ladies' Club of the Muses and a few other patriotic modern-thinking Weimarians shared these sentiments. Ottilie and Adele rushed into the adventure of a minor conspiracy. The wounded man was secretly moved to a place of hiding and secretly he was fed and nursed. Needless to say, the two young women fell in love with the wounded hero, the son of a Silesian fur merchant, bearing the prosaic name of Ferdinand Heinke. Restored to health, Heinke first took some leave in Breslau and subsequently rejoined his unit. Twice more before the end of the year his detachment was quartered in Weimar, where the now recovered young hero revealed himself as something of a ladies' man. However, he showed a certain circumspection with regard to the ladies who adored him: in Breslau there was a fiancée waiting for him.

When Arthur Schopenhauer arrived in Weimar in the late autumn of 1813 Adele was still dreamily involved in this romance of gunpowder and amorous charm – undeterred by the great disasters which Weimar once more had to endure. The allied troops had left their wounded behind in the town. There were epidemics of dysentery and nervous fever. In November 1813 Weimar, with a population of six thousand, had five hundred cases of typhoid. There was a shortage of doctors and there was fear of infection. Twice a day a sulphur fumigation team moved through the town. There were food supply problems; there were numerous suicides. Adele remained unconcerned – initially at least – also by the disasters within the house, by the tensions and quarrels between her mother and her brother.

The memory of Heinke, who had meanwhile finally turned his back on Weimar, became a psychological place of refuge for Adele, more so than for Ottilie. The finding of Heinke was glorified into the dawn of real life. Adele recorded it in poetry: '*Finding* meant life within a life / that otherwise crept

poorly, full of longing', and, 'Courageously you gave up a slave's existence /
for freedom and fatherland, / in foreign parts a sheltering roof awaits you /
. . . Farewell, be happy, man of noble attitude! / . . . / We recognized each
other for all time.' Elegiac Adele surrendered herself uninhibitedly to the
transfiguring and myth-creating force of memory: 'The flowers, sprung
through icy blankets / . . . / *Those* flowers no lapse of time can take from me. /
If their cups close I have lost nothing. / What I have lived, irradiated by
blood-red suns / is now enclosed in my existence.'

Though Adele was so devoutly raising Heinke, the future police president
of Breslau, to the lodestar of her life, she had been compelled, once again, to
yield to Ottilie during the weeks of that star's earthly presence. At the height
of the romance she wrote to Ottilie: 'We really are in a sad position . . . in that
we both love one and the same person . . .: I am . . . keeping silent because I
have firmly resolved to suppress all thought of him and to content myself with
his respect. . . . I shall do everything to discover if he loves you. . . . I flatter
myself that since yesterday I have made myself agreeable to him, more I do
not want.'

So much did Heinke become a myth for Adele that years afterwards he
continued to be the yardstick of her self-examination. 'Ferdinand,' she wrote
in her diary on New Year's Eve 1816, 'have I acted, lived, thought in your
spirit?' Henceforth every man would be measured against Heinke: 'but if I
estimate a man so that alongside Heinke he does not collapse into a hollow
nothing, then I am resolved' (4 March 1817). And after ten years, in August
1823, she wrote: 'I now think of Ferdinand as my destiny, as my hope of the
beyond, as I do of God, without wish, without remorse, without tears. That
was the call of my destiny, I listened to it, and now it is over.'

Whenever Arthur, at the maternal dinner table, derogatorily and contemptuously dismissed the patriotic fervour which flared up also in Weimar after
Napoleon's departure, and in doing so clashed with Gerstenbergk who was
swimming with the tide, Adele would find herself in a conflict of loyalties. On the
one hand, Gerstenbergk seemed to her a weakling compared to Heinke, a
braggart, whose friendship with her mother she did not approve of any more
than did her brother; later indeed she would 'rigidify into ice' at the suspicion
that her mother might wish to ally herself to him. In short, Arthur's dislike of
Gerstenbergk met with her endorsement. On the other hand she felt deeply hurt
by Arthur's derogatory remarks about the so-called freedom fighters; he was
besmirching her idol. What she did not know was that Heinke was actually
being kept informed by Gerstenbergk about Arthur's scenes.

Adele too suffered from that conflict of loyalties, she too felt she was in the
crossfire. She reacted with dismay and terror to the escalation of the disputes
between her mother and her brother. Ultimately, her mother was closer to her
than her brother, and so she finally shared Johanna's outrage. 'My brother,'
she wrote to Ottilie at the time of the great clash, 'has behaved abominably to
my mother, for the time being she does not wish to see him.'

Now and again Goethe would invite Schopenhauer to bigger social evenings, but as a rule at first he was asked on his own to the house on the Frauenplan almost once a week. Between February and April 1814 the invitations became less frequent.

Goethe was not interested in any cosy social contact with Schopenhauer; 'With others,' Goethe once said, 'he would chat, but with him, young Dr Arthur, he philosophized.' Only when he was in an 'appropriate serious mood' did he wish to meet Schopenhauer, that was why he requested him to call only when specifically invited. Goethe intended to work with Schopenhauer. He believed he had found in him an interlocutor with whom he could philosophize about what was then, and had been for some time, most on his mind: his colour theory.

On 16 May 1810 Goethe's extensive work *Zur Farbenlehre* (*On the Theory of Colours*) had appeared in two octavo volumes with a quarto volume of plates. He had worked on the book for two years; in his *Annalen* (*Annals*), looking back to the event, he called the day on which it was published his 'Liberation Day', with an ironical allusion to the fact that the victory over Napoleon could never, to him, be such a day of liberation. While patriotic passions simmered, Goethe was pondering the 'primal phenomena' of light, darkness, and the blending of the two: the turbidity which appeared as colours to our eyes. 'On our right, day – on our left, night; from the combination of the two all things have sprung, among others also ourselves.' He regarded his patriotic contemporaries as especially turbid. He forbade his son August to volunteer against Napoleon. The fact that his Grand Duke so hastily defected from the Emperor at the end of the war filled him with bitterness. Even after Napoleon's defeat he continued proudly to wear the Cross of the French Legion of Honour. It was especially in his role of author of the *Theory of Colours* that he was fond of comparing himself to the great Corsican. Just as the Emperor, revered by him as a figure of light, had had to assume the dark legacy of the French Revolution and to lighten it, so he had inherited a legacy no less dark: that of having to clarify the 'errors of Newton's theory of colours'. In the polemical part of his *Theory of Colours* Goethe indulges in images of military conflict: 'This is not therefore a case of a prolonged siege or a doubtful conflict. Instead we find that eighth wonder of the world [Newton's theory of colours] to be already an abandoned antiquity threatened with collapse, and we are therefore setting about pulling it down without further ado, from gable and roof downward, so that the sun at long last should shine into that old nest of rats and owls.' And as invariably happens with the battles of titans, ultimately they are faced by a whole world of pygmies, to whom they must succumb. During the months and weeks when Napoleon was beaten down Goethe, with growing anger and with growing disappointment, was waiting for the shattering effect of his colour opus. For twenty years the mountain had been in labour, and the public was reacting no differently than if a mouse had been born. His friends had applauded him; a few painters, Runge among them, were inspired by it. But the scientific world dismissed it. 'Experts will find nothing new,' wrote the *Gothaische Gelehrte Zeitung* laconically. The literary public regretted this unnecessary excursion by its great teacher, and the political world had other things to worry about. Why did Goethe not turn to the burning issues of the day, it asked querulously.

Goethe believed – though he did not as a rule say so aloud – that Napoleon fell victim merely to a conspiracy of mediocrity. But exactly the same had now also happened to him, the other titan, with his *Theory of Colours* – as he would say to anyone willing to listen: 'No matter how many devils in the lecture theatres and bookshops oppose me . . . they will not prevent me from declaring aloud what I have recognized as the truth. . . . Anyway, what is that freedom of the press that everyone is clamouring and sighing for if I am not permitted to say that Newton deceived himself in his youth and spent the rest of his life perpetuating that self-deception!'

Needless to say, no one was trying to ban Goethe from publishing. His publisher was exceedingly obliging, even though he must have suspected that the publication would remain on his shelves. Outwardly the work was sumptuously produced, so that at least it would be an ornament to any library. This latter expectation was fulfilled.

When Goethe embarked on his connection with young Schopenhauer he felt misunderstood with regard to what seemed to him his most important work. Later he was to say to Eckermann: 'Of whatever I have achieved as a poet I have no high opinion at all. There were excellent poets living alongside me, there were even more excellent ones before me, and there will be such poets after me. But that in my century I alone am the one who in the difficult science of colour theory knows the truth – that I consider a feather in my cap, and I therefore have a sense of superiority over many.'

Goethe, fond of symbolical stage settings, reacted to this situation of polite silence by adopting the role of guardian of a secret mystery. He had to 'make proselytes', he said on one occasion. One such grateful proselyte had dropped into his life in the person of Arthur Schopenhauer.

In order to understand why the *Theory of Colours* was so important to Goethe one has to consider not so much the results of his researches as the motivation which kept him engaged in this work for decades.

On his Italian journey (1786–8) Goethe had devoted himself to painting with unflagging energy; he wanted to move out of the cave of the subjectively sentimental to the light of objective 'vision'; instead of writing poetry with his heart alone, he wanted to do so with his eyes. But he was forced to discover that he did not have that outstanding talent for painting that he had assumed he possessed. The art of 'self-denial', which he practised so expertly, in this instance took on the shape of the idea that it was necessary, first of all, to explore the essence of colour. He therefore came to the conclusion in Italy 'that the colours as a psychic phenomenon must first be tackled from the side of nature if one wished to find out something about them with regard to art'. Hence the idea to study colours 'scientifically' was largely inspired by a need for compensation. But there were other more important reasons.

Colours to Goethe were the predominant subject of his nature studies going back to his early years in Weimar. The fact as such, as well as the manner in which he pursued the study of natural sciences, takes us to the heart of his understanding of himself and the world.

While still in the Storm and Stress period, he saw 'nature' as the quintessence of subjective emotional personal power. 'Nature' – entirely in Rousseau's sense – confronted convention and social rules. The unrestricted outflow of subjective nature was supposed to bring one into harmony with objective nature. Inner and outer nature were in harmony if one allowed one's own 'nature' to unfold. Anyone surrendering to his 'inner' nature was living dangerously. The waves of spontaneity might break against hard reality. In the uninhibited whirl of his first few years in Weimar, in company with the young Duke, it was still possible to cushion any possible collisions. Spontaneity encountered an area protected by privilege, where one might roam with reduced risks. This worked for a while – until Goethe began to be taken up more by what protected him: the duties of ministerial office and his position in society subjected him to the discipline of the principle of reality. The conflict was exacerbated, tensions grew. Yet Goethe was fond of evading any tragic culmination to a conflict; this time by travelling to Italy. There he practised the art of tolerance: one should do one thing without necessarily avoiding another; one might sacrifice to both deities, the god of poetry and the god of reality; neither should external life he wrecked on internal life, nor the other way about. Subsequently Goethe was to find a formula for it: truth to him was 'a revelation from within, developing outside. . . . It is a synthesis of world and spirit, giving us the most blessed assurance of the eternal harmony of existence.'

Such 'harmony' can exist only if sovereignty has been achieved above the conflicting claims of poetical and reality-oriented existence. His Italian journey helped Goethe to achieve this, as may be seen from his *Torquato Tasso*. Goethe had drafted the play before his journey, when he had not yet found the 'middle voice' between world and poetry. Not until the completion of the journey was he able to finish the play. By then, Tasso was still the poet suffering from his environment, but in contrast to Goethe's first drafts his sufferings were now presented almost entirely as the consequences of a tendency to misjudge the real world, one which in its poetry expresses itself in a subjective, idealistic manner. Goethe prided himself on having outstripped Tasso, for this now became the programme of his life: to be Tasso, the poet, and at the same time Antonio, the man of the world. But how could the poet cling to the world when the world was growing more unpoetical every day? Unpoetical, moreover, not only in the obligations of everyday social and political existence but, above all, in the expectations of the modern understanding of reality, reflected as a paradigm in the victorious advance of the natural sciences. Goethe hoped once more to hold and bind together, in his person, that which was being torn apart by the powerful trends of his age: analytical reason and creative fantasy, abstract concepts and sensory vision, artificial experiment and living experience, mathematical calculation and intuition. Goethe was tormented by the anxiety that poetry might lose its right of domicile in the realm of truth, that 'tender experience' would be banished by the robust, heartless, though pragmatically successful methods of 'science'. Yet in fighting that defensive battle he did not wish to become Tasso, who from the outset stood forlorn against the worldlings. He did not wish to defend frontiers against science but to carry the spirit of poetry into science; he wanted to challenge the claims of science on its own territory; he did not wish to be defensive but to carry the attack into the heart of the opponent's territory. But he only launched that attack, he could only launch it, inspired by his personality ideal: any knowledge that could not be brought into harmony with the multifarious strivings and talents of man, any knowledge in which 'sensuality and reason, imagination and intellect' failed to meet in 'decisive unity', seemed to him knowledge 'unworthy of man', a caricature of the idea of truth. To him truth was bound by the law of a comprehensive existential logic. Truth could have human value only if it remained tied to body and life, i.e. to the range of our senses and our sensuality. Not every kind of curiosity excited his applause. There is a curiosity that takes us away from ourselves and from our world, which turns us towards what is no business of ours, which results in man 'ceaselessly torturing' himself and thus losing himself. Goethe strove for a kind of truth that would not leave us stunned. That was why he did not wish his 'primal phenomena', i.e. those primal forms from which, in his understanding, nature produces its wealth of forms in infinitely numerous variations, to be understood as an abstract concept or category, as a type merely 'thought up' for the purpose of ordering the empirical material. Goethe's 'primal phenomenon' was to remain visual; there had to be a 'primal plant' as a model of all plant varieties. In southern Italy Goethe actually believed he had found it. What nature is, what it can give us for 'our benefit' – that emerges fully from its appearance; it has no ulterior meaning to be first discovered by mathematicized physics or some artificial experiment. As for the latter, Goethe had some very drastic comment to make: 'Nature falls silent on the rack.' He railed against the 'evil' of the new physics: it should be robbed of its prey, it was necessary to liberate 'the phenomena once and for all from its gloomy empirical-mechanical- dogmatic torture chamber'.

For a time Goethe had tried to improve his strained relationship with mathematics, especially with non-visual arithmetic. In Jena he had taken lessons in algebra. Yet the manner in which he dropped this project testifies to that sovereign talent for living that made him a well-rounded Olympian, a man so greatly admired by his contemporaries and by posterity. He justified the discontinuation of his algebra studies with the words: 'I shall not be able to use it for my personality.' Here was that dazzling ignorance in the service of life which Nietzsche had commended in Goethe and without which there would not have been Goethe's Promethean power of creation, a power of creation springing from his formula for life: to create one's own world, bringing together the disparate elements in an equilibrium of happiness, leaving the 'inconvenient' outside without any scruples. Goethe was unable, for instance, to find any kind of rapport with death. Those around him respected it. Frau von Stein stipulated in her last will that her funeral cortège was to bypass the house on the Frauenplan. When Christiane died Goethe withdrew to his rooms, in shaky health. This sovereign gesture of excluding the 'inconvenient' cannot simply be termed 'repression' because it lacks the tight, cramped and cramping element of that concept. This gesture is productively related to a sphere of life to which it lends vital homogeneity. But it can do so only because it remains elastic, because it practises its limitation with some simultaneous irony, because the exclusion also represents a kind of 'renunciation' that implies an acute awareness of what it is that has to be renounced under the gentle force of the law of life that one has acknowledged for oneself. At times, of course, it has its comical aspect, as when Goethe regarded the rainbow – which, according to his theory of colours, should not exist at all – as a 'wicked prank' played on him by nature. Another instance: a famous physicist made Goethe a present of a valuable modern polarization apparatus which would prove the correctness of Newton's hypotheses on the origin of colours, as it diffracted light into the colours of the spectrum. Goethe persistently refused to use the apparatus, just as two centuries earlier the Holy Inquisition had similarly declined to look through Galileo's telescope. Goethe quite simply rejected any information on nature that was obtained with an aid to perception and not by means of our healthy senses. In nature, Goethe maintained among other things, there was only light but no light rays. Rays were produced merely with the aid of an artificial assembly of apparatuses which did violence to light. Hence whatever might be discovered about such an artificial ray of light did not therefore concern the essence of light. One of Goethe's main complaints about Newton was that he did not stage his experiments in open nature but instead forced light to pass through a hole: 'Friends, avoid the darkened chamber / where your light is being pinched.'

If nature study, reduced to human scale, was regarded by Goethe as necessary to the equilibrium of a rounded life generally, then this was particularly true of his colour researches; colours to him were an excellent symbol of life itself. It is the law of life that gives rise also to the colours: polarization and intensification. Polarization means light and darkness. Light – and this has to be said in defiance of Newton – must be seen as the 'simplest, most homogeneous, most indivisible essence known to us': a 'primal phenomenon' in short, beyond which it is impossible to investigate.

Confronting light there is darkness. Light and darkness have not only physical, but at the same time 'meta-physical' reality. They are in conflict with one another. Goethe, once again tending to conciliation, prefers the term 'interplay'. Only that interplay produces colour. Colours are like life, the 'turbid', the mixed, the productive balance of polar opposites. 'Chromatic reflections and parallels,' Goethe noted in his diary. 'Love and hate, hope and fear are likewise only different states of our turbid interior, through which the spirit gazes towards either the light or the shady side.'

Colours to Goethe are subjective and objective at the same time. The activity of the eye reflects the polarity which dominates life generally. 'We believe that here, once more, we observe the great agility of the retina and the tacit opposite which anything living is compelled to utter whenever some definite state is offered it. Thus inhalation presupposes exhalation, and the other way about, as every systole presupposes its diastole. It is the eternal formula of life that applies here too. As darkness is offered to the eye it demands light; it demands darkness when light is supplied to it, and thereby it demonstrates its vitality.'

The discovery of harmony between the particular nature of the eye and the particular nature of light, darkness and turbidity should satisfy us, Goethe suggested. 'For here too we are left with no choice but to repeat that colour is nature in accordance with its own laws concerning the sense of the eye.'

'Nature in accordance with its own laws concerning the sense of the eye' – this then was Goethe's formula, by means of which he hoped to bridge the gap between the subjective and the objective aspects of colour: the 'law' of the eye which can see colour reflects the 'law' of nature which produces the colour.

To young Schopenhauer, who had just radicalized Kant's transcendentalism in his dissertation, such a hypothesis was bound to seem like naive realism. It seems likely that in conversation with Goethe Schopenhauer, somewhat disrespectfully, would have commented on it along these lines. Many years later he was to relate the following episode: 'But that man Goethe . . . was so completely a *realist* that he absolutely could not get it into his head that the *objects* as such exist only to the extent that they are *projected* by the perceiving subject. What, he once said to me, looking at me with his Jovian eyes, you suggest that the light exists only in so far as you can see it? No, *you* would not exist if the light did not see *you*' (C, 31).

This scene admirably reflects the nub of the difference between Goethe and Schopenhauer; a difference which, bearing in mind their points of departure, should not really have surprised either man, seeing that it existed even before their joint work was embarked on. But at first it was buried by a productive misunderstanding: Goethe approved of Schopenhauer's persistent adherence to the principle of visuality as the basic prerequisite of all cognition, though he overlooked the fact that Schopenhauer was limiting the validity of such visualization to the confines of our projecting activity. Schopenhauer in turn was impressed by the universality and the boldness with which Goethe, in everything he did, followed that principle of visuality. He was positively dazzled by the manner in which Goethe applied this principle not only in discourse but actually embodied it existentially ('Jovian eyes'). That, as well as the fact that Goethe derived his colour theory from a detailed description of the origin of the colours in the eye (the physiology of colours) – a point of departure which Schopenhauer could easily accept into his intellectual world – diminished, in Schopenhauer's eyes, the seriousness of the underlying difference.

After a few weeks of common discussion and experimentation in the field of colours Goethe, at the beginning of 1814, jotted down a couplet later to be included in his *Xenien*: 'Gladly I'd continue to bear the teacher's burden / if pupils did not immediately turn themselves into teachers.' In point of fact, Schopenhauer, whose modesty never was his strong suit, was about to mount the teacher's rostrum. Proceeding from Goethe's physiology of colours he intended to develop a complete theory of the origin of colours in the eye, convinced that Goethe might have supplied some illuminating observations but nothing like a theory.

Not until a year after his departure from Weimar was Schopenhauer to write down that 'theory' within the space of a few weeks, interrupting work on his major philosophical project for that purpose. The underlying ideas, however, developed during the months of personal contact with Goethe. In Goethe's *Theory of Colours* the focus was the 'actions and sufferings of light'; Schopenhauer eventually turned these into something different: the 'actions and sufferings of the eye'. Light as a 'primal phenomenon' – that proposition Schopenhauer conceded to his master, without, however, making too much of it; instead he turned to what interested him primarily – the way in which the eye reacted to the (further undeterminable) phenomenon of light. Schopenhauer operated with the hypothesis that colour phenomena resulted from differentiated activity by the retina, triggered off by modified incidence of light. The retina, he claimed, had the 'natural urge . . . to display its activity *fully*' (VC, 60). As each modified incidence of light made only partial demands on the activity potential of the retina, the retina had a tendency to 'supplement' the activity falling short of the optimum: this produced the experience of complementary colours, as well as the strange sense of harmony which complementary colours gave rise to. Here Schopenhauer developed an analogy to musical experiences of harmony, which were similarly due to complementary ratios, in this case of acoustic vibrations.

Pointedly and – like Goethe – in opposition to Newton, Schopenhauer chose this formulation: colour is not the phenomenon of a 'divided ray of light' but the phenomenon of the 'divided activity of the retina' (VC, 72).

In the first edition of his colour theory, published in 1816, Schopenhauer formulated his divergences from Goethe with considerable restraint. Although factually present from the outset, it was only in the second edition of 1854 that they were polemically presented. He wrote, polemicizing against

Goethe's 'primal phenomena' of light and darkness: 'Primary phenomenon properly speaking is only the organic capacity of the retina to cause its nervous activity to separate and successively appear in two qualitatively opposite halves, sometimes equal, sometimes unequal' (VC, 129–30).

With his colour theory Goethe in fact presented the public with a chapter of his grand 'confession', a chapter dealing with his philosophy of life and nature; this explains the numerous ethical, aesthetic and metaphysical reflections in it. Schopenhauer's interest in colours, on the other hand, was, on the lines of his dissertation, one of cognition theory. That was why he called his essay *Über das Sehen und die Farben* (*On Vision and Colour*). In the chapter devoted to vision he repeated and clarified what he had earlier stated in his dissertation: an account of the operation of the 'pure intellect' which, from the stimulation data in the body (in this case the retina), with the aid of the *a priori* causality principle, constructs the world perceived by our senses.

Except for his encounter with Goethe, Schopenhauer would certainly not have concerned himself with the problem of colour. To him this was merely another sphere to which he might apply his cognition-theory hypotheses. Being just then about to penetrate to the core of his philosophical project, the metaphysics of the will, nothing less than his veneration for Goethe could have persuaded him to undertake this new task. He wished to be close to the revered master and to assist him in his fight against Newton with, as he believed, better arguments. Schopenhauer was in the role of the wooer, but he was no yes-man and did not readily oblige. And Goethe, as so often, acted coolly in the face of such wooing for his favour. Others who had experienced the same fate, such as Lenz and Kleist, had been almost broken by it. Not so Schopenhauer. Between the two a strange 'struggle' developed, in the course of which Schopenhauer displayed a kind of self-assurance which, in spite of hurtful rejection, did not turn into resentment. Schopenhauer remained true to himself and to his way of philosophizing, while preserving his veneration for the master. He did not lose himself, either in veneration or in increasingly reserved fits of self-assertion.

The story of that 'struggle' began in July 1815, when Schopenhauer, then in Dresden, sent Goethe the manuscript of his finished essay *On Vision and Colour*.

It was over a year since Schopenhauer had been dismissed by Goethe with the motto: 'If you wish to enjoy your worth / you must give worth to the world.' That amicably reproving parting shot led Arthur to believe that he was entitled to keep up the connection, even though at the time of personal contact it had led to occasional dissonances. Schopenhauer therefore requested Goethe to honour the essay, in memory of their joint work, by becoming its editor.

Goethe was away at the time. He was visiting his native Frankfurt, where the manuscript with its covering letter was sent on to him. He was negotiating with his publisher Cotta about a new collected edition of his works. He met

Freiherr von Stein and accompanied him down the Rhine to Cologne. Ernst Moritz Arndt joined them. In Bonn he spent a few days in the circle of ministers and generals of the Rhine provinces. He received visits from the Tsar's sister Catherine, from the Grand Duke of Mecklenburg, and from the Duke of Cumberland. In Wiesbaden he was presented with a high order; *Werther*'s Lotte, now Madame Kestner, a widow, sent her son to see him. In between these activities Goethe worked on his *West-Östlicher Divan* and revised his *Italienische Reise (Italian Journey)*. He did not therefore immediately find the time or the inclination to reply to Schopenhauer's letter. But on 3 September 1815 Schopenhauer sent him a reminder. He could well imagine, he wrote, that compared with Goethe's travels in the *beau monde* the colour manuscript sent him must seem rather insignificant, but for him, Schopenhauer, it was close to his heart: 'I know from your own lips that the literary whirl has always been secondary to you, that real life has been the main thing. In my case, however, it is the other way about: what I think, what I write, has value for me and is important to me; what I experience personally and what happens to me is unimportant to me, indeed I scoff at it' (CL, 16). Schopenhauer urgently requests Goethe at least to confirm the receipt of the manuscript; if he does not wish to take it up would he please send it back, 'with or without a note'. Would Goethe be good enough to put an end to his torments of waiting and his anxiety that the essay might have gone astray or fallen into third hands?

Clearly Schopenhauer, after a few weeks of waiting, had given up hope that Goethe might seriously discuss his essay or even decide to edit it.

But then, on 7 September 1815, Goethe's reply arrived. It was couched in friendly tones. Goethe pretended to have received the manuscript in 'good time', to have read and considered it. Goethe was exaggerating: in actual fact he had probably just glanced at the essay, for at a later date he was to request Schopenhauer to prepare a brief synopsis of it, so that he could refer to it in his own writings.

Schopenhauer's hopes, at any rate, revived with the receipt of this letter of 7 September, the more so as Goethe promised that he would, as soon as he was back in Weimar, dictate some 'observations as the moment suggested them'. There was no mention of any possible publication. In a letter of 16 September Schopenhauer thanked Goethe for the 'provisional reassurance' his promise to comment on his essay had brought him.

Another month passed before Goethe answered on 23 October. However, this letter did not contain the promised 'observations' on Schopenhauer's essay. True, Goethe declared that he had read the manuscript with 'great pleasure', and he commended the 'soundness' of the presentation; Schopenhauer, he said, was an 'independently thinking individual'. But after these flattering preliminaries Goethe came out with the substance: he had, at the moment, moved too far away from the colour theory to be able to discuss any differences – for surely that was what Schopenhauer wanted. In the meantime, Schopenhauer might get in touch with Professor Seebeck, another fellow warrior in the common cause of colour. With Schopenhauer's permission he would pass on to him the manuscript for an expert opinion. 'It would be my fondest wish,' Goethe wrote, 'for the two of you to get closer together and to work with one another until such time as I have safely returned to the harmonious coloured regions from the quaint spiritual trips which now snatch me first one way and then another [his work on the *West-Östlicher Divan*].' Arthur was disappointed and outraged by this letter. He was disappointed because Goethe neither dealt in substance with his essay nor reacted to the question of editing and publication. He was outraged because he felt brushed aside in the meanest manner by the suggestion of collaboration with Seebeck. In his very extensive reply of 11 November 1815 he muted his outrage but allowed it to shine through in jocularly introduced literary references. Goethe's suggestion had reminded him of the daughter of the vicar of Taubenheyn (a character in a ballad by G. A. Bürger), 'who had claims of marriage to the noble lord, who instead arranged for his worthy huntsman to marry her; or of Jean-Jacques Rousseau, who in his youth, when visiting a noble lady, was asked to stay for a meal but subsequently discovered that he was expected to eat with the servants' (CL, 22).

Schopenhauer did not wish to be treated as a servant at the master's table. The pride with which he rejected Goethe's proposal characterized also the diction and the contents of the rest of this mammoth letter of 11 November. Schopenhauer was positively trying to force Goethe into a corner. As there were differences of opinion on a few points, the error must be either on his or on Goethe's side. If it lay on his own side, 'why should Your Excellency deny yourself the satisfaction, and deny me the instruction, of drawing in a few words the line which in my essay divides the true from the false?' (CL, 19). That still had a respectful and modest ring, but then Schopenhauer continued: 'But I make no secret of the fact that I do not believe that such a line can be drawn. My theory is the unfolding of a single indivisible idea which must be either wholly false or wholly true; it resembles a vaulting from which no stone can be removed without the whole structure collapsing' (CL, 19). Matters with Goethe's colour theory, on the other hand, were quite different: it was the 'systematic compilation of many . . . and various facts, and there a small error may very easily have crept in'.

Schopenhauer was generous with compliments, but at the same time performed an undisguised and massive devaluation of Goethe's colour theory. Goethe had written that 'we begin to theorize with every attentive glance into the world'. He regarded his work as a new type of theory-building. Was he now to be told by Schopenhauer that only Schopenhauer's essay had raised his own rock to the heights of theory? The comparison made by Arthur in order to illustrate his proud self-assessment was not very flattering to Goethe: 'If I were to liken your colour theory to a pyramid, then my theory would represent its apex, the indivisible mathematical point from which the entire structure spreads out, and which is so essential that without it the shape is no longer a pyramid, whereas one may slice off again and again from the bottom without it ceasing to be a pyramid . . .' (CL, 21). Schopenhauer knew that Goethe too was familiar with Aristotle and that he therefore realized that the essence (idea) of a thing (matter) lay in the entelechy of its form. The simile therefore amounted to the suggestion that Goethe should regard his work as 'matter' brought to life only by Schopenhauer's spirit.

Now that Schopenhauer's reaction to Goethe's friendly reserve had soared up to the heights of self-esteem the following sentence flowed from his pen: 'I know with complete certainty that I have supplied the first true theory of colour, the first in the whole history of science' (CL, 20).

It should be remembered that to Goethe his *Theory of Colours* was the work which he believed had earned him a major place in world history. In it he felt like a Napoleon in the realm of the intellect. And now a totally unknown philosopher, not yet thirty, was claiming that it was only he who actually raised that work to the level of a theory. And that young philosopher – this was the peak of impudence – pretended to have done so with a theoretical work that was a sideline for him. The master had spent half a lifetime on the *Theory of Colours*, and his twenty-seven-year-old 'finisher' now had the effrontery to write: 'I have always only treated it [the essay], with the exception of a few weeks, as a sideline while I continually carry with me in my mind very different theories from those concerning colour' (CL, 22).

The astonishing thing about Goethe's reply to that letter, with its curious mixture of suppressed outrage, disappointment, overbrimming pride and sincere reverence, was its relaxed friendliness, with not even a hint of offence or irritation at the young philosopher's not exactly flattering assessment of Goethe's life's work, the *Theory of Colours*. Goethe began by reassuring Schopenhauer: Seebeck had not yet seen the manuscript and, if the author did not wish him to see it, he would not receive it. This was followed, in a tone of sovereign irony, by Goethe's verdict on his disagreement with Schopenhauer. The irony was in the fact that Goethe was playing on Schopenhauer's transcendental philosophical view: from it he deduced the right of error to exist, and the wisdom of allowing roads to part if 'what is one's own' can only thereby be preserved. Goethe wrote: 'Anyone personally inclined to construct the world from the subject will not regret the argument that the subject is always only an individual in the phenomenon and therefore requires a certain share of truth and of error in order to achieve its individuality. Nothing, however, differentiates men more than that the amounts of these two ingredients are mixed in different proportions.'

Schopenhauer refused to accept that by this sentence Goethe had passed judgement on the whole affair, and that no more was to be expected. But what could he expect? Did he expect Goethe to write to him: yes, you have raised my disjointed observations to the status of a true theory; remarkable, young man, how within a few weeks you placed the crown upon my life's work; I hasten to place your work, which has at long last moved mine into the sunlight, before the public?

That was precisely it. The young philosopher was seeking the blessing of his substitute father: you are my beloved son in whom I am well pleased. Go forth. . . . That blessing, of course, Schopenhauer was waiting for in vain. For a while he continued to ask for it – not by humbling himself, not by displaying humility before the throne of the patriarch, but by intensifying the demonstrations of his self-assurance simultaneously with unfeigned respect for Goethe.

Goethe, however, did not reply. At that point Schopenhauer began to give up. On 23 December 1815 he wrote: 'My first, always uncertain, hope that you might, by some sympathy, help that work to publicity is more or less gone: the expectation I entertained in that respect . . . is evaporating after nearly seven months of . . . waiting in vain' (CL, 23). He asked to have the manuscript returned to him, but he did so once more with a grand gesture. The son, denied his father's blessing, now confronted him, addressing him with unparalleled boldness: what is keeping you from me is your realization that truth is on my side and error on yours. By refusing me your favour you display a lack of magnanimity. 'To speak frankly,' Schopenhauer wrote, 'I find it quite impossible to believe that Your Excellency should not have realized the correctness of my theory: for I know that through me truth has spoken – now in this small matter as it will one day in a major one – and your mind is too perfect, too accurately attuned, not to resound at every note. But I can well imagine that a subjective dislike of certain statements, which do not quite concur with some put forward by yourself, should make an examination of my theory distasteful to you, since you are constantly putting it aside and putting it off, and, being unable either to give or to deny me your consent, keep entirely silent' (CL, 23).

Goethe's silence was regarded by Schopenhauer – at least he persuaded himself to believe this – as proof of his own superiority, at any rate in this matter. And he once more repeated the (certainly unintentional) insult to Goethe by calling the colour affair a 'sideline'. Why did he do it?

To him the discussion of the colour problem was in fact secondary to the importance which a personal relationship with Goethe had for him. But in the given conditions such a personal relationship could only be established and maintained on the basis of their concern with colour. The balance of the relationship required that the 'son' should be given a chance to offset the 'father's' superiority in life by out-trumping the 'father' at least in one area. Arthur wanted to earn the paternal blessing by proving that he had something to give to his 'father'. But Goethe did not accept such an assumption of fatherhood – and why should he, considering that he could not tolerate even his real son except in the role of his secretary? However, he showed respect to the 'pupil' now assuming the part of 'teacher'. Otherwise he would have punished Schopenhauer's unmannerly behaviour with devastating dismissal or total disregard.

On 28 January 1816 he sent the manuscript back. In a friendly covering letter Goethe indulged in a daydream, highly flattering to Arthur, of how pleasant it would be to sit together on winter evenings in disputation with one another: the 'conversation . . . does not always have to be unanimous'. At the conclusion of the letter, however, Goethe, who had silently accepted a good many pinpricks from Schopenhauer's arrogance, managed to slap his face. He suggested to the man who was pleased to act as the finisher of his colour theory that he might like to 'briefly sum up his views' so that he, Goethe, might occasionally quote them. Goethe was treating his finisher with condescending casualness, restoring the proper ratio of magnitudes.

In reply Schopenhauer wrote that only from a Goethe or a Kant – and from no one else – would he have tolerated the kind of treatment he had received.

He now had his book on colour printed without Goethe's blessing. On 4 May 1816 he sent him a copy with the remark: 'I would ask you for your opinion if I had not abandoned hope of ever learning it . . .' (CL, 28). A week later Goethe thanked him politely: 'let me hear from you some time.' For Goethe a casual dismissal, for Schopenhauer a painful one.

In his *Annals* Goethe later recorded: 'Dr Schopenhauer joined me as a well-disposed friend. We discussed a good many things in agreement; eventually, however, a certain separation proved unavoidable, as when two friends, having walked together so far, shake hands, one wanting to go north and the other south, and very soon losing sight of one another.'

CHAPTER FOURTEEN

THE WILL AS THE
'THING IN ITSELF'

The great historic battles with their smoke of gunpowder, their noise and their stench of corpses had meanwhile shifted to the west; the domestic skirmishes with his mother, however, were at their peak when in the spring of 1814 Arthur Schopenhauer was looking for a new environment, where he might devote himself to his great work. His choice fell on Dresden. He had, by way of experiment, stayed in that city a few times before, the city then famed as the Florence of the north. Climate, architecture, scenery, atmosphere, its great collections of art treasures, the big library, the social life – all these had appealed to him.

Admittedly, Dresden had no university, but for Schopenhauer, convinced as he was that he had nothing to learn any more from any living philosopher, this circumstance did not carry any weight against his choice. On 24 April 1814 he wrote to Karl August Böttiger, whom he had met at his mother's tea parties and who was at that time Chief Inspector of the Royal Museum of Antiquities in Dresden: 'My better and real life are my philosophical studies, everything else is well subordinated to them, and is indeed no more than peripheral. However, being in the position to choose, I desire a place of residence which would offer me the beauties of nature, the pleasures of art, and the appurtenances of scholarship, and which would also allow me to find the necessary repose. All of these, far though I have travelled, I have never found so happily combined as in Dresden, and it has therefore long been my wish to settle down there permanently. I am therefore very keen on going to Dresden' (CL, 10).

He asked Böttiger to inform him whether Dresden, after the disasters of the war, still offered the same attractions. There was talk about Dresden having suffered a good deal from the recent events. Böttiger dispelled his misgivings, and in May 1814 Schopenhauer moved to Dresden, which became his home for the next four years.

The city had in fact suffered from the war, the traces of which were still visible everywhere. Throughout the previous year Dresden had been at the centre of military operations. In the spring the French had established themselves there – the King of Saxony had been a vassal of Napoleon right to the end. In early May 1813 the French had withdrawn in the face of the approaching Coalition troops, and in doing so had blown up the Augustus Bridge, an architectural monument even then. Dresden was 'liberated': the population lined the streets, the poets composed verses of welcome, school choirs sang. But the 'liberators' were able to hold out for two weeks only. In mid-May the French returned. Napoleon took up temporary quarters in the city. The population lined the streets, the poets composed verses of welcome, school choirs sang. At the end of August the great battle for Dresden was fought. French troops defended the town against assaults by the Coalition. Dresden experienced the worst shelling so far. Over two hundred houses were destroyed or damaged. Several tens of thousands of dead were left lying on the battlefield outside the city. The war, a contemporary complained, had undermined 'all good manners and behaviour' among the people of Dresden; he recorded that 'even from the educated classes . . . women and virgins, otherwise considered respectable and chaste . . . were among the packs of females who walked among the prone and mutilated victims of the battle, as though between the flower beds in a garden, displaying hideous concupiscence.'

Although the French had won the battle they were about to lose the war. Dresden remained besieged.

The city, now without hinterland and weighed down by the burdens of billeting, passed through difficult weeks. Half-starved people pounced on the horses which had starved in the streets. People were knifed outside bakers' shops. Nervous fever and typhoid were rampant. Approximately one hundred people died in the hospitals every day, and the same number again on the streets. Ludwig Richter, the painter of Biedermeier idylls, recalled those days with horror: 'There was a house where those who had died were flung out of the windows of the first and second floors, totally naked, and piled up on big farm carts right to the top. Such a load looked appallingly horrible, with emaciated arms, legs, heads and bodies sticking out, while the carters stepped about on that tangle and worked, with their shirt sleeves rolled up, as if it were logs of wood under them.'

In the spring of 1814, when Schopenhauer arrived in Dresden, the city had not yet recovered from these hardships. Grain supplies were meagre and prices, in consequence, rose. Dresden, known for its cleanliness and affluent appearance, was thick with dirt, the parks were neglected, beggars and war disabled were vegetating in the streets. There were ruins and piles of rubble everywhere. It was to take over a year for the city to recover. It also took the King that long to return from his Napoleonic adventure. On 17 June 1815 he re-entered Dresden, which had decked itself out for the occasion. Once more the inhabitants lined the streets, the poets wrote verses and school choirs sang. The people of Dresden evidently were very broadminded in their political loyalties. Politically orthodox contemporaries reproached them for it. Freiherr von Stein called the people of Dresden 'those soft wordmongers attached to their chattels'; it was 'repulsive to observe,' he wrote, 'that the humiliated state in which their fatherland finds itself, the disasters which have befallen it, concern them less than the inconveniences of the war . . . and the destruction of the Dresden bridge.'

Arthur Schopenhauer probably found this lack of political steadfastness attractive rather than the opposite, since, as we know, he regarded the war as a 'murderous carnival', in which taking sides merely meant making oneself ridiculous in, as a rule, a fatal manner.

Schopenhauer took lodgings at Grosse Meissensche Gasse 35, near the 'Black Gate' through which Anselmus in E. T. A. Hoffmann's *Der goldene Topf* (*The Golden Pot*) rushed out into happiness and disaster. Unlike Hoffmann, who had stayed in the city a mere six months before Schopenhauer came, the young philosopher did not by any means throw himself into the social whirl. He was a frequent visitor to the theatre and the opera, and soon became known there as a person who rushed in hurriedly and usually late, often departed before the end of a performance, and did not shrink from loud expressions of disapproval. Being an admirer of modernized Italian opera, especially of Rossini, he was not greatly impressed by the efforts of the new Music Director, Carl Maria von Weber, who favoured German opera – to Schopenhauer's mind, merely ambitiously dressed-up musical comedy.

Totally engrossed in his work, he made no friends in Dresden, but he was fond of surrounding himself with people who admired him or merely respected him as a stimulating, bizarre figure.

While in the thrall of creative élan he found solitude perfectly bearable. But at moments of relaxation he was sometimes tormented by a sense of loneliness. He tried to escape from it, but without losing himself. It is altogether surprising to see the young philosopher worrying about his identity in a social environment. 'Any *communion* with *others*,' he wrote in his manuscript journal in 1814, 'any *conversation* takes place under the condition of mutual limitation, of mutual *self-denial*; hence one must allow oneself to be involved in a conversation only with *resignation*' (P 1, 95).

That 'resignation' which he imposed on himself he defines elsewhere in his journal as the art of retarded participation. If one cannot bear loneliness one should seek company, but in such a way that both, loneliness and company, are united with one another, 'i.e. one should learn to be lonely also in company, not communicate to others everything one thinks, nor take too literally what they say, but instead expect very little of them both morally and intellectually, and remain indifferent to their opinions, so as not to lose one's equanimity. One should therefore, while in their midst, never wholly be in their company: then one will cease to demand much of them. . . . In this manner, by not getting into close touch with people but always preserving "a distant behaviour", one is neither wounded nor defiled by them, and one can bear them. Seen in this light, company may be likened to a fire at which the wise man warms himself from a certain distance, without reaching into it like a fool who first burns himself and then flees into the chill of loneliness, complaining that fire burns' (P 1, 113).

A person approaching social contact with the fear that he might be 'wounded' or 'defiled' in his value does not readily make friends. The fact that he lacked friends did not alarm Schopenhauer. On the contrary, he turned that lack this way and that until it became an advantage: 'Nothing betrays a greater lack of understanding of people than quoting the fact that a person has many friends as evidence of his merits and value, as if people gave away their friendship according to value and merit! As if they were entirely like dogs who love those who stroke them or give them a few crusts without worrying about anything else! He who knows best how to stroke them, even though they are the ugliest beasts, has a lot of friends.'

This lack of friendship, however, could only be regarded as an advantage by Schopenhauer so long as he failed to explore further the realization which he confided to his journal in 1814. As a variation on Plato's theorem that 'like can only be recognized by like' Arthur wrote: '*Any asset needs to be won in its own field*. . . . Friendship, love and loyalty of people are won by friendship, love and loyalty to them. . . . In order to know how much happiness an individual can receive in his life one need only know how much he can give' (P 1, 101).

Was Schopenhauer's proud self-reassurance of 'I have no friends because none is worth my friendship' perhaps only an attempt to ward off the realization that he was winning no friendships because he could not *give* any? 'How much can I give?' – this question would reveal a weakness behind the loner's strength, i.e. his lack of courage to trust others. Eventually Schopenhauer's mistrust became insuperable because it led into a vicious circle of self-confirmation: mistrust creates distance, and distance creates conditions which are bound to give rise to new mistrust. On 5 March 1820 Adele wrote in her diary about her brother: 'One who has never loved cannot trust.'

In Dresden Arthur Schopenhauer acted the part of a largely unloved, generally respected, sometimes admired, often feared eccentric who, it was said, intended to 'overthrow the whole of philosophy'. No one knew what he intended to teach in a positive way, nor did anyone wish to know, seeing that Dresden's philosophical hunger was sated, for the time being, by Schelling's *Weltseele* (*World Soul*). Schopenhauer's dissertation, meanwhile published, was ignored among his acquaintances. No new message was expected from him, but his vociferous acuity in critical disputations was, according to taste, feared or admired. The theatrical entrepreneur and writer Freiherr von Biedenfeld (1788–1862), later to champion the publication of Schopenhauer's principal work with Brockhaus, said of Schopenhauer, whose acquaintance he had made during his Dresden years, that he was 'of most candid honesty', 'outspoken, rough and tough, exceedingly resolute in all scholarly and literary questions, calling a spade a spade to friend and foe alike, much given to jokes, often a downright humorous ruffian; not infrequently his fair head with its flashing blue-grey eyes, the long fold of his cheeks to both sides of his nose, his rather strident voice with the short, fierce gesticulations of his hands presenting a rather grim aspect'.

Schopenhauer, who wanted 'company', but in a manner that would keep him away from company, felt positively attracted to localities where he could satisfy his disputatiousness. The Italian 'Chiappone' tavern with its smoke-stained ceiling from which dangled Venetian salami, truffled sausages and Parma hams was then the meeting place of Dresden's influential literary circle: men from the *Abendzeitung*, fiction writers of national reputation such as Friedrich Laun, Theodor Hell, Friedrich Kind (the librettist of *Freischütz*) and Clauren. The group also called itself *Liederkreis*, and its impressive publication, the *Abendzeitung*, was enjoying growing, and more than regional, popularity among readers interested in traditional education, people who, whether in politics, philosophy or literature, preferred moderation, a cosy evening's fare after work. Sound common sense was here sound in an especially extravagant manner. The first issue of the paper was adorned by a poem by its publisher Theodor Hell: 'When tired from work / I relax in the evening / wishing to enjoy / poetry's blossom, / am fond of reading / our bards' latest books, / as though sitting among flowers, / breathing their perfume.'

Schopenhauer was a frequent guest at the Chiappone because he loved Italian sausage and because he knew that he was feared by the poetical regulars. Invariably he would cross swords with these local matadors and he would always find grateful listeners and spectators who were anxious to vent their own resentment against those masterminds of daily taste. Biedenfeld reports: 'Although a determined opponent of that *Abendzeitung*, almanach and *Liederkranz* activity, and of all the participants whom he always called the literary clique . . . he yet turned up very frequently in the public spots where these men were wont to spend their leisure. As a rule a quarrel would develop, in which he, with his blunt outspokenness, very much acted the unpleasant fellow, often salting their coffee with the most cutting sarcasm, giving uninhibited rein to his critical humour, flinging the worst morsels of Shakespeare and Goethe into people's faces, and all the while, his legs crossed, sitting at their whist table, so that they made one blunder after another. . . . They all feared him, but not one of them ever dared to repay him in like coin.'

Although Schopenhauer was hurling his thunderbolts in that 'bards' circle', he had an almost amicable relationship with one of its members: with Friedrich August Schulze, known by his pseudonym of Friedrich Laun. In later years Schopenhauer still called him his 'good, dear, loyal old Schulze'. It was Schulze who coined the nickname of 'Jupiter tonans' for the young philosopher and it was he who was reputed to have helped Schopenhauer extricate himself from an '*affaire galante*'. No details of this are known.

In December 1816, however, Schopenhauer, in a letter to his boyhood friend Anthime, to whom he was fond of boasting about his amorous successes, informed him of a love affair; on 1 June 1817 Anthime replied: 'You are, as it seems, very much in love, my good friend; in that situation everything seems beautiful. As an old practitioner I confess to you that I am unconvinced that the faithfulness of your belle will be of long duration. Meanwhile make the most of your illusion.' Maybe this was the 'girl in Dresden' of whom Adele Schopenhauer wrote in her diary on 27 April 1819 that she was '*enceinte*'. Adele was appalled, the girl was from the lower classes, there could be no question of marriage. Arthur, however, Adele remarked, was 'meanwhile behaving correctly and well'.

News from Dresden acquaintances about Arthur Schopenhauer was sparse. What was going on inside him, what was budding inside him – of that they discovered little. The painter Ludwig Sigismund Ruhl (1794–1887), who had painted the philosopher as a young man, was allowed to accompany Arthur on his walks and occasionally was admitted even to the holy of holies, his study. 'We were sitting in your room,' Ruhl later recollected, 'you lecturing to me of this and that, of the expectations you had of the success of your philosophy.' Johann Gottlob Quandt (1787–1859), a wealthy man of leisure and an art connoisseur, was perhaps the only person to whom Schopenhauer opened up a little during those years. Quandt had made Johanna's acquaintance in 1815 and had become a friend of Adele. Time and again Schopenhauer found himself reminded by Quandt of his troublesome family quarrel, but whereas in conversation with others he never referred to his mother and sister otherwise than as 'silly geese', to Quandt he not only ranted about family relationships but also hinted at his sorrows and hurts. At least according to Quandt: 'I believe I observed deep down in his heart the throbbing of an enormous pain that seemed to accompany his memory of a terrible epoch in his life. Obscure though his remarks about this may have been, I yet very clearly saw respect, indeed affection for his mother – though he may not himself have fully realized this – shining through everywhere.'

Yet Schopenhauer's social contacts, his public existence, concealed more than they revealed. He lived, according to Biedenfeld, mainly 'with his books and studies . . . almost wholly isolated and rather monotonously'. Behind the barriers of monotony and isolation, however, unrolled the great adventure in Arthur Schopenhauer's life: the 'ecstasy of conception' and the eventual completion of his great work.

Perhaps it was Arthur's landlady who experienced the most striking manifestations of that – at times downright ecstatic – inner life: on one occasion Schopenhauer returned to the house from the orangery at the Zwinger with a flower in his lapel. The landlady: 'Herr Doctor, you are in bloom.' 'Yes,' replied Schopenhauer, 'if the trees did not bloom how should they bear fruit!'

In retrospect Schopenhauer was to describe his four years in Dresden as the most productive of his life: 'When . . . through favourable circumstances the hour arrived when my brain had its highest tension, then, no matter what object my eye fell upon – it spoke revelations to me.' The whole system, he wrote in a letter near the end of his life, had 'as it were, without any action on my part . . . converged radially like a crystal towards a centre, as I immediately laid it down in the first volume of my principal work.' This first volume he was to offer to his publisher on 28 March 1818 with the words: 'My work, therefore, is a new philosophical system: but new in the full sense of the word: not a new presentation of what existed before, but a chain of thought linked to the highest degree, such as has not previously entered any man's head' (CL, 29). The very extensive manuscript journals of those years show traces of how these 'chains of thought' formed in his mind. Here Schopenhauer's thinking can be seen in another aggregate phase: as a searching and existentially engaged mental process, not yet settled or tamed into a constructive system. His work seeks to solve problems; his manuscript journal allows the existential meaning of the problems to emerge. The journal contains the questions enmeshed in human life – the questions to which his work was to provide the answers.

Schopenhauer, as we know, had gone through the Kantian school, where, in a sense, the spirit of his father, from whom he had escaped into philosophy, caught up with him again. In metaphysical matters his father had shared the childlike humility of Matthias Claudius, acknowledging autonomous philosophical excursions to heaven with grunts of discomfort. With his Kant-inspired critique of all philosophical conceptual constructs of the absolute Arthur remained his father's son.

This critical approach also marked Schopenhauer's dispute with the young Schelling, whom he had studied while still in Berlin and to whom he now returned once more. 'Schelling,' Schopenhauer noted, 'does with his absolute what all pious and illuminated theists did with their God – they stated logical impossibilities about him, which were merely a pictorial expression of the absolute statement: intellect is only a faculty conditioned by the sensory world and valid only within it, whereas I (the illuminated theist) stand on a higher level of consciousness' (P II, 326).

Although Schopenhauer concedes that there is such a thing as experience transcending the intellect, he warns against the attempt to give it intellectual legitimation. For in that case one would lose both: the intellect would talk nonsense, and experience would lose its evidential value. Schopenhauer, as we know, termed the experience at variance with the categories of the intellect the 'better consciousness'. This could only be discussed cautiously, not in the manner of the multitude. Schopenhauer's caution sprang from the same attitude as that with which Wittgenstein, at the end of his *Tractatus*, had this to say about what is truly moving: 'What one cannot speak about one has to be silent about.' Arthur Schopenhauer wanted to know exactly where silence began and how far language, perhaps modified language, was still possible. His notes from 1814 to early 1815 revolve around that problem. Schopenhauer was searching for an appropriate language for the 'better consciousness' and did not shrink from metaphorical presentation. He varied the image of the sphere. With our 'cognition according to the theorem of reason', Schopenhauer argued, we keep going round its surface, never reaching its centre. No matter how extensive our knowledge, the surface area never becomes the volume. Only the 'better consciousness' opens up a new dimension: the surface is converted into a space. It is like entering into the sphere. Further meanings may be derived from that image. How does one get from the surface into the depth? Answer: one has to be heavy, heavy with suffering, only then does one overcome the buoyancy of self-assertion which keeps one on the surface. 'For man to acquire noble sentiments . . . for the *better consciousness* to be active within him, pain, suffering and failure are as necessary to him as weighty ballast is to a ship, which attains no draught without it' (P 1, 87). The ship, of course, should not, on the other hand, sink; it should not therefore be too heavy, but just heavy enough to ride sufficiently low not to be overturned by wind or waves. In this metaphor of moderate depth the 'better consciousness' is certainly still linked to self-preservation.

In contrast to the 'better consciousness' its opposite number, 'empirical consciousness', gradually changed its meaning. Schopenhauer, with Kant, had defined empirical consciousness as that consciousness which relates exclusively to an 'appearing' world, to one 'appearing' to that consciousness. To 'empirical consciousness' Being presents itself as being projected. 'Empirical consciousness' is a mode of perception and cognition. To Kant its inevitable root in the 'appearing', the phenomenal, world is by no means a mark of a false existence. Kant, especially in the second edition of his *Critique of Pure Reason*, had insisted that the 'appearing' world should not be understood as a mere 'appearance' in the sense of delusion or deception. We live in a '*natural* and unavoidable *illusion*' which, just because it is 'unthwartable', is part of our basic anthropological equipment and hence fits us functionally into the world we live in. The fact, therefore, that we are dealing merely with an 'appearing' world, is no problem for Kant in practical terms. It is different with Schopenhauer. With him 'empirical consciousness' acquires a double meaning. On the one hand, in good Kantian manner, it means the limitation, demonstrated by transcendental philosophy, of our faculty of perception and cognition; at the same time, however, it means being chained to a life at the mercy of deception, and hence a false life. In that sense Schopenhauer demotes the 'phenomenal' world to an 'appearing' and hence deceiving world. In order to illustrate this he further develops the metaphor of the sphere. 'Empirical' consciousness, he noted in 1814, is 'like a squirrel running in a treadmill'. Whereas 'empirical' consciousness a moment ago was the probing of the surface of a sphere, it is now being equated with the movement of our unquenchable desire which keeps us trapped in pointless and aimless activity. 'Empirical' consciousness, in Schopenhauer's dissertation still purely a cognition-theory subject, has become an ethical problem. Having lost its transcendental-philosophical innocence it becomes existentialist folly: 'People were just as foolish in the theoretical field as we all are continually in the practical, where we hasten from a desire for gratification on to new desire and thus hope finally to find happiness; instead of going into ourselves just once, tearing ourselves free from desire and dwelling in the better consciousness' (P I, 155).

This note of 1814 defines the decisive antithesis: the 'better consciousness' is to be the salvation from 'volition'. That the empirical world is the phenomenon of the 'will' was a realization not yet expressly formulated at the time. The 'will' was not yet the magic formula for the deciphering of the world, but it was already the name for everything hostile, for what opposed a life in truth. Even before Schopenhauer developed his metaphysics of the will, a consequence of that metaphysics, i.e. the 'denial of the will', had already been present as an agent of salvation. Schopenhauer first *experienced* the will as what he suffered from and what he wished to free himself from, and then he *recognized* the will as the 'thing in itself', as that universal reality supposedly underlying all phenomena. As presented in his principal work, Schopenhauer proceeds from the discovery of the will as the essence of the world to its denial; existentially, however, he proceeds from the denial of the will ('better consciousness') to the realization that it is the will which appears in everything real. Thus while Schopenhauer wished, in the name of his 'better consciousness', to break free from this 'will', he discovered in it the unifying point of all being. This movement, which set the hostile element in the centre of the world, which identified the painfully experienced will as the 'thing in itself', marked the birth of Schopenhauer's metaphysics of the will. Some time about the end of 1814 or the beginning of 1815 Schopenhauer noted down in his manuscript journal those sentences from which all else follows: '*The world* as the *thing in itself* is a great will which does not know what it wants; for it does not *know* but merely *wills*, simply because it is a will and nothing else' (P I, 169).

But Schopenhauer did not go through Kant's school for nothing. Kant remained his theoretical conscience, and that reminded him that our faculty of cognition and representation could never grasp an 'in itself' but always only a 'for us'. This meant that the 'will' identified with the 'thing in itself' could certainly not be that projected will recognized as an 'object' – not the 'will' which Arthur had still placed in one of his four categories of conceivable objects in his dissertation.

How could Schopenhauer uphold the Kantian dogma of the unknowability of the 'thing in itself' and at the same time speak of having solved the 'riddle' of the 'thing in itself'? He overcame this difficulty by realizing how the 'will' had shown itself to him as the 'thing in itself': it was not the imagined, discursively recognized will which he identified with the 'thing in itself' but the will perceived in 'internal experience' and felt in his own body.

Everything would depend on Schopenhauer's ability to clarify the nature of the 'inner experience' and to differentiate it clearly from representing, perceiving activity. His notes now revolved around this problem.

The whole world outside me is given to me only as something imagined, as an idea. There is, according to Schopenhauer, only a single point at which I have access to the world other than by imagination (representation). That point is with myself: when I see my body, when I observe and explain its activity, then what I perceive and recognize is still only imagined, but here, on my own body, I also feel those urges, that desire, pain, or pleasure which simultaneously, in activities of my body, present themselves to my imagination and to the imagination of others. Only within myself *am* I that which appears to me (and to others) as imagined and which, simultaneously, one can reflect on. Only in myself is there this dual world, its obverse and reverse, as it were. Only in myself do I experience that which the world *is*, in addition to being presented to me as imagined, as representation. The world 'outside' has for me only an imagined 'inside'; only in myself am I that 'inside' myself. I am the inside of the world. I am what the world is in addition to being representation. 'They went off outwards in all directions instead of going into themselves, where any riddle can be solved' (P 1, 154).

With this realization Schopenhauer fulfilled an old dream: 'Recognize the truth within yourself . . . *there the heaven touches the earth* (P 1, 17), he had jotted down in 1812. This was not a case of 'self-knowledge' in the traditional moral sense, nor one of self-knowledge in the manner of reflective philosophy which, out of the thought of the subject, comes to know the whole of the objective world. Schopenhauer wanted to make the experience of will on his own body the instrument of comprehending the whole of the world. He thereby performed a double movement: a *contractive* one which immerses itself in his own experience (not in his own thought, as in the case of reflective philosophy), and an *expansive* one which interprets the whole of the world according to the model of this internal experience.

However, the problem which Schopenhauer had earlier addressed in connection with the 'better conscience' now re-emerged. How could one, beyond analytical objectivizing thought (along the lines of the principle of reason), speak about this internally experienced will and its identity with the whole of the world? The identity systems of philosophers like Fichte, Schelling and Hegel obviously could offer no help with formulation. After all, they placed the unifying point into the *thinking* subject, not the willing one. Help and inspiration came, much to his own surprise, from the fragmentary reports of a newly discovered spiritual continent: ancient Indian religion.

The discovery of spiritual India had largely been the work of the Romantic movement. Herder had prepared the way. Kant had shown little understanding. He had scoffed at the Tibetans: they carried papistry to extremes, with the believers eating even the excrement of the lamas. Herder, on the other hand, had commended the profundity of Brahminism, interpreting it as pantheism, with the world being seen as a manifestation of a single spiritual reality (the Brahma). The churchman Herder was commending this kind of religiosity without God, without a beyond, without a childlike faith in reward and retribution. To bustling mid-Europeans he recommended the art of contemplation, of meditation. On the other hand, the tranquil meek soul of India had positively enticed its European ravishers. It was not the spiritual attitude for self-preservation.

The Romantics – the Schlegel brothers, Görres, Baader, Windischmann, Novalis – who seized on anything that promised to burst the narrow confines of analytical and dissecting reason were set on their trail by Herder's hints. Meanwhile other source texts had appeared, admittedly in translations which often mutilated their meaning. The most important was probably the translation, published in 1801, of some written transcripts of pre-Buddhist, Brahminic arcane science, the Upanishads. The Frenchman Anquetil published this collection of sources under the title *Oupnekhat* (a corruption of the Sanskrit 'Upanishads'). The texts were doubly corrupted, as this was a Latin translation of a Persian translation from the Sanskrit.

Schopenhauer's attention had been drawn to this book in Weimar, in the winter of 1813–14, where, in his mother's drawing room, he made the acquaintance of the Jena scholar Friedrich Majer, a Herder disciple, who had made a name for himself as an Indologist.

Many years later Schopenhauer still found extravagant words for this book which he first studied in the summer of 1814. In his last work, *Parerga and Paralipomena* (1851), Schopenhauer admitted in retrospect: 'For how thoroughly redolent of the holy spirit of the Vedas is the Oupnekhat! How deeply stirred is he who, by diligent and careful reading, is now conversant with the Persian–Latin rendering of this incomparable book! How imbued is every line with firm, definite and harmonious significance! ... Here everything breathes the air of India and radiates an existence that is original and akin to nature. And oh, how the mind is here cleansed and purified of all Jewish superstition that was early implanted in it, and of all philosophy that slavishly serves this! With the exception of the original text, it is the most profitable and sublime reading that is possible in the world; it has been the consolation of my life and will be that of my dying' (PP II, 396–7).

For two years, from 1815 to 1817, at the Grosse Meissensche Gasse in Dresden, Schopenhauer, the newly-baked Indian enthusiast, had as his neighbour another as yet totally unknown philosopher, Karl Christian Friedrich Krause (1781–1832), who was trying to blend his thought (which deviated from the mainstream of contemporary philosophy) with Indian wisdom. Krause was even more unfortunate than Schopenhauer in that, even at the end of his life, he did not find recognition. However, by some curious roundabout routes his philosophy reached Spain and Spanish Latin America, where the Indian ethics of compassion, watered down to solidarity ethics under the name of 'Crausismo', became the theoretical concept of social-liberal progressivism.

Krause, unlike Schopenhauer, had a command of Sanskrit and made his own translations. Schopenhauer could get expert advice from his Indologist neighbour, borrow books from him, and generally cultivate the acquaintance. He also learned from him details of meditation techniques. Krause himself practised methodically and encouraged his students to attain 'unity of being' by 'inperience, inspirituation'. He was probably the only person in his day who did not merely, like the Romantics, incorporate fragments of Indian philosophy and religion into his own bold speculations, but actually tried to bring Indian tradition to existential practice.

From 1814, therefore, Schopenhauer studied the Upanishads, regularly read articles on India in *Asiatisches Magazin* and got hold of any literature on India he could. However, his intensive concern with Buddhism did not originate until after the completion of his principal work.

With so much veneration for Indian wisdom one would expect Schopenhauer's notes for 1814 to 1818 to show ample indications of his concern with Indian philosophy and religion. In 1816, at any rate, he admitted to his manuscript journal: 'I confess, incidentally, that I do not believe my teachings could ever have come about until the Upanishads, Plato and Kant were able simultaneously to cast their rays into one man's mind' (P 1, 422).

In actual fact only a few notes in the manuscript journals refer directly to Indian religion or philosophy. Yet these few remarks are of exceptional importance because in them certain elements of Indian thought are directly linked up with major points of Schopenhauer's own nascent philosophy.

The birth and decay of the world, the infinite variety of its forms, are called the 'maya' by the Upanishads. Anything experiencing itself as an individual and trying to assert itself in its individuality is governed by 'maya'. In 1814 Schopenhauer commented on this: 'Man . . . is captive to *delusion*, and this *delusion* is as real as life, as the sensory world itself, indeed it is one with it (the maya of the Indians): on it are based all our wishes and desires, which in turn are only the expression of delusion' (P 1, 104). Two years later Arthur remarked laconically: 'The "maya" of the Vedas . . . the "phenomenon" of Kant are one and the same . . .' (P 1, 380).

As for the 'will', which is within us and simultaneously, as the 'thing in itself', behind all phenomena, Schopenhauer believed to have found a correspondence similarly in the Upanishads: the 'Brahma', the world soul. In the Upanishads Arthur read: 'That from which all living creatures are created, that by which, once born, they live, that towards which they die, and that towards which they hasten – that you should seek, for it is Brahma.' Arthur commented on the passage with the words: 'The will to live is the source and the essence of things' (P II, 396).

The world as 'maya' and 'Brahma' – this appeared to Schopenhauer to be the same as that which his own concept called the world as 'representation' and the world as 'will'. Even the Indian salvation pattern – liberation from the series of forms and relapse into 'nothingness' – seemed to conform with what Schopenhauer calls the denial of the will. What he found especially attractive in the Upanishads was the fact that, apart from the mentioned aspects of the world (maya, Brahma), they contain nothing that corresponds to the Western creator-god, to the beyond, to transcendence, etc. Schopenhauer here found a religion without a God, and that seemed to him, seeking as he did a metaphysics without a heaven, to be a confirmation that he was on the right road.

Such confirmation was about all that Arthur Schopenhauer found during the years of developing his philosophical system. He wanted to find a language of his own. He tried hard to develop his philosophy within the horizon of Western philosophical tradition. His aim was to make his two discoveries – the contractive movement of 'inner experience' of the will on one's own body and the expansive interpretation of the world according to the model of that 'inner experience' – instantly obvious to knowledge operating with concepts. His philosophy, he kept pointing out, though not constructed 'of concepts', had formulated its discoveries 'in concepts'. That was why he used elements from Indian philosophy only by way of illustration. Looking back on the period when his system was beginning to take shape, Schopenhauer later wrote: 'I called the thing in itself, the inner essence of the world, by the word for what we are most familiar with: the will. Admittedly this is a subjective term, chosen out of consideration for the subject of knowledge: yet such consideration, as we are communicating knowledge, is essential. It is therefore infinitely better than if I had called it, say, Brahm or Brahma or world soul or whatever.'

Schopenhauer therefore undertook to *understand* the world as 'will'. The emphasis is on 'understanding'. Understanding is not exposition. This was a distinction Schopenhauer had to make abundantly clear. We proceed by way of exposition when we are searching for causes. That is the way our intellect has to operate. Schopenhauer had demonstrated this in his dissertation. 'Exposition' is part of presenting: we connect objects causally with one another. In that way actions of the will may also be 'explained'. That, too, Schopenhauer had demonstrated in his dissertation: the way the will is moved by motivation. Viewed thus, however, will is not the inwardly experienced will but one object among other objects. In 'understanding', on the other hand, it is not a question of connecting the 'object that is the will' causally with other subjects; understanding does not search for cause and effect, for the *why*, but it comprehends the *meaning*, it asks *what* the will actually is. But what the will is we can experience solely and exclusively within ourselves, where we encounter the will not only as an object of our imagination, our representation, but where we experience it 'from within', i.e. where we ourselves *are* the will. We have to understand ourselves if we wish to understand the world. Schopenhauer's metaphysics of the will is by no means an analytical approach to the empirical world, in competition with natural science, but a hermeneutical approach to existence. It does not explain the causal connections of what is but it asks what Being is.

Schopenhauer drafted the outlines of his hermeneutics by way of demarcation from the natural sciences in a note of 1816:

> Hitherto – and this is the correct way of natural science, to proceed from what is known and through it to explain what is less known – the forces of crude matter were presumed to exist. . . . By these it was hoped to explain ultimately the organization and man's cognition and volition, and one would then have the perfect natural science. One was content to proceed from all kinds of '*qualitates occultae*', abandoning any attempt to elucidate them since one only intended to build upon them and not to undermine them, since one only wished to observe what followed from them, without any hope of further information on themselves. . . . From the very beginning I chose the diametrically opposite road. I too intended to proceed from what is best known, just as they do. But instead of, like them, regarding the most common phenomenon and the most imperfect and hence simplest phenomenon as the best known, even though they could see that it was totally unknown to them, I regard as the, to me, most familiar phenomenon in nature that which is closest to my cognition and which, at the same time, is the most perfect, the highest power of all others, and which therefore most clearly and completely enunciates the essence of all of them: and that is *the human body and its activity*; they tried to explain these by the forces of inorganic nature; I, on the other hand, learn to understand these [the forces of inorganic nature] from the former [the human body and its activity]. I do not, in doing so, proceed by the law of causality, which never leads to the essence of things, but I observe directly the essence of the world's most significant phenomenon, man: I find that, disregarding the fact that he is my representation, man is *will* through and through: will remains as the 'in itself' of his essence. Everyone immediately knows what this is, for everyone is it himself. [P I, 365]

Schopenhauer knew that, by this step, he was using the concept of 'will' differently from the way it was generally understood. The concept of will in the philosophical tradition, as well as in common speech, links 'will' with 'intent', 'purpose', 'aim'. I want something. This something I have imagined, thought up, seen, etc. In any case the 'willed' is already in my mind before I even get to the action of volition itself. Understood in this way, the will is intellectualized. But this is not the way Schopenhauer understood the will. He was, in consequence, bound to encounter misunderstandings, and because the public clung to the familiar concept it probably failed to perceive the new aspect that Schopenhauer intended to present with his modified concept, and in consequence took little notice of him at first. Schopenhauer had to struggle against the current of spontaneous associations of the term 'will'. He was going to accept the intellectualized will only as a borderline case. Will could be accompanied by cognition, but that was inessential. Will was a primary, vital striving and movement which, in the borderline case, might become aware of itself and which only then acquired the awareness of an aim, an intention, a purpose. It is enormously important to understand Schopenhauer correctly on this point, because he might otherwise be accused of projecting the intentional will, i.e. the spirit, into nature, in the style of consciousness philosophy. But the reverse is the case: Schopenhauer does not wish to spiritualize nature but to naturalize the spirit.

Schopenhauer suspected the difficulties of comprehension he would encounter. In 1816 he wrote in his journal:

> I have greatly extended the range of the concept 'will'. . . . Will used to be recognized only where it was accompanied by cognition and where, therefore, a motive determined its expression. But I say that any movement, shaping, striving, being, that all these are manifestations, objectivizations, of the will, in that it is the 'in itself' of all things, i.e. that which remains of the world if one disregards the fact that it is our imagination. [P I, 353]

We attain that 'in itself' of the world if we proceed from our own 'in itself', i.e. from the inwardly experienced will: 'Only by comparison with what occurs within me when I perform an action, and how this follows a motivation, can I understand, by analogy, how those dead bodies change in response to causes, and what their inner essence is. . . . I can do this because I myself, because my body, is the only thing of which I also know the other side, which I call the *will*' (P I, 390). And then follows a bold turn: 'Spinoza says that a stone moved by a push would, if it possessed consciousness, believe that it was moving of its own will. I would add that the stone would be correct.'

We are embodied will, which, moreover, is conscious of itself. Only the consciousness, not the 'being a will', distinguishes us from, for instance, a stone.

What further flights of ideas this leads to will be seen in Schopenhauer's principal work. In his notes, for the time being, he was still considering the problem of method.

As a hermeneutical philosopher he had, as we have seen, distanced himself from the analytical approach of the natural sciences, and of empirical science generally. Even more emphatically he distanced himself from philosophical tradition and from his philosophical contemporaries. 'One of the principal mistakes of all *philosophy* to date,' Schopenhauer wrote in 1814, 'one that is connected with the fact that it was being viewed as a *science*, is the fact that *indirect* knowledge, i.e. knowledge from *reasons*, was sought even where *direct* knowledge exists. Thus, e.g. the identity of my body with my will is a case of direct knowledge' (P I, 209).

That directness, that immediacy, was totally different from the directness from which post-Kantian reflective philosophy proceeded. In the first edition of his *Critique of Pure Reason* Kant had uttered the tentative suggestion that 'the something which underlies outward phenomena might possibly . . . be the subject of ideas at the same time.'

Kant had subsequently done everything to prevent the idea, the subject of cognition, from construing the inwardness (the 'thing in itself') of the external world out of itself. Nevertheless, post-Kantian philosophy, suspecting that fear of error was the error itself, had followed the trail of Kant's tentative suggestion. Fichte, and after him Schelling and Hegel, decided 'to derive the smallest as well as the greatest, the structure of the most trivial blade of grass as well as the motion of heavenly bodies, from consciousness and its *a priori* forms' (Fichte). That was the directness of reflective philosophy: it proceeded from the movement of ideas. That movement should be traced. The subject of cognition should watch himself at work, he should, in a manner of speaking, get behind himself. Fichte and Schelling called this 'intellectual viewing'. Intimate acquaintance with the workshop of ideas opens to us the door to the secret of the world. This, too, was a way of seeking a solution to the riddle of the world – something that Schopenhauer likewise was aiming at. But that was not how Schopenhauer understood his way into himself. Instead of proceeding from the subject of cognition he proceeded from the subject of volition, from the other side of reason.

Earlier, in his dissertation, he had unmistakably declared: the subject of recognizing can never recognize itself. For whenever cognition tries to recognize itself, i.e. when it makes itself the object, the recognizing subject must always already be presupposed. After all, we want to *recognize* cognition. Schopenhauer said in his dissertation: 'The imagining ego, the subject of cognition, being, as the necessary correlate of all projection, a condition thereof, can never itself become a representation or an object. *Cognition of cognition is therefore impossible*' (D, 68).

Schopenhauer had asked himself the obvious question of whether, in his cognition theory, he had not after all attempted a cognition of cognition. His answer was that he had not obtained the structures of our perceiving and recognizing faculty through (object-less) self-reflection, but by abstraction from the different types of object cognition, i.e. not by studying the subject of cognition but by studying the possible objects of cognition.

The realization that cognition of cognition only led to barren duplications had enabled Schopenhauer in his Berlin period to escape from the reflective convolutions of Fichte's philosophy. That by doing so he had cleared a road for himself for a new approach to directness, to the immediacy of the body as embodied will – that he only realized later.

Reflective philosophy had placed the 'thing in itself' into thought; Schopenhauer discovered it in the will. The verso of the projected idea was not the mind watching itself at work, but nature: not nature as an external object but nature experienced within us. His departure from reflective philosophy and his turn to 'nature' thus understood had exceedingly far-reaching consequences: Arthur Schopenhauer did not follow the fashionable drift towards the philosophy of history.

Reflective philosophy, deriving the whole of human and natural life from structures of the mind, had increasingly, from Fichte to Hegel, assigned to the historical process the task of letting the mind find itself. History was interpreted as happening truth: a journey of the mind which becomes alienated among the successive shapes of its materializations, only to return to itself on a higher level, through the operation of the concept and the operation of history. The glance into history is hereby interpreted as a element of progression in the emphatically comprehended historical process itself, as an element of self-acquisition. All this is far removed from Schopenhauer: the will which underlies everything is not the mind materializing itself but a blind, rankly growing, aimless, self-lacerating activity, with no clear direction towards anything intended, towards anything meaningful. Reality is shot through not with reason but with such a 'will'. Napoleon, who had caused such destruction in Schopenhauer's beloved Dresden, was a striking example:

> Bonaparte is in fact no worse than many people, not to say most. He simply had the very common *egotism* of seeking his advantage at the cost of others. What distinguishes him is solely his greater strength of satisfying that will. . . . Because that rare strength was given to him he revealed the whole wickedness of human will: and the sufferings of his age, as the necessary reverse of it, revealed the misery which is inseparably tied up with the evil will, whose manifestation as a whole is this world. [P 1, 202]

There can be no fundamental change nor, in consequence, hope. What remains is: breaking free from will, in philosophical contemplation, in art, and ultimately in the 'better consciousness', later to be called the 'denial of the will'. The 'better consciousness' is the red-hot moment in which the will is extinguished. This is no denial in the Hegelian sense, not a contradiction tending towards reconciliation on a higher plane. The mental pattern of 'dialectic' is alien to Schopenhauer; he clings to the irreconcilable 'dualism' between 'better consciousness' and empirical, i.e. will-determined, consciousness. There can be no more mediation between the two 'than we can transfer a summer hour into winter, or preserve a snowflake in a hot room, or carry a piece of a beautiful dream over into reality, any more than the notes of music, when they have died away, leave a trace behind them' (P 1, 79).

The term 'better consciousness' disappeared from his notes as Schopenhauer found the key concepts for his metaphysics of the will.

However, only the term disappeared – not what it had designated. It had designated, as Schopenhauer now realized, only something quantitatively different: it had meant, on the one hand, that inner-world transcendence, that ecstasy which Schopenhauer now, relating it to the metaphysics of the will, called the 'denial of the will'; on the other hand, the term had described the attitude of philosophical contemplation, of wonder, through which the self-evident became questionable. Wonder stands at the beginning of all metaphysics; denial stands at its end.

Thus the 'better consciousness', which drew together wonder and denial, continued to be present in Schopenhauer's work, albeit incognito, from the beginning to the end.

CHAPTER FIFTEEN

THE WORLD AS WILL AND REPRESENTATION

Schopenhauer concluded his 1818 preface to the first edition of his principal work with the sentence: 'And so . . . I dispatch . . . this book, calmly resigned to the fact that it, too, will fully endure the fate which truth has suffered at all times, with only a brief victory celebration between the two prolonged periods when it is condemned as paradoxical and disparaged as trivial.'

Schopenhauer's philosophy was indeed bound to seem paradoxical in an age which surrendered itself to the renewed metaphysics of the absolute, an age for which the circumscribed 'thing in itself' was full of promise – a promise which called for action and which it was thought might be redeemed by self-reflection and the operation of history. Schopenhauer's contemporaries proceeded from transcendental critique to transcendence: at the bottom or at the goal of Being they discern a meaning, something transparent, something pointing to something meant. The 'thing in itself' is trying to say something to us, it has meaning. Philosophy deciphers that meaning; what is new is the admission that this 'meaning' can ultimately only be found within itself. Schopenhauer, likewise proceeding from transcendental philosophy, does not arrive at a transparent transcendence: to him, Being is nothing other than 'blind will', something vital but also opaque, not pointing to anything meant or intended. Its meaning lies in the fact that it has no meaning but merely is. The essence of life is the will to live – admittedly a tautology, as will is nothing other than life; 'will to live' is thus merely a linguistic duplication. The road to the 'thing in itself', which Schopenhauer also follows, ends in darkest and densest immanence: in the will experienced on one's own body – a paradox for all those who hope to think and work their way outward towards the light.

This realization, however, becomes trivial when placed not at the end but at the very beginning of the road; when a materialistically sober biologism defines the will as a force which produces the multiplicity of living forms out of matter; when the formula 'nothing other than', used in an inflationary manner, is used to reduce all forms of life to chemistry, mechanics and physics. This is the obvious, and therefore trivial, immanence of the natural sciences, which, however, has nothing in common with Arthur Schopenhauer's immanence. Schopenhauer's immanence is of the kind that gives an answer to a metaphysical question (What is the 'thing in itself'?); the immanence of the sciences, on the other hand, is one that precludes any metaphysical question from the outset. Schopenhauer's line of thought leads to the point where traditionally the transit to the transcendental occurs with the question: What is hidden behind the phenomenal world? Schopenhauer, too, asks that question. He sets the stage on which normally only God, the absolute, the spirit, etc., have their entrances. But instead of these exalted figures of meaning-assignment it is the 'will', that immanence *tout court* that steps out of the wings. Yet on this stage Schopenhauer's 'will', which consumes the old metaphysics, must play a metaphysical part. After all, it is metaphysical curiosity which produced the play as a whole. Torn out of this play of meaning in an ultimate metaphysics it might of course happen that Schopenhauer's discoveries are considered trivial because they are misunderstood.

Schopenhauer, therefore, picking up the thread of his dissertation, sets out in the manner of transcendental philosophy: The world is my representation, my imagination. The imagining process comprises both poles – subject and object. These are interrelated concepts: no subject without object, no object without subject. With his transcendental-philosophy prelude Schopenhauer has very carefully prepared the transition to the next act. He wishes to show a way out of this enclosed world of transcendental philosophy, he wants to get to the 'thing in itself' – but first of all he wants to block two of the exits most commonly used by contemporary philosophy. There is no way out either through the subject or through the object. Demonstration of this requires, once more, a thorough examination of the subject–object relationship. In this relationship, Schopenhauer points out, there is no logical priority: the subject cannot be explained from the object, nor the object from the subject. In either case the other is always mentally bracketed and presupposed. By discovering myself as a recognizing subject I have objects, and conversely: I only discover myself as a subject in so far as I have objects. The deceptive ways out, therefore, are the mistaken attempts either to derive the world of objects from the subject (such as, in particular, Fichte's subjectivism) or to explain the subject from the world of objects (as in the materialism of Helvetius and Holbach). Subjectivism is dismissed by Schopenhauer in a few polemical words; the boundary line separating his philosophy from materialist objectivism – with which he suspects his metaphysics of the will might be confused – is, by contrast, drawn very painstakingly:

[materialism] regards matter, and with it time and space, as existing absolutely, and passes over the relation to the subject in which alone all this exists. Further, it lays hold of the law of causality as the guiding line on which it tries to progress, taking it to be a self-existing order or arrangement of things . . . and consequently passing over the understanding, in which and for which alone causality is. It tries to find the first and simplest state of matter, and then to develop all the others from it, ascending from mere mechanism to chemistry, to polarity, to the vegetable and the animal kingdoms. Supposing this were successful, the last link of the chain would be animal sensibility, that is to say knowledge; which, in consequence, would then appear as a mere modification of matter, a state of matter produced by causality. Now if we had followed materialism thus far with clear notions, then, having reached its highest point, we should experience a sudden fit of the inextinguishable laughter of the Olympians. As though waking from a dream, we should all at once become aware that its final result, produced so laboriously, namely knowledge, was already presupposed as the indispensable condition at the very first starting-point, at mere matter. With this we imagined that we thought of matter, but in fact we had thought of nothing but the subject that represents matter, the eye that sees it, the hand that feels it, the understanding that knows it: ... suddenly the last link showed itself as the fixed point, the chain as a circle, and the materialist was like Baron von Münchhausen who, when swimming in water on horseback, drew his horse up by his legs, and himself by his upturned pigtail.

In the third edition (1858) Schopenhauer added: 'Accordingly, the funda-mental absurdity of materialism consists in the fact that it starts from the *objective* . . . whereas in truth everything objective is already conditioned as such in manifold ways by the knowing subject with the forms of its knowing, and presupposes these forms; consequently it wholly disappears when the subject is thought away' (WWR I, 27–8).

The only way of escape from that circle (as also from the circle of subjectivism), according to Schopenhauer, is the discovery of a point at which we have the world before us not only as something imagined, as representa-tion, not only in a subject–object relationship. Realization of the circle should lead us 'to seek the inner nature of the world, the thing in itself, no longer in either of those two elements of the representation [subject and object], but rather in something entirely different from the representation' (WWR I, 31).

This way of proceeding from the circle is an argument for philosophical curiosity, and thus presupposes philosophical prudence. However, a very much more elementary experience points the same way, an experience so elementary that, for that very reason, it has so far been overlooked by philosophical reflection. Schopenhauer, as a latecomer with an upper-middle-class background and scarcely acclimatized to the professional philosophical world, was sufficiently self-assured and uninhibited to turn the spotlight on this experience: if the world is indeed my representation, then surely my everyday contact with it teaches me something else – that the world does not only pass before us (the recognizing subjects) as a representation, but that it also excites within us an 'interest', one that 'engages our attention entirely' (WWR I, 95). Philosophical tradition, having placed man's essence in thought and cognition, had been compelled to derive all 'interest' in the world from cognition. For Spinoza, for instance, even the craftsman's work on an article or the sexual act are primarily forms of 'recognizing'. In such an interpretation our natural urges are darkened cognition. The image of man is designed from his head. As a rule, that reflecting head also makes man, on whom it reflects, begin with thought. Schopenhauer disagrees: 'interest' does not spring from cognition, but it precedes cognition and engages us in a totally different dimension from that of cognition alone. 'What is this world of perception besides being my representation?' (WWR I, 18), asks Schopenhauer, and gives the answer we already know: will.

The will is what we are most certain of. 'Will' is the name for the self-experience of our own body. Our own body alone is that reality which we possess not just as representation but which we ourselves are. As, however, I can simultaneously adopt an observing attitude to my own body, that body is presented to me 'in two entirely different ways. It is given in intelligent perception as representation, as an object among objects . . . But it is also given in quite a different way, namely as what is known immediately to everyone, and is denoted by the word *will*' (WWR I, 100). I can 'explain' the activities of my own body, i.e. derive them causally as one object from other objects, according to the principle of reason. But it is only on my own body that I am, and simultaneously feel, that which I can explain in the act of representation. I can transfer myself into the world of objects and yet, simultaneously, I am the 'thing in itself'. Self-experience of my own body is the only point at which I can discover what the world is apart from its being my representation.

Schopenhauer occasionally referred to the (thus described) will by a term used by scholastic philosophy for God as the greatest certainty: he called the 'will' experienced on one's own body the '*realissimum*'. Just as scholastic philosophy derived all other certainties from God, so Schopenhauer operated with his new '*realissimum*'. The certainty that the external world is more than a mere idea is based on, and justified by, my self-experience of my own body. 'If we wish to attribute the greatest known reality to the material world, which immediately exists only in our representation, then we give it reality which our own body has for each of us, for to each of us this is the most real of things' (WWR I, 105).

For this delicate transition, from the greatest reality of the will experienced on one's body to the external world, Schopenhauer uses the method of 'analogy':

The double knowledge which we have of the nature and action of our own body, and which is given in two completely different ways . . . we shall use . . . as a key to the inner being of every phenomenon in nature. We shall judge all objects which are not our own body, and therefore are given to our consciousness not in the double way but only as representations, according to the analogy of this body. We shall therefore assume that as, on the one hand, they are representation, just like our body, and are in this respect homogeneous with it, so on the other hand, if we set aside their existence, as the subject's representation, what still remains over must be, according to its inner nature, the same as what in ourselves we call *will*. For what other kind of existence or reality could we attribute to the rest of the material world? From what source could we take the elements out of which we construct such a world? Besides the will and the representation, there is absolutely nothing known or conceivable for us. [WWR I, 104–5]

That thought is of persuasive simplicity. The conclusion by analogy is based on the assumption that this dual form of existence (*having* an imagined, a represented world and *being* the will) must be attributed also to nature, unless one wants to limit it merely to the aspect facing our imagining faculty and thereby to reduce it to a phantom – a view which, unless one happens to be a hypersceptical philosopher, marks one out, according to Schopenhauer, as a candidate for the 'madhouse'.

The persuasive plausibility of the thought is due to Schopenhauer's consistent adherence to transcendental philosophy, with its thesis that all of the known and perceived world is our imagination, our representation. But as our representation is not everything, that which remains beyond the reach of representation (Kant's 'thing in itself') must be sought where we ourselves, and to start with *only* we ourselves, are something else in addition to being imagining subjects.

From Nietzsche down to our own day (e.g. von Gehlen) it has been suggested that Schopenhauer's philosophy of the will might have saved itself the transcendental-philosophy detour. The fact, however, is that only the road through transcendental philosophy prevents us from inadvertently speaking of the 'will' as of an object among objects. But that is no longer the 'will' meant by Schopenhauer (the will which one is oneself even before imagining it). The road through transcendental philosophy circumscribes (initially only in a negative way) that part of Being which is not absorbed in representation, in being an object, in causality, etc. To Schopenhauer the 'will' resides in this 'Being without being a representation'. Removed from that sphere the will becomes an object of representation among other such objects and therefore, in the causal chain of objects, an explaining link.

Schopenhauer never tired of warning against such misconceptions. Reference to the will, he emphasized, does not explain anything but merely demonstrates what the world is, in addition to our presenting and handling it as a world which needs (scientific) explanation and which is so explicable.

'We are as little permitted to appeal to the objectification of the will, instead of giving a physical explanation, as to appeal to the creative power of God. For physics demands causes, but the will is never a cause. Its relation to the phenomenon is certainly not in accordance with the principle of sufficient reason; but that which in itself is will, exists on the other hand as representation, that is to say, is phenomenon. As such, it follows the laws that constitute the form of the phenomenon' (WWR I, 140).

Schopenhauer's philosophy of the will does not compete in ideas with the explaining natural sciences. That is why I have called Schopenhauer's method of comprehending the world from an inwardly experienced will the hermeneutics of existence. Schopenhauer's posing of questions is thoroughly hermeneutical where he performs the decisive turn from the representation to the will. In the following quotation the hermeneutical terms are emphasized: 'It will be of special interest to us to obtain information about its real significance, that significance, otherwise merely felt, by virtue of which these pictures or images do not march past us strange and meaningless, as they would otherwise invariably do, but speak to us directly, are understood and acquire an interest that engrosses our whole nature' (WWR I, 84).

Unless one takes the hermeneutical element of this question seriously one misses one of the principal points of Schopenhauer's philosophy – that Schopenhauer approaches reality with an attitude of seeking meaning (and not seeking explanation), merely to discover, while reading in the book of life, that the world does not point to anything lying outside itself but only to himself, the questioner: hence complete immanence.

What aspect then does the world acquire from this point of view? Here are a few examples of this intuitive, hermeneutical approach which rediscovers one's own internal essence in the external world:

> Now let us consider attentively and observe the powerful, irresistible impulse with which masses of water rush downwards, the persistence and determination with which the magnet always turns back to the North Pole, the keen desire with which iron flies to the magnet, the vehemence with which the poles of the electric current strive for reunion, and which, like the vehemence of human desires, is increased by obstacles. Let us look at the crystal being rapidly and suddenly formed with such regularity of configuration; it is obvious that this is only a perfectly definite and precisely determined striving in different directions constrained and held firm by coagulation. Let us observe the choice with which bodies repel and attract one another, unite and separate, when set free in the fluid state and released from the bonds of rigidity. Finally, we feel directly and immediately how a burden, which hampers our body by its gravitation towards the earth, incessantly presses and squeezes this body in pursuit of its one tendency. If we observe all this, it will not cost us a great effort of the imagination to

recognize once more our own inner nature, even at so great a distance. It is that which in us pursues its ends by the light of knowledge, but here, in the feeblest of its phenomena, only strives blindly in a dull, one-sided and unalterable manner. Yet, because it is everywhere one and the same – just as the first morning dawn shares the name of sunlight with the rays of the midday sun – it must in either case bear the name of *will*. For this word indicates that which is the being-in-itself of everything in the world, and is the sole kernel of every phenomenon. [WWR I, 117–18]

To regard these metaphors as no more than stylistic ornament would mean utterly to misunderstand this passage; it is in fact the language that adapts itself most precisely to an experience – the experience that the identical will is alive in all existence.

Another example, one referring to organic nature:

The animal is just as much more naïve than man as the plant is more naïve than the animal. In the animal we see the will-to-live more naked, as it were, than in man, where it is clothed in so much knowledge, and, moreover, is so veiled by the capacity for dissimulation that its true nature only comes to light almost by chance and in isolated cases. In the plant it shows itself quite nakedly, but also much more feebly, as mere blind impulse to exist without end and aim. For the plant reveals its whole being at the first glance and with complete innocence. This does not suffer from the fact that it carries its genitals exposed to view on the upper surface, although with all animals these have been allotted to the most concealed place. This innocence on the part of the plant is due to its want of knowledge; guilt is to be found not in willing, but in willing with knowledge. Every plant tells us first of all about its native place, the climate found there, and the nature of the soil from which it has sprung. . . . Moreover, every plant expresses the special will of its species, and says something that cannot be expressed in any other language. [WWR I, 156]

Elsewhere in his work Schopenhauer went a few steps further. In very bold formulations he tried to express what plants might have to 'say' to one engrossed in regarding them: 'Indeed it is remarkable how the plant world in particular invites one to aesthetic contemplation, and, as it were, obtrudes . . . itself thereon. It might be said that such accommodation was connected with the fact that these organic beings themselves, unlike animal bodies, are not immediate objects of knowledge. They therefore need the foreign intelligent individual in order to come from the world of blind willing into the world of the representation. Thus they yearn for this entrance, so to speak, in order to attain at any rate indirectly what directly is denied to them.' Schopenhauer was inclined to leave this 'idea that perhaps borders on the visionary' undecided, but nevertheless, in a later edition of his principal work, quoted a sentence of St Augustine which hints at a similar thought: 'The trees offer to the senses for perception the many different forms by which the structure of this visible world is adorned, so that, because they are unable to *know*, they may appear, as it were, to want to *be known*' (WWR 1, 201).

As Schopenhauer referred to Augustine, so Marcel Proust was later to refer to Schopenhauer as a kindred spirit in the art of silent communication with plants. One might recall the famous passage in *Remembrance of Things Past* where the narrator, engrossed in the contemplation of a whitethorn hedge, has the irresistible feeling that these blossoms have something to 'tell' him. In this gazing and 'listening' the narrator loses his sense of here and now, as well as the consciousness of himself. His grandfather discovers him and brings him back to the everyday world.

Schopenhauer once had the same experience as the narrator in *Remembrance*. To a visitor he recounted the following anecdote from his time in Dresden: 'walking one day in the glasshouse in Dresden and totally engrossed in the physiognomy of the plants' he had asked himself whence these multifarious forms and colours of the plants originated. What were these plants with their curious shapes trying to tell him? He may have spoken aloud to himself, and thereby, as well as by his gesticulation, attracted the attention of the glasshouse attendant. The man had been curious who the strange gentleman was and, on his way out, had questioned him. Schopenhauer thereupon: 'Ah, if you could tell me who I am I should be greatly in your debt.'

These glances into nature, not explaining but understanding, are part of a contemplative attitude. At the same time, however, this kind of approach, as we recall, is supposed to derive from a transfer of analogy of the internal experience of the will to the external world. Will, however, is dark motion, blind urge, unconscious being. Will may be 'accompanied' by knowledge, but knowledge is not part of its substance. If therefore we wish to experience ourselves as the 'subject of willing' – and we must do so if we wish to comprehend within ourselves the core of the phenomenal world – we are yet far removed from self-oblivious, passionless contemplation. With our experienced will as the '*realissimum*' we are supposed to be able, as with a 'magic word', to 'reveal to us the innermost essence of everything in nature' (WWR 1, 111) – but how that will has changed during its analogous transition to the external world! Out there, the will 'speaks' to us everywhere, but we evidently perceive that allocution only in the attitude of contemplation. The experience of our body sets us on the trail of the secret of the world, but we must meanwhile have lost our link with our body, we must, according to Schopenhauer, have wholly become the 'world eye' if we wish to see the universal spectacle of the will. From the urge of the will to the spectacle of the will – a transition that is far from being self-evident. The mental steps with which Schopenhauer walks the tightrope across reveal not only the philosopher's talent for thinking up ideas but also his intimate motivations.

Schopenhauer has in mind an experience in which the division between ego and world would be eliminated: away from representations, into Being. The goal of that wish for ecstasy has since Kant borne the name of 'thing in itself'. Experience of the will on his own body had revealed itself to Schopenhauer as that 'thing in itself' – or rather: not just revealed itself but painfully forced itself upon him. Immediate, direct self-experience of the will enables me to immerse myself in a dimension which lies *below* the '*principium individua-tionis*'. However, the anti-Dionysian Schopenhauer can derive no pleasure from such an underbidding of empirical consciousness, which is always also an individual consciousness. One is at the mercy of one's body's urges, instincts, desires and pains. This is what the 'thing in itself' is like: because one *is* it one cannot *see* it from outside. The eye cannot see itself. It is around this difficulty that Schopenhauer's metaphysics of the will revolves: from where can one *see* the will, the 'thing in itself', without oneself *being* the will? What is needed is a point which, like the will itself, transcends the boundaries of the individual – for one must get out of the individual if one does not wish to get trapped in the thicket of phenomena. Schopenhauer therefore thinks up a cunning move: the subject of volition, as the sub-individual 'thing in itself', can be viewed only by the super-individual, by the pure subject of cognition; 'pure' meaning: detached from will and hence from the empirical interests of the individual. Thus: will-less contemplation of the will. Between the sub-individual and the super-individual a delicate transaction is taking place: the metaphysical charm of the will (its spacelessness, timelessness and ground-lessness) is to move across into the viewing act, but not the substance of that will, its desires, urges or activity. Schopenhauer is juggling with concepts. Everything will depend on whether, instead of producing conceptual phantoms, he succeeds in demonstrating the existence of such contemplation. What matters is not whether such contemplating is conceivable but whether it exists. And in order to know that it exists one would have to have experienced it in oneself. Schopenhauer has experienced it, and he proposes to talk about it in concepts. His whole philosophy talks about it.

This contemplation had been called the 'better consciousness' in Schopen-hauer's manuscripts. A state of trance: lost to space, lost to time, lost to the ego, immersed in contemplating. One is in a state of rest, and the thing contemplated leaves one at rest. This way one can view the world only if one has no self-assertive interests to defend in it, if for a few moments one has freed oneself from pursuing objectives, from considering advantage, and from wishing to dominate. During such moments, according to Schopen-hauer, we are 'delivered from the miserable pressure of the will. We celebrate the Sabbath of the penal servitude of willing, the wheel of Ixion stands still' (WWR 1, 196), for some moments we enjoy the 'blessedness of will-less perception' (WWR 1, 198). Such contemplation is possible for anyone, and it happens to everyone who, through whatever circumstances, momentarily steps out of the treadmill of his daily life, rubs his eyes in astonishment and asks himself what it is all about. That is the moment of metaphysical activity proper. No conceptual work, indeed no work at all, leads to that point, but a slackening, a ceasing, a suspension of activity. Philosophy, Schopenhauer once said, was really nothing else but the translation into concepts of what everyone has always known when he halts in the above manner: 'Philosophy can never do more than interpret and explain what is present and at hand; it can never do more than bring to the distinct, abstract knowledge of the faculty of reason the inner nature of the world which expresses itself intelligibly to everyone in the concrete, that is, as feeling' (WWR I, 271).

Cognition detached from will, such metaphysical activity proper, is nothing but an aesthetic attitude: the transformation of the world into a spectacle which may be watched with disinterested pleasure. Art, or more accurately the attitude which art invites the observer to adopt, is the paradigm of that manner of experiencing reality: 'The pleasure of everything beautiful, the consolation afforded by art, the enthusiasm of the artist which enables him to forget the cares of life . . . all this is due to the fact that . . . the in-itself of life, the will, existence itself, is a constant suffering, and is partly woeful, partly fearful. The same thing, on the other hand, as representation alone, purely contemplated, or repeated through art, free from pain, presents us with a significant spectacle' (WWR I, 267).

A generation later Nietzsche was to proclaim the same idea, admittedly with a gesture of out-trumping all theories before him. His dictum that the world can be justified only aesthetically meant just that: only transformed into an aesthetic phenomenon can the world be tolerated. When Nietzsche, contrary to Schopenhauer, nevertheless called for an arrangement with the will, then he was referring to a will which he had previously transformed into an aesthetic game. Nietzsche's 'Will to Power' 'screws up its eyes': it observes itself from a sufficient distance to enjoy itself.

In Schopenhauer's philosophy, as in no one else's before him, the aesthetic element is accorded the highest philosophical rank. A philosophy which does not explain the world but offers information on what the world actually is and means, such a philosophy, according to Schopenhauer, derives from an aesthetic experience of the world. In his manuscript journals Schopenhauer expressed this even more clearly than in his principal work. 'Philosophy,' he observed in a note of 1814, 'has so long been sought in vain because it was sought by way of the sciences instead of by way of the arts' (P I, 154).

The reason why the philosophical viewing of the world is aesthetic is that it is detached from will. This will-lessness of viewing not only transforms the object viewed into a spectacle but also brings out what Schopenhauer terms the pure 'objectification of the will' or the 'idea'. The 'idea' here is not a thing of thought; ideas are shapes of the visual world seen from the perspective of contemplation.

Whilst science, following the restless and unstable stream of the fourfold forms of reasons or grounds and consequents, is with every end it attains again and again directed farther, and can never find an ultimate goal or complete satisfaction, any more than by running we can reach the point where the clouds touch the horizon; art, on the contrary, is everywhere at its goal. For it plucks the object of its contemplation from the stream of the world's course, and holds it isolated before it. This particular thing, which in that stream was an infinitesimal part, becomes for art a representation of the whole, an equivalent of the infinitely many in space and time. It therefore pauses at this particular thing; it stops the wheel of time; for it the relations vanish; its object is only the essential, the Idea. We can therefore define it accurately as *the way of considering things independently of the principle of sufficient reason,* in contrast to the way of considering them which proceeds in exact accordance with this principle, and is the way of science and experience. This latter method of consideration can be compared to an endless line running horizontally, and the former to a vertical line cutting the horizontal at any point. The method of consideration that follows the principle of sufficient reason is the rational method, and it alone is valid and useful in practical life and in science. The method of consideration that looks away from the content of this principle is the method of genius, which is valid and useful in art alone ... The first is like the mighty storm, rushing along without beginning or aim, bending, agitating, and carrying everything away with it; the second is like the silent sunbeam, cutting through the path of the storm, and quite unmoved by it. The first is like the innumerable violently agitated drops of the waterfall, constantly changing and never for a moment at rest; the second is like the rainbow silently resting on this raging torrent. [WWR I, 185]

All this is said about art, but it applies equally, without reservation, to philosophy as Schopenhauer understands it. Philosophy merely 'translates' such viewing into another language, the language of concepts. That is why Schopenhauer eventually describes philosophy as intermediate between art and science: with the aesthetic it shares the mode of experience, and with science it shares its concepts; it has not, therefore, won its truth from concepts but has merely 'laid it down in concepts'. This view divides Schopenhauer from Hegel and from an entire philosophical tradition before and after him. There, concepts occupy the top rank; with Schopenhauer it is viewing, contemplation, that holds it. With the others, art – no matter how flatteringly approached – is ultimately only an imprecise expression of truth. For Schopenhauer it is the other way about: concepts are an imprecise expression of truth; art is nearer to truth. That is why Schopenhauer was later able to act as *the* artist's philosopher, for Richard Wagner, Thomas Mann, Marcel Proust, Franz Kafka, Samuel Beckett, and through to Wolfgang Hildesheimer.

Art and philosophy both owe their existence to the ability 'to remain in a state of pure perception, to lose oneself in perception, to remove from the service of the will the knowledge which originally existed only for this service. In other words, genius is the ability to leave entirely out of sight our own interest, our willing, and our aims, and consequently to discard entirely our own personality for a time, in order to remain *pure knowing subject*, the clear eye of the world' (WWR I, 185–6).

For Schopenhauer, therefore, the happiness of knowledge is linked to opting out from the task of coping with practical life, from history, and from the intrigues of sensuality. In an earlier age this was called the *vita contemplativa*, a lifestyle with a respectable tradition: retreat as a chance of finding the truth.

Though unengaged truth formerly enjoyed a high prestige, its standing had greatly diminished at the beginning of the nineteenth century. This was inevitable in an age for which politics had become its destiny, an age which began to believe that history and hence also happiness could be 'made'. The spirit of making had penetrated also into metaphysics.

Kant had placed the 'disinterested pleasure' of art between theoretical and practical reason: in art one might warm up for the higher tasks presented by practical reason. The categorical imperative had startled the sensually inactive as well as the contemplatively reclusive.

The Romantic philosophy of art, on the other hand, placed art at the peak of human spiritual endeavour. It was not to be swallowed up by 'any common purpose or use' (Wackenroder); to this extent it was to remain 'disinterested'. However, it was also given an activist trait: the artist was a microcosmic architect of worlds. In his dreams reality was dreaming. Artistic productivity served as the paradigm of what was later to be called an 'unalienated' life. The imaginary element of the Romantic movement was not only a sphere of salvation and a dream of salvation but also an experimental set-up for successful action. To the Romantics Being was *poiesis*. Romanticism was not a defection from the world of action; it saw itself as an avant-garde project of activist self-realization.

Never before had metaphysics been as enterprising as at the beginning of that century. Reflective philosophy emanating from Kant was a practical philosophy. Kant himself had seen his elaborate transcendental philosophy as a contemporary basis for practical ethics. Even so, to his successors he seemed too timid. To them 'is' and 'ought to' were confronting each other too brusquely. The dualism between 'is' and 'ought to' would have to be conceptually eliminated. The eliminated dualism became a magic formula: 'dialectics'. Being would not only be *ought to*, but 'ought to' would be *being*. Being henceforward was an activity of the ego (Fichte) or of the spiritualized natural subject (Schelling) or of the world spirit (Hegel). All these were scenarios in which the hard-working Being, by dint of its own dynamism (dialectics), was actually moving towards what Kant's imperative had only called for. A reconciled and therefore happy human community was no longer just a regulative idea, something that practical morality was asked to implement, but an immanent perspective of historical development. It was simply on the agenda. Heaven had awakened earth with its kiss and the earth had begun to work. The philosophy of history was henceforth to keep the Protestant work ethic in its holy of holies.

From Schopenhauer's concept of the will, however, the working spirit has been expelled. The will has no aim, it roams as a blind urge. It justifies no hopes. The project of historical reason cannot be entrusted to it. The will keeps one busy, but with slavish work. No future happiness is being fashioned in the workshop of the will; it is better therefore to escape somewhere where one may be inactive. From such a point the spectacle of the will can even be enjoyable. Schopenhauer's 'will' is conceived as much more active than all the spirit subjects from Fichte to Hegel. But its activism is pain without a future, without a promise. Against this background the *vita contemplativa* is bound to acquire quite a different standing from the one it had for the philosophers thirsty for action.

At about the time that Schopenhauer was writing his principal work Hegel began his first Berlin lecture with a reflection on double truth: the truth of 'weekday' and the truth of 'Sunday'. The weekday possessed the 'interest of need': here the problem was coping with practical life, and here one had to tolerate the question: 'What use to me is this knowledge?' On Sunday, however, it is not just the Creator who rests from his labours. It is a day of contemplation. One may look at what one has achieved. The philosophy of Sunday is what tradition terms *philosophia perennis*. Here one does not *have* useful truths but one stands *in* truth. Not use but the happiness of knowledge is the hallmark of Sunday philosophy. In downright ecstatic work Hegel spoke of this dominically self-sufficient theory of Being, which gazes on the hardships of the weekdays from which it has escaped. But Hegel never forgets for a moment that this theoretical pleasure is the 'need' of those who have satisfied their other needs. In this sense he speaks of *philosophia perennis* as a 'need for needlessness'.

'It is a fact,' Hegel said in his Berlin lecture, 'that the need to concern oneself with pure ideas presupposes a long road which the human spirit must have traversed; it is, in a manner of speaking, the need of an already satisfied need of necessity, of needlessness, at which the human spirit must have arrived, of abstraction from matter . . . from the concrete interests of desire, or urges, of the will'. Hegel, who unlike Schopenhauer was not fortunate enough to be relieved of material worries by inherited wealth, and who therefore had to live not only for philosophy but also by it, attempted to bring Sunday and weekday together in his thought. His philosophy of history is a philosophy of the whole week. His consolation is that the weekdays of history, since man is the 'fashioner of his happiness', will tend towards an historical Sunday. On that historical Sunday the spirit will have completed its 'work of transformation', it will have arrived at itself and therefore be free to enjoy itself. (With Marx, as we know, it will go fishing and hunting in the morning, etc.) Meanwhile, however, the world spirit was still 'working', and only in Hegel's mind had it already attained dominical domestic bliss – a circumstance luckily coinciding with Hegel's recent appointment to a highly endowed professorship of philosophy.

To Hegel the working of history was a happening of truth. One forfeited all hope of truth if one opted out as an individual, if one prematurely observed one's own private Sunday. To him it was clear that one had to join in the historical working of the world spirit; beyond that there were only the empty shells of 'supposed profundity'.

After Hegel the working world spirit, as is generally known, assumed ever more solid shape.

Feuerbach saw it in operation in the very practical 'fire and life insurance', and David Friedrich Strauss observed it on a train journey. 'Massive impression of this modern miracle,' he wrote, 'dreamy consciousness during such magical flight. No fear whatever, but a sense of most intimate relationship of one's own principle with such inventions.' To Marx, finally, industry was the 'open book of human essential forces'. But even the activists occasionally experienced misgivings. Strauss wrote in a letter:

> Let us not deceive ourselves, the modern age which has dawned cannot, initially, be joyful for us. The element in which we most liked moving in the past is coming to an end. This is what the creatures of the land and the air must have felt when in Noah's day the waters burst in. For our element, surely, was . . . the theory, I mean the free intellectual activity not aimed at purpose or need. This is now scarcely possible any more, and soon it will even be proscribed.

CHAPTER SIXTEEN

THE GREAT NO

'Free intellectual activity not aimed at purpose or need' (D. F. Strauss) is indeed the 'element' of Schopenhauer's philosophy. Such a synoptic view, such looking at and over the whole of the world and of life, requires a right place and a right time. His experience of the mountains had first provided young Arthur with such an occasion. In his principal work Schopenhauer described the mountain peak of philosophy in these words:

> When, however, an external cause or inward disposition suddenly raises us out of the endless stream of willing, and snatches knowledge from the thraldom of the will, the attention . . . comprehends . . . things . . . without interest . . . entirely given up to them . . . : then all at once the peace, always sought but always escaping us on that first path of willing, comes to us of its own accord, and all is well with us. It is the painless state, prized by Epicurus as the highest good and as the state of the gods; for that moment we are delivered from the miserable pressure of the will. We celebrate the Sabbath of the penal servitude of willing; the wheel of Ixion stands still. [WWR I, 196]

The person thus freed from the 'miserable pressure of the will' is free now to watch the spectacle of the will. The lead actor in this spectacle is the human body. Schopenhauer's philosophy of the body sweeps aside the traditional dualism of body and soul and, in doing so, undertakes something until then unheard of: the body, as embodied will, becomes the fundamental principle of a whole system of metaphysics. 'Every true act of his will is also at once and inevitably a movement of his body. . . . The act of will and the action of the body . . . are one and the same thing, though given in two entirely different ways, first quite directly, and then in perception for the understanding' (WWR I, 100).

The traditional concept of the body–soul dualism had, of course, been based on the belief that the action of the will and that of the body were not one and the same. Ever since Plato 'will' had been defined as a mental-spiritual impulse which governed the body. To Plato cognition was the achievement of disembodied sovereignty. Such cognition had command over the body and became a source of 'pure' will. That will would break the power of the body, which was a power of death, of non-being. Plato called the body a 'tomb'. Western tradition is rich in magnificent attempts at 'thinking the body away'. To do this a mental-spiritual command centre had to be discovered, whose commands the body would obey. Such reasoning is hardly surprising in an age which was at the mercy of the body's fate, with no protection from it. An age without intensive-care units, health insurance or immunization had to protect itself, at least in its imagination, against the attacks of the body. The assertion of the intellect's supremacy was made proudly, but in fact it was a defensive move. The mainspring of this idealism was not, as is often suggested nowadays, hostility to pleasure but fear of death, fear of pain, sickness, epidemics, debility. One was captive to the body because one loved life. The idealistic visionaries of potency attempted to gain power over a body which was regarded as the gate through which death burst in. 'War and insurrections and fighting are caused by nothing other than the body and its desires,' wrote Plato. To St Paul the 'flesh' was subject to the 'law of death'. His longing for salvation, however, was not therefore hostile to the body: to those who walked in Christ's spirit he promised a 'new body'.

There had, of course, always been the Cynics' protest against a spiritualism trying to rid itself of the power of the body. This argued, as a rule, that one felt at home in one's body and could make oneself comfortable in it. But Cynicism, too, was subject to the law of ageing, and as the ills of the body increased so did the need for a sovereignty detached from the body. The body-affirming Renaissance was largely a youth culture.

Noisy endorsement of the body has always adopted a polemical posture and, to that extent, has been a critical complement to the history of idealism. The upside-down laughter-culture of the carnival, whose time-limited outburst calls for a festive liberation of the body, is probably the clearest illustration of this. No one, however, had seriously conceived the idea of seeking salvation and grace in consonance with the body. That has been reserved for our own century, more especially for the most recent decade. A whole generation, searching history for salvation-promising subjects on which to pin its messianic hopes, replaced the (by then dismissed) 'proletariat' with the human body. As earlier with the proletariat, so one should now join up and ally oneself with the body. Histories are being written of the golden age of the body and of its possibly golden future; solidarity with the enslaved body is being preached. A class struggle is being discovered between head and belly. The body has become a carrier of secrets, which, provided one listens attentively, will disclose everything that matters. Its murmured oracles are now listened to and the health-insurance-protected body has been sur-rounded by a whole culture of interpretation. 'Sensing' is now the royal road to truth. The body is the latest metamorphosis in the career of the 'thing in itself'. And, as always, *this* 'thing in itself' is also full of promise.

The reason why Schopenhauer, in his day, was so vigorously moving the body into the centre of his metaphysics was not that he wished to confront the idealist beyond of the soul with a new earthly religion, with a religion of the body, but that he wished to sweep away the illusion that one could escape the superiority of the body. Schopenhauer was far from loving that which dominates everyone, his own body. He did not wish to replace the shattered illusion of salvation by way of the soul with the illusion of salvation by way of the body.

Schopenhauer brushed aside the entire traditional concept of a (soul-spirit) will by differentiating between action of the will and merely intellectual will-intention. 'Resolutions of the will relating to the future are mere deliberations of reason about what will be willed at some time, not real acts of will' (WWR I, 100). Whether a will-intention adopted by reason is actually implemented depends not on the force of reason but on whether this intention stimulates my will as it manifests itself in the totality of my bodily existence. Reason supplies motivations to the will, but how the will reacts to these motivations lies outside the power of reason. The decision is not made prior to the action, in the sense of a causal link between decision and action, but the decision coincides with the action itself. This is preceded by the intention to decide in a certain way. The decision, however, exists only in, and through, the action. 'Only the execution seals the decision,' Schopenhauer declares. Who I am – that I cannot discover from my intentions but only from the realized (and this means always also the embodied) pattern of my life. There is no escape into a spiritual background world which might lend some 'deeper' meaning to my practical life or even give it absolution. The actions of my life are the open book of my identity. What I am I have willed. The will within me is not something that I could 'make'; the will which I am is happening. Schopenhauer argued against the traditional theory of the freedom of the will:

> Freedom of the will therefore consists in man's being his own work in the light of knowledge. I, on the other hand, say that he is his own work prior to all knowledge, and knowledge is merely added to illuminate it. Therefore he cannot decide to be this or that; also he cannot become another person, but he *is* once for all, and subsequently knows *what* he is. With those other thinkers, he *wills* what he knows; with me he *knows* what he wills. [WWR 1, 293]

For Schopenhauer the head, too, is strictly a part of the body. But the thinking of the head is ultimately also just an action of the will. Yet the will which we all are manifests itself with varying strength and perceptibility in our bodies. Even the vegetative life of our bodies is will, whether we notice it or not; as a rule we only notice it when some function is disturbed, as in pain, discomfort, etc. For Schopenhauer man's faculty of cognition does not sever him from the happenings of the will in his own body; indeed he defines cognition as an organ of the will, through which other shortcomings of bodily equipment are compensated. With regard to man's position *vis-à-vis* the rest of nature Schopenhauer writes: 'The will, which hitherto [in non-human nature] followed its tendency in the dark with extreme certainty and infallibility, has at this [human] stage kindled a light for itself' (WWR I, 150). This was necessary to ensure that the 'complicated, many-sided, flexible being, man, who is extremely needy and exposed to innumerable shocks' (WWR I, 151) should be able to exist at all. In our recognizing faculty therefore we remain largely tied to the will: 'Thus knowledge in general, rational knowledge as well as mere knowledge from perception . . . destined originally to serve the will for the achievement of its aims, knowledge remains almost throughout entirely subordinate to its service' (WWR I, 152).

'Against the mighty voice of nature,' Schopenhauer wrote, 'reflection can do little' (WWR I, 281). Schopenhauer gives free rein to his not inconsiderable satirical talent to describe the humiliation of the spirit whenever it clashes with the activity of the body. The most powerful voice of nature, and hence the most suitable occasion for the discomfiture of the spirit is – how could it be otherwise? – sex. Schopenhauer calls the genitals the 'real *focus* of the will' (WWR I, 330). Nature, ruthlessly pursuing its purpose of propagation of the species, usually presents itself to our consciousness and perceptions as the emotion of being in love. Our genitals seek each other, and our souls believe they have found each other. Human beings see themselves as individuals, and that is why they have to be trapped into serving the purpose of their species. This is achieved by the pleasure of the body and the enamoured state of the soul. A pleasurable crossing of the boundaries of individuality takes place. Post-coital depression is often the sobering return from such intermingling. Their purpose achieved, there is no further need for the actors. In the animal kingdom, Schopenhauer argued, nature operates even more 'naively': there the male is sometimes killed after mating, or even kills himself. In the human world, myths connect love and death; the everyday manifestation of this bond, however, is more often the 'plague of domesticity'. 'Nature . . . with all her force impels both man and the animal to propagate. After this she has attained her end with the individual, and is quite indifferent to its destruction; for, as the will-to-live, she is concerned only with the preservation of the species; the individual is nothing to her' (WWR I, 329–30).

That 'knowledge is in the service of the will' is true therefore in particular of sexuality, whose super-individual power keeps the individual on a string. Because that is where the 'focus of the will' is situated, Schopenhauer is ready to discover the secret sexual urges even in remote spheres of life, where one would not suspect their existence. Such 'psychological' observations – groundwork for Freud and Nietzsche – are found in large number in the second volume of his principal work and in his *Parerga*. In the first volume, where the outlines of his entire philosophy are drawn in one great sweep, Schopenhauer does not yet take the time he needs, nor has he yet accumulated the necessary material, to conduct such researches in detail. Sexuality, however, is of central importance, even though initially, in his first volume, he devotes only a few pages to it. Sex, as he experiences it, becomes for him the model of a painfully perceived will generally. This is what lends Schopenhauer's judgements on the will their emotional undertones. An example: Schopenhauer has only just spoken of the stones and their weight which inexorably draws them towards a centre, and immediately, at the cue 'unending striving', he finds a switching point to the unending business of procreation: 'Such also is the life course of the animal; procreation is its highest point, and after this has been attained, the life of the first individual quickly or slowly fades, while a new life guarantees to nature the maintenance of the species, and repeats the same phenomenon' (WWR 1, 164). The procreative process is indifferent to the fate of the individual living creature. The human being, however, experiencing itself as an individual, is unfortunate enough to be aware of that indifference of nature towards him. He discovers this most clearly in sexuality, which promptly throws him back to the animal kingdom. During mating he becomes a creature of his species. This affront 'from below' was hard to bear for Schopenhauer, who otherwise, admittedly 'from above', from the 'better consciousness', was fond of deriding any anxious clinging to the principle of individuation. Let us recall what he had written in his more intimate notes: 'Picture the most beautiful, the most charming couple.... Now look at them at the moment of enjoyment of their lust – all playfulness, all that gentle gracefulness is suddenly gone, all of a sudden vanished at the beginning of the "actus", giving way to deep seriousness. What seriousness is that? The seriousness of the animalic' (P 1, 42). At this 'seriousness' the fun stops for Schopenhauer – the fun of eroticism and the fun of a contemporary natural philosophy with its quasi-erotic perception of nature. In his manuscript journal he calls the natural philosophers – meaning Schelling, Steffens, Troxler and others – 'a special class of fools' who have no actual knowledge of what they are talking about. They have made nature their platonic mistress: all they are capable of is raving about nature in her unrisky presence. 'But just try for once to be wholly nature: the thought is terrible: you cannot find mental rest unless you are prepared, if necessary, to destroy yourself and, thereby, to destroy all nature for yourself' (P 1, 27). This horror Schopenhauer subsequently perpetuated in his principal work in a magnificent image:

> Just as the boatman sits in his small boat, trusting his frail craft in a stormy sea that is boundless in every direction, rising and falling with the howling, mountainous waves, so in the midst of a world full of suffering and misery the individual man calmly sits, supported by and trusting the *principium individuationis*.... The boundless world, everywhere full of suffering in the infinite past, in the infinite future, is strange to him, is indeed a fiction. His vanishing person, his extension-

less present, his momentary gratification, these alone have reality for him. . . . Till then, there lives only in the innermost depths of his consciousness the wholly obscure presentiment that all this is indeed not really so strange to him, but has a connection with him from which the *principium individuationis* cannot protect him. From this presentiment arises that ineradicable *dread* common to all human beings . . . which suddenly seizes them, when by any chance they become puzzled over the *principium individuationis*. [WWR I, 353]

What to Schopenhauer is a 'dread' is a delight to Romantic natural philosophy, to which Schopenhauer is often presented as standing close. Novalis, for instance, uses the same image of the sea, but what Freud was to call the 'oceanic sensation' of self-dissolution is to Novalis something alluring:

Whose heart would not leap with joy when the innermost life of nature in its full richness comes into his mind! When that powerful sensation, for which language has no other name than love and ecstasy, spreads within him . . . as, trembling in sweet fear, he sinks into the dark tempting womb of nature, when humble personality consumes itself in the tumbling waves of pleasure and when nothing is left but a focus of immeasurable procreative vigour, an all-engulfing vortex in the great ocean.

For Novalis, as for Schopenhauer, the individual becomes a 'humble personality' under the impact of the super-individual forces of nature. The Romantic spirit experiments with the ecstasy of self-surrender ('and I will not practise caution . . .' – Eichendorff). Schopenhauer had criticized these gatecrashers of Dionysus for lacking the strength for an illusionless look at that tempting element of self-dissolution. For in pursuit of our inner nature we do not reach any sheltering 'realms of our mothers' (Goethe). We experience no pacification but upheaval. 'Yet our earth presses closely against us, its life and working has an inner kinship with us,' wrote the Romantic Steffens. No, said Schopenhauer; we cannot be friends with an earth that is not interested in us at all, which by our death merely preserves the life of our species. We may be nature through and through – to this extent he agrees with the Romantics – but for that very reason we are at the mercy of its mercilessness, its jungle-like struggles, its discords.

Thus everywhere in nature we see contest, struggle and the fluctuation of victory, and later on we shall recognize in this more distinctly that variance with itself essential to the will. . . . This universal conflict is to be seen most clearly in the animal kingdom. Animals have the vegetable kingdom for their nourishment, and within the animal kingdom again every animal is the prey and food of some other . . . since every animal can maintain its own existence only by the incessant elimination of another's. Thus the will-to-live generally feasts on itself, and is in different forms its own nourishment, till finally the human race, because it subdues all the others, regards nature as manufactured for its own use. Yet . . . this same human race reveals in itself with terrible clearness that conflict, that variance of the will with itself, and we get *homo homini lupus* [man a wolf to man]. [WWR I, 146–7]

The will-dominated individual cannot be anything but egotistical, and society therefore – entirely in the spirit of Hobbes, who likewise made *homo homini lupus* the anthropological foundation of his political theory – is a latent state of war among egotisms. With a surprising, though in itself plausible, move Schopenhauer links the concept of individual egotism to his basic transcendental-philosophical reflections: although everything is 'in itself' will, the individual (in whom the subject of volition and the subject of cognition coincide) sees the will in everything outside himself only as an 'idea'; solely in himself does he experience the will also as an inner reality. In other words: that which underlies all phenomena, the will, 'i.e. what is actually real, it finds immediately only in its inner self' (WWR I, 332). It follows therefore, according to Schopenhauer:

that every individual, completely vanishing and reduced to nothing in a boundless world, nevertheless makes himself the centre of the world, and considers his own existence and well-being before everything else. In fact, from the natural standpoint, he is ready for this to sacrifice everything else; he is ready to annihilate the world, in order to maintain his own self, that drop in the ocean, a little longer. This disposition is *egoism*, which is essential to everything in nature. But it is precisely through egoism that the will's inner conflict with itself attains to such fearful revelation. . . . Therefore, whereas each individual is immediately given to himself as the whole will and the entire representer, all others are given to him in the first instance only as his representations. Hence for him his own inner being and its preservation come before all others taken together. Everyone looks on his own death as the end of the world, whereas he hears about the death of his acquaintances as a matter of comparative indifference. . . . In the consciousness that has reached the highest degree, that is, human consciousness, egoism, like knowledge, pain and pleasure, must also have reached the highest degree, and the conflict of individuals conditioned by it must appear in the most terrible form. Indeed, we see this everywhere before our eyes, in small things as in great. At one time we see it from its dreadful side in the lives of great tyrants and evildoers, and in world-devastating wars. On another occasion we see its ludicrous side. . . . But it appears most distinctly as soon as any mob is released from all law and order; we then see at once in the most distinct form the *bellum omnium contra omnes* [the war of all against all] which Hobbes . . . admirably described. [WWR I, 332–3]

Against this background Schopenhauer now developed his theory of the state, which in fact followed Hobbes: the state fits 'muzzles' on the 'beasts of prey', and although this does not make them any better morally, it renders them 'as harmless as a grass-eating animal' (WWR I, 346). The state is an altogether defensive institution of compulsion. Everybody wants to commit wrongs, nobody wants to suffer wrongs. As Schopenhauer's basic anthropological category is not morality but the will, there is for him, primarily, no such thing as a sense of justice but only the pain of suffering an injustice. This pain consists of an infringement, an injury, a violation of the individual's own sphere of will. The individual, himself ready at any time to infringe the spheres of will of others, must, at the same time, be interested in having his own sphere of will protected against such infringements. He must therefore be deterred from committing such infringements himself; this deterrence simultaneously protects him against the infringements of his own sphere by others.

Schopenhauer explicitly contradicts all theories, developed by Kant's successors, which expect the state to accomplish a moral improvement of man (Schiller, Hegel) or which regard the state as a kind of higher human organism (Novalis, Schleiermacher, etc.). The state, according to Schopenhauer, protects the individual against himself; it cannot improve him. The state is a social machine which, at best, couples collective egotism with a collective interest in survival.

> The state is so little directed against egoism in general and as such, that, on the contrary, it is precisely from egoism that it has sprung, and it exists merely to serve it. This egoism well understands itself, proceeds methodically, and goes from the one-sided to the universal point of view, and thus by summation is the common egoism of all. The state is set up on the correct assumption that pure morality, i.e. right conduct from moral grounds, is not to be expected; otherwise it itself would be superfluous. Thus the state, aiming at well-being, is by no means directed against egoism, but only against the injurious consequences of egoism arising out of the plurality of egoistic individuals, reciprocally affecting them, and disturbing their well-being. [WWR I, 345]

To this end Schopenhauer calls for a state equipped with strong instruments of power; however, it should remain a power of the external world. Just because he does not concede to the state any moral competence, he denies the state any business in the inner world of its citizens or any right to give orders there:

> will and disposition, merely as such, do not concern the state at all; the *deed* alone does so. . . . Thus for the state the deed, the occurrence, is the only real thing; the disposition, the intention, is investigated only in so far as from it the significance of the deed becomes known. Therefore,

the state will not forbid anyone constantly carrying about in his head the thought of murder and poison against another, so long as it knows for certain that the fear of sword and wheel will always restrain the effects of that willing. The state also has by no means to eradicate the foolish plan, the inclination to wrongdoing, the evil disposition, but only to place beside every possible motive for committing a wrong a more powerful motive for leaving it undone, in the inescapable punishment. [WWR 1, 344]

Schopenhauer wants a functioning state machine – not, like the Romantics, a state as an institution for meaningful life. Schopenhauer's teacher Schleiermacher had written: 'Whoever regards man's most beautiful artifact [the state] . . . as no more than a necessary evil . . . is bound to perceive as a restraint what is designed to provide for him the highest degree of life.' To Schopenhauer the state is in fact a 'necessary evil'.

Entirely in line with Hölderlin's warning, 'What has made the state a hell is that one wanted to make it a heaven', Schopenhauer does not want a state with a soul, one that might then wish to reach out for the souls of its citizens. Uncompromisingly he defends freedom of thought. The criterion of state-supporting thought is ruled out. Schopenhauer therefore poured scorn on Hegel, whom he accused of having manufactured his whole philosophy from the slogans and directives of the Prussian State Ministry.

In connection with his theory of the state Schopenhauer also developed some very bold theses on the subject of property. In what respect and to what extent, Schopenhauer asks, should the state protect property? Translated into his terminology the question reads: To what extent does an individual's property belong to his sphere of will? Schopenhauer, consistently proceeding from the plane of the body-linked will, replies: 'For *property*, that is not taken from a person *without wrong*, can, in view of our explanation of wrong, be only what is made by his own powers. Therefore by taking this, we take the powers of his body from the will objectified in it, in order to make them serve the will objectified in another body' (WWR 1, 335).

In short: property deserving to be protected in the same way as the inviolability of the body exists only as the 'fruit of labour'. The 'moral right of property' is based 'simply and solely on elaboration' (WWR 1, 336). Hence property accumulated without such work would be theft.

Schopenhauer, still living on his father's inheritance, now presents to us the spectacle of that conflict in which the intellect always looks foolish when it clashes with self-interest. His own theory of property places the sinecurist Schopenhauer in the wrong; he therefore has to modify his theory to accommodate himself. He achieves this with a single sentence – even his excuses are laconic – which robs the just-developed theory of property of all incisiveness and radicalism: 'The morally established right to property, as deduced above, by its nature gives the possessor of a thing a power over it just as unlimited as that which he has over his own body. From this it follows that he can hand over his property to others by exchange or donation and those others then possess the thing with the same moral right as he did' (WWR I, 337).

He had, therefore, by having his father's inheritance 'transferred' to him, been installed in his father's sphere of will; he is also, in terms of ownership, flesh of his flesh and can therefore assert his 'unlimited power' over the property incorporated into him. In consequence, he would later regard the 1848 Revolution as the *émeute* of a *canaille* out to deprive him of his lawful property.

In his analyses of right and wrong and of the state Schopenhauer always emphasizes that he does not wish to develop any moral maxims, that he is only describing, only observing, the actual state of affairs. The world is ruled by the will, there is no morality that could effectively check it. Schopenhauer is consistent therefore in using as the starting point of his argument not any sense of justice, but evidence of pain when injustice is suffered – injustice being interpreted as an infringement of the body-linked sphere of the will. To him there is no comparable inner evidence that could lead one to do right. Only fear of suffering a wrong can provide a certain counterpoise to the potentially uninhibited greed of one's own will, which does not respect the sphere of will of others. Any such internal evidence as has from time to time been claimed to exist ('conscience', 'categorical imperative') is to Schopenhauer no more than the speculative phantasm of wishful thinking taking itself for reality.

Schopenhauer was of course aware that – especially since the French Revolution – periodically recurring attempts had been made to improve not only human coexistence but man himself. With undisguised viciousness Schopenhauer would point out that all so-called 'progress' had only served to torment the patient – mankind – but had not healed him. 'Infamous' and 'foolish' was his description of the optimism which so smugly asserted that the history of mankind had been at work for thousands of years in order to ensure a place in the sun for whatever generation happened to be at the helm. Considering the horrifying dimension of most recent history Schopenhauer in fact seems to have been the only philosopher who, with his pessimism, matched his age. History to Schopenhauer is not an enterprise tending in one direction but – viewed from an appropriate distance – a huge carnival of the unchanging same. He who stands on the platform of the metaphysics of the will must discover, according to Schopenhauer:

> that in the world it is the same as in the dramas of Gozzi, in all of which the same persons always appear with the same purpose and the same fate. The motives and incidents certainly are different in each piece, but the spirit of the incidents is the same. The persons of one piece know nothing of the events of another, in which, of course, they themselves

performed. Therefore, after all the experiences of the earlier pieces, Pantaloon has become no more agile or generous, Tartaglia no more conscientious, Brighella no more courageous, and Columbine no more modest. [WWR 1, 183]

Nothing new under the sun: the will ultimately always performs the same spectacle everywhere; the wisdom of self-preservation demands that at least one should not allow oneself to be fooled too painfully. Politics, the state, the law – these for Schopenhauer are areas where the superiority of the will has to be handled with care. The task of politics can only be the avoidance of the greater evil.

In an age which proclaimed politics as 'destiny' (Napoleon), in an age when the *whole* person aimed at fulfilment through politics and when, conversely, politics reached out for the whole person, Schopenhauer was pleading for a greatly slimmed-down concept of politics.

Schopenhauer's judgements on history, law, politics, etc., were admittedly made from the perspective of a non-participating observer. Only for such an observer does everything turn into a carnival. The philosopher will laugh last, to make sure no one laughs at him. He safeguards himself against Ash Wednesday by avoiding the carnival. That is Schopenhauer's strategy of happiness.

All the analyses of everyday and historical human life assembled in the preceding three books of his principal work are – how could it be otherwise? – inspired by that great 'no' to which Schopenhauer dedicated the fourth, final, book.

So far Schopenhauer has acquainted us with the will as the non-transgressible power of reality. And now comes the 'denial of the will'. Where does it come from and where does it lead to?

Schopenhauer has given us a foretaste of what this denial of the will is in his essay on art, which, as he understands it, produces an instant of will-lessness both in the artist and in the person allowing art to affect him. This means that both during the creation of a work of art and during the viewing of it there is always an effect of will-denial at play. But how, to reformulate our question, is the denial of the will even thinkable as a possibility in Schopenhauer's metaphysics of the will?

The will, that 'thing in itself' within us, surely is not at our disposal; surely the will is our Being which we cannot transcend. It should not be forgotten that Schopenhauer knows such ecstasies of will-lessness even prior to all comprehending ability. That is why he never tires of emphasizing: 'As the knowledge from which results the denial of the will is intuitive and not abstract, it finds its complete expression not in abstract concepts, but only in the deed' (WWR 1, 384).

He does not want to conjure up the denial of the will as a possible attitude conceptually, yet he would like to make it conceptually comprehensible – within the conceptual framework of his metaphysics of the will.

If he wishes to remain within that framework Schopenhauer will have to interpret the denial of the will as an event of the will itself, and not as the effect of some cognition independent of the will, let alone dominating the will. The radical immanence of his metaphysics of the will rules out any transcendental intervention of superior powers – the very thing Schopenhauer would scoff at if discovered in others. Schopenhauer therefore will not really have to speak – though he does so at times – of the will being 'broken' by cognition but of it 'fading away', of its 'turning', of its 'turning upon itself' – a process which may be accompanied by the ecstatic world cognition of denial as an epiphenomenon. In short: Schopenhauer will have to make the denial of the will comprehensible primarily not as a process of cognition but as a process of being. Because the will is all, it cannot be denied by anything other than itself. To the metaphysician of the will the denial of the will can be thinkable only as self-suspension of the will.

Schopenhauer uses his theory of pity to prepare the transition to a comprehended mystique of will-denial.

Pity to Schopenhauer is not a moral demand but the name of an experience, accompanied by powerful sentiments, that flares up now and again – the experience that everything outside myself is likewise will and that it suffers all sorrow and all pain just as myself. To him who feels pity 'the veil of Maya has become for the person who performs works of love, transparent and the deception of the *principium individuationis* has left him. Himself, his will, he recognizes in every creature, and hence in the sufferer also' (WWR I, 373). Pity is individual self-experience of the will without individual self-assertion of the will. Pity is the ability, at certain moments, to extend the intensity of own-body will-experience beyond the boundaries of one's own body. The will within me retains all its strength but it no longer acts on the frontline of self-assertion; it is in a state of strange dispersion: it is no longer concentrated on its own body but it swarms out and can no longer distinguish own from strange: '*Tat twam asi!*' (All this is you!)

From this experience of the identity of pity, defined in this ancient Indian formula, Schopenhauer guides us to the mystique of denial, which is higher than all reason and is folly to the wise.

> If that veil of Maya, the *principium individuationis*, is lifted from the eyes of a man to such an extent that he no longer makes the egoistical distinction between himself and the person of others . . . then it follows automatically that such a man, recognizing in all beings his own true and innermost self, must also regard the endless sufferings of all that lives as his own, and thus take upon himself the pain of the whole world. No suffering is any longer strange . . . to him. . . . He knows the whole, comprehends its inner nature and finds it involved in a constant passing away, a vain striving, an inward conflict and a continual suffering. Wherever he looks, he sees suffering humanity and the

suffering animal world, and a world that passes away. Now all this lies just as near to him as only his own person lies to the egoist. Now how could he, with such knowledge of the world, affirm this very life through constant acts of will, and precisely in this way bind himself more and more firmly to it, press himself to it more and more closely? Thus, whoever is still involved in the *principium individuationis*, in egoism, knows only particular things and their relation to his own person, and these then become ever renewed *motives* of his willing. On the other hand, that knowledge of the whole, of the inner nature of the thing-in-itself, which has been described, becomes the *quieter* of all and every willing. The will now turns away from life; it shudders at the pleasures in which it recognizes the affirmation of life. Man attains to the state of voluntary renunciation, resignation, true composure and complete will-lessness. [WWR I, 378–9]

This central passage of Schopenhauer's transition is inadequately formulated, because it gives rise to misunderstanding.

How could one, Schopenhauer asks, 'given such knowledge of the world, affirm' this life 'by constant acts of the will'? As if any knowledge could in itself have the power to cut the bond which ties us to the will. Schopenhauer argues as if the denial of the will were, after all, ultimately a question of intellectual consistency. This is very nearly a return to Kantian philosophy: 'virtue' out of the power of moral reason, radicalized into world-denying ascesis. The 'perfect knowledge of one's own nature' was to become the 'quieter of all and every willing', Schopenhauer writes. He guards himself against a relapse into devout rational Kantianism by recalling the distinction between 'abstract' and 'intuitive' knowledge. There is a gulf between the two. 'Intuitive' knowledge is to do more with inspiration than with discursive comprehension, more with conversion than with conviction. Old Matthias Claudius with his Pietist 'rebirth' is drawn upon for illustration. Schopenhauer refers to the saints and ascetics who realize that great denial in their own bodies and lives. This is it: denial does not have to express itself in any special intellectual knowledge; it is embodied in one's actions and way of life. Any information on it is an incomplete translation, it takes on the language of the day: 'according to the dogmas' which a person has absorbed into his reason the denying attitude will interpret itself in very different ways, according to whether that person is a Christian, an atheist, a Buddhist, etc. Dogmatic self-exegesis takes place for the 'satisfaction of his faculty of reason' (WWR I, 383). Denial itself, however, is not the work of rational understanding. Schopenhauer goes back to the Christian terminology of 'chosen grace' in order to make it clear that the mystery of denial is not the fruit of decision but something that happens to one, something one does not arrive at but that comes over one. However, Schopenhauer's definition of the role of knowledge in the act of denial remains equivocal, and even contradictory. One moment he writes: 'For if the will-to-live exists, it cannot, as that which alone is metaphysical or the thing-in-itself, be broken by any force. . . . The will itself cannot be abolished by anything except *knowledge*' (WWR I, 400). A few lines further down, however, the power of such knowledge is, quite consistently, interpreted as a natural power of the inverted will: 'Nature leads the will to the light, just because only in light can it find its salvation' (WWR I, 400). The denial of the will is thus itself an action – a last action? – of the natural history of the will. Seen thus, the denial of the will is not a triumph over the will to live but the mystery of its self-extinction. 'Thus,' Schopenhauer writes at the very end, after a good deal of vacillation on the issue, 'the effect of the sedative is ultimately a liberating action of the will' (WWR I, 405).

With that 'bliss' of denial, when everything comes to rest, when in the disinterested gaze the world is reflected as if in a motionless, undisturbed sheet of water, when my body no longer consumes me and is only a 'glimmering spark' (WWR I, 390) – then, according to Schopenhauer's murmured remark, that extinction may after all harbour within itself a glorious arrival: 'Behind our existence lies something else that becomes accessible to us only by our shaking off the world' (WWR I, 405).

Schopenhauer's work concludes with these sentences: 'We freely acknowledge that what remains after the complete abolition of the will is, for all who are still full of will, assuredly nothing. But also conversely, to those in whom the will has turned and denied itself, this very real world of ours, with all its suns and galaxies, is – nothing' (WWR I, 411–12).

Did Schopenhauer know what he was talking about? He was no saint, and no ascetic either. Even in later years he did not become the Buddha of Frankfurt. His own body, far from wasting away to a 'glimmering spark', had been cherished and cosseted with almost hypochondriac care. Nor was he chaste; even his terrible fear of venereal disease was unable to restrain him. He was an expert on denial, so long as it did not affect his own will. That he effectively asserted, often in a positively berserk manner. Yet he also had moments of 'better consciousness'. He had peered over the fence of self-assertion but he remained an outsider with regard to that ecstasy of denial which the conclusion of his work invokes. And because he was an outsider he was particularly concerned with the moment of crossing the frontier – and that, to him, was art. The most moving passages of his work are the ones devoted to music, that frontier phenomenon *par excellence*. In music, the 'thing in itself', the will, is present as pure play, without embodiment. Everything is present once more, as though prior to a parting, but the phenomenal world has already disappeared: 'Music . . . is also quite independent of the phenomenal world, positively ignores it, and, to a certain extent, could still exist even if there were no world at all' (WWR I, 257). Music is the whole world all over again, but incorporeal. It surrenders the 'heart of things' (WWR I, 263), in it 'the deepest recesses of our nature find expression' (WWR I, 256). The 'thing in itself' really starts to sing in music.

All these, however, are the perspectives of an outsider. The will is not denied; it has merely, in art, lost its overwhelming power for some instants. Seen through art, the will offers a 'significant spectacle' – 'free from pain' (WWR I, 267).

One does not have to disappear in denial; one may remain here if, through art, a chance is offered of seeing the world as if one had left it already.

Live 'as if' and deny 'as if': this was the balancing act performed by the totally unascetic and totally unholy Schopenhauer. Before greedy Arthur consumes his opulent midday meal at the restaurant he plays his flute for an hour: Rossini's 'celestial music'. Schopenhauer's 'better consciousness' knows only a time-restricted ecstasy. Holiness and prolonged ecstasy are things he shuns. This, unfortunately, Nietzsche did not learn from him. Because Schopenhauer wishes to be present at the ultimate, at denial, the penultimate, i.e. art, to him becomes the ultimate. Besides, being a philosopher, he wants to talk about it all. These are sufficient reasons for remaining on firm ground. Besides, he had to await the public's reaction to the work just launched upon the world: perhaps there would, after all, be a positive reaction to his message of denial.

CHAPTER SEVENTEEN

FIRST ITALIAN JOURNEY

In the spring of 1818, before he had completed his manuscript, Schopen-hauer, through the mediation of Freiherr von Biedenfeld, made contact with the publisher Brockhaus. The previous year Brockhaus had published Johanna Schopenhauer's (by then fourth) book, *Ausflucht an den Rhein* (*Excursion to the Rhine*). The family quarrel, however, prevented Schopen-hauer from making use of his mother's business connection, even though her name opened the door for her as yet unknown philosopher son. His overbrimmingly self-assured covering letter alone would scarcely have done so: 'My work, therefore, is a new philosophical system: but new in the full sense of the word: not a new presentation of what existed before, but a chain of thought linked to the highest degree, such as has not previously entered any man's head' (CL, 29). His philosophical precursors and contemporaries were brushed aside in strong words. His book, he wrote, was as far removed from the 'meaningless verbosity of the newer philosophical school' as it was 'from the expansive flat twaddle of the period before Kant' (CL, 29). Strictly speaking, his work was beyond price, since his whole life was invested in it. He therefore expected of the publisher, above all, a dignified presentation of the work: good printing, careful proofreading, high-quality paper. The honorarium he demanded was 'insignificant': one ducat per sheet, i.e. forty ducats for the whole book. The publisher would not, in the long run, be taking any risks, because 'the book ... will ... be one of those which subsequently become the source and mainspring of a hundred other books' (CL, 29).

Schopenhauer did not enclose a sample: Brockhaus was to buy a pig in a poke. And Brockhaus did.

Friedrich August Brockhaus was a bold businessman who had led his publishing house to economic success within a few years. His *Konversations-Lexikon*, which he had bought for a song from the bankrupt publisher Leupold and completed under his own management in 1811, proved a gold mine. Brockhaus was a shrewd enlightener who did not shrink from conflict with the censor. At the time of the Napoleonic occupation he maintained contacts with the patriotic opposition. He published the *Deutsche Blätter*, between 1813 and 1814 the semi-official paper of the anti-Napoleonic coalition. When it was no longer dangerous to do so, in 1814, he republished the essay 'Deutschland in seiner tiefsten Erniedrigung' ('Germany in her Deepest Humiliation'), on account of which the bookseller Palm had been executed by firing squad on Napoleon's orders a few years earlier. For Brockhaus the risks had to be calculable; he was not a man acting on the spur of his beliefs. Brockhaus's ambition was to be represented in all genres of literature. He published ladies' almanacs, travel books, *belles-lettres* and scientific works. The prestige of philosophy attracted him. Philosophical titles were still rarities on his list. The philosophizing son of one of his lady authors therefore fitted well into his programme. On 31 March 1818 Brockhaus wrote to Schopenhauer: 'Your highly esteemed proposal . . . flatters me' (Corr 14, 224). Schopenhauer thanked him and requested a formal contract. He warned the publisher that there might be difficulties with the censorship, as his work conflicted with the 'dogmas of Jewish-Christian belief' (CL, 31). If the worst came to the worst the book would have to be printed and published elsewhere, perhaps in Merseburg, where there seemed to be a more liberal atmosphere. The publisher certainly would derive no disadvantage: 'After all, it is well known that a ban is by no means a misfortune for a book' (CL, 32).

Schopenhauer urged expeditiousness. The book should be published in time for the autumn fair; after that he wished to go on a journey, to Italy. In the summer Schopenhauer delivered the manuscript by the contractual date and impatiently awaited the first galley proofs. Arthur was still unfamiliar with publishing practice, for after a mere fortnight he felt it necessary to urge Brockhaus on. When a week later no galleys had arrived Schopenhauer for the first time turned offensive. Brockhaus was not even to think of treating him like 'the authors of the *Konversations-Lexikon* or similar poor scribblers'. With these he had nothing in common except that he 'also happens to use pen and ink' (CL, 38). The publisher of the *Konversations-Lexikon* did not react to this insult. Without comment he sent Schopenhauer the first galleys. This was not enough for Schopenhauer. At that rate the book would not be ready in time for the fair. Angrily he referred to the agreed timetable. 'Nothing is more awful to me than having to deal with people whose words do not deserve credence' (CL, 40). As evidence of the publisher's good faith he wanted his honorarium straight away. And then followed the sentence with which Schopenhauer finally wrecked the relationship between himself and the publisher: 'Moreover, I hear from various quarters,' he wrote to Brockhaus, 'that you are as a rule slow with the payment of honoraria, or indeed altogether fail to pay' (CL, 41). Brockhaus replied: 'If you claim that you . . . heard that I am slow with the payment of honoraria . . . you will, so long as you do not give me the name of at least *one* single author, whom I could challenge on this point, permit me to regard *you* as *not* a man of honour' (Corr 14, 243). Schopenhauer did not react to this.

In a further letter he again had something to complain about. Brockhaus thereupon broke off relations. He had the book printed as per contract, but refused to have anything further to do with that 'chained dog', as he called Schopenhauer in conversation with others. In his final letter of 24 September 1818 he wrote: 'I had been . . . expecting proof of your slanderous allegations in your earlier letter, or else a retraction of these, but as neither the one nor the other is contained in it, and as, in accordance with my statement, I do not henceforth regard you as a man of honour, there cannot in future be any correspondence between us, and I shall not even accept any letters from you, which anyway in their divine rudeness and rusticity would suggest a *vetturino* [coachman] rather than a philosopher as their author. . . . I only hope that my fears that by printing your work I am printing only waste paper will not come true' (Corr 14, 244).

When it became likely that the book would not be ready for the autumn fair Schopenhauer gave up waiting and, in October 1818, embarked on his long-planned Italian journey. At the beginning of 1819, in Rome, he was to hold his book, fresh from the press, in his hands.

His relations with Brockhaus had been wrecked quite simply because he, Schopenhauer, impatient and panicky, was unable to wait for the moment when he would step on the stage to face his public.

But before setting off for Italy Schopenhauer once more wrote to Goethe, whose *Italian Journey* had been published a year earlier. He had, Schopenhauer said, accomplished his 'day's labours' and would probably never achieve anything 'better or weightier'. He was now off to the land 'where the lemons are flowering' and 'where the No, No of all literary journals will not reach me' (CL, 34). Schopenhauer requested Goethe's 'advice' or 'suggestions' concerning his impending trip to Italy. As with the *Theory of Colours*, Schopenhauer wished to follow the trail of his surrogate father also as a tourist. Such a motivation should have seemed familiar to Goethe, who had himself followed his father by travelling to the south.

Goethe's reply was brief and friendly, but without 'advice' or 'suggestions'. He would read the work of his 'esteemed contemporary' (CL, 501). Goethe enclosed a letter of introduction – to Lord Byron.

Byron was just then in Venice, where Arthur arrived at the beginning of November 1818.

Byron was working on an Armenian–English grammar, he was involved in a love affair with Countess Guiccioli, and every day in the morning he galloped along the Lido. That was where Schopenhauer saw him. Schopenhauer was in the company of a woman who, at the sight of the mounted Don Juan, uttered high-pitched shrieks of delight. Schopenhauer became jealous and refrained from using Goethe's letter of introduction to make the nobleman's acquaintance. He was to regret it later: once more the 'womenfolk' had kept him from something important. In Italy, as he was to tell an acquaintance later, he 'enjoyed not only her *beauty* but also her *beauties'* (C, 133). This was probably something of an exaggeration, for in another conversation Schopenhauer, looking back on his Italian journey, admitted: 'Just think of it, at the age of thirty, when life was smiling at me! And as for the women, I was very fond of them – if only they would have had me' (C, 239).

Whether his companion on the Lido 'would have had' him we do not know; perhaps Schopenhauer did not know himself; at any rate he had Byron's rivalry to fear. In spite of such worries Arthur was happy: a 'marvellous mellow mood' (Corr 14, 249) had come over him in Venice, he wrote to his sister Adele.

Venice in autumn: Goethe had described the 'joyous sight' it offered to the traveller leaving the 'misty north' behind: 'Sailing across the lagoon in bright sunshine and watching the gondoliers on the gondolas' planks, lightly floating, colourfully attired, poling, outlined against the light-green surface in the blue air, I saw before me the best, freshest picture of the Venetian school.'

The Venetian Republic no longer existed. The winged lions of St Mark now no longer guarded the Doge but the Austrian Governor, Prince Metternich. As there were fears of a Carbonari conspiracy – Byron himself was suspected of being involved – the town was swarming with Austrian police spies. Nevertheless it kept its sensuality and serenity. With patrician self-assurance and with Goethe's introduction in his pocket Schopenhauer attended the glittering Venetian parties. Having so recently emerged from the gloom of his Dresden study, he had to accustom himself afresh to this new world. As everything attracted his attention, he noted in his travel diary, he was afraid of attracting everyone else's. Soon, however, he became 'assimilated'; he stopped 'having to concern himself with his person and turned his attention purely to his surroundings', to which, 'through objective, disinterested observation, he now felt superior instead of being oppressed by them as before' (P III, 2).

Arthur was now open to impressions but he remained introspective – so much so that even amidst the colourful autumnal world of Venice he continued to ponder his gloomy mysticism of denial. Venice, where the carnival season was just beginning, offered a picture of colourful and high-spirited affirmation of the will to live. The phenomenal world was getting at him. Denial was 'in no way conceivable', he noted in his travel diary. That could only be expressed in 'darkness and silence' (P III, 2). But for that there was too much light and too much noise in Venice. With restrained euphoria Schopenhauer took part in the bustle, though always careful not to lose his 'superiority'. At the end of November he left Venice. By the time he got to Bologna he was tormented by the thought of not having sufficiently helped himself to the pleasures Venice had offered him. In his travel journal he rationalized this feeling into a thought on human destiny generally: 'Just because *all happiness is negative,* what happens is that when at last we feel totally at ease we are not properly aware of it but allow everything to pass by softly and gently, until it is gone and its by then positively experienced absence reflects the vanished happiness: then we realize that we failed to hold on to it, and our sense of loss is accompanied by remorse' (P III, 3).

Schopenhauer arrived in Rome at the beginning of December and stayed there until the end of February. He spent his time in what Goethe had called 'the capital of the world' doing the usual things: the ancient architectural monuments and the Renaissance works of art had to be viewed. For Goethe the day he first saw Rome had been a 'second day of birth, a true rebirth'. Schopenhauer looked around conscientiously but he felt nothing like rebirth. His journal records a few reflections on painting and ancient architecture, and some criticism of the 'halfness and falsity' of contemporary art. Nevertheless, Schopenhauer too celebrated a 'second day of birth': it was in Rome that he finally received the first copy of his book. In February he learned in a letter from Adele that Goethe had received the book and had 'immediately' begun to read it. Ottilie – Adele reported – had told her that 'father is sitting over the book and reading it with an eagerness she had *never* seen in him before'. Goethe had said that 'now he had a joy for a whole year; for he was now reading it from beginning to end and he thought it would probably take that much time' (Corr 14, 250).

That of course was an extravagant promise. Even for Schopenhauer Goethe did not set aside his habit of only reading the beginnings of contemporary books. Yet his first dips into The World as Will and Representation had actually stimulated him. He gave Adele a slip of paper on which he had marked a few passages which had given him 'great pleasure'. The first of these commended passages dealt with 'anticipation', the anticipation of beauty in the artist's soul. The artist, Schopenhauer had written, let nature speak where in reality it only stammered. This idea, flattering to any artist, was instantly taken up by Goethe. In the first part of the Annals he said: 'As the poet pre- creates the world by anticipation'.

Schopenhauer, holding in his hands a deluxe copy of his work and a letter from Adele with the sentence, 'At least you are the only author whom Goethe is reading in such earnest manner' (Corr 14, 151), now felt elevated to that company of the spirit where the geniuses nod to one another and converse with each other across the centuries. Such feeling called for lyrical expression. After many years the thinker once more turned poet: 'From long-harboured deep-felt pain / It rose up out of my innermost heart. / To hold to it I struggled a long time: / But now I know I have succeeded. / Act now whatever way you please: / You cannot threaten my life's work. / You may delay it but cannot destroy it: / Posterity will raise a monument to me' (P III, 9).

During those weeks Schopenhauer indulged in prose also: notes on the subject of 'genius' were becoming frequent in his travel diary. Thus he wrote: 'A scholar is someone who has learned a lot; a genius is someone from whom mankind has something to learn, something it did not know before' (P III, 5). Schopenhauer, however, had a problem: the German artists' colony in Rome, where he was a frequent guest, showed little inclination to recognize him as a genius. At the Café Greco, the centre of that scene, he was actually known only as the son of his now famous mother. Even the news of the family quarrel had reached Rome. One of the café's regulars wrote to his relations back home: 'I have seen a lot of Schopenhauer. . . . There is a good deal of prejudice against him here, mainly with regard to his relationship with his mother. . . . Germans being what they are, he has managed to make enemies of nearly all of them by his paradoxes, and I have frequently been warned against seeing him.'

This letter was from Karl Witte, a friend of Schopenhauer's from his Göttingen days. Witte, born in 1800, had been a much admired child prodigy in Göttingen. At the age of ten he entered the university, where he studied first mathematics and then law, and took his doctor's degree at sixteen. A year later, his attempt to get an assistant professorship in Berlin ended in failure: the students would not listen to the boy who was supposed to teach them. The Ministry granted him a scholarship of which Witte was then availing himself in Italy. The relationship between Witte and Schopenhauer must have been fairly close, for a brief note from Arthur to Witte begins with the words: 'My dear! The picnic is off. I'll collect you at half past four to go to the Ermine [a Roman tavern]' (CL, 42). It was there, at the Trattoria dell'Armelino and at the Café Greco, that Schopenhauer would sit and irritate people. The crowd of artists who met there, as well as the locale itself, were described ten years later by Felix Mendelssohn in a letter to his father:

> They are frightful people if you see them sitting in their 'Caffé Greco'. . . . This is a small dark room, about eight steps across, and on one side of the room one is allowed to smoke tobacco but not on the other. There they sit all around on the benches, with their wide-brimmed hats, big mastiffs by their sides, their necks, cheeks, whole faces covered in hair, producing a terrible fug . . . being rude to each other; the dogs ensure the spread of vermin; a necktie, a frock coat would be innovations – any part of the face the beard leaves free is hidden by spectacles, and thus they drink coffee and talk about Titian and Pordenone as if they were sitting by their sides and they too wore beards and storm-hats! At the same time they make such sickly madonnas, feeble saints, milksops of heroes that sometimes one feels like bringing one's fist down.

In this Nazarene-German company of lovers of madonnas and milksops Arthur Schopenhauer was bound to be a jarring element. One evening he spoke approvingly of Greek polytheism: a Mount Olympus full of gods surely gave an artist a rich choice of individualities. Such praise of paganism was considered outrageous at the Café Greco. One of the company objected: 'But we have the twelve apostles!' Whereupon Schopenhauer said: 'Spare me your twelve philistines from Jerusalem!' (C, 46).

On another occasion Arthur proclaimed that of all nations the Germans were the stupidest. That was too much for the patriotic clientele of the café. They called on each other: 'Let's throw the fellow out!' Schopenhauer probably made off on his own accord first. Back home he noted in his travel journal: 'If only I could get rid of the illusion that I should regard that brood of toads and vipers as the likes of me, I should be a lot better off' (P III, 8).

The German colony in Rome did not suffer from that illusion: Schopenhauer was by no means regarded as their kind of person. In his presence they were afraid of him, and away from him they mocked him. One of the Café Greco clientele wrote home: 'Among the German travellers who have since arrived here I notice Schopenhauer, son of the learned book author . . . Johanna Schopenhauer of Weimar. He really is a pretty complete fool. . . .' After all that annoyance Schopenhauer avoided his fellow countrymen and sought contact chiefly with the rich English tourists. These people travelled in comfort, with several baggage coaches, carrying with them good wine, bedding and chamberpots. With such a company of tourists Arthur in March 1819 set off south for Naples, where, according to Goethe in his *Italian Journey*, one might not only, as in Rome, study, but also live and love. Schopenhauer did not give himself much time, because in April he was back in Rome, staying there for a few days before continuing to Florence, where he remained a month. Only here, and not in Naples, did the 'magic arms of love' brush against him again.

Chief Government Counsellor Eduard Crüger, an acquaintance of the philosopher during his final years in Frankfurt, reported that 'in Florence Schopenhauer was engaged to a lady of noble family, but broke off the engagement on learning that she suffered from tuberculosis' (C, 197). The comedy playwright Georg Römer likewise later referred to Schopenhauer's intention to get married: he would, he reported, 'have married partly from inclination, partly from a sense of duty . . . had not an insuperable obstacle intervened, which, despite all the pain it caused him, must nevertheless now be regarded as fortunate "as a wife is not fitting for a philosopher" ' (C, 71).

There is, however, some doubt whether that affair really occurred in Florence. To Adele, at any rate, Schopenhauer in a (non-extant) letter must have expressed similar intentions in connection with his Venetian adventure in November 1818. For in May 1819 Adele wrote to her brother: 'Your affair there [in Venice] is beginning to interest me, may it end happily – your beloved is rich, even of noble family, yet you believe she will wish to marry you?' (JSS 77, 160).

Matrimonial plans with regard to a rich Italian woman 'of noble family' – surely this cannot be the Venetian girl Teresa Fuga, with whom Schopenhauer got involved during his first stay in Venice, whom in May 1819 he informed of his return to Venice, and who subsequently wrote him a letter, addressed to one Arthur Scharrenhans and containing a tempting offer:

Dear friend! I received your letter with great pleasure and learned that you have not forgotten me and that I am much in your thoughts; but believe me, my dear, I too have not forgotten you . . . ; I love you and wish to see you, do come, I am looking forward to embracing you and spending a few days with you. I have a friend already, but he is forever leaving Venice and only visits me now and again – in any case he leaves for the country on Sunday, where he will be staying for fifteen to twenty days; you can therefore come without fear, I await you with all my heart; I no longer have a relationship with the 'impresario', I have long had this other friend; and as for Englishmen who have fled England and come to Venice out of desperation, I have no flirtations with them any more either.

Among all these flirtations, Englishmen, impresarios and other friends Teresa was to keep a small gap open for her Arthur, whose surname she could not remember – for a few days. If this was the affair Schopenhauer represented to Adele as one leading to marriage he must have bragged a good deal, or else indulged in considerable illusions.

Adele, who once wrote in her diary, 'As I love, no one probably will love me,' considered herself especially competent to differentiate in amorous sentiments between 'superficial' and 'deep'. Moreover, she did not trust men, and her brother Arthur was no exception. Her comment on his adventures was: 'May you not totally lose the ability to esteem a woman, while dealing with the common and base ones of our sex, and may Heaven one day lead to you a woman for whom you can feel something deeper than these infatuations . . .' It gave her 'some inward pain', she wrote to Arthur on 22 May 1819, 'that in one single letter there are two love affairs without love, and that all this is not yet what I would have wished for you'. Adele here writes like a sister whom her brother has made his intimate confidante. This is surprising as, at the time of his break with his mother and his departure from Weimar on 22 May 1814, relations between brother and sister had also suffered a good deal. Adele then wrote to her friend Ottilie von Goethe: 'My brother behaved abominably to my mother.' Schopenhauer, however, did not want to drag his sister into the breach and soon resumed his correspondence with her, not in order to pour out his heart to her – in 1816 Adele noted in her diary: 'I know nothing of my brother' – but to prise his sister out of his mother's sphere of power. He seemed to have urgently advised her to get married in order to leave home. Adele was not particularly pleased with such advice; in the summer of 1814 she complained to her friend Ottilie: 'Arthur has written to me. . . . I cannot get married, not for a long time, perhaps, or probably, never. Arthur is pestering me. . . .' Adele was certainly on the lookout for a husband but the right man would not come along. Small wonder that initially she postponed reacting to her brother's injunctions. 'I ought to have long answered . . . the pending letters. . . . The one to Arthur, in particular, will not come right,' she confessed to Ottilie in the summer of 1815.

A year later Adele decided on a plan of her own: she would move in with her brother in Dresden; not to be helped – Adele was very proud – but in order to help. She had a feeling that Arthur had to be brought out of his, as she assumed, grim seclusion; besides, she would try to work towards a reconciliation between him and their mother. No doubt she also looked to a chance of avoiding her mother's friend Gerstenbergk for a while. Schopenhauer did not think much of the plan; while he wanted to prise Adele away from his mother, he did not want her near him. He must have written a very abrasive letter, for Adele, in despair, noted in her diary: 'outrageous answer. I was so upset I ran straight to Ottilie. . . . And, oh, I had set such hopes on my plan of going to Dresden; everything I built up so laboriously has been pulled down.'

After this disappointment the correspondence between brother and sister lapsed for some months. In October 1816, on a visit to Mannheim, Adele heard this sentence from the stage of the theatre: 'You may lose everything, every friend – you will still have your brother.' That put her in the right mood. 'I wrote my letter to Arthur gently and softly,' she noted in her diary.

Schopenhauer replied, announcing the early completion of his work. He must have told Adele something about it, certainly enough to awaken the fear in her that by his brusque manner he might find himself at loggerheads not only with his family but also with the spirit of his age and with religious and moral practices. In the summer of 1818 Adele wrote to Ottilie: 'This morning a letter from my brother: in August he goes out into the world, leaving his book to come out, which I fear like death. . . . Arthur is heavily on my mind.'

On his Italian journey, however, Schopenhauer, relieved of his work and immersed in a milder climate of life, began to confide in his sister more than ever before. Admittedly there was another sound reason: as his affair with a Dresden lady's maid had entailed consequences – the woman became pregnant and, while Schopenhauer was in Italy, gave birth to a daughter – his sister's willingness to help was very useful to him. And because in this matter he supposed that she might really do something for him, he took her into his confidence. That must have been in the spring of 1819, because on 27 April 1819 Adele noted in her diary: 'His girl in Dresden is *enceinte*; I am appalled – but he is meanwhile behaving correctly and well.' Schopenhauer would therefore have admitted paternity and promised financial support. But Adele nevertheless remained sceptical. She enjoined her brother: 'Do not accept your duty in the customary narrow sense, to which the wickedness of you men likes to reduce it – I had rather the child had not been born, but now it is here you should care for it.'

Schopenhauer had probably hinted that he would like Adele to look after the child a little and also after the young mother. 'If there is anything I can . . . do for the girl, say so openly,' she replied, immediately offering help: she might send money to its mother – but visiting her, no, that was really not on. Anyway, it was being said that the woman was meanwhile living with another man. Arthur had odd ideas if he expected her to call there.

In the late summer of 1819 the child died. Adele to Arthur: 'I am sorry that your daughter is dead, for if the child had lived it would have given you joy in the future.'

Adele wrote these lines on 8 September 1819, by which time Schopenhauer had returned to Germany and was staying in Dresden. Meanwhile, however, disaster had befallen the Schopenhauer family. The banker Muhl in Danzig, where Arthur's mother and Adele had their whole fortune and Arthur one-third of his, suspended payments in May 1819 and requested his creditors to continue and to accept a settlement, otherwise there would be the threat of total bankruptcy. Schopenhauer heard about this from Adele at the end of May, while in Venice. Adele was greatly alarmed: she spoke of an 'overthrow' of her 'whole destiny on earth'. Adele had every reason to worry. Her mother's share of the fortune had already severely shrunk as a result of her ostentatious Weimar lifestyle. Adele's share of the wealth had meanwhile become the basis of both their maintenance – indeed of their future. It did not look as though Adele could restore her fortune by marriage. Gerstenbergk had offered to help, but the Schopenhauers did not wish to accept. Notice was given to the lady's maid, the cook and the manservant. A substantial sum of money was borrowed for a journey to Danzig. For a settlement it was best to be on the spot. From Danzig Adele wrote to Arthur: 'It pains me here in high society to have to attend all the parties . . . because I am forever thinking of closing time! A new road, a new life! . . . We shall live very simply on what is left to us, I want to earn my own requirements so far as my health permits. . . . If the worst comes to the worst, but only the *worst*, I will leave my native land and go to *Russia* as a governess. . . . I cannot, I *will* not marry without affection; everyone knows his strength, that which weighs on thousands is nothing to me, that which thousands bear would crush me.' Adele kept Arthur *au courant* to the best of her ability. Under the seal of confidentiality she hinted that Muhl had offered her and her mother special terms. 'My plans,' she wrote on 8 September, 'aim at receiving back at some *future* time, when Muhl has recovered, part of the money that I am now losing.' Arthur should keep calm as a creditor, she requested, and, if an official settlement were offered, accept it. Only if none of the creditors opposed it could the settlement be reached. 'Accept . . . the firm assurance that . . . your *advantage* shall be as close to me as my own. That, when I can no longer do anything for you, I try to pursue my advantage, you will understand; but I give you my word that I will sooner set aside *my* advantage than suffer any detriment being done to you. Calmly continue to trust me.'

But that was just what Schopenhauer was not prepared to do. The hints about special terms had aroused his suspicions.

Initially, being only partially affected by the threatened bankruptcy, he had spontaneously offered help. He would divide 'what was left to him' with his mother and sister, he wrote. With this letter to his sister Schopenhauer had enclosed another to his mother, containing the same offer but with hurtful words: 'even though neither in his son nor in his daughter have you respected the memory of that man of honour, my father' (JSS 77, 140).

Adele tried to conceal the enclosed letter from her mother, but her mother read it and 'a horrid scene ensued', as Adele noted in her diary. 'She [Johanna] spoke of father in a way which nearly broke my heart, said frightful things about Arthur and uttered that "actually he should have been *dependent* on her".'

Adele wanted to escape this witches' cauldron of hostilities: at first she wanted to throw herself out of the window. In her diary she wrote: 'To die was a game compared with the gigantic load of suffering – but when I felt the frightful urge within me God gave me good sense and strength.'

Under these circumstances Arthur's offer, needless to say, was not accepted. Nor did he repeat it; on the contrary, his mistrust was now aroused. It was directed against Muhl, who he rightly supposed wished to save himself by a settlement. But it was directed also against his mother and sister, who, he believed, were not beyond cheating him by agreeing special terms with Muhl. In actual fact, there were special arrangements. Johanna, in addition to a 30 per cent settlement, was to receive a life annuity of 300 *Reichstaler* 'by way of some compensation', as it was put in the deed executed on 8 July 1820. Johanna, moreover, received a genuine painting by Paolo Veronese, for which, however, she did not succeed in finding a buyer.

As Adele saw it, these arrangements were not directed against Arthur. For him, she believed, there was simply no more to be had. After all, she had written to him 'that, when I can no longer do anything for you, I try to pursue my own advantage'.

Adele, free from any sense of wrongdoing, was deeply hurt by Arthur's distrust. His cordial letters from Italy were still all too fresh in her mind. She wrote: 'I do not wish to be raised to the heavens one moment and be condemned the next; it is time you had a clear idea of my nature – if not, give me up.'

Unfortunately, however, Adele was saddled with the task of winning her mistrustful brother over to the settlement. He refused stubbornly. Adele implored him: the settlement might fail, in which case all would be lost; did he want to ruin everybody, including his mother and sister? Schopenhauer became even more determined: what Adele did not understand, he, as a former merchant, understood very well: this was a game of poker, where one had to keep one's nerve. Anyone wanting to go for a settlement must surely, as Muhl must do, allow for the failure of such a settlement. But there would be a settlement even if he, Schopenhauer, did not participate in it – Muhl's own interest would demand it. That was why Schopenhauer had decided on a different strategy. He ignored Muhl's payment problems, simply hanging on to his bills of exchange and waiting. Once Muhl had re-established his affairs he would collect his claims. Meanwhile he would not oppose the settlement. On the contrary: it was in his interest for the settlement to come about because only thus would Muhl regain solvency.

It was a delicate combination: Muhl would become solvent again at the expense of Johanna and Adele, and Schopenhauer would recover his assets at the expense of Muhl's manoeuvre. Only *because* his mother and sister would lose three-quarters of their fortunes would Schopenhauer save 100 per cent of his. Of course he risked losing everything in the event of Muhl remaining insolvent in spite of the settlement, and he also risked the settlement not materializing because of his refusal to participate in it. This was a risk into which he was also drawing his mother and sister. Schopenhauer had no wish to harm either of them, but even more was he determined to avoid being the loser himself, and this fear was far greater than any sense of family solidarity.

He experienced a grim satisfaction when things in fact worked out exactly as he had assumed they would. Muhl became solvent again, and a year later, on 1 May 1821, Arthur presented his bills with these words: 'Just in case you are thinking of pretending to be still insolvent, I will prove the opposite to you by the famous syllogism which the great Kant introduced into philosophy in order to prove man's moral freedom, i.e. the conclusion from having to do to being able to do. In other words: unless you pay up voluntarily I shall sue for the bill. You observe that one can be a philosopher without, therefore, being a fool' (CL, 69).

No, Schopenhauer was no fool. In addition to being an expert on the 'better consciousness' he was also quite adept at the 'empirical consciousness'.

He turned out the winner in this business. But it lost him his short-lived cordial relationship with Adele. On 9 February she noted in her diary: 'At last Arthur's letter, which shattered me. I cannot answer it yet, instead I wrote him a few lines of farewell. Because my soul has parted with him.'

CHAPTER EIGHTEEN

THE UNATTENDED LECTURER

Arthur Schopenhauer would later maintain that he only applied for a university post because he believed that, in view of Muhl's collapse and the impending loss of his fortune, he had to supplement his income by teaching. A temporary emergency – which subsequently proved rather more harmless than at first he had assumed – therefore induced him, for a while, to live not only for philosophy but also by philosophy.

In fact, however, there were other motivations as well. As he wrote to Professor Lichtenstein in Berlin in December 1819, he wished 'at long last to get . . . into practical life' (CL, 44).

More diplomatically, and therefore more circumspectly, he formulated another motive: he now wished to challenge the philosophical spirit of the age and to put it in its place also from an academic standpoint. Schopenhauer was not yet content to work solely for posterity. He wanted to reach his contemporaries, and this meant that he felt like Hercules faced with the task of cleaning out the Augean stables of his age. In his letter to Professor Blumenbach in Göttingen he clothed this intention in the careful phrase: 'Having now served . . . my apprenticeship and also my journeyman years, I believe . . . that some person or other might now well learn something from me' (CL, 43). With his letters to Lichtenstein in Berlin and to Blumenbach in Göttingen Schopenhauer, from Dresden in December 1819, was trying to sound out the situation at these two universities. With both of them he was familiar from his student days, which was why he had shortlisted them for his future career. For a brief time in the autumn of 1819 he also thought of Heidelberg, where, on his return from Italy, he had arrived in July 1819.

What attracted him to Heidelberg was the scenic beauty of the region; besides, there was a vacant chair at the university: a little over a year earlier Hegel had been called to Berlin from Heidelberg. Schopenhauer would also have good support there: his schoolfriend from Gotha and fellow student from Göttingen Ernst Anton Lewald had meanwhile become Professor of Classical Philology at the University of Heidelberg. The other aspects of Heidelberg held little attraction for Schopenhauer: there, in that bastion of German Romanticism, the waves of patriotic fervour had risen to especial heights following the assassination of Kotzebue by the fraternity student Sand in Mannheim on 23 March 1819. Patriotic sentiments in the town and among the students first of all manifested themselves in savage anti-Semitic excesses. The reverence shown to Sand particularly in Heidelberg could still be observed there many years after the event. The executioner Braun – who had turned melancholic at the thought of having had to execute such a pious and noble man – used the planks and beams of the scaffold on which Sand had been executed to build himself a shack in his vineyard near Heidelberg. There the fraternity students used to meet in secret. And it was in Heidelberg that the trade in relics flourished: people fought for the wood shavings spattered with the martyr's blood. Pipes and coffee cups with Sand's portrait were on sale.

None of this was to Schopenhauer's taste. He stayed for a month and then continued his journey in the direction of Dresden. *En route* he stopped in Weimar, on 19 and 20 August. He called on Goethe, entering his room unannounced. Goethe, just then in conversation with another visitor, greeted him coolly, asking 'how he, whom he had still supposed in Italy, was making such an impromptu appearance here?' and requesting him to come back in an hour. Schopenhauer did not expect such a reception. Adele's account of the sympathy Goethe had shown to his book was still fresh in his memory. When he returned an hour later he made no secret of his disappointment. But Goethe must have been conciliatory and put him at his ease again, for Adele noted in her diary: 'received . . . a letter from my brother with an account of his stay in Weimar, with his delight at his reception at Goethe's, a surmise of what love might give him, of what might have been made of him'.

Goethe and Schopenhauer spent an evening and a morning together. Schopenhauer spoke of his travels and his plans. Soon they got back to their old subject, the theory of colours. Goethe demonstrated a few experiments. In his *Tages- und Jahreshefte* Goethe recalls this encounter, which was to be their last, in friendly words: 'A visit by Dr Schopenhauer, a usually misjudged but difficult-to-know deserving young man, stimulated me and proved instructive to both sides.'

From the end of August 1819 Schopenhauer was back in Dresden, where his memories of the city were gilded afresh by his productive phase there. A few days after his arrival his daughter, only a few months old, died – not a shattering experience for Schopenhauer. His worries concerned his own academic future. Where would he have the best prospects? Lewald wrote from Heidelberg that no obstacles would be placed in his way, though his philosophical work was still totally unknown there. The fine autumn promised a good vintage, otherwise things were quiet again – apart from excesses against the Jews.

Schopenhauer was now tending more towards Göttingen and Berlin. Göttingen, he wrote to Blumenbach, was 'the most worthy, and perhaps the leading, university in the world' (CL, 43), distinguished above all by the successes of the empirical sciences – but what were its requirements of philosophical speculation? Could he expect to find a public there? he asked Blumenbach. Schopenhauer's Göttingen mentor in the natural sciences replied that there was no doubt Schopenhauer would be favourably received by his colleagues, but whether he would find a public was exceedingly uncertain, as there was no indication 'that another presentation of philosophy was being missed'. In short: Göttingen had no need of philosophical renewal. Lichtenstein's answer from Berlin was more encouraging. Although Lichtenstein, too, wrote, 'I am not aware of any definitely uttered statements about your writings,' he continued: 'but you may be assured that they are esteemed here in accordance with their worth.'

In his letter to Lichtenstein Arthur had listed the reasons which, to his mind, spoke for and against Berlin. The 'higher intellectual culture' of a big city would make it easier to find a public not exclusively made up of students. Removal from Dresden to Berlin was more easily accomplished than, for instance, to Göttingen or Heidelberg. Against Berlin was the 'high cost of residence' and its 'fatal situation in a sandy desert' (CL, 45). Schopenhauer decided in favour of Berlin because in his answer Lichtenstein had made a tempting observation: 'Since Hegel has been here philosophical studies seem to be finding more friends.'

Schopenhauer was attracted to the lion's den. He wanted to face up to the great contestant who, so far, had ignored him. While still in Dresden he requested the Dean of the Berlin faculty to announce his lectures straight away in the catalogue of courses. He wanted to teach 'universal philosophy, i.e. the teaching of the essence of the world and of the human spirit', and as for the hours of his lectures, no doubt the 'most suitable would be . . . those when Herr Professor Hegel has his principal course' (CL, 55).

Schopenhauer underestimated the power of the Hegelian spirit in a positively foolhardy manner. Whereas well over two hundred students were crowding into Hegel's lectures, no more than five keen types wished to be instructed by Schopenhauer in his first semester on the 'teaching of the essence of the world'. It did not greatly help Schopenhauer that in his first lecture he proclaimed himself an 'avenger' who had come to liberate post-Kantian philosophy, stuck as it was in 'paradoxes' and corrupted as it was by 'uncultured obscure language' (LTR, 57), from the stranglehold of its tormentors. His message was heard but not believed. Belief was given to Hegel, against whom the whole of Schopenhauer's proclaimed avenging was directed.

Schopenhauer the avenger was bound in that situation to seem like a sectarian preacher opposing the towering power of the Hegelian church. It was only a slight consolation that, after his inaugural lecture in a trivial controversy about the concept of 'motive' – the only personally conducted controversy between the two – he proved himself the more knowledgeable in the natural sciences.

In the spring of 1818 Hegel had been appointed to the chair vacated by Fichte's death four years previously. The Prussian Minister of Education Altenstein, a comparatively liberal politician, was one of the philosopher's admirers and supported his call to Berlin. What Altenstein appreciated about Hegel, and what also excited and fascinated a public which had been stirred by the upheavals of the past few years and now wished to relax a little, was the significant manner in which Hegel was processing the modernization impulses of the French Revolution, while at the same time combining them with a conservative state-supporting attitude. When Hegel's *Philosophie des Rechts* (*Philosophy of Right*) appeared in 1820 with that famous sentence from the introduction: 'what is reasonable is real; and what is real is reasonable,' Minister Altenstein congratulated the author with the words: 'It seems to me that you are giving . . . philosophy the only correct position with regard to reality, and therefore you will most assuredly succeed in preserving your listeners from the ruinous illusion which rejects that which exists, without having properly understood it, and which, especially with regard to the state, indulges in the arbitrary erection of vacuous ideals.'

Hegelian philosophy had sold its soul to the project of modernism, i.e. thinking in terms of historical progress and societal reason, but at the same time stood against any 'arbitrariness of presumptuous subjects'. Thus Hegel, for instance, described the philosopher and fraternity student Fries, who was persecuted by the state authorities, as a 'warlord of that shallowness which calls itself philosophy' and which presumes to let the state, that structure developed over the centuries through the 'labour of reason, to congeal into a pap of the heart, of friendship and of enthusiasm'.

Hegel found this power-protected polemical attitude entirely compatible with the sentiments which, to the end of his days, made him drink a glass of red wine in memory of the French Revolution on every 14 July. The Revolution to him remained a 'glorious sunrise', the 'colossal discovery of the innermost essence of liberty'. As late as 1822, at the very time when Hegel called on the Prussian authorities to do something about a literary periodical in which his philosophy had been criticized, he had this to say about the French Revolution: 'As long as the sun has stood in the vault of the sky and the planets have revolved around it no one had ever seen man standing on his head, that is: standing on the idea, and building the world in accordance with it.' On another occasion Hegel admitted that it had only been the Revolution that had produced modern philosophy, and hence, above all, his own.

Revolutionary action by individuals or social groups was rejected by Hegel; instead he placed the revolutionary impulse in the throbbing heart of the world spirit, which performed its work without the philosopher having to interfere. All he had to do, and all he could do, was formulate in concepts that which was happening anyway; and what was happening anyway was the inevitably progressive historical process, a history of the spirit's finding itself in the material reality of the life of society. The Whole was the True, because the Whole was *becoming* the True. In his preface Hegel presented his *Philosophy of Right* as the philosophy of the past future: 'As for saying anything about *instruction* on what the world should be like, philosophy anyway always comes too late. It only emerges as the *thought* of the world at a time when reality has already completed its formative process and has accomplished itself. . . . If philosophy paints grey on grey, then a form of life has aged, and with grey on grey it cannot be rejuvenated but only recognized; Minerva's owl only begins its flight at the onset of dusk.' To Hegel history is in fact the world's judgement. History will put an end to everything outdated, to everything that opposes the spirit's urge for self-realization. It requires no wild rebels, no rabble-rousers, no demagogues; indeed it does not require any 'arbitrariness of the subject', which anyway insists only on the narrow-minded interests of individual freedom. Such 'arbitrariness' only destroys itself, and there is no great loss in helping the process along a little. Hence Hegel's declaration of loyalty to a state which was just about to pull the 'demagogues' out of circulation. In a letter to Niethammer Hegel had this to say about it: 'I cling to the belief that the world spirit has commanded our age to advance; such a command is obeyed; that being advances like an armoured, serried phalanx, irresistibly and with such imperceptible motion as the sun moves forward, through thick and thin; countless light formations opposing and supporting it clash along the flanks, most of them do not even know what it is all about, and only receive blows on their heads as if from an invisible hand.'

Hegel conspired with the world spirit and therefore had no need, unlike Fichte before him, to involve himself in the actions of the day. Hegel had raised Fichte's existential activism to a Napoleonic level. He did not fritter himself away in '*petites batailles*' but sat at the general's command post. It so happened that Napoleon was quite near when Hegel gave birth to his *Phänomenologie des Geistes (Phenomenology of Spirit)*, the work that was to establish his reputation.

The year was 1806, and Hegel was still in Jena, working feverishly on the completion of his book. Napoleon with his army was moving against Prussia, and Jena feared the worst. And the worst happened: Napoleon entered Jena. As he was writing the final passages of his work Hegel could see from his window the soldiers bivouacking in the marketplace and stoking a huge fire with the boards and posts of market stalls and butcher's tables. Wisps of smoke entered through the cracks around his window. That night he completed his work, writing those famous sentences which conclude the *Phenomenology of Spirit*:

> The *goal*, Absolute Knowing, or Spirit that knows itself as Spirit, has for its path the recollection of the Spirits. . . . Their preservation, regarded from the side of their free existence, appearing in the form of contingency, is History; but regarded from the side of their [philo-

sophically] comprehended organization, it is the Science of Knowing in the sphere of appearance; the two together, comprehended History, form alike the inwardizing and the Calvary of absolute Spirit, the actuality, truth and certainty of his throne, without which he would be lifeless and alone. Only

> from the chalice of this realm of spirits
> foams forth for Him his own infinitude.

That night Jena was in flames. The French had set fire to the residence of the Muses and there was looting. Hegel stuffed his *Phenomenology* into his pocket and fled. When he returned he found his apartment devastated, with not a piece of underwear or clean paper left. And yet, what was all this compared to having seen Napoleon, the man who had caused all this to him: 'I saw the Emperor – that world soul – ride forth through the city to reconnoitre. It is indeed a wonderful sensation to see such an individual, here concentrated at one point, mounted on a horse, reaching out over the world and dominating it.'

One is reminded of Heinrich Mann's obedient subject Diedrich Hessling in *Der Untertan*, who, most hurtfully insulted by a smart lieutenant, proudly remarks: 'There's no one like him!' Hegel, likewise, though badly ruffled by the world spirit, did not cease to admire him.

For the world spirit, in particular, it is true that you cannot make an omelette without breaking eggs. In Jena Hegel was one of the eggs. In Berlin he had moved a lot closer to those who were making the omelettes.

Hegel was in love with history: 'The True is the Bacchantic ecstasy in which no member is not drunk.'

It had all begun at the Tübingen abbey school, when, upon news of the storming of the Bastille, Hegel and his roommates Schelling and Hölderlin planted a freedom tree in the Neckar meadow. Euphoria at a progressive history that could be 'made' burst even through the Kantian barrier against metaphysics: there was no reason why our *consciousness* should be thought of as separate from *being*, as Kant had taught. The power of history, as imagined on the Neckar meadow, suggested a different definition of being: 'being' is the spirit's 'own'; to the revolutionary-minded theology students the 'spirit', like Christ, comes into its 'own'. Hegel decided to lend a hand to ensure that 'his lot' accepted it, the spirit. The time of the sacrifice on the Cross was over. In the circle of his friends, Hölderlin contributed the idea that thought should rescind the primal separation of judgement: that is, its separation from being. The great impetus for conciliation was seeking a kind of reason that recognized itself in its 'otherness', in nature and in history. In his *Phenomenology of the Spirit* Hegel was to characterize that reason as one which 'rakes through all innards of things' and 'opens all their veins', so that it might 'leap out from them and face itself'.

As, however, the history of the quarter-century following the Revolution brought a lot of disappointment to the enthusiasts of Revolution, everything for Hegel depended on his establishing belief in the reason of history in such a way that it could never be disappointed again. The betrayed lover was consoling himself by being privy to the 'ruses of reason'. Hegel's entire energy was directed towards designing a system of historical reason that was immune to disappointment. In a political memorandum written in 1802, i.e. shortly after the transformation of the Revolution into Napoleonism, Hegel argued:

> The ideas contained in this work can have . . . no other purpose or effect than an understanding of *that which is*, and thereby to promote a calmer view, as well as a more temperate acceptance of it in contact and in words. For what makes us violent and sorrowful is not that which is, but the fact that it *is not* as *it should be*. If, however, we recognize that *it is as it must be*, i.e. not according to arbitrariness or accident, we also accept that it should be that way.

With his statement Hegel had arrived at himself: there was no need to make demands on reality, since what was reasonable was happening anyway. What 'should be' was consumed by 'what is'. Every disappointment brought us nearer to the truth, dissolved pure 'opinion' and made us ripe for complicity with objective reason. In Berlin, eventually, Hegel raised that 'ripeness', for himself personally, to cosiness.

Looking back on Hegel's last decade in Berlin, a personal witness of those years, Rudolf Haym, wrote: 'One has to recall that period in order to understand what the real dominance and validity of a philosophical system is about. One has to picture . . . that grand gesture and that conviction of the Hegelians, who, in complete unsmiling seriousness, were airing the question of what the further content of world history could possibly be, now that in the Hegelian philosophy the world spirit had reached the goal, the knowledge of itself.'

It was in this cosy certainty that the world spirit had arrived that Hegel, during his Berlin years, wrote his great works: the *Philosophy of Right*, the *Geschichte der Philosophie* (*History of Philosophy*) and the *Philosophie der Geschichte* (*Philosophy of History*), and that he revised the *Logik* (*Logic*) and the *Enzyklopädie* (*Encyclopaedia*) – while living the life of a solid citizen. Philosophy, he used to say, should 'remain in the lecture theatre', and anyone making his personal acquaintance was at first astonished at the platitudinous, ordinary, and indeed shallow conversation Hegel clearly liked to indulge in. Heinrich Hotho made Hegel's acquaintance in the twenties and described him as follows: 'His prematurely aged figure was stooped . . . a yellow-grey dressing gown fell carelessly from his shoulders, over his meagre body, to the ground; there was no outward trace either of impressive distinction or of captivating charm, a trait of old-fashioned respectability and probity was what emerged most from his whole bearing.'

No scintillating head, no eloquence: a man struggling hard with his words, and what he uttered was often barely comprehensible because of his marked

Swabian accent. People would guess what his 'sumpn' might be, until they discovered that it meant the weighty philosophical category of 'something'. That was not how one had imagined the world spirit. If, on the other hand, it was a case of attacking the Catholics, then this Swabian Protestant, which he always remained, could display a very sharp tongue. In one of his lectures Hegel had permitted himself a joke. When a mouse gobbled up a consecrated host, he said, then, according to the Catholic teaching on transubstantiation, it accepted the body of the Lord and therefore should be adored.

After this stupid remark the Church demanded that the state should take Hegel to task. He defended himself by arguing that as a Lutheran he had a duty to unmask papist idolatry. He said the same in front of his students. A chaplain among the audience stared menacingly at the professor. Hegel, unshaken, remarked: 'Your looking at me like that does not impress me.'

As a philosopher Hegel very nearly wore official uniform. The *Jahrbücher für wissenschaftliche Kritik* (*Annals of Scholarly Criticism*), which he founded in 1826, was originally to have a representative of the state as a co-editor. This did not come about, but the publication was nevertheless run like a government body. That was why Börne attacked it: here was a threat of state control of the spirit.

The 'persecution of demagogues', which began after 1819 and resulted in the arrest of several Opposition thinkers while others, such as the Berlin theologian de Wette, were hounded from office, produced a political calm in Berlin during the twenties. Student fraternities remained banned. There was drinking, but no political talk; there was work but no debate. The student Ludwig Feuerbach wrote to his father from Berlin in 1824: 'there is probably no other university where such universal application reigns, such a sense of something higher than mere student affairs, such striving for scholarship, such peace and quiet, than here. Other universities are veritable taverns compared to this place of work.'

Hegel's philosophy, which presents the world spirit, too, as at work, fitted very well into that mood. Work should be followed by relaxation. But art, if it wished to be more than relaxation from work, was in a poor way.

It was the theatre and the opera which benefited most from the recession of political culture. These two art forms, being social collecting points on a large scale, operated as safety valves. Rahel Varnhagen wrote: 'A city without a theatre is to me like a man with his eyes shut, a place without a breath of air, without direction. In our days and in our cities it is the only universal area where the circle of joy, of the spirit, of the participation and reunion of all classes is drawn.' And Minister Bernstorff observed laconically: 'After all, one must leave one bone to those snapping dogs!'

Passion for the theatre experienced a new climax. Here, also, was the great debate which could not take place elsewhere. *Der Freimütige* (*The Candid Speaker*), a much-read entertainment journal, put up letter boxes in the Berlin streets where theatre reviews, which were in fact subsequently published, could be posted. Hegel, too, wrote reviews of performances.

Taste had changed: times had never been so bad for high culture. There was a boom in light entertainment. Between 1815 and 1834 the Berlin National Theatre staged 56 tragedies and 292 comedies. When Napoleon was conquering the world, the tragedy of destiny appeared in Germany. After his fall, the end of great deeds and great tragedy also meant the end of such weighty subjects on the stage. Light entertainment became even lighter. Actors reaped triumphs in farcical parts. But the decor grew ever more splendid. E. T. A. Hoffmann's *Undine* benefited from that trend. Schinkel was its stage designer. That magnificence was subsequently outclassed by the performance of Weber's *Freischütz* (1821). But the most impressive staging of all was that of Spontini. Here elephants appeared on stage and cannon were fired.

The predilection for lightweight entertainment made the public receptive also to the light-footed. The ballet dancer Fanny Essler was said by Berliners to be 'dancing world history'.

Schopenhauer arrived in a city which was trying to recover from the stresses of the past three decades. As in the foyer of the theatre, among the confusion of voices, the most recent events were already dying away, impressions of the tremendous events that had been witnessed were fading to everyday triviality. Hegel's grand philosophy was bound to seem like an expansive, cosy review of events which once held everyone breathless and which were now over. A time of harvest: one reviewed and preserved one's stock. The Biedermeier period.

Yet the spirit of the age was more sophisticated than at first it appeared. As if nothing had happened, Restoration policy after 1815 still tried to force life into the outmoded order of the eighteenth century. But too much had happened. There was something forced, something contrived, about the belief in the durability and reliability of traditional forms. One accepted life as it was, but with a faint sense of shifting ground. Convictions were beginning to half-close their eyes, morality was squinting. One might duck, one might pull in one's horns, but one settled down comfortably and enjoyed looking out from one's 'secret little room' (Eichendorff) into open nature, where abysmal things were happening, where 'twilight' reigned. During those years Hoffmann's tales were highly popular, and Professor Wolfart publicly produced his somnambulists. Schopenhauer, too, hastened to watch.

A reviewer in the *Literaturblatt* lamented the loss of 'naivety', of 'tenderness', of 'heroism'. From this new perspective of the twenties even the playfulness of Romantic irony seemed 'heroic'; after all, that was concerned with the whole, with the elevation of the self-powerful ego. All that, the writer lamented, had now been replaced by mere sophistication, by cheap effects and by absurdity.

Sophistication marked even the attempts at strenuous solidity. The earlier

Romantic delight in loss of orientation now flipped over into delight in putting down roots. Friedrich Schlegel and Clemens Brentano were received into the Catholic Church, Hoffmann became a Chamber Court Counsellor, and Hegel became a loyal supporter of the regime. A lot of loud pedal was being used – and not just on the pianoforte which was invading all bourgeois living rooms.

On these rocking foundations – with everyone pretending that they were solid – a great deal of talking began. Never before had there been so much snug togetherness, never before had so much been written and read. Clubs, associations, round tables and ladies' circles shot up like mushrooms in Berlin. There was the Lawless Society, which, according to Hoffmann, pursued no other objective 'than to eat a good midday meal in the German tradition'. A Society for the German Language grew up around the Gerlach brothers. Hoffmann met his Serapion brethren, Clemens Brentano founded the Society of Cockchafers which devoted themselves to 'poetry and aspirations'. There was the league of Philarten, who, so they claimed, wanted to 'awaken the soul from its sleep'. Meetings were held in Friedrichstrasse of the Debating Club for Unresolved Questions.

These were in part societal forms with a political undercurrent, which compensated for the strangulation of public opinion. But even more so, they reflected a cosy attitude, where literature provided a pleasurable *frisson* and a touch of the unsolid.

Literary life in Berlin was in a sorry state. At the Café Royal a handful of students would meet in order collectively to finish Goethe's *Faust*. Evening entertainments featured men who, in response to cues called out from the floor, would compose poems. A certain Otto Jacobi, a law court official, threatened to cover the whole of German history, starting with Charlemagne, in several dozen plays. He was outdistanced by Ernst Raupach, who within the next ten years was engaged in writing fifty plays for the Berlin stage, about the history of the Hohenstaufen dynasty. All of them were produced. Publishers of ladies' albums and almanacs organized authors' competitions: reader demand actually outstripped the large supply of competent authors. The university, young Feuerbach had written to his father, was a 'place of work'. That was a fact. In contrast to what Wilhelm von Humboldt, the founder of Berlin University, had envisaged, the university was concentrating on practical vocational training. But even application and industry were still moving on uncertain ground. Molelike, honest application still wished to be reassured about things great and whole: how everything came to be and how it now was. Those about to become tiny wheels and tiny cogs retained enough curiosity and disquiet to wish to know how the machine worked and what it was all for. But this curiosity was not pushed to the point of allowing oneself to be disquieted. Such safety-first curiosity was readily satisfied in Hegel's course. That was why veterinary surgeons, insurance brokers, civil servants, operatic tenors and commercial clerks were rushing to his lectures. They may not have understood Hegel too well, but surely it was enough to know that there was one person who understood it all and found it good. This then was the mood and the public demand. Small wonder that Schopenhauer with his message cut no ice here.

To begin with, there was Schopenhauer's return to Kant. Kant's transcendental critique of cognition was quite simply regarded as outdated. What the world really was – that, by then, was believed to be accurately known. The need for comfort called for that belief; besides, history had ceased to be confusing and had calmed down again. Respect for the unknowability of the 'thing in itself' had vanished, as had fascination with the demonic element, so strikingly represented by Napoleon. Added to this was the fact that the empirical discovery of nature, untroubled by theory, was on the advance. Its triumphs made the scruples of reason seem increasingly pointless. The spiritual blend of empirical-pragmatic sobriety and Hegelian speculative zeal, which remained compatible with Protestant–Christian orthodoxy, denied all prospects to a metaphysics of the will which was based on a radicalized Kantian critique of cognition and which was thoroughly atheistic.

One either understood the metaphysics of the will and rejected it *because* one understood it, or one dismissed it because one misunderstood it and therefore failed to see its originality. To begin with the latter: a few reviews of Schopenhauer's work which initially appeared saw the metaphysics of the will as warmed-up Fichte; i.e. the 'will' was understood as a force of the spirit, of reason – a crucial misunderstanding, against which Schopenhauer had expressly warned in his work. The 'will' was not understood in the way intended: as the other thing beside reason. No matter how much Schopenhauer spoke of urges, of will in nature, of nature within us, one was at best prepared to hear Schelling's 'nature' in it. But in Schelling's 'nature' the spirit-subject was still inherent – the desire, the urge which found its highest, its self-aware shape in the spirit, in consciousness. If, on the other hand, one understood Schopenhauer's metaphysics of the will correctly, then it must have seemed extremely disturbing to an age which philosophically was in the thrall of Hegelian panlogism. That reason, in Schopenhauer's system, should be a mere epiphenomenon, that it was not the motive force behind nature and history, that reality in its core, as a 'thing in itself', was something non-reasonable – that his contemporaries refused to accept.

The originality of Schopenhauer's approach was either misunderstood, or else it was understood but rejected as deviant and not worth discussing. Schopenhauer's position against panlogism made him appear out of step with the passion for historical thinking, a passion massively aroused by Hegel. Unlike the majority of his contemporaries, Schopenhauer refused, and had to refuse, to interpret history as a progressive happening of truth. His viciously ranting invectives against history as a carnival and costume ball of always the same passions and opinions made him look like a philosophical fossil from pre-modern times.

Then there was Schopenhauer's pessimism and his denial of the world, which sounded mystical and too Indian. They had to be rejected, if not as outrageous, then at least as bizarre – if only because of the undisguised atheism inherent in these opinions.

Schopenhauer was in fact lucky in that he was not yet being taken seriously as a philosopher. Had he been taken seriously, then his affront against religion – something a philosopher could not afford during the Restoration period – would not have gone unpunished. State and university authorities normally intervened in far more harmless instances, though of course only if the voice blaspheming against the national religion was actually heard. Kant had experienced this in the past, and Fichte after him; during Schopenhauer's Berlin years one Eduard Beneke was thus disciplined – incidentally, a reviewer of the *World as Will and Representation* who had been greatly reviled by Arthur. Later, nearly the whole of the Young Hegelian or Left Hegelian school was put under an academic teaching ban on the grounds of alleged atheism.

Hegel, whose historicization of religion had provided the detonator for subsequent explosions of religious critique, was watching his step very carefully, afraid of the charge of atheism. In his Berlin lectures on 'Philosophy and Religion' he observed: 'Philosophy has been accused of placing itself *above religion*: but this is incorrect in fact . . . it merely places itself *above* the *form of faith*, its content is the same.' Even so, the hardline faction of Lutheran orthodoxy in Berlin did not trust the loyal state philosopher any further than they could see him. The figures around Bishop Eylert and around Hengstenberg's *Kirchenzeitung* (*Church Journal*) maligned him at court – at first without success. Schopenhauer's metaphysics of the will, on the other hand – a teaching which declared the will to be the only substance, without a creator-god and purpose in the world, hence the purest form of atheism – did not even penetrate to those circles, and his teaching of the denial of the will was so Indian and abstruse that not even Bishop Eylert, who had ears everywhere, was alarmed by it. In a memorandum dated 1819, which weighed heavily on the university politicians, Eylert had railed against the 'eccentric arbitrariness' of modern philosophy, 'which, with a presumptuous mania for innovation, is building and destroying systems, and in this ever airy alternation confuses both language and concepts'. Schopenhauer's 'eccentric arbitrariness' was then still *hors concours* and attracted no disciplinary measures, especially as his theory was not one of those 'systems' of which, as Eylert wrote, it was to be feared that they might 'exceed their sphere' to become 'revolutionary politics'.

Schopenhauer's philosophy of art must similarly have seemed strange to his contemporaries. The days of the Romantic philosophy of art were over after 1815. Artists' euphoria had given way to realistic sobriety. The 'wild men' of the turn of the century were dead or held official posts. Importance was now, more modestly, attached to the entertainment value of art; the public wanted it to be pleasing rather than adventurous. Artists wanted to arrive without departing on flights of fancy. Hegel had taught that art, after all, was an underdeveloped stage of the spirit, one that was far surpassed by religion and philosophy, one – above all – that had to obey the commands of the objective spirit, i.e. ultimately the state. Art, like religion, was being sucked into relativist historical thinking and questioned as to its worldly usefulness and moralizing force. The Muses, too, were to work within and for bourgeois life. In short: there was no longer the élan or the carefree readiness to place art at the top of possible hierarchies. Art was to be a servant, decorative and useful.

Not so Schopenhauer: he neither treated art historically nor considered its usefulness in the realistic sense. Schopenhauer, as we know, took seriously – and in an unparalleled radical way – Kant's definition of the enjoyment of art as 'disinterested pleasure'. Schopenhauer loved art not as an ornament, or as a relaxation in life, but he loved it in opposition to life, as a pre-manifestation of salvation from the hardships and pains of the will to live. With Schopenhauer the entire force of the religion of art was brought back, but in a totally atheistic metaphysics of art. Future generations of artists – from Richard Wagner to Proust and Samuel Beckett – were to feel elevated by such a philosophy. Now, however, was a time of artistic restraint. One did not aim at the whole, nor did one want to disappear in the totally other. 'Feet on the ground' was the slogan.

The style of his philosophy also marked Schopenhauer as an outsider. The attitude of the individual thinker is emphasized too aggressively. In the first edition of his principal work the polemical attacks on his contemporaries are still rather tame. The brusqueness and near-hostility, however, lies in his gesture of haughty ignoring: Schopenhauer quotes the classical philosophers of antiquity, the middle ages, and modernity as far as Kant. He engages in discourse across millennia, implying that the philosophers of the present might be forgotten. In his writings Schopenhauer appears as a man who, aloof from the mutterings and the turmoil of the day, has thought through everything afresh, from first principles and independently: a great philosophy built up by his own hands and – away from academic business – at his own desk. This philosophy, no matter how learned it seems, lacks the smell of the academic stable. The non-cerebral nature, the clarity and the beauty of Schopenhauer's language were conspicuously outside the framework of professorial discourse. There is even a hint of naivety, of carefreeness, almost of ingenuousness, about his philosophy. Let us remember the manner in which Schopenhauer had his first Berlin lectures advertised: 'Arthur Schopenhauer will present universal philosophy, i.e. the teaching of the essence of the world and the human spirit.'

Even more striking is what might be called the 'existential' aspect of Schopenhauer's philosophy. It is perhaps least evident in his 'ethics', in his teaching of the renunciation of the will. He himself points out that neither is 'the saint a philosopher' nor the 'philosopher a saint'; philosophy instead – as a 'sculptor' representing a 'beautiful person' need not himself be beautiful – need only offer a reflecting image of the inner nature of the world' and of real life in it (WWR I, 383). Kierkegaard was later to observe critically that Schopenhauer had not lived what he had taught.

Nevertheless, Schopenhauer's point of departure, in contrast to his contemporaries, was existential through and through; simply because he linked the philosophical interpretation of the world to the undeceivably and unmistakably unique experience of his own body. No matter whether a world-spanning picture of the will was subsequently to be designed – what the will actually is, that can only be *experienced* by each individual in his own body–spirit identity. Schopenhauer speaks of the identity of the subject of volition and recognition in the individual. I may know that the world is representation *and* will, but I can *experience* it only at one single point in the world, and that point is myself. I may think the thoughts of others, the world as an idea enters into me and I myself am an idea to others – to that extent I am always also outside, with others, with history, etc. But I cannot leave my body, and I cannot enter into anyone else's body. It is in this bodily identity that the whole density of being is concentrated in happiness and in suffering.

All around Schopenhauer, however, different philosophies were proclaimed. In them, being is *outside* in the objects and in the things, in the historical process, in the march of the spirit; what is nearest, one's own body, either becomes an alien thing, dissected by the distanced searching gaze, or something even more remote that is first deduced from the categories of the spirit. The spirit, in that case, is what matters: that it happens to be located in my body is accidental. Schopenhauer, too, can think the individual away in his cosmos of the will, but he does not forget for a moment that it is ultimately the existing individual that thinks itself away. The whole world, which is mine, is balanced at the peak of individual existence. That is why Schopenhauer has called this identity of the subject of volition and the subject of recognition in one individual the most amazing riddle, *the* philosophical problem *par excellence* (WWR I, 102).

This then was what Schopenhauer in the summer of 1820 intended to present to a handful of students at the University of Berlin. Next door Hegel was addressing a packed lecture theatre. The following winter semester Schopenhauer might as well have packed his bags: for lack of interest no lecture materialized. It was an existential disaster for Schopenhauer. Would his philosophy help him to cope with it? Schopenhauer had made a philosophy. What was that philosophy now making of the philosopher?

CHAPTER NINETEEN

DISAPPOINTMENT IN BERLIN

About 1823 Arthur Schopenhauer noted in his secret daybook, *Eis Eauton*:

> If at times I have felt unhappy, then this has been largely due to a *méprise*, to a mistaken identity: on those occasions I regarded myself as someone other than who I am, and lamented that person's misfortune: e.g. a *Privatdozent* who is not made a professor and has no audience, or one of whom a philistine here speaks ill or a gossip there talks scandal, or the defendant in that bodily injury suit, or the lover whom the girl he particularly wants rejects, or the patient housebound by his illness. . . . I was not any of these, all this is alien material from which, at best, the coat was made which I wore for a while and then took off in favour of another. But who am I really? He who wrote the *World as Will and Representation* and provided a solution to the great problem of existence. . . . That is who I am, and what could challenge that man in the years he still draws breath? [P IV, 2, 109]

Here we have a catalogue of the major and minor disasters of those years: the collapse of his university career, the suit for damages following charges of bodily injury inflicted on the seamstress Marquet, the unsatisfactory development of his affair with the chorus girl and dancer Caroline Richter, known as Medon, and his nervous disease and ear trouble which confined him to his room for a whole year. But we have here also, moreover in pointed formulation, Schopenhauer's strategy for dealing with it all. What is happening to me, Schopenhauer is saying, is not really happening to me because *I am someone else*. I am the author of a great philosophical work. Outside in the world there is the social masquerade, the play-acting, the comedy. Whenever Schopenhauer cuts a poor figure in it he withdraws to his work-ego. But there is something curious about that work-ego: it no longer is an 'ego'. First, Schopenhauer says: I am not out there, I am my work. Then he says: My work is something other than just my ego. In his manuscript journal he wrote (about 1825):

What guarantees me the genuineness and hence the everlastingness of my philosophical theses is that I did not make them at all, but that they made themselves. They originated within me entirely without my help, at moments when all volition in me had, as it were, fallen soundly asleep. . . . Only what at such moments of totally will-free knowledge appeared within me, I wrote down as a mere spectator and witness and used it in my work. This warrants its genuineness and guards me against doubt in the face of a lack of all sympathy or recognition. [P III, 209]

Hegel had said the same about himself: that the absolute spirit had settled within him. The difference was that Hegel was believed, whereas Schopenhauer was left on his own – in spite of, and because of, this bold self-reassuring manoeuvre. Arthur would have to mobilize considerable amounts of thought to make such self-reassurance proof against disappointment. Fortunately for him, he was not lacking in ideas: necessity is the mother of invention, and besides, there were enough arguments in his own philosophy to explain away the lack of attention paid to it – in other words, to rationalize that lack.

'*My age*,' Schopenhauer noted in his journal in 1820, 'is not the sphere of my activity but only the soil on which my physical person stands, yet that is only a very insignificant part of my whole person' (P III, 14). That 'whole' person towered above his age. One could not see it any more than one can see a mountaintop from a cloud-covered plain. Schopenhauer is always out to devalue the present and his contemporaries. It was not as if significant figures could not exist even then, but their voices were being drowned by the ephemeral sounds of the day, which, in an age increasingly obsessed with writing and reading, swelled to a continuous roar. A century before Ortega y Gasset Schopenhauer diagnosed a 'revolt of the masses' in the world of discourse. For the masses, which are increasingly finding means of expression as well as an audience, the only thing that counts is that which supports self-preservation, that which supports life-affirming illusions. The ordinary person – Schopenhauer refers to 'factory products' or 'bipeds' (P II, 73) – is afraid: he seeks the safe anchorage of a philosophy that flatters and reassures him. Hence the belief in a deity, a belief continuing under various guises, in a deity that looks after man and – if possible through man – guides everything towards the best possible solution, no matter whether that deity is called 'history', 'absolute spirit', 'nature', or later 'the proletariat'. The true philosopher, on the other hand, lives 'dangerously but in freedom': neither the old nor the newly costumed certainties provide any protection. The meaningless homelessness simply has to be survived. Naturally, this was not anything for 'public opinion', which was looking for very palpable certainties. That was why the 'flitting will o' the wisp of public opinion' must not be made one's 'lodestar' (P III, 71).

A philosophy whose insights are gained in thinking in opposition to the will to live has nothing to say to those – and they of course are the great majority –

who demand knowledge in the service of life. This idea underlies all the varieties of argumentation with which Schopenhauer tries to brush off his displeasure at the fact that his philosophy has remained without resonance. It is an idea well anchored in the core of Schopenhauer's philosophy. From it stems his positive attitude to esotericism, because esotericism permits a proud reinterpretation: I was never talking to those who now ignore me. My truth, dismissed by the marketplace, is not for the marketplace. In his manuscript journal he reflected on the secret cult of the Greek mysteries: 'The *mysteries* of the ancients are an excellent invention, in so far as they are based on the idea of selecting, out of the large crowd of people to whom the whole truth is simply inaccessible, a few, to whom the truth is then communicated within certain limits, and from these again a few, to whom much more is then revealed because they can comprehend more, and so forth' (P III, 211).

The esoteric attitude can be linked to a particularly sophisticated or would-be sophisticated intention – as evinced by the history of the secret societies of the late eighteenth century – but it can also stem from a pre-modern concept of truth. In an age which has increasingly become used to associating truth with 'effectiveness' (with an audience, in history, as command over nature, etc.) and hence with 'usefulness', any refusal to acknowledge the empirical criterion of success or a majority decision as a criterion of truth, together with the endeavour to emphasize the bliss of knowledge rather than the utility of truth, is almost bound to lead to an elitism of the spirit. This can be observed in Schopenhauer. Nietzsche admired him for it and followed him in it, with the knowing smile of the too-clever-by-half.

Schopenhauer, however, despite his esoteric and haughty attitude, rather naively insisted that with his philosophy he had served 'mankind': 'Contrary to man's nature and right I had to divert my strength from service to my own person and the promotion of my own well-being, in order to make a present of them to the service of mankind. My intellect belonged not to me but to the world' (P IV, 2, 107).

No matter how high-flown these thoughts about 'service to mankind' may have been, they also served some very limited, private, purposes. Thus, in 1822, Schopenhauer used them to justify his selfish procedure in the matter of his inheritance, thereby putting the seal on his break with his family: 'For this reason I was also entitled to watch carefully to ensure that the support of my paternal inheritance, which had to carry me for so long and without which the world would have received nothing from me, would remain to me also in old age' (P IV, 22, 107).

In his reflections of the 1820s Schopenhauer did not only have to rationalize his lack of success with the public; nor was he only looking to his philosophy for protection against disappointment. He not only berated his public and buttressed his self-assurance, he also pursued self-clarification. Although he felt that he had accomplished his great task there were still numerous problems which would not let him rest and which he wished to clarify. These reflections would subsequently be incorporated in his later publications, especially in the second volume of his principal work.

The equation of 'will' and 'thing in itself' – the core of his philosophy – would not let him be. 'Will' was only 'in a sense' the thing in itself. In his *Brieftasche (Pocket Book)* he wrote in 1824: 'To *recognize the thing in itself* is a contradiction because all cognition is *representation*, whereas the thing in itself means the thing to the extent that it is *not*' (P III, 778).

And yet: the 'thing in itself', he argued, was the 'will' to the extent that the experience of the 'emergence of the act of volition from the depth of our inside' (P III, 36) was the point at which the representation could most clearly comprehend the in-itselfness of reality, because it was experiencing it in its own body. The essence of the world, the 'thing in itself', is understood by us according to its only just knowable aspect: 'but just because the will is the most immediate phenomenon of the thing in itself, it evidently follows that if the remaining phenomena of the thing in itself were brought to us equally close, i.e. if their cognition were raised to the same degree of clarity and immediacy as our will, *they would present themselves just as the will does in us*. I am therefore entitled to state that the inner essence of every thing is *will*, or that *will* is the thing in itself' (P III, 36).

Schopenhauer went on probing: 'but where does the will come from?' (P III, 68). He cut himself short: that was a meaningless question. One could not ask questions beyond the existence of the will. *What* something means, we may discover by asking; *that* it is at all lies beyond all question. While philosophy had so far placed the spirit or God, i.e. the essence, before existence, Schopenhauer now reversed the relationship: *existence* comes before *essence*. In his journal he jotted down the bold sentence: 'the inner essence of the world is not a recognizing one' (P III, 70). The *existence* of the will is rather like a black hole swallowing up the light of knowledge. His philosophy must therefore, Schopenhauer conceded, leave a 'host of questions' unanswered, 'but,' he continued, 'our thinking does not even have forms for the answers which that kind of question would demand' (P III, 70). Schelling in his late years would brood over the same *aporia*, over the riddle of *that*.

Should one 'complain' about the 'darkness in which we' have to 'live our lives'? Schopenhauer asks himself and answers

> This complaint is unjust and arises from the illusory mistaken belief that the entirety of things originated from an *intellect*, that it had existed as a *representation* before becoming real, i.e. that it had to have sprung from *representations* and hence had to be open to the representation and exhaustible through it. In reality, however, everything we complain that we do not know is probably not in itself *knowable*. For the representation in which all knowledge lies is only the

outward side of our existence, something added to it, something that was not necessary for the preservation of the existence of the things generally, of the entirety of the world, but merely for the preservation of each animate individual. [P III, 183]

In short: To Being, both recognition and being recognized are external.

In recognition there is differentiation, separation, individuation. But are these also differences in Being itself? – that is the next question. Let us take our own Being.

> What does everyone know of himself? His body, visually through his senses; next, internally his volition and a continuous sequence of acts of the will triggered off by representations: that is all. The substratum of all this, however, the actual willing and knowing is not accessible to us at all: we only look outwards; inside everything is dark. . . . Judging by the part that falls within our knowledge, everyone is completely different from everyone else: but is it therefore certain that the same applies with regard to that part which is the essential, and which remains unknown to everyone? Why should not the essence of everyone, in regard to this totally unknown part, be the same and identical, even though, in regard to the knowable part, it presents itself as distinct? [P III, 283]

On the side of our Being averted from knowledge we are all the same, because we are all 'will'. How uncomfortable Schopenhauer really was with this idea emerges from a note in his manuscript journal from 1823: 'An optimist bids me to open my eyes and to see how beautiful the world is with its mountains, plants, air, animals, etc. These things are admittedly beautiful to *behold*, but to *be* so is something entirely different' (P III, 172).

This is Schopenhauer's philosophical passion: to escape from *being* into *seeing*.

When the subject ceases to *be* will it has the chance of *seeing* the patent secret of the world, the omnipresence of the will. Here then is the delicate transition in Schopenhauer's metaphysics of the will: having originated in the 'hot zone' of the internally experienced will, it has arrived at a cooled-down cosmos of the will which offers itself only to sober knowledge, severed from will at least for some moments. The supra-individual (the 'better consciousness') catches sight of the sub-individual (the will in nature). The trained merchant clerk determined this constellation in an almost accountant-like manner: the will disappears in the subject in order to be able to emerge the more clearly in the object: the minus on the one side becomes the plus on the other.

As for the will-less subject – should it not be pitied for its lack of being? Schopenhauer observed: 'The true essence of man is the will: representation is something secondary, something added later, something, as it were, external: and yet man finds his true salvation only when the will has disappeared from consciousness and representation alone is left in it. The essential, therefore, is to be extinguished and its phenomenon (representation), its addendum, is to remain. This needs a lot of thought' (P III, 236).

Nietzsche was to give it 'a lot of thought', arriving at the conclusion that life could be justified only as an aesthetic phenomenon. Schopenhauer in his own reflections was led once more to the close link between his metaphysics and his ethics: if even the recognition of truth required a sobriety freed from the urge of the will, then the being in truth would have to realize an even more complete and enduring liberation from the troubles of volition. The realization of truth is, simultaneously, the de-realization of the will's vital force. Schopenhauer conceives a truth that is opposed to life. Nietzsche would take him up at this point, but with a significant reversal: as truth cannot be lived, the philosophical rehabilitation of the will must be pursued for deception; for what ultimately matters is no longer truth but power, living power.

In pursuing the 'true salvation' of pure seeing liberated from will, Schopenhauer knew quite clearly whom he wanted to escape from: Dionysus. Small wonder that Nietzsche, this inside-out Schopenhauer, would throw himself into the arms of this god of erotic salvation.

The 'thing in itself' is most clearly comprehended in the will, but where is the will most clearly experienced? In the sex act, was Schopenhauer's answer, more bluntly than ever before, in his journal: 'If I am asked where the *most intimate knowledge* of that inner essence of the world, of that thing in itself which I called the *will to live*, is to be found? or where that essence enters most clearly into our consciousness? or where it achieves the purest revelation of itself? – then I must point to the *ecstasy in the act of copulation*. That is it! That is the true essence and core of all things, the goal and the purpose of all existence' (P III, 240).

This was written by Schopenhauer in 1826. His love affair with the chorus girl and actress Caroline Richter, known as Medon, had been going on for five years.

He had met the nineteen-year-old woman in 1821. That was when he noted in his secret journal *Eis Eauton*: 'As the real time of inspired ideas is over for me and as my life henceforth is most suited to teaching, it should therefore be exposed to all eyes and have a foothold in society such as I cannot acquire as a bachelor' (P IV, 2, 106).

Caroline Richter, however, was not the woman with whom he would have that 'foothold in society'. On the suburban stages of Berlin she took the roles of 'second leading lady': in real life she compensated for this by maintaining relationships with several lovers at a time. Her beauty and the loose lifestyle of the theatre enabled her to do so. Schopenhauer, a keen theatre-goer, had fallen in love with her but was always subsequently tormented by jealousy. Ten months after he had set out on his second Italian journey in May 1822 Caroline gave birth to a child. Arthur, who remained attached to Caroline until the end of his life – he even remembered her in his will – always maintained his hostility to that child of 'infidelity'. His testamentary provisions specifically excluded Carl Ludwig Gustav Medon, as Caroline's son born in March 1823 was called. And when Schopenhauer in 1831 wished to leave Berlin together with Caroline, the project came to nought because of his refusal to meet Caroline's wish to take her son with them. Schopenhauer went to Frankfurt on his own, disappointed and hurt.

Caroline Richter had come to Berlin in 1819, at the age of seventeen, and, presumably through the support of some highly-placed person was engaged as a chorus girl at the National Theatre. A Secret Secretary Louis Medon made her pregnant, and she gave birth to her first son in the early summer of 1820; henceforth she called herself 'Medon'.

There are no letters extant from Arthur to Caroline, and there is virtually no documented information on their liaison, which after all lasted for ten years; only a few letters from Caroline to Arthur at the beginning of the 1830s, when he was already living in Frankfurt, have been discovered. In these letters Caroline complains about Schopenhauer's refusal to accept her son; she makes it clear that she would have liked to have accompanied him and that his mistrust hurt her. Having supported her financially, he no doubt had accused her of letting herself be kept by other gentlemen, for she replied: 'that I have not been frivolous, of that my debts will best convince you.'

Periodically Caroline suffered from violent chest pains, which caused her to give up her post at the National Theatre in the mid-1820s; thereafter she appeared sporadically at suburban theatres, sometimes even in leading roles.

Caroline's mysterious illness also deterred Schopenhauer, who, if his reports are to be believed, had once before, in Italy, taken flight from a tubercular woman.

Caroline for her part tried to dispel her lover's misgivings about her health by pointing out – in a manner bound to goad his jealousy – 'that I am not sick,' she wrote in 1832, 'is proved to you by the man who is so keen to marry me.'

Schopenhauer was torn one way and another: by fear of the possible illness of his mistress, by jealousy, by the fear of losing his independence if he founded a family, and by doubts as to whether Caroline was in fact the right woman for such plans.

His journals testify not only to his philosophical reflections during those years but also to the effect this love affair was having on his inner life. Inevitably the joys and pangs of love were processed into his philosophical thought. To quote an example: 'The very first appearance of a new individual is, strictly speaking, the moment when his parents begin to *love* one another, i.e. to desire each other with entirely individual affection: at that moment, in the encounter of loving glances, is the new individual formed: it is, in a sense, a new idea; and just as all ideas strive vehemently towards emergence in the phenomenon and avidly seize the substance thereto, as handed out to them by the law of causality, so this special idea of a human individual also strives most vehemently towards emergence as a phenomenon, and that vehemence is the passion of the two future parents for each other' (P III, 138).

As Schopenhauer noted down these observations in 1822 – which are subsequently restated in his *Metaphysik der Geschlechterliebe* (*Metaphysics of Love between the Sexes*) – one such 'special idea of a human individual' was 'striving towards emergence' in Caroline. But this 'idea', as he soon had to observe with mortification, was not his.

During his second Italian journey, from 1822 to 1823, he was tormented by a sense of guilt: should he not have bound Caroline more firmly to himself? Such worries were even transformed into poetry: 'But a thousand times harder it is to see / That what fortune had placed in our hands / Our stupidity has clumsily shattered' (P III, 159).

Under a southern sky, however, he permitted himself more mellow thoughts: surely, he reflected while full of doubt about Caroline, monogamy was rather an imposition for a woman: 'For a woman, limitation to *one* during the short time of her flowering and fitness, is an unnatural state. She is expected to save for one what he cannot use and what many others desire from her: and she herself is expected to suffer deprivation at that failure. Think of it!' (P III, 163).

The woman, therefore, according to Schopenhauer, should be allowed to have several men simultaneously, and the man, in exchange, to have several women in succession. 'In monogamy, man at one time has too much and in the long run too little; and the woman the other way round' (P III, 162). Because of this, 'men are half their lives whoremongers and the other half cuckolds.' In Caroline's case Schopenhauer had to reconcile himself to the role of 'cuckold'.

That a lover very often lacked prudence was something Schopenhauer experienced to his loss. Lack of prudence precipitated him into a bizarre misadventure involving a woman.

Schopenhauer was expecting a visit from Caroline on 12 August 1821. His neighbour from the flat next door, the forty-seven-year-old seamstress Caroline Marquet, was sitting with her women friends in an anteroom. Schopenhauer did not wish any prying witnesses to his reunion. Anyway, his neighbour had no right to be in the anteroom which was part of Schopenhauer's apartment: something alien was here interfering in his own sphere of will. Schopenhauer ordered the three women to leave the room. The Marquet woman refused. What followed next was described by Schopenhauer in the statement he made in the lawsuit brought against him by the seamstress:

> Eventually I threatened to throw her out, and as she defied me this is what in fact happened, but not in the way that I seized her by the throat with both hands, which is not even conceivable, but that I gripped her, as was most purposeful, around her whole body and dragged her out,

even though she resisted for all she was worth. Outside she screamed that she would sue me and she also screamed for her things, which I then hurriedly chucked after her: but as one little piece of something had been left behind, which I had overlooked, this had to serve as a pretext for her having the temerity to come back again into the *Entrée*: then I threw her out again, although she was resisting most violently and shrieking with all her might, in order if possible to rouse the whole building. As I therefore threw her out of the door for the second time she fell – I believe, deliberately. For it is the way of such people that, when they realize that *active* resistance does not get them anywhere, they resort to the *passive* side, in order to *suffer* as much as possible and to have a lot to sue about, and her earlier clamour that she would sue me entirely points in that direction. However, I declare the allegations that I tore the plaintiff's bonnet off her head, that she fainted, or indeed that I kicked her and beat her with my fist to be totally false and mendacious. Not a word of this is true, and anyone with only a slight knowledge of me will realize *a priori* that such rough brutality is quite unthinkable given my character, position and education. [CL, 75]

The Court, however, the *Kammergericht* where the Marquet woman argued her claims for damages, did not concede, either *a priori* or *a posteriori*, that the 'brutality' alleged by the seamstress was 'quite unthinkable' on the part of the accused philosopher.

The *Kammergericht* sentenced Schopenhauer to a fine of twenty *taler* for 'slight injury to the person without appreciable damage'. Caroline Marquet, however, was not satisfied with that. On the grounds of allegedly 'being paralysed down the whole of her right side and only being able to use her arm with difficulty and for a short time' she laid a new action with the *Instruktionssenat*, having discovered that Schopenhauer was a man of means. She claimed annual maintenance as well as payment of treatment costs. She also pleaded for Schopenhauer to be arrested. The case was beginning to acquire monstrous dimensions and was to drag on for years. The court eventually found in favour of the plaintiff. While Schopenhauer was still away on his travels his fortune on deposit with a Berlin bank was attached by order of the court. This happened in 1825, by which time the case had been running for three years. In order to have his money freed from attachment and to lodge an appeal against the judgement Schopenhauer hurriedly returned to Berlin. He was successful: the court of appeal dismissed the claim to maintenance. The Marquet woman in turn appealed to the *Obertribunal*, which upheld her claims. Schopenhauer lodged a submission to the Minister of Justice, but unsuccessfully. After five years of hearings final judgement was handed down on 4 May 1827: Schopenhauer had to pay Marquet fifteen *taler* each quarter throughout such time as the physical handicap the seamstress claimed to have suffered from his blows and her fall

persisted. Caroline Marquet lived another twenty years and, as Schopenhauer once grimly remarked, was 'shrewd enough not to stop the trembling of
her arm'.

Schopenhauer had come to Berlin in 1820. After a mere two years – whose
balance sheet may have shown the gain of a mistress but also failure as a
university teacher and a tiresome lawsuit – he had had enough of the city. As
he wrote to Adele on 15 January 1822, he was considering a move to
Dresden: 'as my fortune is sufficient for my now moderate needs I shall
probably spend the rest of my life, whose greater half is over anyway, in
Dresden, engaged as always in my studies and thoughts, until perhaps I am
called to some university chair' (CL, 79). Yet he hesitated to make a final
decision about the next phase in his life. He was reluctant to give up his
academic position in Berlin, even though for the time being it had shrunk to a
notice of his lectures in the course catalogue. He granted himself a waiting
period: he would once more travel in Italy. 'If I am not known or esteemed in
Italy,' he wrote to Friedrich Osann, a friend from his Weimar days, 'then I
know the reason why. If the same is the case in Germany, then I must deduce
it first, and the reasons do not make me love Germany' (CL, 82).

Schopenhauer set out on 27 May 1822. He appointed Friedrich Osann to
be his listening-post. While he, the philosopher, was living under the southern
sun, not reading the *Jenaische Literaturzeitung*, Osann, as his 'trustee in
Germany', was to look out for 'any mention of me in books, journals, literary
periodicals and such like' (CL, 83). Osann would not find this an onerous
task. Things remained quiet.

In contrast to his first visit to Italy, Schopenhauer did not intend to 'bustle
about as a tourist in a hurry', but, after an extensive 'inspection' of
Switzerland, travel via Milan to Florence in order to live there 'very quietly'
for a while (CL, 84). He kept to his plan: having spent June and July 1822 in
Switzerland, he arrived in Milan on 17 August, left the city two weeks later,
and from 11 September 1822 until May 1823 he remained in Florence – very
much at ease. In what for him was almost a serene mood he wrote to Friedrich
Osann on 29 October 1822: 'Again the Great Bear stands low in the sky –
again dark-green foliage in a motionless air stands out in sharp contour
against the deep blue sky, solemnly and melancholically – again olives, vines,
pines and cypresses make up the landscape in which countless small villas
seem to float – again I am in the city whose pavement is a kind of mosaic; . . .
and again I walk each day across that curious square populated by statues.'
This account concluded with the words: 'With Italy you live as with a lover:
today in violent quarrel, tomorrow in adoration; with Germany you live as
with a *Hausfrau*, without much anger and without much love' (CL, 87).

We do not know exactly how Schopenhauer spent this time. He provides
scant information. A later friend of his, Carl Bähr, has only this to report: 'He
associated almost exclusively with lords and did nothing but read Homer'
(CL, 512). His letters to Osann mention a Dominican with whom

Schopenhauer walked in the Boboli Gardens and whom he joined in 'sighing over the decline of the monasteries', and the 'candlelit ancestral hall of the villa of an English lady' to whom he had been 'paying court' (CL, 88). He had diligently attended the theatre, the opera and the museums in Florence, he wrote; he called it 'service to the Muses'. He had been 'more sociable than for a long time'. He had had occasion to watch 'intentions' and their tormenting 'boredom' at close quarters; he had 'gained in experience and judgement of people' (CL, 92).

'It was an enjoyable time and I shall always think back to it with pleasure,' he wrote to Osann from Munich on 21 May 1824. A year had passed by then since his return from Italy – a very bad year. He reports on it to Osann: 'I got here [to Munich] a year ago, and about six weeks later, when I wanted to continue my journey, a chain of illnesses began which kept me here all winter. Haemorrhoids with fistula, gout and a nervous complaint succeeded one another; I spent the whole winter indoors and suffered greatly' (CL, 92).

This short piece of information hid a serious crisis in Schopenhauer's life, perhaps the most difficult until then. In Italy he had been able to live with a natural incognito; back in Germany the incognito forced upon him hit him badly. Nothing had stirred in the meantime: he simply did not exist for the public as a philosopher. For him on the other hand, that philosophy, the work he had produced in the years of 'inspired idea', existed in an almost crushing way. The work which the world refused to notice was casting its shadow on him and even discouraging him: I shall never again achieve anything like it, he often admitted to himself in a dejected mood. At such times he felt as if he had outlived himself.

In his *Brieftasche (Pocket Book)* we find this kind of note from those days of heavy depression: 'If it is said that life, from end to end, is nothing but a continuous lesson, whose results, moreover, are mostly negative, I might answer that, for this reason alone, I should have preferred to be left in the calm of self-sufficient nothingness, where I would have no need of lessons or anything else.' Or: 'For the evils of life one consoles oneself with death, and for death with the evils of life. A fine situation' (P III, 170).

The bad winter in Munich was followed by a spring without promise. His hands still shook, and he hardly awoke properly during the day. His right ear was 'totally deaf'. At the end of May 1824 he roused himself to undergo treatment àt Bad Gastein; he stayed there for a month. After that he did not return to Munich – he feared its 'hellish climate' as much as he did the 'sandy desert' of Berlin where nothing now attracted him, not even his Caroline who had meanwhile borne another man's child.

He decided to spend the summer in Mannheim, but, to be on the safe side, he first inquired from Osann whether the 'ladies' – meaning his mother and sister – were not going there as well. At all costs he wished to avoid an encounter. Osann evidently informed him that the coast was clear, because in July and August 1824 he stayed in Mannheim. From there, still avoiding

Berlin, the arena of his defeat, he travelled to Dresden in September 1824 and spent the winter there.

That winter again he had a lecture advertised in Berlin – purely *pro forma*, on the assumption that nobody, or not enough students, would register for it. The assumption was correct.

He put out feelers for a new kind of activity. He proposed to Brockhaus a new translation of Sterne's *Tristram Shandy*. Brockhaus declined. He was equally unsuccessful with a project for the translation of Hume's popular-philosophical writings on the critique of religion. During his months in Dresden he even drafted a few sentences for the preface to that translation which would never materialize – sentences suggesting the way Schopenhauer intended to use Hume to advance his own cause: 'A future age will understand why I am trying, by means of a new translation, to draw my own age's attention to the present work of the excellent David Hume. If my contemporaries were able to appreciate my endeavour it would be super-fluous' (P III, 177). In a second draft of the preface he undisguisedly hinted at his resignation with regard to his own writings: 'As for my qualification for this small work, this consists solely in that I have rather a lot of leisure, considering myself relieved now from processing my own ideas for communi-cation, as experience has confirmed what I foresaw and predicted, to wit, that they would find no readers among my contemporaries' (P III, 182). Although at first Schopenhauer had no success with his translation projects, he was not discouraged. Towards the end of the 1820s he was to make a translation of the maxims of life of the early-seventeenth-century Spanish sceptic Gracián. This translation was not to appear until two years after Schopenhauer's death.

Another translation project – no doubt the most important and the most ambitious for Schopenhauer – likewise failed to materialize at that time: in 1829 an anonymous article appeared in the *Foreign Review*, voicing the need for an English translation of Kant's principal works. Schopenhauer reacted promptly. He requested that the editorial office put him in touch with the anonymous author, offering himself as the translator. The author – revealing himself as Francis Haywood – replied with a counter-proposal: he, Haywood, would make the translation himself and Schopenhauer might then examine it. Offended, Schopenhauer addressed his offer direct to the editor of the *Foreign Review*, but without success.

It was, of course, not for the money but in order to achieve some minimum of public literary impact that Schopenhauer tried his luck as a translator. The only success he was able to score in this field was as the translator of his own work. For the collection *Scriptores Ophthalmologici Minores* he produced a translation of his essay 'On Seeing and Colours' into Latin. It was published in 1830, one of the few external occasions to feed Arthur's pride. Another occasion was a brief note by Jean Paul in his *Kleine Nachschule zur ästhetischen Vorschule* (*Little Finishing School to the Aesthetic Preparatory School*), published in 1824. He spoke there of:

> Schopenhauer's *World as Representation and Will*, an inspired philosophical, bold and many-sided work, full of acuity and profundity, but with an often hopeless and bottomless profundity – comparable to a melancholy lake in Norway, within whose dark encircling wall of steep rocks one never sees the sun but, in its depth, only the starry daytime sky, over which no bird and no cloud passes. Fortunately I can only praise the book, but not endorse it.

This was the judgement of one of the mentors of the Romantic movement which by then was ancient history. As for the other, Ludwig Tieck, Schopenhauer made his acquaintance in Dresden during the winter of 1824–5 and clashed with him. Karl von Holtei, another close friend of Arthur's mother, was present and later recorded in his memoirs:

> I took great care not to tell her [Johanna Schopenhauer] that I had met the above-mentioned eccentric [Schopenhauer] in Dresden, in Tieck's house, a few years before, and why I had been horrified by him. Arguments developed between him and Tieck, about various philosophical systems; gradually, via Jacobi, whom Tieck loved, they led to religious quarrels; and when, in the course of them, Tieck spoke of God, Schopenhauer, as if stung by a tarantula, leapt up, spinning like a humming top and repeating with sneering laughter: 'What? You need a God?' An exclamation which Ludwig Tieck could not forget to the end of his days. [C, 53]

In the spring of 1825 Schopenhauer returned to Berlin after an absence of three years. The tiresome Marquet lawsuit required his presence, but he was probably drawn back also by Caroline Medon, for he instantly got in touch with her again. According to Wilhelm Gwinner, Schopenhauer's executor, he even once more considered marrying her.

In Berlin the situation had hardly changed for Schopenhauer. Hegel continued to ride high. This was not even, at first, changed by the triumphant return to Berlin in 1827 of Alexander von Humboldt, the explorer and globetrotter. Even this opponent of all speculation, this idol of the education-hungry middle-class ladies – even Hegel's wife hastened to attend Humboldt's lectures, much to the chagrin of her husband – and of the botanizing aristocracy paid his respects to Berlin's Swabian-speaking philosopher king. Humboldt indeed directed some pinpricks against a 'metaphysics without knowledge or experience', but when Hegel got wind of this and got Varnhagen von Ense to ask Humboldt how such remarks were to be understood, Humboldt sent the indignant philosopher his lecture manuscript, in which Hegel found nothing objectionable. What he could not know was that Humboldt had cunningly sent him the wrong text. There was no way of getting the better of Hegel – least of all for Schopenhauer. After two years he was once more looking for a new haven. He had not completely written off a university career, in spite of all his crushing disappointments. Now even the university beadle behaved impertinently to him. The beadle, Schopenhauer stated in his complaint to the faculty, was behaving 'with such conspicuous insolence' that one was tempted even 'in the early morning to doubt his sobriety' (CL, 102).

In September 1827 Schopenhauer inquired of Friedrich Wilhelm Thiersch, a senior official of the Bavarian educational system, with whom he had been acquainted since his stay in Munich, whether there might possibly be a place for him at some university in 'southern Germany', or whether such a place might be created, so that 'he could, after all, have some impact on the outside world'. He was thinking of Würzburg, whose 'beautiful surroundings' and 'serene and mild climate' (CL, 105) he appreciated.

Thiersch supported Schopenhauer and encouraged him to submit a formal application, whereupon the Bavarian Ministry of Education started inquiries. The Bavarian envoy in Berlin reported that Schopenhauer 'enjoys no reputation whatever either as a writer or as a teacher . . . so that the above-named Schopenhauer, whose appearance is well known to me as not very attractive, would not represent a great gain for the university of Würzburg' (CL, 516). Inquiries were also made of Savigny, whose answer was likewise unfavourable: 'You ask, finally, about the *Privatdozent* Dr Schopenhauer. I can express no opinion about his writings because I do not know them at all; but as far as his person is concerned, he has always struck me as very presumptuous, and moreover I have heard more against him than in his favour' (CL, 516).

Nothing came of the Würzburg project. Schopenhauer next tried his luck at the university of Heidelberg. He wrote to Georg Friedrich Creuzer, a famous scholar in the field of antiquity and mythology. He wished, Schopenhauer said, 'to have a position in bourgeois society' (CL, 106); might that not be possible in Heidelberg? Creuzer advised him against it: interest in philosophy was on the decline in Heidelberg. Creuzer made no secret of his doubts about whether Schopenhauer was the right man to reverse that trend.

Embittered by months of unsuccessful applications Schopenhauer was advised by Adelbert von Chamisso, whose acquaintance he had made, not to paint the devil too black – a good grey was sufficient. But Schopenhauer stuck to his view: those were pitch-black devils who had conspired against him.

Naturally, during these years he had never given up hope that his work might after all be received as it deserved. He forced himself to be sceptical in his expectations, but even so he was over-optimistic. In 1821 he wrote the first draft of a preface to the hoped-for second edition of his work. He calculated that this new edition would be needed in 1828. Too soon, as it turned out. That year Brockhaus, in response to his inquiry, informed him that of the 1800 copies of the first edition 150 were still in stock: how many copies had in fact been sold it was no longer possible to say as a considerable number had been pulped several years earlier.

In response to this information Arthur sketched out a new draft of the preface to the second edition, which he now dated for 1836. In this draft he reviled the public as 'dull contemporaries' and haughtily pretended that being ignored had actually been of advantage to him: 'For he who loves truth and knows its enjoyment needs no encouragement: the reaction of outsiders, whether supporting or opposing, very easily confuses' (P III, 524). The second edition, he wrote, was intended for posterity, not for the 'crowd . . . of monkeys'. Who was included among those 'monkeys' emerged from a further, perhaps the most vicious, draft of the preface, written in 1830: they were the people who had fallen for that 'windbag Fichte' and for the 'clumsy charlatanry of Hegel' (P IV, 1, 13). Not to have been noticed by these, he claimed, he considered a distinction.

All this may sound like sovereign bitterness, but it also reveals, in its forced manner, the misery and the deep hurt of a man misunderstood. The dedication 'To the Manes of my Father' is tuned to a different key. Schopenhauer intended to have this dedication precede the text of the second edition. The first draft of it was written in 1828, just after his last efforts to find an academic post had failed and when he had been informed that sales of his work had totally died; at a time, therefore, when he had gleaned nothing but rejections in his role of translator as well, and when, in consequence, he realized that he would be unable, in the foreseeable future, to establish a position as a solid citizen by his own achievement, by his own work. What he was in bourgeois life, he was through his father; that he could live for philosophy without having to reach out for the breadbasket – that, too, he owed to his father. By the yardsticks of bourgeois society he was a failure: he was able to live only in the shelter of the fortune inherited from his father. And so he wrote these sentences:

> Noble, excellent spirit! to whom I owe everything that I am and that I achieve. Your active providence protected and carried me, not only through helpless childhood and rash youth, but into manhood and to this day. By putting a son like me into the world you ensured at the same time that he would prevail and develop in a world such as this. You considered the possibility that he might not be exactly gifted for ploughing the soil . . . and you seem to have foreseen that your son, you proud republican, would lack the talent . . . for crawling before ministers and counsellors in order basely to beg for a piece of hard-earned bread, or to fawn on puffed-up mediocrity, or humbly to join the adulatory entourage of charlatan quacks. . . . Therefore I consecrate this work to you, a work which could have come into being only in the shadow of your protection and to that extent it is also *your* work. . . . And everyone finding in my work any kind of joy, consolation or

instruction, let him hear your name and know that if H.F.S. had not been the man he was, A.S. would have perished a hundred times . . . [P III, 380]

Arthur would spend several more years polishing this dedication. He would omit the remark that 'A.S. would have perished a hundred times', and eventually he would drop the dedication altogether. Who or what had enabled him to live not by philosophy but for philosophy – that was to remain unrevealed in the published prefaces to the second and third editions (1844 and 1859).

Schopenhauer's years in Berlin ended in farce. Just before leaving the city in August 1831, fleeing from the cholera epidemic, he proposed marriage to a seventeen-year-old girl. At a boating party he presented grapes to the girl, Flora Weiss. Flora reports: 'But I didn't want them. I felt revolted because old Schopenhauer had touched them, and so I let them slide, quite gently, into the water behind me' (C, 58).

Arthur called on her father, who was flabbergasted: 'But she is only a child!' He left the decision to his underage daughter. Arthur, needless to say, had dropped tempting remarks about his wealth. The daughter, however, as handed down by the family, 'felt such violent dislike of S., only intensified by his small presents, that there could be no doubt about the failure of his wooing' (C, 59).

It was almost twenty years since Arthur had written in his journal: 'What makes us almost inevitably into ridiculous figures is the seriousness with which we treat the present whenever it has about it a necessary appearance of importance. Probably only a few great spirits got over this, and from figures of ridicule became those who laughed' (P I, 24).

CHAPTER TWENTY

FLIGHT FROM BERLIN

In his final year in Berlin Schopenhauer had a dream. 'And in order to serve truth in every form and unto death I am writing it down,' Schopenhauer recorded in his journal, 'that during New Year's night from 1830 to 1831 I had the following *dream* which indicates my death in the present year. From when I was six to when I was ten I had a bosom friend and permanent playmate of exactly the same age, by name of Gottfried Jänisch, who died while I, in my tenth year, was in France. Over the past thirty years I have probably thought of him exceedingly rarely. Yet in the night mentioned above I found myself in a country unknown to me, a group of men stood in a field, and among them a slim tall adult man who, I do not know how, had been made known to me as the same Gottfried Jänisch, and he welcomed me' (P IV, 1, 46).

Cholera was raging in Berlin. Schopenhauer took the dream as a warning: he would die unless he fled. His uncertain relationship with Caroline Medon, whom, as he discovered at their parting, he loved after all and therefore wished to take with him, delayed his departure. Anyway, where was he to flee to? He decided on Frankfurt, initially for no other reason than that he had been told that the city was 'cholera-proof'.

Shortly after his arrival there, in September 1831, Arthur had another dream: 'my parents, as I believe, were present; and it indicated that I would survive my now still living mother; my dead father was carrying a light in his hand' (P IV, 1, 47).

A few weeks later he was sick and became bedridden, and he spent a bad winter. Totally isolated in the strange city, he lived in a furnished flat on the Untermainquai. He did not leave the house and no one came to see him. He was gripped by fear of death and by unbearable loneliness. His thoughts were revolving around Caroline. He pestered his friend von Lowtzow in Berlin with questions: How did she spend her time, who was keeping her? He begged Lowtzow to keep an eye on her. Lowtzow tried to dispel Schopenhauer's mistrust and was generous with sermons: one only made one's life needlessly difficult by not struggling through to being trusting; his lack of trust had destroyed his relationship with Caroline.

Schopenhauer was beginning to doubt whether Frankfurt had been the right choice. Mannheim held good memories for him: he had recovered there from a serious illness and depression in 1824. He had also made some friends there, albeit casual ones. He therefore decided to move once more: in July 1823 he transferred to Mannheim.

He stuck it for a year. He joined the Harmony Society, an association of local dignitaries with its own premises and library. But its social gatherings did not mute the helpless anger with everything and everybody that would sometimes engulf him. Returning late at night to the house of the shoemaker Michael Reuss, where he was lodging, he would occasionally wake the neighbours by striking his walking stick against the furniture. Challenged about causing such tumult, Schopenhauer replied: 'I summon my spirits' (C, 64).

In 1833 he drew a balance sheet on the cover of his account book of the reasons in favour of his staying in Mannheim and those in favour of returning to Frankfurt. He decided on Frankfurt. The balance was tipped by such reasons as: 'You are less restricted and less bothered by company provided by accident and not by your choice, and you are free to sever or avoid displeasing contacts'; 'better cafés'; 'more Englishmen'; 'no floods'; 'a skilful dentist and less bad physicians'; 'a healthy climate'; 'less spied on'.

After his one-year intermezzo in Mannheim Schopenhauer returned to Frankfurt on 6 July 1833; apart from short, as a rule one-day excursions he was not to leave the city until his death in 1860.

The former 'Reich city' had been declared a 'free city' following the Congress of Vienna. A relatively democratic constitution was adopted: the still predominantly patrician Senate was confronted by a Citizens' College, a kind of second chamber, and by a 'legislative body', half of whose deputies, at least, were freely elected by the citizens.

The city was the seat of the German League's parliament, an assembly of delegates from those princes whose territories were wholly or even partially on German soil. The republican city was thus the venue of the great palaver which, under Metternich's stage management, was just then discussing the suppression of republican and libertarian tendencies. The numerous princely envoys, patronizing the elegant quarters and *tables d'hôte* – Bismarck, the Prussian envoy, was a regular at the Englischer Hof, where Schopenhauer had his lunchtime headquarters – added a touch of the big world to the solid bourgeois milieu. Frankfurt at the time had approximately 50,000 inhabitants, half of whom belonged to the electable and electing citizenry. The poor lived in the crooked and dark little streets of the old city, while the well-to-do inhabitants were moving out into the new residential areas on the fringe of the city, where generous parks, gardens and avenues had been laid out on the old levelled fortifications.

Frankfurt was not only the political capital of the German League but also the hub of the Central European capital market: the seat of the Rothschilds. 'Money is the god of our age, and Rothschild is its prophet,' Heine wrote of that Amschel Mayer von Rothschild who, wearing a frock coat and standing on a straw mat he brought along with him, dictated the quotations at the stock exchange every Monday. He lived in a magnificent townhouse on the Zeil, while to the end of her life his mother remained in the little shop in the Judengasse.

Frankfurt was the centre of Europe, Schopenhauer once remarked in a conversation; 'everything comes here to Frankfurt. Here you see and hear what is going on in the world' (JSS 68, 112). Arthur Schopenhauer, having now opted for a stationary life, no longer needed to seek out the great world: at the Englischer Hof he could watch it move past him. The Trade Fair city was swarming with foreigners, a fortunate circumstance for Schopenhauer, who did not think very highly of the Frankfurt tribe: 'It is a small, stiff, internally crude, municipally puffed-up, peasant-proud nation of Abderites, whom I do not like to approach' (JSS 68, 112).

Frankfurt did not yet have a university, but the sciences, especially the modern natural sciences, met with approval and support. An efficient sense of reality was in favour. There was a Physical Association, a Geographical Association, a Historical Museum and, most important of all, the *Senckenbergische Naturforschende Gesellschaft* (Senckenberg Nature Research Society), of which Schopenhauer was a member. This society had built up a large natural science library – Schopenhauer was to use it extensively for his essay 'Der Wille in der Natur' ('Will in Nature', 1835) – and maintained what was then probably the most important scientific collection. It was to the latter that Schopenhauer referred with his remark that 'rare natural phenomena' were 'anyway always first demonstrated in Frankfurt am Main' (JSS 68, 112).

The city was highly receptive to modernity, to innovation. The first few streets were asphalted. The grateful citizens thereupon serenaded the city architect, that 'widely experienced, indispensable' official. New water mains were laid: now they reached the upper storeys. The same year, 1828, saw the start of gas lighting. By Constitution Day 1845 the job was accomplished: the streets of the city centre and the windows of the elegant shops were lit up. But contrasts remained. Within the city boundaries there were peasants who had not even yet adopted cattle-shed feeding, but drove their cows and pigs through the streets to pastures outside the city. At the church of St Nicholas, the Nikolaikirche, the desiccated ox-heads from the butchers' previous guild day were still on display. Stinking open sewers still ran along the streets and the bleating tones of the nightwatchman were still heard. When it rained hard the German League still had to wade through flooded streets to their place of assembly. Their Excellencies urged the Senate to make some improvements. The Senate, in order to remedy at least the worst filth in the streets, recommended that the 'portable bath establishments', which carried bath water to private houses, should on their return journey use the waste water to sprinkle the streets.

Factories were springing up all round Frankfurt, but within the city the guilds were still powerful, limiting the number of artisan enterprises and endeavouring to preserve traditional manufacturing techniques. Journeymen unable to find employment were spreading dissatisfaction. Saint-Simonian ideas, reaching Frankfurt from France, were discussed in political clubs. The assembly of the German League heard complaints about the 'corrupted spirit' said to have invaded its host city. During the weeks following the July 1830 revolution in France there was noisy disorder in the city. At the traditional 'exodus' for the grape picking, observed with riflemen's festivities and fireworks, a disturbance occurred during which several soldiers were wounded and the residences of some envoys pelted with dung. In 1833 a handful of students occupied the Frankfurt *Hauptwache* to proclaim 'Germany's freedom'. Their proclamation passed unheard: they were overpowered and jailed.

Schopenhauer records these activities of the *canaille* with alarm: he was worried about his wealth, which ensured his outwardly peaceful and independent life and enabled him to devote himself wholly to philosophy. And yet he wanted to face the danger. In the reading room of the Casino Society he studied the *Frankfurter Oberpostamts-Zeitung* and *The Times* every day after lunch. There he learned what was brewing in his immediate surroundings as well as in the big world. He was anxious to take precautions; his need for security was great. Whenever an officer turned up at the Englischer Hof, the normally rather disgruntled philosopher could be very obliging and courteous.

Schopenhauer remained a Prussian subject. He never applied for Frankfurt citizenship. As a 'non-citizen resident' he had no vote, which did not worry him in the least. As a 'permissionist' he was content to have been granted the right of residence and was happy with the low taxes he had to pay. During the first few years he changed his place of residence frequently. He lived in Alte Schlesinger Gasse, on Schneidwall (Untermainquai), in Neue Mainzerstrasse, and in the 'Hanging Hand' house in Saalgasse, a narrow little street leading from the Fahrtor to the Weckmarkt behind the cathedral. In 1843 he moved into Schöne Aussicht 17, near the bridge over the Maine and the corner of Fahrgasse. There he lived for many years, until in 1859, because of a quarrel with his landlord over a poodle, he moved to the house next-door, a 'far bigger and more beautiful lodging'. A year later he was to die there. All those years his household was run by housekeepers. After 1849 Margarethe Schnepp performed this task to his 'excellent satisfaction'. Margarethe was remembered in his will. In his very first years in Frankfurt Schopenhauer established a strict routine to which he would adhere to his death. The first three hours of the day were devoted to writing. If more than that was asked of the brain, he said in justification of the routine, ideas would turn colourless and lack originality, and style would deteriorate. One could tell that that 'nonsense scribbler' Hegel had often brooded more than ten hours over his pandects.

After his three hours of writing Schopenhauer would pick up his flute. He would play for an hour '*con amore*', in his later years almost only Rossini, whose entire works he owned in an arrangement for flute. He used to go out for his lunch, at first to the Zum Schwan inn or the Russischer Hof, and later, almost regularly, to the Englischer Hof, built by Salin de Montfort on the southern side of the Rossmarkt. It was to the Englischer Hof that his admirers would direct their pilgrimages in years to come, as well as the curious who were seeking his acquaintance or merely wanted to gawp at the by then famous philosopher.

Schopenhauer had an enormous appetite; his neighbours at table were amazed. He would spoon up the rich sauces. Sometimes he would order double helpings. He refused to be disturbed during his meal. Over coffee he was at last ready to make conversation and occasionally would remain sitting there until five o'clock. He appreciated the kind of chance acquaintances that came about at table. The writer Hermann Rollet, one such casual acquaintance, met the philosopher in 1846; this is how he described him:

> He was a well-built and – albeit according to a somewhat outdated cut – invariably well-dressed man of medium height with short silvery hair, with whiskers trimmed in an almost military style, otherwise always smooth-shaven, of a rosy complexion and with bright, usually amused and exceedingly intelligent blue-flecked eyes. His not exactly handsome but intelligent features often wore an ironically smiling expression. However, he usually displayed an introverted and, when he uttered anything, sometimes almost baroque nature, whereby he daily supplied some considerable material to the cheap satire of a frivolous part of the otherwise very decent, but in terms of mental qualities very mixed, table company. Thus this often comically disgruntled, but in fact harmless and good-naturedly gruff, table companion became the butt of the jokes of insignificant men about town, who would regularly – though admittedly not ill-meaningly – make fun of him. [C, 88]

As for Schopenhauer's table talk from his early Frankfurt years, when impatience still outweighed imperturbability, we have a less well-meaning account from the pen of the musical writer Xaver Schnyder von Wartensee: Schopenhauer, he reports, would frequently boast of his good and numerous teeth as an outward indication of being superior to the 'common biped'. He praised science for producing a 'marvellous invention' against venereal disease: one dissolved a pinch of chloride of lime in a glass of water and bathed one's penis in it after coitus. Thus one remained protected against infection – this he had, in a loud voice, explained to all at table whether or not they wanted to hear it. When berating his poodle Schopenhauer would address it as 'you, sir' and the while cast angry sidelong glances at his neighbours. Schnyder also recounts the episode which caused a breach between him and the philosopher:

We were engaged in an argument on a musical matter when the serving
waiter had been standing for quite a while at Schopenhauer's side with a
dish, offering him beef, which he, in the heat of the argument, failed to
notice. So I said to him: Well, do help yourself at last *a priori* so that I
can help myself *a posteriori*. With a glance full of unspeakable fury and
contempt Schopenhauer screamed at me: These are sacred expressions
you have just used, which must not be profaned, expressions whose
importance you do not understand. [C, 62]

Henceforth Schopenhauer avoided all conversation with Schnyder and had
his place laid at the other end of the table, in order to be safe from such
'ignoramuses'.

After an ample midday meal he would go to the reading room of the Casino
Society, which was likewise situated in the Rossmarkt. Then followed, as a
rule, a prolonged brisk walk, whatever the weather, sometimes with a
muttered monologue under his breath, taking no notice of passersby, and
accompanied by his poodle. He would sometimes spend a long time at
panoramic points outside the city. Children at play did not know what to
make of him and occasionally threw balls at him.

He spent his evenings at home, reading. He avoided parties and never
received visitors at that hour. During the first few years he frequented the
theatre, the opera and concerts. As an attentive listener he requested the
conductor and manager of the theatre to take measures against the noise,
especially disturbing during the overture, of late arrivals inconsiderately
slamming the doors to their boxes or letting fall the tip-up seats. If the actions
of the unpunctual could not be controlled, then at the least the doors and
hinged seats might have some cushioning fitted to them. 'The Muses and the
audience will be grateful to you for improving matters' (CL, 218), he wrote to
the manager.

Schopenhauer found the noise of everyday life disturbing. He regarded this
as evidence of his intelligence. Noise was distracting: anyone causing or
seeking out noise proved that his head was not made for the silent effort of
thought. In the second volume of his principal work he would later develop
his philosophy of noise nuisance:

Actually, I have for a long time been of opinion that the quantity of
noise anyone can comfortably endure is in inverse proportion to his
mental powers, and may therefore be regarded as a rough estimate of
them. Therefore, when I hear dogs barking unchecked for hours in the
courtyard of a house, I know what to think of the inhabitants. The man
who habitually slams doors instead of shutting them with the hand, or
allows this to be done in his house, is not merely ill-mannered, but also
coarse and narrow-minded. . . . We shall be quite civilized only when
our ears are no longer outlawed, and it is no longer anyone's right to cut
through the consciousness of every thinking being in its course of a

thousand steps, by means of whistling, howling, bellowing, hammering, whip-cracking, letting dogs bark, and so on. [WWR II, 30]

Schopenhauer's sensitivity to noise went deep; it pervaded his whole
existence.

He believed that in his work he had – in so far as that was at all possible –
clarified the Whole. Where insight did not penetrate began night, which to
him held no allure but only fear. The universe of his work, however, was
reassuringly spacious. By contracting himself, in practical life, around his
work he found the everyday world outside to be a nocturnal jungle, where a
thousand dangers were lurking. 'In order to live in a solitary way one has to
have a lot of the god in one or a lot of the beast,' Montaigne had said. In his
work Schopenhauer was a god. But he had to summon all his strength not to
become, at the same time, a frightened beast. To his secret journal *Eis Eauton*
he confided:

Nature has played its part to insulate my heart by endowing it with
mistrust, irritability, violence and pride in a measure almost incom-
patible with the '*mens aequa*' of the philosopher. I have inherited from
my father that fear which I myself am cursing . . . and fighting with all
the will-power I possess, but which on the slightest occasions over-
comes me with such force that I see vividly before me misfortunes which
are merely possible, or even barely imaginable. A terrible fantasy
sometimes intensifies this inclination to an unbelievable degree. Even as
a child of six my parents, returning one evening from a walk, found me
in the depths of despair because I suddenly assumed I had been
abandoned by them for ever. As a youngster I was tormented by
imagined diseases and quarrels. While a student in Berlin I thought for a
time that I was consumptive. At the outbreak of the 1813 war I was
haunted by the fear of being pressed into military service. From Naples
I was driven by fear of smallpox, from Berlin by fear of cholera. In
Verona I was seized by the *idée fixe* of having taken poisoned snuff.
When I was about to leave Mannheim [in July 1833] I was seized,
without any outward reason, by an indescribable sense of anxiety. For
years I was haunted by fear of a criminal suit because of that . . . Berlin
business, or the fear of losing my fortune and of challenging the division
of my inheritance *vis-à-vis* my mother. Whenever there was a noise at
night I would start from my bed and grab my sword and pistol, which I
always kept loaded. Even when there is no cause for alarm I carry
within me a permanent inner anxiety which makes me see dangers
where none exist. It magnifies the smallest annoyance into infinity and
makes dealings with people exceedingly difficult for me. [P IV, 2, 120]

Schopenhauer's propensity to fear gave rise to a need for rituals for
domesticating the everyday world. At his bank he requested that it should

always be the same clerk who brought him his interest to his lodgings. His shoemaker had to work strictly to Schopenhauer's directives. His desk was scrupulously tidy. Woe to the housekeeper if she should attempt to overthrow that world order. Under his inkwell he secreted gold coins, as emergency money for a moment of danger. He had all the books in his library bound as upright octavo volumes. For important items he devised little hiding places. Interest coupons were kept in old letters and notebooks. Personal notes were given false headings in order to mislead snooping eyes. Visitors without appointment were often turned away. Walking to his barber cost him self-conquest. Who could tell if his throat was not to be cut? His Buddha statuette was guarded like the apple of his eye. He nearly drove his housekeeper out of the house on one occasion because she had dared to dust the figure. He drank wine in modest amounts. He never allowed himself to walk unsteadily.

His style of thinking and his language were along the same lines. Hegel had once said: 'The True is the Bacchantic ecstasy in which no member is not drunk.' Certainly, Schopenhauer would have answered, if truth were a delirium of concepts. But he prided himself on having developed a metaphysics which never left the firm ground of *viewing*. One must surrender only to such concepts as still revealed their visual origin, the firm ground from which they were abstracted. Concepts which abandoned that firm ground, such as the notion of the 'absolute', of 'timeless being', etc., were like paper money, whose cover was highly uncertain. 'With concepts of this sort,' Schopenhauer wrote in the second volume of his principal work, 'the firm ground that supports the whole of our knowledge trembles, as it were. Therefore philosophizing may occasionally, and in case of necessity, extend to such knowledge, but it must never begin with it' (WWR II, 85).

Schopenhauer was a master at utilizing the semantic wealth of language. He was the greatest stylist among the philosophers of the nineteenth century. But he wanted to rule, to control that wealth. Surrendering to the dynamics of language, the way Nietzsche did, was not his way. He listened to language and sensed its specific movement, but he wished to capture its energy in the elastic grid of the structure of its periods. The power of language was to drive *his* mill. The world was the tumult of will, and because there was no overarching metaphysical order nor a time-dynamic tending towards salvation and progress, there was left for him only the magic of an order-creating language. That was why he believed that what can be known at all can be known clearly, and what can be said at all can be said clearly.

Only in this clarity can the feeling for the margins be sharpened, where the knowable merges into darkness and the utterable into the unutterable: 'Whatever torch we will kindle and whatever space it may illuminate, our horizon will always remain encircled by the depth of night' (WWR II, 185).

Part of Schopenhauer's endeavour to consolidate and circumscribe the order of his life was the fact that after his flight from Berlin, feeling himself to be a survivor, he again resumed contact with his mother and sister.

Correspondence with his sister had never quite ceased, but with his mother there had been no exchange of letters since 1819. The outward occasion for the letter which Schopenhauer wrote to his mother towards the end of 1831 was a financial matter. But he no doubt slipped in also some remarks about his personal well-being, for his mother responded with well-intentioned advice: 'Lead an orderly life, avoid catching cold, and at the slightest touch of feeling off colour take to your bed, drinking camomile . . . is best' (25 January 1832). Or: 'Two months in your room without seeing a single person, that is not good, my son, and saddens me, a man cannot and should not isolate himself in that manner' (1 March 1832).

Schopenhauer's tone *vis-à-vis* his mother remained matter-of-fact and remote; references to business matters still held an ironically offensive undertone. Schopenhauer made it clear that ultimately it was only joint marauding expeditions in matters of inheritance that kept the family pack together. The only extant letter from Schopenhauer to his mother from the 1830s contains this passage: 'No doubt you will have received the pleasant and important news of, if I may use such an expression, a welcome killing to be made in Danzig: (at this point all-round family congratulations, with compliments). However, I am of the humble opinion that we should not pounce on it too avidly but first look around *for more*' (22 July 1835; CL, 142).

His mother and Adele had by then given up residence in Weimar. Their means were no longer adequate to the running of an elegant establishment. Weimar society was fobbed off with health reasons: they could not bear the climate. In 1829 the Schopenhauer ladies moved to the Rhine. They spent the summer months in a villa in Unkel and the winter in Bonn. Adele's well-to-do friend, Sybille Mertens-Schaaffhausen, the wife of a banker, a dilettante archaeologist and art collector, had arranged their change of domicile.

Johanna Schopenhauer was then at the peak of her career as a writer. In 1831 her collected works were published by Brockhaus in twenty-four volumes. Authorship had become her livelihood. Their extravagant lifestyle and the loss of their capital owing to the difficulties of the Muhl banking house had almost completely eroded not only her part of the inheritance but also her daughter's part, which she administered. The financial future of Adele, still unmarried, was insecure and Johanna had by then lost any clear idea of her income, her assets or her debts. She knew that she was in debt to her daughter, whose money she was not supposed to have touched, and that was why she disinherited Arthur to make sure what little she left would all go to Adele.

By the mid-1830s, however, the author Johanna Schopenhauer was beginning to be forgotten. Financial worries were increasing. Schopenhauer did not discover this from his mother but from his sister. His mother fell ill and Adele looked after her. But the Schopenhauers had not been totally lost sight of in Weimar. The Grand Duke granted Johanna a small pension. In the autumn of 1837 mother and daughter moved to Jena. Johanna embarked on writing her memoirs. She had got to the point of Arthur's birth when she died on 16 April 1838.

Adele had undergone a miserable time during those years. She had been under her mother's whip, and when her mother fell ill she had nursed her.

Annette von Droste-Hülshoff, a friend of Sybille, had occasion in the 1830s to observe the two Schopenhauer ladies at close quarters. The portrait which Annette painted in a letter to Sophie von Haxthausen in 1837 is not very flattering to Johanna Schopenhauer:

> Listen, Sophie, your memory is like a sieve, otherwise you would have remembered what I told you about Adele: that everybody preferred the mother, that Adele is being regarded as quite objectionable, and also is objectionable, and that for a very long time I could not stand her, but that, if one has known both of them for *a long time and closely*, the mother's character is as unworthy of respect as that of the daughter seems truly venerable. Admittedly, Adele is vain and at times quite ridiculous, but she is incapable of hurting a fly, there is no base spark in her, and she is capable of the greatest sacrifices, which moreover she makes every day, and, what is more, entirely without boasting. She will without hesitation deny herself any pleasure she might have looked forward to for a long time, she will hand over the money she has saved up over a long period to fulfil some favourite wish whenever she can help a needy person or a friend by doing so. With the most touching patience, without complaining to her closest friends, she bears the unreasonableness of a mother who, admittedly, can be extremely agreeable, but who . . . when she is alone almost dies of boredom and ill humour, and who, despite all her fussing around her daughter, does not care a damn how she feels, who bullies her all day long and who – as I witnessed myself on several occasions, when her boredom had grown excessive – makes her get up, though laid low with a fever, and accompany her to a party; who eats up her daughter's fortune (everything belongs to Adele) in delicacies and otherwise spends it on her amusement, with an outrageous indifference, and who, when one points out to her that she is reducing Adele to penury, coldly answers that Adele is popular, that somebody or other would take her into their home. How do you like that? And Adele does not rebel, she tries to conceal her domestic misery in every way possible, and altogether behaves better than one in a thousand would. Surely these are qualities for the sake of which one may overlook a little pitiful sentimentality and vanity, especially as Adele is so honest and decent and not at all of an enamoured disposition, and only wishes to be taken as interesting by ladies as well as gentlemen. Do not think that she has bribed me by declarations of love.

Schopenhauer, as we know, had no reason to complain about his mother: her will to live had not impeded his own, it had merely prevented her son from acting the successor patriarch after his father's death. Adele, on the other hand, had been crushed by her strong mother and prevented from leading her own life. And she derived no benefit from her brother's bitterness about their mother. Arthur did not come to Adele's help, he did not help her stand up to her mother.

Adele was still on the lookout for the man in her life. The picture of the hero of 1813, the former hussar and subsequent Breslau police official Heinke, had meantime faded. A medical student, Stromeyer, was vaguely paying court to her. Immediately she made him a present of her most precious possession, a special edition of *Iphigenie* given her by Goethe himself. With that present in his baggage the future famous surgeon left town and married another woman. A relationship of several years' duration with the promising young scientist Gottfried Osann – his brother Friedrich Osann was a friend of Arthur's – came to a melancholy end in 1826. They were by then half-way betrothed. The man's family was not pleased with the connection, or perhaps these were only Adele's fears. At any rate the two parted. Osann, possibly out of spite, married a servant girl. In the year of the break-up Adele fell out of the carriage on a journey to Jena. Rumour had it that she attempted suicide.

When, after a prolonged silence, Schopenhauer in 1831 once more wrote to Adele, she replied at once and foreshadowed an extensive letter in which she would lay out her life before her brother. She wrote that letter on 27 October 1831. In it she recounted the story of the past few years: unhappy love, shortage of money, farewell to Weimar, life in Unkel and Bonn. Her soul had fluctuated between 'madness and death'. Now all had gone quiet inside her:

> not a single passionate sensation moves me, no hope, no plan – hardly a wish, for my wishes touch on the impossible. Hence I have learned to watch them fly and move away like birds in the blue air. Life displeases me, I have a horror of *old age*, I have a horror of the *lonely life* which is my certain lot, I will not marry because I will scarcely find a man who would harmonize with me. . . . I am strong enough to bear this emptiness, but I should be sincerely grateful to the cholera if it rid me of the whole history without too violent pain.

With a very intimate turn of phrase she drew her brother into her own death wish. She wondered, she wrote, why Arthur was clinging to life so long and had fled from the cholera in such panic.

'Virtually no one knows me,' she continued, 'for my soul has a social attire like those Venetian veils and masks, there is not much to be seen of myself. Why bore people? For the most part they only want superficial words, and if I have to mix in society I give them those.'

She hinted that she would like Arthur to search her out, to look behind her 'social attire'. But she did not wish to trouble her brother, she would come closer to him if he for his part were ready to open up to her. She did not want to push him: 'Do not be afraid of any spying, whatever you conceal of your affairs I shall never attempt to discover.'

But for Schopenhauer this was again too importunate. He did not want to know about the whole unhappiness of his sister. He resisted being drawn into her pitiful life. That was not hardheartedness but a fear of being drawn into a compassion which, touching as it would on his own depression, would paralyse him. He therefore struggled against it. Such almost compulsive compassion emerged where Adele needed it a lot less: with her toothache that she had written to him about. 'That you should torture yourself so about my toothache,' she replied with some surprise, and also with a sense of disappointment that Arthur did not wish to know about her other troubles.

Schopenhauer had a panicky fear of being claimed by Adele. He did not wish to be responsible for her. Time and again Adele felt bound to dispel her brother's fears on that account: 'I am certain to survive my mother, but in no way will you find me clinging to you insecurely or confusedly! I know I shall be far, far poorer than you, but be quite reassured, I shall help myself, and if one day I die all alone, you will inherit from me, tidily and in good order, whatever is still left.'

Adele had taken the first step by opening her heart to her brother; Schopenhauer, alarmed, had blocked her approach and denied her any glance into his own mind. Matters therefore stopped at the business level. He advised Adele in money matters. But he did send his sister a sealed copy of his last will. Adele found this almost impossible to believe and sent the document back when an opportunity arose. But Schopenhauer returned it to her.

In 1840 Adele paid a passing visit to her brother. The encounter was friendly, but such that neither was anxious to repeat it. Although another meeting had been arranged on Adele's return journey, this did not materialize.

Adele spent the last decade of her life under the care of her loyal friend Sybille in Bonn and in Italy, where she tried her hand at literary work. In the streets of Florence the youngsters would mock the hideously ugly old woman and her girlish behaviour. Society, too, turned its nose up at her, but soon she was accepted because she had *esprit* and because she had been a 'darling' of the old Goethe.

Adele's sad life ended in 1849. Her brother had seen her for a last time in Frankfurt a few weeks before her death. On her dying day, 20 August 1849, she wrote a letter to Arthur. It was touchingly businesslike: 'Permit me, in the event of my sudden death, to let my friend Sybille Mertens distribute these (to you useless) things among the friends of my youth, in accordance with my wishes which are known to her. You would gain very little to your advantage by selling them.'

CHAPTER TWENTY-ONE

ON THE WILL IN NATURE

On 30 April 1835 Schopenhauer once more inquired of Brockhaus what the situation was with regard to sales of the first edition of *The World as Will and Representation* and whether, at long last, a second edition might be considered. 'Though you may not actually believe me, I am not giving up hope of living to see the second edition myself and of enriching it by the many thoughts that I have put down since 1819' (CL, 141).

Brockhaus replied that unfortunately there had lately been no demand for the work at all, which was why stocks had largely been pulped.

A new edition was therefore out of the question. That summer Schopenhauer resolved to present the 'many thoughts' which had accumulated in his manuscript journals to the public in an independent work. He did not even offer it to Brockhaus. A Frankfurt bookseller undertook its publication. Schopenhauer had to contribute to the printing costs and, of course, waive any honorarium. The study appeared in 1836 in a print run of five hundred copies. It was entitled *On the Will in Nature*. Its subtitle was *A Discussion of the Confirmations which the Author's Philosophy has Received from the Empirical Sciences since its Publication*.

Schopenhauer had always insisted that his metaphysics was not in competition with the natural sciences. The notion of the 'will' must not be used to patch up faulty chains of explanation: 'We are as little permitted to appeal to the objectification of the will, instead of giving a physical explanation, as to appeal to the creative power of God. For physics demands causes, but the will is never a cause' (WWR I, 140). It is the internal aspect of all causation processes; it is the interpretation of the materials which are linked to one another by explanations. 'The aetiology of nature and the philosophy of nature never interfere with each other; on the contrary, they go hand in hand, considering the same object from different points of view' (WWR I, 140).

Schopenhauer had conscientiously followed recent scientific research, primarily in the fields of physiology and comparative anatomy, and had come to the conclusion that, in particular, observations on the instinctive behaviour of animals and the analysis of functional connections of organisms tended to support his interpretations.

He noted with satisfaction that some researchers were using the concept of 'unconscious will' for characterizing certain vital processes. Later he discovered that the physiologist Brands had even borrowed from him without acknowledging this to his readers. Schopenhauer was annoyed, not only because he felt robbed but because he was anxious to see empirical research advance to the boundary where the metaphysics of the will and the natural sciences met. 'But this my metaphysics,' Schopenhauer wrote in the preface to *On the Will in Nature*, 'proves itself to be the only one having an extreme point in common with the physical sciences: a point up to which these sciences come to meet it by their own paths, so as really to connect themselves and to harmonize with it' (WN, 215–16).

As yet, Schopenhauer did not have to point his essay aggressively against so-called vulgar materialism, which would not be triumphant until the 1850s – at the end of the wild years of philosophy – when it would proclaim such notorious explanations of the world as its being determined by 'pressure' or 'thrust', and utter such pearls of wisdom as 'Man is what he eats.' For the second edition of his 'nature' book, however, in 1854, he was to write a preface castigating that fashionable materialism as 'veritable barbers' assistants' and pharmacists' apprentices' philosophy'.

In 1836 – Hegel's owl of Minerva was still abroad even though a new day was dawning – Schopenhauer was arguing chiefly against the spirit of philosophy. In doing so he not only resorted to arguments from the area of the empirical sciences, but he intended once more, 'after seven years of silence', to outline briefly his own basic philosophical stance. In the chapter on 'Physical Astronomy' he succeeded in doing so with such cogent clarity that in years to come he would describe it as simply beyond improvement. At issue are the two types of experience of the world: objective knowledge, which asks for causalities, and internal knowledge, which becomes aware of its own being as will, and with that 'self-assurance' casts its light into the inward aspect of the external world. Causal explanation, Schopenhauer argued, was reasonably successful for inorganic and vegetative life. Our intellect has to presuppose (*a priori*) that causality exists also with regard to other, 'higher', life phenomena, but it becomes increasingly difficult to apply it to animalic life or to ourselves.

> Just at the point where the outwardly directed light of the understanding with its form of causality, gradually yielding to increasing darkness, had been reduced to a feeble, flickering glimmer, behold! we are met by a totally different light proceeding from quite another quarter, from our own inner self, through the chance circumstance that we, the judges, happen here to be the very objects that are to be judged. . . . But, just at this point, the observer receives from his own inner self the direct information that the agent in them is the will – that very will, which he knows better and more intimately than anything

that external perception can ever supply. This knowledge alone must be the philosopher's key to an insight into the heart of all those processes in unconscious Nature, concerning which causal explanation – although, here, to be sure, more satisfactory than in the process last considered, and the clearer, the farther those processes were removed from these – nevertheless had still left an unknown x, and could never quite illumine the inside of the process, even in a body propelled by impact or attracted by gravity. . . . We can surely hardly avoid recognizing *the identity of this x*, even on the lowest degrees of the scale, where it was but faintly perceptible; then higher up, where it extended its obscurity more and more; and finally on the highest degrees, where it cast a shadow upon all things – till, at the very top, it reveals itself to our consciousness in our own phenomenal being, as *the will*. The two primarily different sources of our knowledge, that is to say the inward and the outward source, have to be connected together at this point by reflection. It is quite exclusively out of this connection that our comprehension of Nature, and of our own selves arises; but then the inner side of Nature is disclosed to our intellect, which by itself alone can never reach further than to the mere outside; and the mystery which philosophy has so long tried to solve, lies open before us. . . . What makes the knowledge, that this is indeed the case, so difficult, is the circumstance, that we know causality and will in two fundamentally different ways: causality entirely from outside, quite indirectly, quite through the under-standing; will entirely from inside, quite directly; and that accordingly the clearer the knowledge of the one in each given instance, the less clear is the knowledge of the other. Therefore we recognize the essence of the will least readily, where causality is most intelligible; and, where the will is most unmistakably evident causality becomes so obscured, that the vulgar mind could venture to deny its existence altogether. . . . The more a thing is given us as mere phenomenon, i.e. as representation, the more clearly does the *a priori* form of representation, i.e. causality, manifest itself: this is the case in inanimate Nature; conversely, the more immediate our knowledge of the will, the more does the form of representation recede into the background: this is the case with ourselves. That is: the nearer one side of the world approaches to us, the more do we lose sight of the other. [WN, 317–21]

What Schopenhauer calls 'that x or the real interior' which is left as an unresolvable remainder in all objectively explanatory knowledge, and of which we become most clearly aware in the direct consciousness of will-pervaded vitality, is that Archimedean point of self-reassurance for which an entire Western philosophical tradition had been searching under a great variety of names. Religious faith was one kind of such self-reassurance. That was why 'knowledge' had to content itself with a 'handmaiden' role. Faith was more than knowledge, it was participation in Being. In such participation Being is experienced as 'leaving be' and as 'being able to be'. Being is opposed to making, it is something one receives; a grace that makes us free.

In the modern age this experience begins to break up. Thinking is faced with the task of producing that self-reassurance out of itself. Since Kant there has been no ontology which did not take its point of departure from the subject which 'thinks' that ontology. 'Being recognized' becomes the key category of being. Whatever else belongs to our being alive but remains in the dark, acting ineffectively, appears from this perspective as a lesser being, not as something fundamental. Because one tries to make everything from oneself one is afraid of what allows one to *be*. Ontology becomes a cabinet of mirrors: anyone who asks about Being encounters the likes of himself on all sides; or in other words, the questioner discovers that whatever it is that is asking the questions within him also answers them. Such answers, naturally, are then devoid of mystery and remain in the area which Schopenhauer calls 'imagining', 'representing'.

In Schopenhauer, however, there still lives a memory of what reassurance of Being actually means: what matters is not that Being which can be known and which is Being only to that extent – but the Being which *is* prior to all knowledge: the back of the mirror within ourselves. These are Schopenhauer's turns of phrase, by means of which he hopes to get at the back of knowledge and known Being: we know something, but in addition and primarily we *are*. The world around us, nature and people, act upon us; they are, without any doubt, real. But turn around as much as we like, they always are reality *for us*, reality acting *upon us*; they are, as Kant put it, 'phenomena' or, as Schopenhauer terms it, 'representations'. This changes nothing about the fact that, of course, we ascribe to them an independent reality; we proceed from the assumption that they are equally as real as ourselves – but we only proceed from that assumption. The 'something else' can never become as real for us as we are ourselves. We transfer the Being experienced in ourselves – what Schopenhauer calls the *realissimum* – to everything which we are not. When Schopenhauer asks what the world is, beyond being our representation, and when we answer that it is, as we are ourselves, *will*, then that question is not primarily about an additional dimension of knowledge (knowledge always is representation), but about something different from knowledge, about *reassurance of being*. Schopenhauer bursts the framework of transcendental philosophy because that is a framework for recognizing activity only, and he has to break that framework of recognizing activity if he wishes to clarify the manner in which we have always possessed experience of being and in which we can understand, from a merely recognized (phenomenal) world, its actual being, which we ourselves are also.

There was a time when there used to be wonderment that anything is at all, and that nothing is nothing; such wonderment concealed within itself the question about being. What is Being? What is 'I am'? So long as such questions still dared to be posed there existed mysticism and those magnificent cathedrals of metaphysics.

Our modern concretized cognition has attained impressive definition: what exists can be dissected into minute components, from which that which lives is built up. That 'unknown x', to which Schopenhauer refers, seems to have disappeared because of an increase in our ability to concretize also, apparently without any remainder, our own vitality which Schopenhauer calls the 'will'. Thus, for instance, the language of psychoanalysis, borrowed from hydraulics, has lately become the language of the intimate.

Concretizing knowledge turns back to the subject of knowledge and makes it into a 'thing among things' (Foucault). Simultaneously the power of 'making' is growing. The old question of Being has become a question of practicability. The question of why something is and why nothing is nothing nowadays contains no moving wonderment; instead it has acquired pragmatic meaning in a civilization whose capacity for destruction is gigantic.

It is not therefore surprising that hardly anyone any longer understands what Being is, what the question about Being was about, and whence the great wonderment came. Nor does it come as a surprise that a highly involved and complex philosophy – Heidegger's – had to be created, one which broods over nothing else but this 'oblivion of being', one which attempts nothing other than to make the meaning of the question about Being comprehensible again.

That 'unknown x' which is hidden 'behind' everything and which we ourselves *are* is what Schopenhauer calls the 'will'.

After Schopenhauer philosophy was to manage without that 'x'. In his day, however, the question about Being was still alive, even though it was itself undermining its vitality, because post-Kantian philosophy had equated that 'x' with the spirit. Thinking was no longer understood as an attribute of Being but, the other way about, Being was perceived as an attribute of thinking. We can comprehend Being in thinking because Being is itself of the same kind as thinking. Thinking related to Being was coming into its own. In this spirit the great neo-metaphysical world systems of Fichte and Hegel were still possible. But as the 'point of unity' was located in thinking and not in Being, it was all in fact the first act of the disappearance of Being in the 'made'. This metaphysics follows the working spirit which it observes producing nature and culture. In Hegel's philosophy the question about Being is, basically, posed in terms of production technology: How did the spirit (which, after all, we are ourselves) manage it? And the question about the 'spirit' in turn points back to the producing individual. But no metaphysics can prevail if, at the same time, it is unmasked as a 'producing' one. What was bound to happen happened.

In October 1829 Hegel had been elected Rector of Berlin University. The government's confidence in him was so great that he was simultaneously given the post of State Plenipotentiary for the Control of the University – an office created after the Karlsbad Decrees. By this personal union Hegel personified a veritable synthesis: he represented the autonomy of the academic spirit and at the same time he represented the power which crushed that autonomy.

Hegel's term as Rector covered the July 1830 revolution in France, a dividing line also for intellectual and political culture in Germany. Initially, however, all was quiet. On 3 August 1830 the King's birthday was observed. Hegel made a speech. Although events in France aroused lively sympathy, there were no signs anywhere so far of tendencies directed against the domestic government. Varnhagen reports: 'The 3rd August . . . was celebrated until late at night with great jubilation on all sides, and our public, inspired through all its classes by massive sympathy for the cause of the French people, seemed for this very reason to wish to demonstrate the more clearly its affection for its Prussian ruler.'

During Hegel's term, which ran to the end of 1830, only one student had been jailed by the police for wearing a French cockade. Other breaches of discipline did not give rise to serious alarm: twelve students had smoked where smoking was not permitted, three had fought duels, fifteen had intended to fight duels, thirty had behaved rowdily in taverns – but all these offences had been committed without political motives. That then was the scene, at least on the surface – yet the events of 1830, the second great revolution beyond the Rhine, produced profound effects. Among other things, they would result in (from then on continuous) attempts to turn Hegel upside down; they would induce a new generation enthusiastically to invest in the momentous future of this life everything it had inherited from that most recent metaphysics.

This was reflected in an increase in political discussion, something Hegel complained about in one of his last letters. 'At present, however,' he wrote to his disciple Goeschel on 13 December 1830, 'the enormous political interest has devoured all others – a crisis in which everything that used to be valid seems now to have become problematical.' This was exactly what was happening: anything valid in the past was now being questioned. Yet the method of questioning was derived from Hegel, who died of cholera in the autumn of 1831.

In the summer of 1830 Heine, then in Helgoland, welcomed the events in France in these words: 'I can no longer sleep, and the most bizarre nocturnal visions race through my overheated mind. Waking dreams . . . enough to drive anyone crazy. . . . Last night I was rushing through all the German lands and mini-lands, knocking at the doors of my friends and disturbing people's sleep. . . . Some fat philistines, snoring all too revoltingly, got a meaningful jab in their ribs from me, and with a yawn they asked: "What's the time then?" In Paris, dear friends, the cockerel has crowed, that is all I know.' For the next decade and a half the cockerel would not cease crowing – also in philosophy. In 1844 Karl Marx would conclude the introduction to his *Critique of Hegel's Philosophy of Law* with the words: 'Philosophy cannot realize itself without the abolition of the proletariat; the proletariat cannot abolish itself without the realization of philosophy. When all internal conditions are fulfilled, the *German resurrection day* will be proclaimed by the *trumpeting of the Gallic cockerel.*'

What mattered to Marx, as it did to the whole cultural scene after 1830, was '*realization*'. The new literary generation – Gutzkow, Wienbarg, Heine, Börne, Mundt – had torn itself loose from the 'airy realm of dreams'. Romanticism, they said, had poeticized reality: the task now was to realize poetry. The philosophers, for their part, pointed out that until then the world had merely been interpreted: the task now was to change it. Gutzkow, a spokesman of the movement which called itself 'Young Germany', versified in his drama *Nero*: 'And now at last, instead of empty fantasy / of the false spirit glow / of a sophistically dream-befuddled age / Let a true, pure / and better reality arise.'

The basic pattern of critique was as follows: philosophy and poetry have already given us the dream of a reality, which we now have to pull down to earth. What we dreamed of, that we must now do. The treasures we have squandered to heaven must now be brought back and made our possessions. But this is possible only – according to the movement – if we understand three things. First, we must realize that we have been repressing ourselves. So the slogan now is: emancipation of the flesh. 'I have a great awe of the human body, for the soul is inside it,' Theodor Mundt wrote in his *Die nackte Venus* (*Naked Venus*). Second, we must understand that the creation of the right life is an enterprise which does not need to justify itself before tradition, nor must it let itself be fobbed off by promises of the future. Everything must be decided here and now. To be 'modern' is the programme of the movement. 'The old is dead, and what is true is modern,' Glasbrenner wrote. The 'circumstances of the present inspire us', the 'moment exercises its rights', others wrote. Goethe, who died in 1832, carried little weight in these circles. Everyone was tired of the calls for moderation of that 'stability-preaching fool' and 'prince's lackey'. The demand of the humanities that everyone should develop his 'personality' was no longer sufficient, because the third thing that had to be understood was that liberation was not to be had through individual effort but was a collective undertaking. Thus one kept encountering the slogan of the 'literature of movement'. 'We, the men of the movement,' Heine wrote with faint irony in his *Die romantische Schule* (*The Romantic School*). In the 1840s this awareness of belonging to a movement intensified into party awareness. Everyone was questioning everyone else's 'position', and the slogan was 'Take a stand!' The head was to seek the heart of the movement – at first, simply, the 'people', later, with Marx, the 'proletariat'. The fact was that, in the meantime, a social movement had emerged – at the Hambach Festival in 1832, and in the Weavers' Revolt in 1844. On the other hand, of course, the peasants were taking Büchner's *Hessischer Landbote* (*Hessian Rural Messenger*), which called on them to rise, to the nearest police station.

The activists of the 1840s looked back with contempt on the columnists of the 1830s: they, surely, had created storms in a teacup, gestures of vanity and self-overestimation. Freiligrath, the writer, had proclaimed: 'The poet stands upon a higher outpost / than on the ramparts of the party.' Herwegh, the activist, answered him in a poem entitled *The Party*, which contained the passage: 'Party! Party! Who would deny her / who was the mother of all victories! / How can a poet thus defame the word, / the word that gave birth to all that is magnificent? / . . . / Even the gods descended from Olympus / and fought upon the ramparts of the party!'

The 'personal note' was, if possible, avoided. Heine, for instance, was in disgrace for, allegedly, being smug and chasing sparkling effects. In an age given to polemics Heine replied: 'Because I am so good at sparkling / you think I cannot also thunder? / How wrong you are!, for I possess / a talent, too, for thunderclaps.'

The 1840s witnessed a competition of radicalisms. There were those notorious duplications: the critical critique, and then, from Marx, the critique of critical critique. Real reality. True socialism. The competition was fought with extraordinary acerbity: the 'parties' pounced on each other. Herwegh condemned Freiligrath. Engels went to war against Heine. Heine against Börne, and the other way round. Feuerbach criticized Strauss, Bauer criticized Feuerbach. Stirner was to outdo them all, but then came Marx, who swept them all into one bag: *Deutsche Ideologie* (*German Ideology*). In 1835, when Schopenhauer put the final touches to his *Will in Nature*, the opening of Germany's first railway line between Nuremberg and Fürth was not the only major event. In the sphere of the spirit two events of striking modernity occurred. They were – what else – events of revelation. Veils were being torn off. The thrust was towards real reality.

One of these events was Gutzkow's novel *Wally, die Zweiflerin* (*Wally, the Doubting Woman*). This was about the 'emancipation of the flesh'. Wally's admirer says to his beloved: 'Show me that you have no secrets from me, not one, and we shall have become one, and I shall be consecrated for my whole life!' Wally and the author resist. Then they both yield. And so, for the duration of a few lines, the author lets his heroine Wally stand 'exposed' by a window. The German League, however, did not forgive the author such obscenity. The novel was banned, and the favourable opportunity was seized to put all other publications of the 'Young Germany' movement on the Index as well.

The ban had been justified not only by reference to such improper nudity; offence had also been taken at Wally's doubts. Not only in the window scene does she show herself a champion of naturalness, but also in matters of religion. She supports the religion of the heart against the traditional dogmas of Christian faith. 'We shall not have a new heaven or a new earth; but the bridge between the two, it seems, must be built afresh,' the author makes Wally write in her diary.

The second great unveiling concerned the religious theme exclusively: David Friedrich Strauss's *Das Leben Jesu* (*The Life of Jesus*) appeared in 1835. Scarcely another book in the nineteenth century produced a similar sensation.

Strauss, a disciple of Hegel (he had visited the master shortly before Hegel's death) drew a radical conclusion from Hegel's religious philosophy. Hegel had taught that philosophy 'merely places itself above the form of faith, the content is the same'. This means: philosophical reflection identifies religion as a definite form of the spirit's self-revelation in history. But only in philosophy has this spirit, stripped of its religious form, come 'pure' into its own. Strauss now took this *historicization* of religion seriously and drew from it the kind of conclusions that Hegel, anxious to appease the powers that be, had refrained from drawing. Using the improved methods of textual criticism developed since the Romantic Age, Strauss extracted the image of the 'real Jesus' from Biblical tradition and differentiated this historically definable figure from the Christ of tradition. This 'Christ' he regarded as a myth, and this myth in turn contained truth. This 'truth' was understood in the Hegelian sense: the myth was an account of the idea of true humanity, an idea which, over a considerable period of time, had crystallized around one real person. In detail, Strauss interpreted the myth as follows: in Christ the idea of the human species is expressed. The 'God become man, the . . . infinite spirit turned into glory'. The God-man, born of a real woman but begotten by an invisible father, was the synthesis of spirit and nature. The miracles performed by Christ were a mythical expression of the fact that 'the spirit is ever more completely taking control of nature, and that nature is reduced, *vis-à-vis* it, to the powerless material of its activity.' Christ's sinlessness meant that the 'course of humanity's evolution is a perfect one, that impurity always only attaches to the individual, but is eliminated in the species and in its history'. In consequence, Christ's ascension was nothing other than a mythical promise of a glorious future for human progress.

Overnight *Das Leben Jesu* became the Bible of the educated middle class, which was firm in its faith in a future in this world. The historic impact of the book – well above 100,000 copies were sold within a few years – was due to a combination of two factors in a way typical of the age. First, there was the gesture of unveiling: through the veil a 'real' core was being reached, i.e. a demystification was being performed. Second, something was being discovered as 'reality' that gave rise to optimism about the future: the idea of progressing mankind. Strauss was the author of the encouragement which Feuerbach a little later formulated like this: The 'candidates for the beyond' should now at long last become 'students of this world'.

Over the years Strauss proclaimed his 'religion' of progress in this world, which underlies his critique of religion, with growing contentment. A generation later Nietzsche would take this as the point of departure for his crushing critique: this, he would say, was 'systematic philistinism come to power'. Nietzsche, of course, wished to experience the tragic sense of life in the happening of secularization. Strauss, however, was far removed from such grand gestures. With his 'tiptoeing carpet-slipper enthusiasm' he established himself in a world which he never ceased to believe existed for his benefit. Nietzsche poured scorn and mockery on one dictum from the aged Strauss, one that might equally well have been uttered in his youth: 'We demand the same piety for our universe as the old-style pious had for his God.'

As a result of Strauss's critique of religion the Hegelian school eventually split up: the conservatives or Old Hegelians were opposed by the Left or Young Hegelians. The latter were unreservedly dedicated to the project of modernity: they radicalized the critique of religion and from a critique of heaven they proceeded to a critique of the earth.

In 1840 came the second bombshell: Ludwig Feuerbach's *Das Wesen des Christentums* (*The Essence of Christianity*; in George Eliot's translation *The Essence of Religion*).

Feuerbach went beyond Strauss in that he interpreted the process of mythologization discovered in religion by Strauss as a kind of alienation of man from himself. Whatever is best in man, his hopes, his awareness of his potentialities, the potential wealth of his essential forces – all these he 'projects' into a heaven. From what it might be itself mankind made its gods, by whom it then allowed itself to be ruled. What was possible was perverted into what had to be done. The gods were products of men, and the products had gained power over their producers. It was the task of criticism to reveal the projective character of religion. This was the restoration of self-assurance, the recovery of the treasures squandered to heaven. Theology had to be brought back to its core: to anthropology. With his critique of religion Feuerbach tested his method of inversion: man becomes the creator and God the creature. With this method Feuerbach next attacked Hegel, practising what today is called 'deconstruction'. From the abysses of Hegelian philosophy he worked his way up to a kind of surface – a surface which Rousseau had reached before him when he reversed Descartes's 'I think, therefore I am' into 'I am, therefore I think.' Except that for Feuerbach 'I am' means: I am my body.

But Feuerbach speaks of the body differently from Schopenhauer. To Schopenhauer body and will are exchangeable concepts. Inwardly experienced corporeality is, as the self-experience of the will, the *realissimum* which simultaneously throws us into the tumult of the entire cosmos of the will, where there is no happiness, no satisfaction, but only endless and aimless activity and desire. As we are body, we are always at the focal point of the tragedy of being.

When Feuerbach, in line with the spirit of his age, turns Hegel upside down and struggles out of the convolutions of thought to the perception of bodily being, then his effort – again in line with the spirit of the age – is presented as a salvation for this world. With Feuerbach there is a promise of salvation in the body. He calls it 'the supreme *principium metaphysicum*, the secret of creation . . . [the] foundation of the world'. Feuerbach, like Schopenhauer, criticizes the absolutization of the 'thinking ego'. Instead he emphasizes the body-ego as a basis also of all cognition. With our thought we comprehend what possibly exists. Thought deals with the possibility of being. But what is, we experience only with our senses. The senses alone are in alliance with the present and in opposition to all forms of escape into the imaginary. The senses give us reality, with them we receive reality, and with them we create reality: 'it is in sensations, indeed in the most common daily sensations, that the deepest and the highest truths are hidden. Thus love is the true *ontological* proof of the existence of an object outside our heads – and there is no other proof of being than love and sentiment generally. Only that which by *being* gives you *pleasure* and by *non-being* gives you pain – that alone is.'

Love experienced with the whole body assures us of the reality beyond the limits of the body. Feuerbach criticized Hegel on the grounds that his spirit-reality was ultimately only a gigantic monologue of a solitarily thinking ego. A definite everyday existential provocation had not yet turned into a philosophical system with him: at the very point where the ego met the likes of itself, other egos, the ego was confronted with something entirely different – the 'you'. 'The individual as such does not have in himself the essence of man, *neither as a moral nor as a thinking creature*. The essence of man is contained only in the community, in man's unity with man – a unity, however, based only on the reality of the distinction between I and You.'

Feuerbach was aiming at a tough mystification: talk about a 'subject', if only by the suggestion of language, presupposes the identity of everything that is 'subject'. Against this, Feuerbach developed the exceedingly simple but fundamental idea that the entirely 'something other' than the ego still belongs to the world of many egos, and that this 'something other' is the 'great distinction' between I and You.

This daily experienced distinction – just like the body – is simply un-prethinkable. It comes before all thinking.

Like the body philosophy, so the philosophy of the You leads with Feuerbach into the grandiloquence of liberation: across mystifications, 'projections', 'alienations' the need was to discover the 'real'. This discovery would help develop the real against the obstacles of self-deception. Feuerbach's philosophical anthropology had no wish to make postulates, rather to criticize those dogmas and postulates which prevented the anthropological reality from coming into its true self-expression.

Feuerbach said of himself: 'God was my first thought, reason my second thought, man my third and last thought.' For Feuerbach these are not degrees of disillusionment. We ourselves, he taught, are still hidden from ourselves, that is why we made for ourselves a God, an absolute reason, etc., and submitted to them. We still have to discover ourselves. That will be our liberation. We are afraid of our bodies because we have made them strange to us. Let us appropriate our bodies! We are afraid of the 'other' because we experience everything outside not as a 'You' but as a deviation from our own 'egos'. Why do we not understand that the 'You' opens up the chance of an adventure, the mystery of love, the mystery of community?

For Feuerbach the road from God via reason to man is a road towards the light. He speaks in downright sacred language of his holy of holies – the body, you, community – demonstrating that in a sense he has also retraced the road from God to man, going from man to the divine, or, more accurately, to deified man. Thus he calls the bodily senses the 'organ of the absolute', and he writes as follows about 'you' and 'community': 'Solitariness is finiteness and limitation; association is freedom and infinity. Man by himself is man (in the ordinary meaning); man with man – that union of ego and you is God.'

Then there was Karl Marx. He too belongs to the history of that 'Pre-March' movement, a movement which, in its search for reality, turned Hegel's metaphysics inside out and, by doing so, believed to have advanced to a 'real reality'.

Just as Feuerbach had 'discovered' the body, the You and community, so Marx 'discovered' the social body and its focal point: the proletariat. In an epoch of political upheaval it provided the political impulse: the libertarian rights of the French Revolution had not yet arrived in Germany. There was also a social experience: the urban squalor of early capitalism. Not even from a student of law and philosophy in Berlin could it remain hidden, especially as it manifested itself in hunger revolts and destruction of machinery. Nevertheless, Marx did not come to philosophy from real misery, but the other way round: from a critique of philosophical misery he came to real misery. His was a philosophical passion which turned towards social sufferings. It was the *thought* thrusting towards reality. The middle-class son was attracted by the proletariat because he had assigned a philosophical role to it. Just as with Feuerbach one never feels that he is talking about a real body but that, instead, one has the body presented to one's eyes in a philosophical role, so with Marx one is not dealing with a real proletariat but with a category with countless legs. Marx's dictum, aimed against Feuerbach and the entire philosophical tradition, 'The philosophers have only *interpreted* the world in different ways, what matters is to *change* it,' ultimately means: change is the continuation of philosophy by other means. Change is the most advanced form of interpretation. 'Praxis' is philosophy in action – yet it is and remains philosophy. If Marx had been described as a social politician he would have taken this as an affront.

In the 1840s Marx was busy freeing himself of Hegel. In his dissertation about Epicurus and Democritus he sketched out a philosophical scenario which he suggested was being re-enacted at the time with himself playing a part in it. The 'Platonic and Aristotelian philosophers, expanding towards totality', had been followed by others, such as Democritus and Epicurus, who had once more tackled the spiritual universe with very simple, elementary, questions and, by doing so, had exploded it. This task, the ambitious young philosopher hinted, had now, in view of Hegelian totality, fallen to himself. A way back to simplicity had to be found, though this was exceedingly difficult: Being determined consciousness.

But what was Being? For Marx it was man in metabolism with nature, i.e. man at work and man socialized in work. It was in work that man expressed his essential forces, it was through work that he created himself and society – but that work was accomplished in 'alienated form', 'as a natural growth'. Man was still trapped in the realm of necessity; he had not yet worked his way through to freedom. The products which man produced, and the social relationships he entered into, had power over him. This was Feuerbach's critique of religion all over again, but, as Marx put it, it had to push forward from the critique of holy alienation to a critique of unholy alienation:

> It is therefore the *task of history*, now that the *yonder world of truth* has disappeared, to establish the *truth of this world*. It is, above all, the *task of philosophy*, which is in the service of history, now that the *saintly form* of human self-alienation has been unmasked, to unmask self-alienation in its *unsaintly forms*. Critique of heaven is thus transformed into a critique of earth, the *critique of religion* into a *critique of law*, the *critique of theology* into a *critique of politics*.

There was a philosophical ferocity at work in this critique – a return to the passion of the wild years of philosophy – but it was, at the same time, a critique which regarded itself as the final one. Once more, for the last time, philosophy – and then let philosophy disappear in realized happiness. With Hegel, Minerva's owl had set out on its flight when reality was ready for it; with Marx her owl was to fly towards the dawn of a new day. 'Critique,' Marx wrote, 'has plucked to pieces the imaginary flowers on his chains not in order that man should now wear his unimaginative, hopeless chains, but in order that he should cast off his chains and pluck a live flower.'

The 'live flower' was what Novalis had sought in dream. And Marx, out-trumping the Romantic movement, proclaimed: 'The reform of consciousness consists *solely* in . . . rousing the world from its dream about itself, in *explaining* to it its own actions . . . it will then be seen that the world has long had the dream of something that it needs only to be aware of in order truly to possess it.'

Every dream will yet be outshone by real possession – that is the great promise of Marxian philosophy. It is the apotheosis of the glorious future of human freedom. That trumpet call also reached Schopenhauer's ears. But to him such optimism was an 'unscrupulous' way of thinking. 'A philosophy,' Schopenhauer said in 1858, in conversation with the French philosopher

CHAPTER TWENTY-TWO

THE MYSTERY OF FREEDOM

Hegel had said of philosophy that it was its age formulated in ideas. This dictum was not only a philosophical ennobling of history, it also' lent the topical diagnosis of each period a philosophical dignity, as well as encouraging it to philosophize on, and for, the political skirmishing of the day. Thus his famous sentence, 'What is reasonable is real, and what is real is reasonable', had political effects – in opposite directions. One side took the statement as a justification of existing conditions, while the other side – men like Ruge, Bauer, Engels and Marx – understood it as an encouragement to make what merely existed into a 'reality' by bringing it into harmony with 'reason'. For the one side the statement formulated an 'is' state, and for the others a 'should be' state. Common to all, however, was the conviction that society and history represented a decisive dimension of the truth-event: thus the overcoming and outbidding of Hegel was still carried out in his footsteps.

After Hegel, therefore, there was a new kind of philosophy. Prior to him, philosophy was dominated by the direct juxtaposition of the individual and the whole: God and man, or man and nature, or man and Being. Men in the plural, people, were not a special category but merely a summation of all the attributes which could be shown to exist in the individual. The concept of 'humanity' was used not so much to designate a plural, historically dynamic subject, but was used in the sense of 'what is human'. That is why it was still possible in the eighteenth century to say that everyone had a duty to respect the 'humanity' within him.

After Hegel, if not before him, a new in-between world was inserted between that duality of 'the individual and the whole': *society* and *society in action*, in other words: history. This in-between world fed on the substance of the earlier antipodes: the old metaphysics of the whole, of Being, disappeared in a metaphysics of society and history, and talk about the individual became meaningless and pointless because the individual was now seen as socially and historically determined. The in-between world of the social-historical admits of only one point beyond: of 'nature' relating to man, of anthropology. As the creature of a natural species, however, man is even less than an individual creature; moreover, in Marx for one, the concept of the social-historical is so dominant that even 'nature' seems to be involved in it.

Henceforward there would be no escape from this in-between world of the social-historical on the one side and 'nature' on the other. One was struggling on the leash of natural necessity and of social necessity. The argument was merely about which of these necessities was the dominant. Hegel, and Marx after him, believed in the victory of social necessity over natural necessity. Hegel spoke of the 'spirit that finds itself', and Marx of the 'abolition of naturalness'. To both of them this was a road to freedom. Both of them understood 'freedom' as a social product of history.

The materialists, on the other hand, believed in the superiority of natural necessity. But they too, as a rule, secularized the old metaphysical promise of salvation: they interpreted the evolution of history as an upward development.

For philosophical thought at the beginning of the machine age, therefore, the remaining dimensions of Being, nature and society began to transform themselves into a kind of 'machine'. To these 'machines' one might entrust the manufacture of a successful life, always on condition that one behaved appropriately. For Hegel this meant 'Freedom is the recognition of necessity' and in the *Communist Manifesto* we read: 'What the bourgeoisie therefore produces, above all, are its own gravediggers. Its fall and the victory of the proletariat are equally inevitable.' This victory will be 'inevitable' if the 'machine' of historical regularity is allowed to run undisturbed. Disturbing factors must be eliminated, and only for that reason must there be a 'party' to carry such 'manifestos' to the people.

There were quite a lot of 'freedoms' to be fought for at the time against political oppression and social hardships: freedom from semi-feudal imposts on the peasantry, freedom from the guilds' constraints on artisan journeymen and on manufacturers, freedom from internal customs duties which were strangling the market, freedom of speech, freedom from state arbitrariness, freedom of political organization and action, freedom for the sciences, freedom of self-determination also in the moral sphere, etc.

It was thought that implementation of these demands would require a prolonged period of time. A struggle planned over a long period called for strategies. Actions were being planned, alliances calculated, forecasts of likely developments made. All this involved the participants in presumed constraints and demanded loyalties to 'great' objectives which must not be frivolously jeopardized by extemporization. Freedom movements intending to get the social 'machine' to work for them have to impose certain restraints upon themselves: hence the polemics against 'irresponsible' elements like Heinrich Heine, hence the condemnation of Luddite-like actions, hence also Marx's and Engels's attacks on the theoreticians of instant freedom, such as Max Stirner and later Mikhail Bakunin. Nevertheless, to him who has freedom as a goal before him, the world will open up.

Curiously, though, the consciousness which, in front, is trying to clear the road to freedom, practises, at the rear, a kind of large-scale deprivation of freedom. The freedom-seeking consciousness seems to know exactly by what social or natural determinants the supposedly free and spontaneous action is surrounded. That is modernity: a longing for freedom and, simultaneously, an awareness of a necessity of Being shown to us by the sciences – a curious mixture of naive spontaneity and disillusioned cynicism. The pincer movement of sociology and psychoanalysis leaves no real room for freedom; in our self-interpretation we appear as an economic character mask, as a social role player, as nature-driven – a continuous string of humiliations for any consciousness of freedom. Nevertheless, the longing for freedom remains alive, especially also in those who are good at sociologically and psycho-analytically exploring the reasons for their spontaneity. Perhaps this is due to the fact that one's longing for freedom exceeds one's courage and ability to take responsibility. One desires the freedom to do anything one wishes, one desires unimpeded satisfaction of one's needs, but when matters go wrong, when the consequences have to be borne, then discursive deprivation of freedom has its great moment: one can explain that things had to happen the way they did, and one is free from responsibility. The highly developed culture of the ability to explain operates in a dangerous grey area: the boundaries between explanation and excuse are fluid. One can even place the ability to explain *ex post facto* at the very beginning of an action, in the sense of preventive absolution in the event of failure. This event is anticipated, and one prepared for 'not having been the one'.

Thus this 'in-between world' of the social-historical, raised to new philosophical dignity, is on the one hand the arena of a truth-event concerned with growing freedom, while on the other it contains mitigations and excuses for the disasters of freedom. Nowadays we cannot simply stand before the existence of the radically evil. (The Hitler phenomenon, for example, has to be explained: a bad childhood, necrophilia, petit-bourgeois *angst*, capitalist interest, modernization shock, etc. Ultimately these are perhaps also means of tranquillizing our own horror.)

Yet the culture of exculpating explanation is not new. In earlier centuries metaphysical need had similarly been fond of presenting that which was as something which necessarily had to be, as a cosmos. Long before the real order and its laws and necessities were understood, there existed a *presumption of order*. Being and chaos simply were not conceivable alongside each other. Newton spent half a lifetime arguing against the thesis – recently revived by Velikovsky – of freely roaming planets. In doing so he relied not so much on the laws of gravity he himself had discovered as, to be on the safe side, on God. And even Diderot had to suffer furious attacks because he had dared to place chance at the heart of the world. One would have preferred to see a devil there, for he would, in his own way, be predictable and necessarily consistent (the Marquis de Sade very impressively demonstrated such a 'negative' theology).

The metaphysical concept of necessary Being, the religious understanding of God – both of these are anticipations of the scientific concept of necessity. Today, as then, we operate with a prior presumption of order, also and especially when the manner of the operation of order is not yet understood in detail. Faith has been secularized into a hypothesis of explicability.

It was due to the power of the presumption of order in the pre-modern age that 'freedom' became one of the most sensitive problems even then. On the one hand, the free will of the human creature was needed so that the evil in the world should not be attributed to the good Creator. On the other hand, the creature could not stand up to the Creator, as in that case the Creator would have lost his omnipotence. Hence there could be no free will and hence the fact that man so persistently abandoned God's path must have somehow been necessary and planned by God. The problem had been argued about from St Augustine to Leibniz, often with the aid of the stake and the rack.

St Paul taught: 'Christ made you free from the law of sin and of death.' Luther took over this interpretation. Man was subject to original sin; man, unfree, was slave to Evil; but ever since Christ's offer of grace man had been able to choose: man was free to be liberated by and in his faith. Man was shackled by the sin of the flesh, but the spirit was free to be liberated. There was no freedom that man could take for himself, there was only the freedom which man might receive. Freedom was not our action but a 'letting it happen'. As, however, man was free to reject the gift of freedom through grace, he was responsible for his unfreedom in original sin. It was a bold way of linking unfreedom with responsibility, and a considerable contrast to our present day, when we rather tend to associate freedom with non-responsibility. It was a long haul from the metaphysics of self-responsibility to the empiricism of unaccountability.

The problem of freedom was *the* challenge, not only to theologians but also to philosophers. As freedom was being suspected of getting God into difficulties, the philosophers had to deal with it. A secret resentment could thus be satisfied. Philosophy, normally degraded to the position of hand-maiden, was able to come to the aid of a threatened God or else, if it so pleased, get him into even greater difficulties.

Spinoza analysed the sense of freedom as an illusion of immediacy: one felt free in one's decisions and actions only as long as one remained in such immediacy. Freedom, therefore, consisted only in 'people being . . . aware of their volition, while being ignorant of the causes which determined them'. That was freedom as self-deception. The discovery of causes, however, was also freedom, and indeed real freedom, because, according to Spinoza, it was freedom from self-deception. We are free when we have freed ourselves of the illusion of freedom. And in this freedom to criticize freedom we become part of that exalted necessity which is the Whole.

Descartes, too, thought in a roundabout way when the issue was freedom. He differentiated between free action and arbitrary action. 'Arbitrariness' is a human urge not controlled by reason and not furnished with 'causes' by reason. In that respect 'arbitrariness' is what is causeless in us. What is causeless is what is not 'necessary'. Our mind, however, resides in the 'necessary'; hence 'arbitrariness' is something alien that does violence to our mind. And because our mind is the most human (because the most divine) element within us, 'arbitrariness' must endanger that most human aspect itself. In 'arbitrariness' one loses one's autonomy, becoming the victim of a happening which one has not oneself brought about but which takes one for a ride. Hence arbitrariness is unfreedom and necessity is freedom.

Thus and similarly philosophy had for centuries turned and twisted around a problem which is in fact a mystery: the problem of freedom. In that hot and dark zone philosophical discourse starts spinning.

Kant did not solve this problem of freedom, he did not resolve the mystery – on the contrary, his merit was to have demonstrated the fundamental insolubility or unresolvability of the problem of freedom.

There is and must be – according to Kant – a double perspective: if we experience ourselves as creatures in time, then every 'Now' is linked into a time chain, i.e. with what precedes it. But as we are always only Now and what has just passed is no longer 'in our power', we can never have in our power that which, as the past, determines our present Now. This applies, as we have said, to self-experience in time. But 'time', according to Kant, does not belong to the world 'in itself' but is only a form of perception by our (inner) sense. The 'in itself' of the world and our self is without time. Admittedly we cannot picture such 'timelessness' since 'time' is an irreducible aspect of our perception. Yet there is, according to Kant, one single point, one single experience, which lifts us out of the determining time chain, in so far as this lies behind us, and links us with what is not yet and what will be in the future. No matter how much our Now may be determined by the Before, we experience it as linked with what might be if we so wish. A kind of inverted determination: we determine ourselves through what we wish to let happen. This wish, however, according to Kant, must not be aided by any urge. For in that case we would remain victims of our sensuality, which has power over us. That is why that 'will be' must be a 'shall be'. The 'shall be' should be equipped not with the secret natural force of volition, but the other way about: the 'shall' rises against the natural urge of 'will' and from its own strength produces a will. You are willing something because you should. You should will. The 'shall', moreover, need not consider the 'can', but, being absolute, it proves its strength by producing the 'can'. Kant does not argue from 'can' to 'shall', but from 'shall' to 'can'. 'Whatever you should do you can do', is the acute imperative of conscience. In conscience, and only there, are we snatched out of the realm of necessity. The 'thing in itself', which we ourselves are, announces its presence in our conscience. Here we are allowed to grasp a corner of our transcendental existence; here we experience something of the 'absolute spontaneity of freedom' (Kant), which we ourselves are.

However, the mystery of freedom is not thereby solved, but it remains obscure because the double perspective of self-experience does not disappear. Any action motivated by a 'conscience' thus understood is, from an empirical perspective, an action from prior determining causes, deriving from them *necessarily*, and must therefore be understood as an unfree action. Even 'conscience' may be seen, from an empirical perspective, as one causality among others. Yet our 'conscience' reminds us at every Now that we can also act differently because we should act differently. We have a paradox here: conscience makes us free because it does not give us freedom. And conversely: thinking in causality gives us freedom by enveloping us in necessary Being.

Kant called the dimension of Being revealed to us through conscience our 'intelligible' Being. To him the tension between our empirical and our 'intelligible' Being is at near breaking-point. Why this must be so and why that tension must not be relaxed, and how one can live with it – to explain this is the purpose of Kant's entire transcendental philosophical enterprise. It requires philosophical and practical skill to balance in Kant's manner on the point of the problem. His successors for the most part were unable to keep this balance. They crashed and fastened themselves to one of the tension-sustaining poles; some to the empirical and others to the 'intelligible' Being. We shall deal first with the 'intelligibles', the metaphysical philosophers of the subject.

Fichte's argument, like subsequently that of Sartre, proceeded entirely from the 'absolute spontaneity of freedom' (Kant): 'But he who becomes aware of his self-sufficiency and independence of anything which is outside him – and this is achieved only by, independently of anything else, making something of oneself – such a person does not require things as props for his Self, and cannot require them as they would undo that independence and turn it into empty appearance. The ego which he possesses, and which interests him, abolishes that faith in things.'

In 1809, following his break with Fichte – a break which caused a sensation among the interested public – Schelling published his essay 'Über das Wesen der menschlichen Freiheit' ('On the Nature of Human Freedom'), projecting the delicate Kantian dualism of freedom and necessity, which was valid only for human experience, into Being generally. Being and God, however, as with Spinoza, were interchangeable concepts. In contrast to Spinoza, however, Being for Schelling was not a cosmos of things but a universe of processes, of happenings, of activities. 'Things', so to speak, were crystallizations, condensations of happenings. This consolidation into things must therefore be resolved again into its underlying processes. Thus Schelling in an inspired formulation developed his notion of the unconditional: 'Unconditional is that which cannot be made into a thing at all.' This sentence is first found in

Schelling's youthful writings and, in a very Fichtean manner, is moulded around the 'ego'. In his essay on freedom of 1809, however, Schelling went beyond Fichte. It was necessary to show, he argued, 'that everything real (nature, the world of things) is based on activity, life and freedom . . . that not only is ego-ness everything but that, conversely, everything is also ego-ness.'

That 'everything', the whole of Being, and especially 'nature', are to be understood as 'I', as 'ego'. The ego-ness of the whole is called 'God' by Schelling. Hence the dark mystery of freedom, as man experiences it in himself, must become a mystery in Being itself, in God. Kant's duality of necessity and freedom in self-experience becomes an all-embracing ambivalence in Being, in God.

'Only he who has tasted freedom,' Schelling wrote, 'can experience the desire to make everything analogous to it, to expand it over the whole of the universe.' Yet the same applies to the experience of necessity. It, too, is of such evidence that it is expanded 'over the whole of the universe'. Being is tied into an order, in rules and laws, i.e. in necessities – but the ultimate cause of this regulated order is spontaneity. That is Schelling's central idea. Regulated Being is the result of the self-constraint of absolute spontaneity, which Schelling called 'God'. In the world as it presents itself to us, Schelling writes, 'everything is rule, order and form; but always the ruleless lies at the bottom, as though it might burst through again some day. . . . This is the unfathomable basis of reality, the unresolvable remainder, that which, even with the greatest effort, cannot be resolved in understanding but forever remains at the bottom.'

Absence of rule at the bottom: freedom, therefore, is the abyss of Being and, at the same time, the abyss in man. Schelling's wide-sweeping metaphysical gesture aims at that abyssal self-reflection. Just as Sigmund Freud at a future date would, when reasoning about the abyssal urges in man, find himself talking about Moses, Oedipus, Electra and other mythological VIPs, so Schelling found himself caught in narrative outbidding of the unprethinkable. He 'tells the story' of the two types of essence in God: of God the chaos figure, who in his creation and in his creature calls himself to order, as it were, and yet remains a rebel against his orderly self.

Schopenhauer for his part called Schelling to order. In his 'Preisschrift über die Freiheit des Willens' ('Competition Essay on the Freedom of the Human Will', 1841) he commented on Schelling's 'freedom' essay as follows: 'It is mainly occupied with a minute description of a God, with whom the worthy author appears to be intimately acquainted, for he even describes his origin. The pity of it is, that he does not give us a single hint as to how he struck up the acquaintance' (FHW, 174).

That, however, is not correct. Schelling made his 'acquaintance' with the abyss in God, in Being, through his intimate acquaintance with the abyssal in himself. Schelling's 'freedom' essay is so bold just because it monumentalizes the mystery of the self-experience of freedom into a metaphysics of chaos as the basis of the world and in so doing, even before Schopenhauer, objects to the post-Kantian practice of extracting panlogism from the subject. Having discovered that nature can be a destructive, disastrous force in man, Schelling attempted to redefine afresh the essence of nature generally. Among all Schopenhauer's contemporaries he was the one who came closest to Schopenhauer's notion of the will: 'Volition is primal Being,' Schelling wrote, 'and to it alone apply all its predicates: causelessness, eternity, independence of time, self-affirmation.'

For Schelling, too, the will is no longer a function of understanding, but the other way round: understanding is a function of the will. Thus the order of understanding is shattered by chaos-producing will, but – and this is Schelling's last word on the subject – the 'spirit' in which 'love' operates is stronger still. 'Yet love is the highest. It is what existed before the cause and the existing existed (in separation). . . .' Once more Schelling came round. One layer further down, below the abyss, there was 'love', 'divine love', which tied and supported us.

We are shackled by necessity – first level. We discover our freedom in which, simultaneously, the threatening abyss of chaos opens – second level. Lower still, we experience ourselves being carried and tied by the feeling that nothing, after all, matters and that everything is for the best – third level. In other words: You must – You can – *You may*.

The mystery of freedom. In Schelling's essay the whole obscurity of the problem was once more magnificently spread out. That perhaps was its finest aspect.

In 1838 Schopenhauer took up the problem of freedom.

In 1837 he had, in the *Hallische Literaturzeitung*, come across a competition organized by the Royal Norwegian Society for Learning in Trondheim. Just then 'freedom is the banner' (Freiligrath) was true everywhere. So the question fitted well into the general trend: 'Can the freedom of the human will be proved from self-awareness?' Encouraged by a small success which had just come his way, Schopenhauer got down to dealing with the question.

In the summer of 1837 he had written an extensive letter to the editors of a new edition of Kant, Professors Schubert and Rosenkranz, urging them to base their edition on the first, undoctored, edition of the *Critique of Theoretical Reason*. The second edition (1787), Schopenhauer had demonstrated in detail, had considerably toned down the original radicalism of the text, and had made concessions to religion and common sense. The editors followed his advice and, in their preface, even published the key passages of his letter. Schopenhauer was at least now entitled to regard himself as a recognized authority on Kant. That was reassuring and somewhat mitigated his irritation at another piece of news in June 1837, when the publisher of his *On the Will in Nature* informed him that only 125 copies had been sold by then.

In a newly stimulated spirit of adventure Schopenhauer worked on his entry for the competition. He had not yet completed it when he learned about another competition, likewise concerned with the problem of philosophical ethics. The Royal Danish Society for Learning posed the rather cumbersome question to the philosophical community, '*Is the source and basis of morality to be sought* in an idea of morality lodged directly in the consciousness (or conscience) and in the analysis of other basic moral concepts deriving from it, or does it lie at some other level of cognition?'

Schopenhauer dispatched his essay for the first competition towards the end of 1838. In January 1839 it was awarded first prize. Schopenhauer, delighting in such a distinction 'like a child' (Hornstein) and impatient for his medal, during the next few months kept besieging the Norwegian Resident in Frankfurt. Meanwhile he was working on the second competition. In the early summer of 1839 he dispatched his essay and, certain of his victory and full of impatience, wrote to the 'highly esteemed Society' in Copenhagen in July 1839: 'I request you to notify me by post of my victory as soon as possible. As for the prize awarded to me, I hope . . . to receive that from you through the diplomatic channel' (CL, 675).

The highly esteemed Society in Copenhagen, however, had other ideas. It did not consider Schopenhauer's essay – the only one received in response to the competition advertisement – to be worthy of the prize. The author, they said, had not answered the question. 'Moreover,' the gentlemen in Copenhagen wrote, 'we cannot pass over in silence the fact that several outstanding philosophers of the modern age are referred to in so improper a manner as to cause serious and just offence.'

Schopenhauer had the two essays published by a small Frankfurt bookseller and publisher in 1841, under the joint title *The Two Fundamental Problems of Ethics, Treated in Two Academic Prize Essays*. On the title-page Schopenhauer specifically described the first essay as 'crowned in Trondheim on 26 January 1839' and the second as 'not crowned in Copenhagen, on 30 January 1840'. That was intended as a resounding slap in the face – but it was not until a decade later, when he began to be famous, that anyone was impressed by it.

In those two essays Schopenhauer could not presuppose knowledge of the whole of his metaphysics – entries had to be anonymous – but had to develop his position 'inductively', proceeding from the question as posed. The Norwegian Society's question 'Can freedom of the human will be proved from self-awareness?' was answered by Schopenhauer as follows: No matter how much one rummaged in one's self-awareness, one could not find freedom there but only the illusion of freedom.

To make this assertion he had to clarify first what was to be understood by 'self-awareness'; one had to know, surely, in which sphere one was to search for the existence or non-existence of free will.

Schopenhauer therefore began by defining 'self-awareness': this was the awareness that was left if one disregarded the 'awareness of other things'. 'Awareness of other things' fills us almost entirely; what then does the 'rest' contain? As the term implies, awareness of one's own 'self' (in so far as it is not some 'other thing'). Schopenhauer asks: 'How does man become aware of his own self?' and replies: 'entirely as of something willing.' The self of which the not-'outward'-directed awareness becomes directly aware is a willing self. That which 'wills' in a person is not exhausted by realized acts of will or 'formal decisions' but embraces the wide area of all 'emotions and passions', such as 'all desiring, striving, wishing, longing, yearning, hoping, loving, rejoicing, exulting, etc., as well as the contrary affections, such as relucting or repugning, detesting, fleeing, fear, anger, hatred, grief, suffering' (FHW, 95). These strivings of the will and excitements of the will, inward though they may be, always of course relate to something external, at which they are directed or by which they are excited. That external something, however, no longer comes within the sphere of self-awareness but belongs to that of the 'awareness of other things'. This differentiation is not as academically hair-splitting as it might seem, because Schopenhauer can explain the illusion of freedom from the strict definition of the concept of 'self-awareness' (an awareness directly accompanying the event of the will): if self-awareness is a direct awareness of the event of one's own will, then it cannot reach any further than that internally experienceable event itself. Self-experienced will stands at the beginning of self-awareness and must do so because awareness must initially be switched off against external things which might stimulate the will by motivation, causation, etc.

The statement of self-awareness about the actions of one's own will, 'which anyone may listen to within himself', may, 'reduced to their bare contents', be formulated as follows: 'I can do what I will: if I want to go to the left, I go to the left; if I want to go to the right then I go to the right. All depends upon my Will: therefore I am free' (FHW, 102). Self-deception, said Schopenhauer. What remains unclear, he said, is whether the will itself, the will which inside myself I always experience only once it has become action, is free. If I am free to do certain things, am I then also free to will? There can be no answer to this question from the perspective of direct self-awareness, because for that self-awareness the will is something primal. Indeed, the will is so primal to self-awareness that, strictly speaking, one only knows what one wants when one has already willed it. There is only *ex post facto* awareness of one's own will.

Information on whether the will itself is free cannot therefore be obtained from self-awareness – that would only lead us into a 'dark interior', where the will has always lived within us; that information is available only if we step out of our direct self-awareness in the direction of awareness 'of other things'; i.e. if we observe ourselves as a thing among other things, from outside. Then the scenery will change. Then there will be a whole world of things, people, etc., all around me, acting upon my will, conditioning it in its stirrings, supplying objects to it, suggesting motivations to it. The relationship between that 'environment' and my will must, from this perspective, be viewed as a strictly causal one, Schopenhauer argues. Man acts just as a stone falls or a plant reacts – necessarily, in response to certain motivations. Motivation is the causality passing through knowledge in its broadest sense (i.e. also through unconscious perception). As definite motivations enter its 'range of vision', the will cannot react otherwise than in definite directions. Between the motivation acting upon the will and the action of the will there is a strict causality, a necessity which rules out freedom. However, man 'by means of his faculty of thinking, can alternately and frequently represent to himself the motives, whose influence upon his Will he feels, in any order, and can thus put them before his Will – which is what we call *deliberating*; and this capacity for deliberation renders possible a far greater *choice* than is open to the animal. This, no doubt, makes him *relatively free* – free, that is, from the immediate compulsion of the sensibly-perceived objects which at the *particular moment* are acting upon his Will as motives – a compulsion to which the animal is wholly given over; whereas he is determined inde-pendently of present objects, by thoughts, which are *his* motives. It is no doubt this *relative* freedom that cultivated but not deep-thinking people really have in mind, when they talk of that freedom of the Will which so obviously gives man the advantage over the animal' (FHW, 121).

According to Schopenhauer, therefore, there is my will, which I am myself; this is my 'character', whose identity cannot be discovered from within but which nevertheless is as firm, as definite and as immutable as the identity of a stone. And then there is a whole world which acts upon that will and moves it in one way or another, just as a stone, hurled with a certain force, will describe a definite trajectory before falling to the ground. The stone must fly when it is thrown, and I must 'will' in a particular way when my will is moved by certain motivations.

Schopenhauer thus paints a picture of a universe of merciless necessity – but, as we have said, from the perspective of the awareness of 'external things', i.e. from the perspective of an objectivized awareness.

Yet Schopenhauer does not stop there. In an involved way he returns to direct self-awareness, and what at first appeared as an illusion of freedom is now granted its truth. 'Having recognized, then,' he writes as he approaches his conclusion, 'as the result of the foregoing exposition, that man's action has not a particle of freedom, but is invariably under the dominion of strictest necessity, we are hereby led to the point at which we can grasp *true moral freedom*, which is of a higher species' (FHW, 183). Like Kant, Schopenhauer now refers to man's awareness of being the agent of his own action and to the feeling of responsibility arising therefrom – a feeling that clings stubbornly to the direct awareness, even when, and especially when, this awareness can make excuses for itself by explaining. 'Thanks to that awareness no one, not even a person totally convinced of the above demonstrated necessity governing our actions, would ever think of using that necessity as an excuse for an offence, or of shifting his responsibility on to those motivations, whose presence in fact made the action inevitable' (FHW, 183). Needless to say, Schopenhauer realizes that attempts to shift the blame are invariably made. What he is trying to say is this: The exoneration does not work, the feeling of responsibility will not ultimately be suppressed; no matter in what distorted form, it maintains its probing presence. In a radical way we are responsible for ourselves. Schopenhauer arrives at the unprecedentedly paradoxical formulation: '*Freedom*, which is consequently not to be met within the *operari* [action] must therefore lie in the *esse* [Being]' (FHW, 188).

Thus, at the end of the examination, the initially rejected illusion of freedom and the sense of sovereign power come into their own. These findings of direct self-awareness reveal a surprising truth: 'The undeniable consciousness of absolute independence and originality, that accompanies all our deeds, (notwithstanding their dependence upon motives) and makes them *our* deeds will therefore not lead us astray: really it goes beyond the deeds and originates higher up, including as it does our existence and essence itself, from which, under the influence of motives, all deeds necessarily proceed. In this sense that consciousness of autonomy and originality, as also of responsibility, which accompanies our actions, may be compared to a hand that points to a more distant object than the one nearer in the same line, to which it seems to point' (FHW, 189).

In what direction that feeling is pointing, the feeling which, despite our realization that our actions are determined, makes us feel responsible – that Schopenhauer can hardly hint at in this essay, because otherwise he would have to unfold his entire metaphysics of the will. But he lets this much be understood: at the bottom of the paradoxical sense of guilt, of the paradoxical feeling of responsibility, lies the *guilt of individuation*, the sense of guilt that one is who one is, and that, through what one is, through one's mere existence, one is a particle of the inwardly torn cosmos of the will, a cosmos which consumes itself in universal conflict. Our direct self-awareness, entirely pervaded as it is by the self-experience of this simultaneously driving and consuming will, is aware of this guilt both in a feeling of freedom and responsibility and in a feeling of remorse.

Returning to direct self-awareness and there discovering the hidden truth of illusion, Schopenhauer once more describes that circle of an immanent metaphysics which even in the critique of experience does not betray experience. He returns to the existence of evidence within direct self-awareness after having first dissolved that evidence (the feeling of freedom and responsibility) in *explaining* (chain of necessities). He returns in order now to try to *understand* this evidence – which, despite all explanations, refuses to disappear – by asking what it *means* if the voice which declares me guilty, which labels us the agent of our actions, which burdens us with responsibility, refuses to be silent.

Here again are the two dimensions: the soothing, and indeed exculpation, by *explaining*, and the persistent disquiet which seeks to absorb into *understanding* that 'unknown x' which remains after every explanation. Schopenhauer resolves the illusion of freedom by an explicatory reference to necessary Being, but presently returns in a circle to the Being of this *necessary* Being. And the analytically resolved initial experience of freedom now means: with me and in me this Being always begins anew.

Heidegger in this context will speak of 'tranquillity' and Adorno of that 'non-identity' which militates against the compulsion of an objectivizing identity.

Schopenhauer's immanent metaphysics 'never tears itself entirely from experience, but remains the mere interpretation and explanation thereof' (WWR II, 183). This is how Schopenhauer formulates his metaphysical programme in the second volume of his principal work. With regard to the free-will problem this means: Explanation tells me *why* I do or have done something. Understanding asks what I really *am* to be doing such a thing.

It will be seen that for Schopenhauer, too, freedom remains a mystery. A mystery, however, which at the same time is so close to us, such a daily occurrence, that an entire exculpation culture is required to dodge it – such as the myth of the subject agent 'society/history', to which we might delegate our responsibility, from which we claim freedoms so that we may get rid of our freedom.

At the end of his 'freedom' essay Schopenhauer had referred to 'true moral freedom'. His second, 'uncrowned', prize essay was concerned with the 'foundations of morality'.

He showed great self-assurance in his introduction: 'Anyone who has seen how none of the roads chosen so far has led to the goal will be the more disposed to join me along a very different one, one which has not so far been seen or else has been contemptuously rejected; perhaps because it was the most natural' (FM in MW, 640).

To begin with, Schopenhauer reviews the roads which do not lead to the goal, especially that of Kant. His criticism may be reduced to two aspects: criticism of an overestimation of reason in questions of morality, and criticism of the secret alliance between morality and selfishness.

On the first point: The foundations of morality have long been sought in the intellect, but erroneously. Under the 'seriousness and pressure of life' nobody will heed such an intellectual morality. Such a 'morality' confronting the more-than-powerful will, confronting the passions, would be as an 'enema syringe in a conflagration' (FM in MW, 670). The '*a priori* house of cards' of Kant's 'practical reason' is of no use, because man was not of such a nature that it would occur to him 'to look around or inquire about a *law* governing his will, a law to which it would have to submit and which it would have to obey' (FM in MW, 669). Kant, according to Schopenhauer, had altogether committed the unpardonable mistake of moralizing his excellent insights into the *a priori* of our recognizing faculty. He had made the error of transferring to the moral sphere the power of theoretical reason which captures the matter of experience in its categories. He had construed a reason which, in the same *a priori* way as theoretical reason governs experience, in the form of moral reason was supposed to govern practical action. The result was what moral doctrines had always been in a more or less disguised manner, to wit – and this is the second aspect of Schopenhauer's critique – a theoretical justification of egotism.

Egotism was nothing other than the natural power of the existence of our will. Will was in itself egotistical, desiring its own 'well-being or ill-being' and requiring no moral prop. Egotism was occurring anyway. A morality which served selfish interests was no morality, but egotism in moral disguise. Anyone performing good deeds in the expectation of a reward in the beyond was therefore acting not morally but egotistically, a creditor granted a loan because he was speculating on a large interest in the beyond. Even Kant, according to Schopenhauer, had, after much vacillation, held out the promise of a reward to those who obeyed his categorical imperative and thereby based his morality on egotism.

In his critique of moral appearance Schopenhauer, like Nietzsche after him, is a master of psychological unmasking: he tracks egotism along its secret paths and unmasks pretence and forgeries. His definition of actions of 'genuine moral worth' is concise. They are actions 'of voluntary justice, pure love of our neighbour and real nobility of soul' (FM, 208). They are actions occurring against the urges of egotism, actions not aimed, even by round-about routes, at one's own advantage. Yet – and this is a crucial point for Schopenhauer – even such actions require a motive force; the 'enema syringe' of mere intellect would never achieve them. Morality, Schopenhauer said in his introduction, had a basis which had been missed because it was the most natural: compassion.

Compassion might be 'natural', yet for Schopenhauer it remained a 'mystery' leading to the heart of his metaphysics.

In his 'freedom' essay Schopenhauer had encountered the *guilt of individuation*; now he was concerned with the *pain of individuation*.

Compassion was an occurrence still within the sphere of the will itself, and not in that of reflection. In compassion the 'veil of maya' is torn; at the sight of another's sufferings I experience 'the barrier between Ego and Non-ego' being 'for the moment broken down', and I share the sufferings of the other in a way in which normally I only 'feel my own suffering' (FM, 247).

In compassion I am painfully linked to a world full of suffering. This is Schopenhauer's reasoning: Being is suffering because it is will; and snatched out for a few instants from the limitations of the individual, from the limitations of egotistical self-assertion of *my* will, I become free to participate in suffering Being. In the case of compassion this fusion takes place not as a contemplative universalist approach but as involvement in a specific individual 'case'. This is something one must have experienced if action is to stem from it. Compassion cannot be preached. One either has it or one does not. It is a kind of tie with Being, higher than all the reason of self-assertion. Compassion is a happening in the dimension of the will: will, suffering in itself and, faced with the pains of others, momentarily ceasing to will itself within its individual limitations.

To Schopenhauer compassion is a 'primal phenomenon and the border stone beyond which only metaphysical speculation may dare to step' (FM, 224).

Schopenhauer's ethics of compassion has rightly been called a 'practical mysticism' (Lütkehaus). Compassion springs from the spiritual overcoming of the *principium individuationis* and does not bank on reward in the next world, let alone in this. It is 'selfless' in the most radical sense; above all, however, it is solidarity 'in spite of history'. Compassion does not hope for a historical overcoming of suffering or misery. The tense relationship between sweeping theories of improvement and individual acts of pity is well known. As a rule they are denounced because they hold out no prospect of realization, and because they merely divert attention from the 'principal evil', which, it is claimed, could be liquidated by the practicable strategic action of 'emancipation'. From this perspective, compassion looks like sentimentality *vis-à-vis* the 'symptoms'. The energy which ought to be used for the hard task of dealing with the roots is instead stirred into 'pap for the heart'. Max Horkheimer was to refer back to Schopenhauer's ethics of compassion when he argued against the supra-strategic instrumental reason of 'emancipation': 'Be mistrustful of anyone who asserts that one can either only help the great whole or not at all. This is the lifelong lie of those who do not in fact wish to help and who invoke grand theory in order to talk themselves out of their responsibility in a specific individual case. They rationalize their inhumanity.'

Schopenhauer's ethics of compassion is an ethics of 'nevertheless'; without any backing or justification from the philosophy of history, and against the background of a metaphysics of hopelessness, it pleads for that spontaneity which would at least mitigate the perennial suffering. It encourages opposition to suffering and, at the same time, makes it clear that there is no chance of eliminating suffering. It is, as Lütkehaus has accurately put it, a 'practical philosophy of the as if'.

Schopenhauer's pictures of universal suffering were not only on a vast canvas but also testified to a sharp eye for the social hardships of his day. In the second volume of his principal work he portrays the world as a 'hell surpassing that of Dante by the fact that one man must be the devil of another' (WWR II, 578). Such a 'hell' is caused by 'boundless egotism' or even deliberate 'malice'. Schopenhauer refers to 'negro slavery' and continues: 'However, we need not go so far; to enter at the age of five a cotton-spinning or other factory, and from then on to sit there every day first ten, then twelve, and finally fourteen hours, and perform the same mechanical work, is to purchase dearly the pleasure of drawing breath. But this is the fate of millions, and many more millions have an analogous fate' (WWR II, 578).

In the revolutionary year of 1848, however, when that social misery depicted by Schopenhauer in the lurid colours of outrage suddenly erupted, became rebellious, built barricades, and here and there took up arms, Arthur Schopenhauer reacted with merciless fury and fear.

In March, as elsewhere in Germany, there were social and political disturbances in the city of Frankfurt.

Towards the end of 1847 the Prussian envoy had first addressed a warning to the Frankfurt senate against the excessive growth of political associations: rebellion was being preached there, revolt against the status quo, communist and socialist ideas were being spread, and the bourgeois public was lending its ear to the 'democratic agitators'. The police department replied that in so prosperous and wealthy a city as Frankfurt there was no dissatisfied proletariat; the poor were being well looked after, the bourgeoisie was inspired by a community spirit and loyally supported the city's constitution of 1816. In a free city the 'demagogues' would have no success.

That, however, was by no means the case. March 1848 supplied the proof.

The demands raised throughout Germany were to be heard in Frankfurt also: freedom of the press, freedom of assembly, curtailment of the power of the predominantly patrician Senate, extension of the rights of the Citizens' College, emancipation of the Jews, trial by jury.

Associations sprang up like mushrooms after rain – the Monday Ladies' Circle, the Citizens' Association. The Gymnasts' Association now called itself the Workmen's Association. The members of the Singers' Circle put on black-red-and-gold caps. An Artisans' Congress was held. A 'solemn protest of millions of unfortunates against the free practice of trades' was adopted: this called for a regulation of labour on a guild basis against the 'French freedom' of capitalism. The master craftsmen were still calling the tune. From May 1848, however, the far more radical *Frankfurter Arbeiterzeitung* appeared. Its editors were expelled: they had fulminated against the 'liberal moneybags'. In nearby Offenbach a resolution was adopted which caused a sensation in Frankfurt the following day: 'The German workers are not yet communists, they do not desire a war against the wealthy or against property, they merely demand employment and a wage sufficient for their maintenance in exchange for their efforts and work, they demand personal freedom, a free press, and equality of rights; and therefore they want peace.' The Frankfurt working men's associations felt encouraged to raise the demand that workers' deputies should be admitted to the parliament at St Paul's church. They described themselves as the 'best, most honest, most loyal and most moral' members of the nation. Their tone was becoming more confident and more menacing: 'Against the wretched machinations of the princes, the moneyed aristocracy, the bourgeoisie, and whatever other names the enemies of the people may have,' a leaflet distributed in the city trumpeted. Meanwhile the first freely elected parliament in Germany was meeting at St Paul's church and discussing the canon of human rights. Above the doorway a slogan proclaimed: 'The fatherland's greatness, the fatherland's happiness, / O return them, bring them back to the people.'

In March 1848 Schopenhauer, as he reported to Frauenstädt in a letter of 11 July, had immediately resorted 'to all kinds of restrictions', cut down on his expenditure and cancelled his orders for books. One had to keep one's possessions together: 'when a storm threatens one strikes all sails' (CL, 231).

The parliament in St Paul's church had meanwhile elected a *Reichs-verweser*, a Reich Lieutenant, pending the election of an emperor – the Archduke Johann. To Schopenhauer this was a silver lining on the horizon. He had been through a terrible time, he wrote to Frauenstädt in July 1848: 'I went through terrible mental agonies these past four months, from fear and worry: all property, and indeed the entire legal state of affairs in jeopardy! At my age that kind of thing hits one badly – seeing the staff, by which one had traversed one's whole life and which one had proved worthy, now shaking' (CL, 231).

Schopenhauer's growing dislike of the revolution had many layers of motivation and many facets of manifestation. Sometimes he was gripped by panic that the revolution might rob him of the property which enabled him to live for philosophy. At other times his dislike turned to mad fury. On these occasions Schopenhauer became a figure of fun even at the Englischer Hof, that favourite venue of conservatives and constitutionalists. He was over-doing his 'democrat bashing', they felt. Even his 'darlings', according to a report by Robert von Hornstein, 'the aristocratic officers of the *table d'hôte* of the Englischer Hof, whom he pampered as the saviours of society, did not always treat him properly'. Schopenhauer raised his glass to the blood-spattered counter-revolutionary, the 'noble Prince Windischgrätz', and loudly regretted his 'excessive sentimentality'. As for Blum, a radical democrat, 'he should not have had him shot but hanged' (C, 222).

In September 1848 the parliament in St Paul's church approved the armistice of Malmö. Prussia had gone to war with Denmark, which had made territorial claims on Schleswig. The war had been seen as a patriotic action and Prussia's retreat was now viewed as a betrayal. Parliament's approval was regarded as evidence of its impotence and its lack of a sense of national honour. Added to this was the general annoyance and disappointment of those who had harboured higher social and political expectations of March 1848.

On 18 September 1848 all this erupted violently. An outraged crowd attempted to storm parliament. Barricades were put up in the streets and live ammunition was used. Two prominent representatives of counter-revolution, Prince Lichnowsky and General Auerswald, were brutally killed by the mob. One of them had his head chopped off, the other had his arms broken and was then used as a rifle target. Ernst Moritz Arndt, by then an old man, lamented: 'The flood which has burst upon us had been dammed up by stupidity, greed and lust for power over a generation; it has burst through and washed the mud and filth from the lowest depths upon our heads.'

Schopenhauer was unlucky enough to get caught up among the warring parties that day. He made a statement to the police authorities on the events, intended to contribute to the identification of the rebels:

> On 18 September this year, at approximately half past twelve, I saw from my window a large rabble armed with pitchforks, poles and a few rifles, with a red flag carried ahead of it, advance across the bridge from Sachsenhausen. . . . Approximately eight or ten men armed with rifles . . . remained, some of them, in the curved recesses half-way across and behind an overturned cart, and with the greatest calm and deliberation fired into the roadway, always taking aim with the greatest care. One of these snipers, who wore a grey vest and a big red beard, was especially active . . . [Corr 16, 164]

In a letter to Frauenstädt Schopenhauer reported a significant detail:

> suddenly voices and hammering on the locked door to my room: thinking that it was the sovereign *canaille* I barred the door with a pole: now there were dangerous blows against it; suddenly the thin voice of my maidservant: 'it's only a few Austrians!' I open at once to these dear friends: twenty tall Bohemians in blue trousers rush in in order to fire at the sovereign ones from my window; soon, however, they change their mind: it would be better from the house next door. From the first floor the officer reconnoitres the rabble behind the barricade: I immediately send him my big double opera glasses. [CL, 234]

Schopenhauer's rage against the 'sovereign *canaille*' was directed principally against its intellectual spokesmen. To that extent his dislike was, in a sense, 'philosophically' justified, because he referred to the 'world-improving pretensions' and the 'infamous way of thinking' of optimism. To him the 'sovereign *canaille*' was a misguided mob which believed that their miserable lives were the fault of state institutions and that happiness would come to them if the existing state were destroyed and another put in its place. To Schopenhauer this was left-orientated Hegelianism for the people. The state was not a machine for progress; if one tried to turn it into such a machine one would inevitably be practising the deification of the state. Schopenhauer defended the authoritarian state by pointing, as we would say today, to the danger of 'totalitarianism'.

In his 'morality' essay of 1841 he had formulated what he regarded as the sole purpose of the state: 'to protect each from all, and the whole community from foreign enemies. Some German philosophasters of this mercenary age have sought to turn it into an institution of education in morality and of edification. Behind this attempt lurks the jesuitical aim of abolishing personal freedom and individual development, in order to make each man a mere wheel in a Chinese governmental and religious machine. But this is the way which formerly led to Inquisitions . . . and religious wars' (BE, 233–4).

This deification of the state was what Schopenhauer saw at work among the 'rabble' behind the barricade; and that was where he also located the second 'infirmity of the age': crude materialism. The illusion, he said, was being indulged in that the satisfaction of material needs in itself represented a way out of the misery of human existence. The spokesmen of the movement, Schopenhauer observed, were in fact 'students gone wrong', more accurately 'Young Hegelians', who have 'sunk to the absolutely physical point of view which leads to *edite, bibite, post mortem nulla voluptas*, and to that extent may be described as bestialism.'

However, none of these 'philosophical' reasons for his dislike can explain Schopenhauer's occasional outbreaks of fear and berserk rage. The hard core of these was and remained fear for his property.

During those very days of revolution he was seized by a fury of self-preservation and self-assertion, which made him totally blind to the torments of social hardship and political oppression, torments for which he had found such moving words in his philosophy of compassion. There he was sitting at Schöne Aussicht No. 17, defending his *principium individuationis* in a way that would have done credit to Don Quixote. For his possessions were in no way threatened, and no one had any designs on his person. Yet he anxiously guarded his purse.

He needed that purse in order not to have to live *by* philosophy, in order not to have to consider publishers, ministries or the paying public – that was what he explained to anyone wishing to listen, and that was how he justified himself to himself. The argument was true, yet it also concealed a profound untruth. Because what should make him independent, his purse, was precisely what prevented him during those weeks from living, at least up to a point, in line with the insights of his philosophy – the philosophy of compassion, the philosophy of 'practical mysticism'. His philosophy certainly does not imply sympathy with the revolution, but it does imply a deep understanding of its social and political motivations. That understanding should have stopped him from offering his opera glasses as a telescopic rifle-sight. During the revolution Schopenhauer certainly shrank to the self-preserving will of a philosophizing coupon-cutter.

Three years later compassion was back again. On 26 June 1852 in his last will and testament he appointed as sole heir the 'fund established in Berlin for the support of Prussian soldiers disabled in fighting against the mutiny and rebellion in the year 1848 and for the maintenance and restoration of

CHAPTER TWENTY-THREE

THE MOUNTAIN COMES TO THE PROPHET

Schopenhauer as well as his possessions survived the revolution. The revolution, however, died. It had not really been pushed very far: the constitution of a constitutional monarchy was adopted and an offer was made to the King of Prussia to become henceforward hereditary German emperor by the grace of the people. That was on 28 March 1849. The King, however, persuaded of his own mission by the grace of God and the legitimacy of the Habsburgs as emperors in Germany, declined. The parliamentary crown of 'dirt and clay' was to him a 'dog collar with which they want to chain me to the Revolution of 1848'.

Frederick William IV had sound political reasons: by accepting the constitutional crown of the New German Reich he would have risked opposition from Russia and Austria to the point of war. But what decided him was his reluctance to ally himself with the liberal revolution, however domesticated it might have become.

Following the King's refusal a section of the St Paul's church parliament abandoned support or championship of the Reich constitution they had themselves adopted. The constitutionalists departed from Frankfurt, leaving behind a powerless left-wing rump parliament which transferred to Stuttgart. But there the Württemberg government closed the assembly premises on 18 June 1849, and that was the end of the history of Germany parliamentary government for the time being. During those weeks rebellions flared up here and there in connection with the so-called Reich constitution campaign. In Dresden, for instance, the Schopenhauer disciple Richard Wagner mounted the barricades together with Bakunin. By means of massive military intervention, courts martial, the death penalty, high-treason trials and hard-labour sentences the governments once more restored law and order. Richard Wagner, with the *Ring of the Nibelung* in his head, fled to Switzerland. Schopenhauer in Frankfurt could draw a breath of relief: the 'sovereign *canaille*' was no longer causing disturbances outside Schöne Aussicht No. 17. Schopenhauer resumed his regular lifestyle: writing in the morning, flute before lunch, luncheon at the Englischer Hof, newspapers at the Casino in the afternoon, then a walk, reading in the evening, and before going to bed a devotional period with the Upanishads. The poor orphan of philosophy had not yet stepped out from the dark. But the moment was near.

In March 1844 the second edition of his principal work, expanded to two volumes, had been published. The publisher had at first made difficulties but eventually he had yielded. Schopenhauer, however, had to waive his honorarium. 'Not to my contemporaries, not to my compatriots – to mankind I present my now completed work,' he wrote in the preface. What he and his publisher had suspected happened: the 'resistance of the dull world' was not yet to be overcome. The book had only a single review of any importance, that by Carl Fortlage in *Jenaische Literaturzeitung* of 1845. The review, somewhat condescendingly, praised the work as 'a traditional and supplementary link' between Kant and Fichte. This was not exactly flattering to a philosopher who believed himself to have inaugurated a new era in philosophy.

When Schopenhauer in August 1846 inquired about the sales of his work he received this reply from Brockhaus: 'To my regret I can only tell you that I made a *bad* deal with it, and you will excuse my not going into further details.'

Nevertheless, a handful of supporters began to collect around Schopenhauer in the 1840s. His 'evangelists' and 'apostles', as he called them – and not only as a joke.

The 'arch-evangelist' was Friedrich Dorguth (1776–1854), an *Oberlandgerichtsrat*, a senior judge, in Magdeburg. This jurist, formerly a *Regierungsrat* in Warsaw and acquainted there with E. T. A. Hoffmann, likewise a *Regierungsrat*, pursued philosophy as a hobby. With voluminous 'critiques', one of 'idealism' and another of 'real-idealism', he assailed a public which did not wish to know about it. Towards the end of the 1830s he discovered Schopenhauer and loudly proclaimed: 'I cannot forbear from acknowledging Schopenhauer as the first real systematic thinker in the whole history of literature.' Needless to say, Dorguth's paeans had little effect.

The next 'evangelist' was the Berlin philosopher Julius Frauenstädt (1813–79). As a student he had never heard about Schopenhauer, but later in a philosophical encyclopedia had come across a few lines mentioning the 'ingenious and original *World as Will and Representation*'. He had bought the book and had been swept away by it. In 1841 he proclaimed in the *Hallische Jahrbücher*: 'Schopenhauer, to my knowledge, is so far the only one among the new philosophers to offer a *pure* philosophy, as profound as it is acute; even though it has so far attracted little or no attention, it has a secure future for all that, as indeed he himself is fully aware and assured.'

The second edition of his principal work in 1844 won Schopenhauer two new disciples, the ones who were his favourites: Johann August Becker (1803–81) and Adam von Doss (1820–73).

Neither of them were of the philosophical profession; they were both lawyers. Becker, an attorney in Mainz, approached Schopenhauer with a letter in 1844. He wished to put a few 'doubts' to him and in so doing revealed such an intimate acquaintance with Schopenhauer's work that Schopenhauer was prepared to enter into a detailed discussion by correspondence with him, one which Schopenhauer himself regarded as valuable. Becker had introduced himself not only with his doubts but also with a malaise about post-Kantian philosophy. This earned him Schopenhauer's favour. Becker remained the only person for whose sake Schopenhauer would occasionally leave Frankfurt: on fine summer days he would travel to Mainz by train. To his regret, however, Becker remained an 'apostle' and could not be encouraged to appear as a writing 'evangelist'.

Adam von Doss was a more active person.

This newly qualified lawyer, upon reading *The World as Will and Representation*, undertook a pilgrimage to Frankfurt. Schopenhauer received him and was charmed by his acolyte's youthful enthusiasm. He called him his 'John the Apostle' and, wishing to stimulate his as yet small following, gave Frauenstädt an account of the pleasant visitor: 'In accurate knowledge of all my writings and in conviction of my truth he is *at least* your equal, if not your superior: his zeal defies description and made me very happy. . . . I tell you, a fanatic' (CL, 240).

Although Doss was not an 'evangelist' either, he was an 'apostle' who wrote letters to educated and well-known people with whom he was not even personally acquainted, urging them at long last to read Schopenhauer.

The outwardly most active member of this group of believers, Julius Frauenstädt, was the one Schopenhauer treated worst, even though he called him his 'arch-evangelist'. Frauenstädt was his reliable assistant: he busied himself publishing, writing commentaries on his master's teachings, arguing with opponents. He would scan books and journals for mentions of Schopenhauer and faithfully report his findings to him. He would get Schopenhauer the books he wanted and occasionally help out with news of stock exchange quotations. Nevertheless he was frequently put in his place by a surly Schopenhauer. Frauenstädt was a somewhat unstable, rash and highly strung person whose intelligence was not up to his curiosity. In consequence he would get entangled in all kinds of misunderstandings. Thus he transfigured the 'will', probably in order to make it more acceptable to the theologians, into something transcending experience and absolute. Schopenhauer rebuked him: 'My dear friend, I have to remind myself of your numerous and great merits in propagating my philosophy in order not to lose my patience and composure. . . . In vain, for example, have I written to you not to seek the thing in itself in cloud-cuckoo-land (i.e. where the God of the Jews resides) but in the things of this world – in the table at which you write, in the chair under your arse. . . . My philosophy is never concerned with cloud-cuckoo-land but with *this* world, i.e. it is *immanent*, not transcendent' (CL, 290).

When Frauenstädt on one occasion objected to his ruffianly 'yelling' –

Schopenhauer had accused him of flirting with the morality of 'bestial' materialism – Schopenhauer broke off the correspondence. Frauenstädt, however, loyal soul that he was, continued to be his evangelist. A few years later, in 1859, he had his reward from Schopenhauer, who appointed him the heir to his writings and to his literary estate.

In the still small group of apostles and evangelists Schopenhauer enjoyed the position of head of his own church. It was a church in diaspora, which Schopenhauer, the critic of philosophical dogmatism, oversaw with a strict eye. He found criticism, especially from within his community, difficult to bear: they should 'let the Word stand', he said. When he was told that members of his community were meeting one another he would say: 'Where two are gathered together in my name, there am I in the midst of them' (C, 139).

Prior to his breakthrough to fame Schopenhauer cultivated these conventicle-like, conspiratorial contacts which flattered his vanity, grown abrasive by long years of public indifference. This vanity was obliged to endure some hurtful rejections right into the early 1850s.

In 1850 Schopenhauer completed *Parerga and Paralipomena*, on which he had been working for the past six years. They were 'secondary works' and 'leftovers', or, as he put it, 'sporadic yet systematically arranged thoughts on a variety of subjects'; they included the subsequently famous 'Aphorismen zur Lebensweisheit' ('Aphorisms on Practical Wisdom').

On 26 July 1850 Schopenhauer offered the book to Brockhaus: 'I do not propose to write anything after this book because I am wary of giving the world sickly children of old age, who would indict their father and diminish his fame' (CL, 242). The work, he explained, was 'incomparably more popular than anything so far': it was, so to speak, his 'philosophy for the world' (CL, 244). Brockhaus was unconvinced and turned it down. Other publishers similarly showed no interest. At this point Frauenstädt intervened and persuaded a Berlin bookseller to publish *Parerga*. The two volumes appeared in November 1851. That was the turning point. With this 'philosophy for the world' Schopenhauer would at last make his breakthrough – but not by himself and not by his own strength: the changed spirit of the age met him half-way. Thus they were finally united – Schopenhauer and his time.

The common belief that following the failure of the revolution the cultural scene was dominated by *Weltschmerz*, disillusionment, general disheartenment and pessimism, and that Schopenhauer's great moment had come for that reason, is not in line with the facts.

Of course there was, among the activists, especially among the more radical of them, disappointment, dejection and a sense of futility, and to that extent Schopenhauer's philosophy fell on fertile ground. Herwegh is a good example. This minstrel on the 'ramparts of the party', a militant activist – he took part in the military rebellion in Baden in April 1848 – engrossed himself in Schopenhauer's writings after his flight into Swiss exile and also succeeded in filling his friend Richard Wagner with inspiration from Schopenhauer's philosophy.

But among the broad educated middle-class public – and that was the milieu where Schopenhauer's 'philosophy for the world' began to make an impact – there was little sign of a basically pessimistic mood. On the contrary: belief in progress was widespread and possibly still growing. Admittedly it was changing its appearance: it became, as contemporaries put it, 'realistic'. No more extravagant demands or airy speculations; extremes now appeared ridiculous. It was time to stop making exaggerated claims on reality and to practise patience. The subjective trend of the spirit was replaced by the 'objective' trend in things and circumstances. From all corners, from the world of politics, of literature, of scholarship, of everyday life and indeed of philosophy now came the call: Back to the firm ground of facts! The liberal Ludwig August von Rochau published his *Grundsätze der Realpolitik* (*Principles of Realpolitik*) in 1853, making a present to his age of a durable catchword for a policy of the practicable, for a policy of change through adaptation to existing conditions, or, more specifically, the Prussian solution of the 'national question'. Marx, too, endeavoured to base himself on the firm ground of facts. The messianic mission of the proletariat was being eclipsed; with laborious meticulousness he dissected the social body, whose soul was the *Kapital*. The question arose for him: perhaps history was, after all, made not by people but by structures?

In the early 1850s a number of vulgar-materialist bestsellers flooded the book market: Moleschott's *Kreislauf des Lebens* (*Circulation of Life*), Vogt's *Bilder aus dem Tierleben* (*Pictures of Animal Life*), and above all Ludwig Büchner's *Kraft und Stoff* (*Energy and Matter*). These went into action against metaphysics, against speculative ideas generally, by referring to facts in their most concrete form. Thought, it was explained, was to the brain roughly what gall was to the liver or urine to the kidneys.

The smug complacency of this materialism was expressed, on a higher philosophical plane, by Czolbe in 1855: 'It is simply ... proof of ... presumption and vanity to attempt to improve the perceptible world by the invention of a suprasensory one and, by adding a suprasensory part, to attempt to make man into a creature elevated above nature. Dissatisfaction with the phenomenal world, the most basic reason for the suprasensory view, is certainly not a moral reason but a moral weakness.'

These reflections lead to the statement: 'Be content with the world that is given to you.' To Czolbe, and to many of his contemporaries, there was such a thing as a moral duty to 'realism'.

Fontane, too – and with him a whole literary movement – accepted an obligation towards reality. Only a few years after he had got himself a wooden rifle from a theatrical property department during the revolution of 1848 he formulated his aesthetic programme as follows:

Realism is what characterizes our period in every respect. Doctors are rejecting all hypotheses and combinations, they seek experience; politicians (of all parties) are turning their eyes to real needs and are locking up their models of perfection in their desks. . . . This realism of our age not only finds its most decisive echo in *art* but possibly finds no such conspicuous expression in any other area of our life. . . . Realism is the sworn enemy of all rhetoric and extravagance; . . . it excludes nothing except the mendacious and the contrived.

In philosophy, Hegel was now passé. In the pre-March era he had been 'put on his feet' again. But the 'reality' one had hoped to attain thereby had a strange air about it, and access to it remained speculative: both Feuerbach's 'body' and Marx's 'proletariat' contained a metaphysical surplus value. 'Reality' was what one discovered if, in a manner of speaking, one backed down the road of speculation again, with Feuerbach, with Marx, or with the late Schelling. The speculative heritage could not be simply ignored; it had to be removed. 'Reality' was a longed-for objective, not that obvious reality of 'post-1848 philosophy', which could go stale very quickly once the first phase of dealing with it was over.

Hegel was so definitely passé that his work could simply be thrown away without its texture having first to be dissolved. Typical of the age was Friedrich Albert Lange's verdict of 1875: 'Excesses of conceptual Romanticism.'

Progress was to be achieved on the basis of reality – in philosophy, in politics, in literature, in science. Mainly in science. The chemist Justus Liebig demonstrated how it should be done. In his Giessen laboratory he opened up the field of 'organic chemistry' to exact experimental science. His discoveries unleashed an avalanche: agrochemistry, artificial fertilizer farming. His practical success enabled him to polemicize with unprecedented acrimony against the remnants of natural philosophy in medical training. He called natural philosophy the 'pestilence of our century', and continued: 'If a man kills another in a state of madness he is locked up; yet natural philosophy is to this day permitted to train our physicians and to impart to them that state of madness which will permit them, with a clear conscience and in accordance with principles, to kill thousands.' It is clear that old scores were being settled. For too long the exact sciences had stood in the shadow of the speculative ones. The dammed-up resentment was now able, in the new era of 'realism', to take its revenge.

The soil of facts was being deep-ploughed in order that reality might prosper.

As for the facts: first, these had to be established through experience. This, for Hegel for instance, was by no means self-evident. To him, the specific was not yet fully discovered when it was confirmed by experience: it still had to be captured in a construing concept, only then was it something 'real'.

Second, one must make sure that experience was not deceptive. It had to be controlled experience, it had to be experimentally repeatable. This meant it had to be communicable. This was the immanent democracy of the empirical sciences: truth is what, under given (experimentally produced) conditions, lies within everyone's experience. In scientific empiricism there is no such thing as a hierarchy of experience, no aristocracy of the spirit, but, in line with the trend, there are only employees of a research process. In an involved way a bourgeois progressive demand – the demand for equality – was being pursued at the heart of empirical science. It was not therefore surprising that the idea of progress had to be kept alive not only by the practical results of the empirical sciences but also by their structures of experience.

Third, these 'facts' had to be dissected, atomized, if one wished to discover what constituted them; perhaps the newly discovered elements could then be recombined into new 'facts'.

'Life', that great, synthesizing, all-embracing concept, could now be discussed quite differently after the discovery by physiologists of the cell as the smallest unit of life. This was almost a rebirth of Leibniz's theory of monads, but as the organism was explained as a process of (likewise newly discovered) cell division there was no need to go back to Leibniz's 'prestabilized harmony'. Even what was hostile to life could now be localized in a small unit: bacteria had been discovered. Medicine was going into battle against them, with Rudolf Virchow as the general.

What permitted life and what permitted death had been transformed into something that could be observed under the microscope: nature without metaphysics. The presumption of a 'life force', however spiritual, was discredited. Equally discredited, under pressure from Darwin's teaching on evolution, were whatever remnants still existed of belief in Creation.

Darwin's great work *On the Origin of Species by Means of Natural Selection*, published in 1859, had given ample support to the spirit of (realistic) adaptation to the world as it was. It was just those adaptive modifications of living creatures to their environment and their resulting greater chances of survival in the 'Struggle for Life' which Darwin had raised to the motive force of the history of evolution, which, in view of the reward of survival for the adapted, might properly be interpreted as a history of material progress – admittedly progress which did not favour the weak. English economic liberalism was here reflected in the contemporary view of nature. Subsequently this was to be called 'social Darwinism'.

The other great demystifying and 'realism'-promoting trend of the age was historicism. Historicism treated truth in a Napoleonic manner. All 'spiritual principalities' were mediatized by it. Philosophy was replaced by histories of philosophy. A period poor in literature produced great histories of literature. Ranke's fame penetrated even into elementary-school primers. In historicism the (metaphysical) question about Being and the meaning of Being was reduced to the questions of what something had become. One knows enough if one knows how something has come about. Truth was being fragmented into a historical game of 'truths'. The plural proved to be the great strength of relativism.

And yet this 'realism', which was so impressively reaching out to all spheres and which in fact was nothing other than a new secularization drive, had an empty kernel. At the Scientists' Congress in Göttingen in 1854 a major dispute arose. One group of scientists tried to save the 'soul' and had to suffer being accused of 'blind faith'.

The fact that, amidst a rampant materialism and naturalism, some scientists were barricading themselves behind the 'soul' was a symptom of a malaise that was bound to heighten a receptivity for Schopenhauer's metaphysics. For it represented a way of thinking which had long been in opposition to the recently dismissed philosophy of the spirit, while at the same time refusing to embrace unlimited materialism and naturalism. Of course it was possible to misunderstand Schopenhauer in a materialistic way, but his metaphysics of the will was too obviously at variance with the crude materialism of the spirit of the age. Another dimension opened up: some thought they could discover in Schopenhauer a darkened vitalism. This vitalism lent the empirically sober 'immanence', to which one now owed allegiance, the 'depth' which the malaise was calling for.

In Schopenhauer, readers found an encomium of a sober sense of reality, of materialistic explanation, and a justification, based on Kant, of why our empirical curiosity must follow this road. They found a confirmation of what they were, materialistically, doing. Simultaneously, however, they found in Schopenhauer the empirical proof that this approach to reality was not the only one. Even the materially visualized world still remains an idea. Schopenhauer inaugurated a new renaissance of Kant and opened up the possibility of a 'materialism as if'. One could endorse strictly empirical science, one could surrender to the materialistic spirit, but one need not be totally captured by it. With Schopenhauer's 'Beyond' of the self-experienced will one could now withstand the pull of a materially interpreted immanence.

Even more effective than this 'as if' materialism was the 'as if' ethics which Schopenhauer sketched out with his 'philosophy for the world'. After 1850 his 'Aphorisms on Practical Wisdom' rapidly became the Bible of the educated bourgeoisie.

Schopenhauer's 'real' ethics had, as we know, led to the mystery of compassion: to fusion with the sufferings of all existence, to the breaching of the wall of the individuation principle, to disarmament in the struggle for self-assertion. By allowing the sufferings of another to enter into it, the individual is already in secret alliance with the great renunciation of the will to live. The compassionate will is a will which is about to 'turn'. None of this, as has been said before, can be commanded, nor is it demanded by any practical wisdom; it either happens or it does not. It is a relaxation of egotistical tensions and hence, measured by the reason of self-preservation, is unreasonable. The ethics of compassion is not concerned with the pursuit of one's own happiness. By contrast, the 'as if' ethic, mapped out by Schopenhauer in his 'Aphorisms', is of a totally different character. Here we have an 'adaptation' to the principle of self-preservation and to the wish to spend one's life, as far as possible, 'happily'. Yet Schopenhauer can only offer an instruction for the happy life with reservations. His 'higher metaphysical-ethical point of view' leads to renunciation of life – as he reminded his readers in the introduction: 'Consequently, the whole discussion here to be given rests to a certain extent on a compromise, in so far as it remains at the ordinary empirical standpoint and firmly maintains the error thereof' (PP I, 313).

The underlying pessimism is toned down, and the (elsewhere criticized) wisdom of survival and self-assertion is pragmatically revalued upwards. Let us, for once, assume that life is worth living – how then should it be lived so that the attainable optimum of happiness is extracted from it? This was the question the 'Aphorisms' attempted to answer. This was 'philosophy for the world'. It set aside the metaphysical scandal. It reduced the esoteric No to life to a muted exoteric Yes: if we cannot avoid participating, then let us at least do so with all necessary scepticism, with resistance to disappointment; let us at least keep our stakes in the game low and give as little credit as possible. If we have to be, or wish to be, participants in the comedy or the tragedy of life, let us at least make sure that we are 'simultaneously spectators and actors' (PP I, 439).

Schopenhauer encourages an attitude of the 'as if'. Today we might say: 'You don't stand a chance, but take it anyway.'

That relative 'happiness' – where was it to come from?

Schopenhauer lists three sources: it derives from 'what a person is', from 'what a person has', and from 'what a person represents'. These are the three dimensions – one's own Being, one's having, and one's standing – in which, according to Schopenhauer, the comedy of the pursuit of happiness is enacted.

In the style of the Stoics Schopenhauer ranges these factors according to their reliability and certainty. What can one take from me, what do I depend on, over what do I have the least power?

'Standing' is the reflection of my existence in the eyes of others: this is what I have least power over. To expect happiness from that source means building on the least secure ground. Besides, we might easily lose ourselves in trying to be something in the eyes of others.

What we 'have' gives us comfort and shelter (Schopenhauer is clearly thinking of his own position), but we may easily be robbed of it. Moreover, 'having' has a reversing power. Ultimately 'having' could have us. The best plan is to 'have as if one did not'.

Arthur Schopenhauer pleads for 'retreat', for a shortening of the front line in order to expose a smaller area to attack. The gain in happiness from such a 'retreat' is that 'it restores to a man his true self' (PP I, 359). We should discover what we are, and that we may miss ourselves but never escape from ourselves. The ideal is a kind of self-sufficiency: to derive enjoyment out of oneself, from one's intellectual gifts, one's fantasy, one's imagination, from one's temperament and from the ability to exert a beneficial influence on all these through a deliberate development of our personality, through self-education. Naturally, in so doing one is bound to come up against the power of one's will, which is not idle but, in the form of desires, tries to drag us into the world of possessions and into the world of others. Such self-sufficiency requires a muting of the will. There must be a predominant composure, stemming not solely from practical wisdom harnessed to the reality principle but containing an admixture of the denial of the will. To this extent Schopenhauer after all, in a sense, presupposes that 'higher metaphysical-ethical point of view' which he is actually endeavouring to exclude.

In an existentialist manner Schopenhauer extracts the Self from the world of the 'non-essentiality' of possession and of one's standing with others, but eventually, in the predominant part of his 'Aphorisms', continues to reflect on the clashes with the 'external' world. This is quite logical: with the Self so vigorously extracted, the thousand threads linking us with the external world are painfully felt. Schopenhauer admits it himself: the world of others within ourselves is the 'thorn', the one we find it most difficult to extract from 'our flesh' (PP I, 358). Thus Schopenhauer, unlike the ancient Stoics, pays tribute to the superior power of society. But he clings to his belief that happiness does not exist through society but only in spite of society.

Schopenhauer has some advice on how to squeeze the modicum of happiness out of the society in which one is entangled. The most important piece of advice, the one from which all others follow, is formulated in an image he had first noted down in his manuscript journal forty years earlier. 'Society can also be compared to a fire where a prudent man warms himself at a proper distance, whereas the fool comes too close and then, after scorching himself, rushes out into the cold of solitude, loudly complaining that the fire burns' (PP I, 430).

The famous parable of the porcupines from his *Paralipomena* – he had first related it to his one-time adored Karoline Jagemann in the early 1830s – contains the same lesson: 'A group of porcupines on a cold winter's day crowded close together to save themselves from freezing by their mutual warmth. Soon, however, they felt each other's spines, and this drove them apart again. Whenever their need for warmth brought them more closely together, that second evil intervened, until, thrown this way and that between the two evils, they discovered a moderate distance from one another at which they could survive best' (PP II, 651). All other advice is related to this practical skill of 'moderate distance'. One should take one's solitude with one into society. Schopenhauer pleads for politeness, which he calls a 'tacit agreement that we shall mutually ignore and refrain from reproaching one another's miserable defects, both moral and intellectual' (PP 1, 462). He recommended that everyone should keep his secrets because one could be fairly certain that some day they would be used against one – even by people one loves at the moment. He warned against the folly of national pride, because it 'betrays a want of *individual* qualities of which he might be proud, since he would not otherwise resort to that which he shares with so many millions' (PP 1, 360).

All his advice presupposes society as a network of latent hostility, of reciprocal ill will. Love and friendship may be fortresses of good will, but as a rule they are razed to the ground more quickly than one realizes. It would be wise to include love and friendship among the possessions which one should have as if one did not have them. And the kind of love which is consolidated by marriage is in an even worse way. Schopenhauer dismisses it with a grim and laconic remark: 'I have not included wife and family in *what a man has*, for they have him rather than he has them' (PP 1, 352). Marriage, therefore, is nothing to do with the economy of moderate happiness.

Schopenhauer not only dispenses advice; in his 'Aphorisms' he also, from a relaxed distance, paints a last self-portrait: for instance when he describes the care which one should devote to health, one's most precious possession. He revealed the dietetic regime of his way of life by giving advice on how a prudent management of one's property keeps the risk of loss low, by reflecting on how one should train oneself for dying, or by reasoning about vanity and thirst for fame. Not having met with recognition for such a long time, Schopenhauer knows very well what he is talking about in these passages: 'From the point of view of eudemonology, fame is nothing but the rarest and daintiest morsel for our pride and vanity. But in most men these exist to excess, though they are concealed; perhaps they are strongest in those who are in some way qualified to acquire fame. Such men, therefore, have to wait a long time in uncertainty regarding their outstanding worth before the opportunity comes for them to put this to the test and then experience its acknowledgement. Till then, they feel as though they have suffered a secret injustice' (PP 1, 398).

Subsequently, shortly before his death, Schopenhauer appended a hand-written addition: 'Our greatest pleasure consists in being *admired*; but the admirers, even if there is every cause, are not very keen to express their admiration. And so the happiest man is he who has managed sincerely to admire himself, no matter how. Only others must not cause him to doubt this' (PP 1, 298).

Schopenhauer indeed managed to admire himself for a long time until eventually he received admiration from outside – and mainly for his 'Aphorisms'.

Why, especially, for this work?

Schopenhauer's 'philosophy for the world' offers pessimism at half price: it shows through everywhere as an underlying attitude without, however, the radical conclusions of denial being drawn. The great malaise is certainly hinted at, but presently it is again excluded, for the sake of life. Schopenhauer shows how one can struggle on in spite of everything. After all, he himself struggled on. The result is a doctrine which, because it expects the worst, is wise enough always to discover the lesser evil. 'Longing for happiness' is tuned down to a prudent 'apprehension about misfortune' (WWR I, 427).

Schopenhauer's success was with those who did not wish to commit themselves totally to any project: either to a culture of despair or to one of progress. Schopenhauer's first followers were very sound, solid and mostly moderately successful people in everyday life. Is Schopenhauer's 'philosophy for the world' therefore a Biedermeier philosophy? Certainly, if a refusal to draw radical conclusions from a doctrine deserves to be pilloried as Biedermeier. But I doubt it. Nietzsche would later develop the idea that there are truths which one would be wise not to wish to 'materialize', which one had better remain silent about, which, in any event, one should not place under the constraint of consistency. Why consistency at all?

Thought should be absorbed in action, it is claimed; one should be consistent and live in accordance with recognized truth. However, does not such a call for consistency ultimately lead to self-censorship? In the end one only dares to think what one believes one can also live; or, conversely, one wants, at any price, including that of destruction, to live something merely because one has thought it. In one instance one misses radical thought and in the other one sacrifices pure thought to the confusion of live action. Should one not forcibly tear thinking and action apart, so that both thought and action can each come into their right and their truth? Spinoza once said, in this connection: 'Only if I am not allowed to do everything can I think everything.' Given therefore that radical thought must be protected against the compromises of action, and action against radical thought, then surely what has to be renounced is consistency.

There are truths that can be lived and others that cannot. One should cling to both – but one can do that only if one abandons the dangerous illusion of their mutual convertibility. It is a delicate act of equilibration. Only those free from vertigo will dare cast a glance into the depths. Only those sure of their will to live will have the courage to think the abysmality, the negativeness of life, through to the end. This was Schopenhauer's position: for him the idea of the denial of the will was protected against the will. He remained a spectator of denial and, out of the environment of a growing cultural malaise, he attracted others who joined him as spectators. In that position one was safe from total involvement: from Yes one could escape into No, and the other way round. 'Life as if' was still the best tactic against all kinds of fanaticisms, self-made prisons and ambitious projects aiming at the Whole and, for that reason, leading to such disastrous results.

Schopenhauer's is a double-bottomed philosophy. It involves itself with the pragmatic aspect of life and of individual self-assertion, yet at the same time it declares that the individual is nothing much 'really', that life generally is nothing much 'really', and that nothing 'really' matters. It was this double-bottomed character which, far beyond the influence of Schopenhauer's philosophy of art in the narrow sense, so influenced the artists of the second half of the nineteenth century and down to our day. It addresses an aesthetic sense, an aesthetic attitude to life. It lends to the seriousness of life an underlying sense of vanity. Although everyone 'must act in life's great puppet play' and feel 'the wire which also connects him thereto and sets him in motion' (PP ii, 420), philosophy grants him a view of the whole of the theatre. For a few moments one ceases to be an actor and becomes a spectator. That is a philosophical moment, and simultaneously an aesthetic one: non-participatory viewing, without being involved in blinding seriousness. It is from this attitude that Thomas Mann's irony springs. He was aware of it and expressed gratitude to Schopenhauer for that insight into the world's 'just about being able to be'.

This aesthetic perspective also provides the picture with which Schopenhauer opens the second volume of his principal work: 'In endless space countless luminous spheres, round each of which some dozen smaller illuminated ones revolve, hot at the core and covered with a hard cold crust; on this crust a mouldy film has produced living and knowing beings – this is empirical truth, the real, the world' (WWR ii, 3).

It is obvious that, once one has adjusted to this perspective, one cannot speak of the pretentious life and bustle in the 'mouldy film' other than with irony or even crude comedy. 'Anthropofugal thought' is what Ulrich Horstman called it, suspecting in it an enjoyment of self-extinction.

But are these declarations of nullity from an aesthetic perspective real anticipations of the annihilation campaigns of a universally hostile seriousness of life? Perhaps the opposite is true; perhaps the aesthetic declaration of nullity can so *relax* the seriousness of life that it feels no wish to rush into real campaigns of destruction.

Scopenhauer certainly produced such a 'relaxing' effect. Like Thomas Mann's irony, so the humour of the great German realists of the second half of the century owes much to Scopenhauer. This is true of Wilhelm Busch, of Theodor Fontane, of Wilhelm Raabe.

After reading Schopenhauer, Wilhelm Busch in a letter explained out of what contrasts he derived his own humour: 'In the upper storey sits the intellect, watching the hustle and bustle. It says to the will: "Let it be, old man! There'll be trouble!" But the other won't listen. Disappointment; brief pleasure and prolonged worries; old age, sickness, death, they don't wear it down, it carries on. And if it makes it jump out of its skin a thousand times, it'll find a new one that'll serve.' Busch does not even shrink from applying his master's distancing perspective to the master himself: 'Abstention is the enjoyment of things which we cannot get.'

Fontane was initiated into Schopenhauer's double-bottomedness by the 'apostle' Wiesike, a rich landowner in Plauen, who had set up a kind of chapel to his revered idol and who gave a party each year on Schopenhauer's birthday. Fontane, who was a guest in 1874, reported: 'Finally, after coffee had been declared on all sides to be the principal poison of mankind, the company got down to drinking it.'

In 1888 Fontane confessed to his son how he dealt with Schopenhauer's pessimism:

> One can train one's pessimism . . . to be cheerful. Moreover, one can really be cheerful with it. . . . One ultimately discovers a law in everything, one convinces oneself that it was never otherwise, and one finds, for one's own person, contentment in work and fulfilment of one's duty. To look matters hard in the eye is only momentarily terrible; not only does one soon get used to it, but one actually discovers a not inconsiderable satisfaction in the knowledge gained, even though one's ideals may have been shattered by it.

Fontane wrote these lines while working on *Der Stechlin*.

The last words of the dying Stechlin are: 'The ego is nothing – with that one must be permeated.' The character of Melusine in the novel bears the name of a water sprite who found herself marooned among the bipeds and who had eventually to return to her watery element. The Countess Melusine in the novel stops the gendarme Uncke from hacking a hole in the ice of the frozen lake. She fears that a hand might reach out from it, to seize her and drag her down. No, there is no reliance on the ego, the elemental carries it away. Old Stechlin has become wisely reconciled to it and has found quiet contentment. Will is everything, in continuous repetition. If anywhere in the world the Gallic cockerel crows, it also emerges from the water of Lake Stechlin.

At about the same time Wilhelm Raabe wrote his *Stopfkuchen* – one long homage to the Frankfurt philosopher. The main character, Heinrich Schaumann, lies 'in the shade of the hedge' of his 'Red Rampart', watching the world's bustle from a proper distance, while the sun shines on his belly. A former school friend, Eduard, arrives from the 'world' outside; Raabe had marked him with an emblem: he operates along the 'principle of sufficient reason', i.e. he is an empiricist driven about the world by his unquenchable longings. Heinrich Schaumann remains where he is, clearly in alliance with the author: 'In the end, surely, it comes to the same whether one remains lying in the shade of the hedge and lets the world's adventures come to meet one, or whether one lets oneself be sent forth . . . in order to find them outside.' Faced with the 'overabundance of stars' which this Buddha of the 'Red Rampart', lying in the shade of his hedge, sees above him, the 'brotherhood of the earth' shrinks considerably. Those then are the moments of 'cosy contempt for the world'.

There is no doubt that with this 'realist' the underlying pessimism acquires especially cosy traits.

Another of Schopenhauer's disciples, certainly the greatest of them, Friedrich Nietzsche, launched an attack against that cosiness. He believed he had to defend Schopenhauer against 'carpet-slipper' pessimism. 'Ethical air, Faustian smell, the Cross, death and the grave' – these, according to his own words, attracted him to Schopenhauer: the obstinate intellectual aristocrat, out of step with his time, not caring about the fashions of the intellectual scum.

Nietzsche found Schopenhauer's radicalization of Kant a considerable encouragement. When the boundaries of cognition are so narrowly drawn, philosophy is free to be a poetry of ideas. It was not only Richard Wagner, but also Schopenhauer, who lent the 'timid eagle' (Ross) the courage to provoke the philological 'shopkeepers' with his *Birth of Tragedy*.

Nietzsche remained in Schopenhauer's wake. He took on his metaphysics of the will and, in a heroic gesture, formulated it as the *Will to Power*. To Schopenhauer's No he responded, his voice breaking, with Yes. Sloterdijk very sensitively perceived that this forced Yes was due to the fact that Nietzsche first of all had to persuade himself that he was 'able to be'.

In connection with the death of God – in Schopenhauer he was given a quiet matter-of-course funeral – Nietzsche also sounded a loud clarion call. His grief at the loss was mingled with the pangs of the birth of a new God: Zarathustra. The God of perfect immanence, of the ever-same, of ceaseless return. '*Circulus vitiosus Deus*' was his name in Nietzsche's *Beyond Good and Evil*.

Nietzsche rejected Schopenhauer's anti-Dionysian *unio mystica* of compassion. His supermanhood, his vanquishing of the poor dissociated ego, his absorption in the energy flow of life was achieved, in Nietzsche, as the eroticism of cognition and of Being. To that extent Nietzsche and Schopenhauer were simultaneously antipodes yet shared the insight that Being should not be thought of either as a monstrous ego (subject) nor as 'dull matter' (object), it was an id.

This ontology of the id was to be later, at the end of the century, psycho-hydraulically remoulded and milled down. Thus Schopenhauer's philosophy led to the science of the soul, which was now totally abandoning all metaphysics. In this way the id was objectivized into an object among other objects and found itself the target of therapeutic measures. Schopenhauer, from his inwardly experienced will, had gained the certainty of Being, i.e. a metaphysics going beyond objectivized empiricism. Today, by contrast, one seeks conversation with 'one's' subconscious. This suddenly becomes irrepressibly garrulous and blurts out all those boring stories one has previously taught it. Once more disenchantment.

Some odd aspects of the impact of Schopenhauer's work in the second half of the nineteenth century are associated with the names of Eduard von Hartmann and Philipp Mainländer. Eduard von Hartmann, a discharged officer, could not really get to the bottom of what Schopenhauer had written about the denial of the will. 'Denial' – a mystery to Schopenhauer himself, one that could not be explained but only demonstrated in great ascetics and saints – that 'denial' had to be underpinned, or 'systematically performed'. For this 'systematic' performance Hartmann resorted to none other than Hegel. The result of this curious synthesis was a monstrous work – *Die Philosophie des Unbewussten* (*The Philosophy of the Unconscious*, 1869) – which presents a meticulously depicted historical three-stage theory of the disillusionment of the will to live. Its quintessence was that the individual will to live could not deny itself of its own accord; that, in good Hegelian fashion, had to be left to the historical process. Hartmann commends the 'force of the pessimistic consciousness of mankind'. The pessimistic world spirit, still operating 'unconsciously', would come to itself as soon as it had eliminated all illusions of happiness – the illusion of happiness in the Beyond, of happiness in the future, and of happiness now – and thereby would reclaim the world into itself and disappear. 'As yet,' Hartmann admits, 'our knowledge is far too incomplete . . . for us to form an idea of the end of that process with any degree of certainty.'

The busy operation of the pessimistic world spirit strikes us as comical, as does the almost optimistic ease with which Hartmann correctly performed his denial – yet today, in the age of the bomb, we take note with a certain unease of his grand historical perspective of the self-extinction of mankind.

Philipp Mainländer, a truly sad person, constructed a philosophy of the will to die. The will to live, he argued, only existed in order to consume itself, to become nothing. Mainländer had evidently allowed himself to be inspired by the newly discovered law of entropy.

So that no one should deceive himself that he was only rejecting the grapes which hung too high, Mainländer developed a programme of universal happiness, which would make everyone realize that the good things of life were not worth having. His *Philosophie der Erlösung* (*Philosophy of Redemption*, 1879) deals with the 'solution of the social': one had to disillusion those who were suffering privation by giving them what they wanted. They would then become convinced of the vanity of life, and that would be the end of everything.

Mainländer himself did not want to wait that long. He chose suicide.

These uninviting 'systems of denial' accompanied the building zeal of the period of economic growth like a shadow and copied its impressive gesturing. Today the zealous No, which sounds so eager for adventure, is toned down to doubt, to scepticism. One asks oneself whether philosophy is up to the experiences of Auschwitz and Hiroshima. Perhaps it is with Günther Anders. The praxis philosophy of the Frankfurt school certainly continues to cling, though cautiously, to a utopia of reconciliation. Horkheimer, above all, construes an 'as if utopianism', and what rattles in his ideas is not Hegel but Schopenhauer. 'Theoretical pessimism,' Horkheimer says, 'could be associated with a non-optimistic practice which, remembering universal horror, would try to improve the possible in spite of everything.'

Adorno, who did not think much of Schopenhauer, remained strangely linked to him in a different way: in reflecting on music. Adorno tried to capture in art, more especially in music, the shrunken remnant of what was once metaphysical 'truth' about life. To him music did not depict anything lying outside it. That was why in its own logic it performed the 'logic' of the moment in history. In Schopenhauer's terminology this means: music is not the copy of a phenomenon, but in it operates the will without matter, without phenomenon, without reference to anything else. Music is a will-event without matter, which is why it speaks from the 'heart of things' – it is the sounding 'thing in itself'. It refers to nothing outside itself, it is entirely itself. Adorno's formula for this was: 'Works of art are self-identity free from the constraint of identity.'

Just as Adorno was seeking the 'truth' of the Whole in music, so Schopenhauer's metaphysical curiosity found contentment in music: 'Whoever has followed me and has entered into my way of thinking will not find it so very paradoxical when I say that, supposing we succeeded in giving a perfectly accurate and complete explanation of music which goes into detail, and thus a detailed repetition in concepts of what it expresses, this would also be at once a sufficient repetition and explanation of the world in concepts . . . and hence the true philosophy' (WWR I, 264).

For Schopenhauer as for Adorno reflection on music touches on the mystery of the world, for the very reason that music does not picture the phenomenal world but itself is directly that of which the world is the phenomenon.

What was, to a musician, flattering in this musical philosophy had been taken up with enthusiasm by Richard Wagner in Schopenhauer's lifetime. In other respects he wanted to 'improve' Schopenhauer: he wanted to redeem will by – not surprisingly – love.

More strictly than Wagner, Schoenberg (to whom Adorno referred) later took up Schopenhauer's philosophy of music by demanding that music had to abandon all imaging. Its 'truth' was purely self-related.

This was the same Viennese scene at the turn of the century where Ludwig Wittgenstein, in analogy to Schopenhauer's musical philosophy, developed his logical mysticism in the *Tractatus Logico-Philosophicus*. Like Schopenhauer, Wittgenstein separates a kind of 'better consciousness' from logical thought. Wittgenstein, like Schopenhauer, wants to mark out the boundary between the utterable and the unutterable. The logic of language, which we use to point to what, outside it, 'is the issue', is itself also 'the issue'. It is self-referring, it plays its language games. The games of language are to Wittgenstein what music is to Schopenhauer. Language 'says' something by pointing to things, and simultaneously it shows itself; it *shows* itself as something that can produce 'meaning' without being 'meaning' itself.

Music speaks of itself, language speaks of itself. While they are doing so there is accomplished through them that unutterable Being which we always are but which we cannot bring before ourselves and therefore can never see or say. We should have to be *outside*, but in that case we *are* not. When we let music speak of music and language of language we may be coming close to that boundary.

The will – this '*ens realissimum*' of Schopenhauer – which plays in music, is it not about to disappear in this playing? Is its playing not a rehearsal of that which, from the perspective of the will, is 'nothing', but from which, conversely, everything which is the will is also 'nothing'? 'What one cannot speak about one must be silent about' (Wittgenstein).

CHAPTER TWENTY-FOUR

THE COMEDY OF FAME

Not long before his death Schopenhauer observed: 'Mankind has learned a few things from me which it will never forget. . . .' We have learned from him, but we have also forgotten that we have learned anything from him.

Schopenhauer is the philosopher of the pain of secularization, of metaphysical homelessness, of lost original confidence. No 'heaven has softly kissed earth, so that in its blossomed gleam it now must dream of it'. Heaven is empty. But there is still a metaphysical wonder, as well as horror at the merciless immanence of the will to live that knows no Beyond. Schopenhauer swept away the substitute gods (natural reason, historical reason, materialism, positivism) at a moment when the flight into these new 'religions' of the practicable was only just beginning.

He tried to think the 'Whole' of the world and of human life, without expecting salvation from that Whole. He asked: How can one live when there are no prescribed horizons to meaning and no guarantee of meaning? In this way he attempted to live his life, a life without warranty, versed in the wisdom of the lesser evil.

He brought the great affronts to human megalomania together in his thought and he thought them through to the end.

The cosmological affront: our world is one of countless spheres in infinite space, with a 'mouldy film of living and knowing beings' existing on it. The biological affront: man is an animal whose intelligence must compensate for a lack of instincts and for inadequate adaptation to the living world. The psychological affront: our conscious ego is not master in its own house.

Nearly a century before Freud, Schopenhauer turned round the philosophy of consciousness which had dominated Western thought. In Schopenhauer there is, for the first time, an explicit philosophy of the unconscious and of the body. Being determines consciousness. But Being is not, as with Marx, the social body but our own real body, which makes us the equals of everything and, simultaneously, the enemies of everything that lives. Schopenhauer spoke of the body, of the will, of life – without messianism. Our body will not redeem us, nor will our reason. He drastically demonstrated the impotence of reason in the face of the will. But he was 'the most rational philosopher of the irrational' (Thomas Mann). He realized that one had to support the weak, i.e. reason. He had nothing but contempt for the folly of trying to free that giant, the will, for oneself. He certainly was not going to be the tail wagging the dog.

Schopenhauer dreamed a different dream: perhaps reason might detach itself, if only for a few moments, from will, so that the will might relax into playing and reason into pure seeing. He dreamed this dream in philosophy, in art, and above all in music. Never before and never since has such moving philosophy been made about music as by Schopenhauer.

His greatest dream however was the denial of the will, its disappearance. He dreamed it by combining, as no one before him, the Western tradition of mysticism with the teachings of Eastern wisdom. There were in his life moments of self-disappearance, his 'better consciousness' which had allowed him to feel what otherwise he could only speak or write about.

He intended with his work to rend the veil of maya and — what irony — it was through that work that he remained fettered to the '*principium individuationis*'. Penetrating into areas where everything may remain unspoken and unheard, he wished to be listened to; he was unable to take this single paradoxical step forward. He did not acquire the tranquillity of silence and laughter. He did not become the Buddha of Frankfurt. He found it hard to bear the silence around him. He wanted an answer, he listened for the tapping signals. When these began to swell into a roar he was ready to die.

Arthur Schopenhauer was no Buddha, and fortunately for him he did not force himself to be one. Shrewdly he avoided the tragedy of trying to chase his own inspirations, his own insights. Schopenhauer did not mistake himself for himself. Insights and inspirations of a certain force and evidential value are something living that passes through us, an anonymous happening that one cannot take possession of through one's ego. And if, nevertheless, one attempts to do so the result will be compulsion, a stage set; anything living will come to a halt and one will go to the dogs, even if one is unaware of it. There is no profit in trying to take oneself by one's inspired word, in trying to 'realize' it, to 'translate' it, to 'appropriate' it. One should let the Self happen. Letting the Self happen instead of appropriating the Self is the secret of anything creative. Schopenhauer realized that, and therefore he was able, without misgivings or fear, to be surprised that it was something different that produced in him the best of his philosophy. In the last years of his life he once said to Frauenstädt: 'Do you think . . . that one can at each moment render to oneself account of what one has done? Sometimes I marvel how I have been able to accomplish all that. For in ordinary life one is not at all that which one is at the heightened moments of production' (C, 124).

He did not trouble to make these two lives congruent. By not doing so he probably did a service both to 'productivity' and to 'ordinary life'.

His 'ordinary life', however, was drawing to a close. After the publication of his *Parerga* and after the reprinting of his *Westminster Review* article in the *Vossische Zeitung* Schopenhauer suddenly found himself at the centre of not only philosophical interest. The number of visitors wishing to be received by him was growing. Curious persons turned up at the Englischer Hof to eye the philosopher. Richard Wagner had an invitation to Zurich extended to him: as a political refugee Wagner could not himself come to Germany. Schopenhauer declined the invitation. The libretto of the *Ring of the Nibelungs*, which Wagner had sent to him with a dedication, led Schopenhauer to remark to an intermediary: 'Thank your friend Wagner for me for sending me his Nibelungs, but he should give up his music, he has more genius as a poet! I, Schopenhauer, remain faithful to Rossini and Mozart . . .' (C, 199).

Friedrich Hebbel called on him. Schopenhauer told him this lovely parable of the comedy of his fame: 'I feel strange with my present fame. No doubt you will have seen how, before a performance, as the house-lights are extinguished and the curtain rises, a solitary lamplighter is still busy with the footlights and then hurriedly scampers off into the wings – just as the curtain goes up. This is how I feel: a latecomer, a leftover, just as the comedy of my fame is beginning' (C, 308).

Some of it really was comical. A silent follower, August Kilzer, searched extensively for the first edition of the principal work – because of the passages later omitted: the first Schopenhauer researcher. Another acquired three sets of his works: one for his own devotion, another for his son, and the third to lend out. Someone tracked down the inscription which Schopenhauer had scratched into the windowpane of his room in Rudolstadt in 1813. The previously mentioned landowner Wiesike purchased the first portrait of Schopenhauer and built a house specially for it. A pastor sent him eulogistic epigrams. A cartwright requested him to recommend some reading matter. A gentleman in Bohemia placed a fresh wreath on his portrait every day. The cadets of a military training establishment burned the midnight oil secretly reading his *Metaphysics of Love between the Sexes*. From nearby Homburg came the members of an association which, with German thoroughness, was dedicated to the practice of pessimism. Even the philosophical profession had its rendezvous. As Schopenhauer's surliness was well known, they mostly confined themselves to visiting the Englischer Hof incognito to participate, from a neighbouring table, in his table talk. One of the philosophy professors, however, actually ventured into the lion's den. He was told the scorpion story by Schopenhauer: when scorpions see a light and there is no escape into darkness they turn their own venomous sting against their head and die. 'You see, my friend, the burning candle – that is my philosophy. And the scorpions, which have been pinching long enough, should now, when they can no longer escape the light, also have the courage to extinguish themselves' (C, 181). The Hegelian Rosenkranz, definitely with malice, called Schopenhauer the 'newly elected emperor of philosophy in Germany'. In German university departments a start was made on Schopenhauer's exegesis. The philosophical faculty of the University of Leipzig held a competition on the subject 'Exposition and Critique of Schopenhauer's Philosophy'.

Arthur Schopenhauer was amazed at the response which his writings found also among women. A young lady in Silesia dedicated a poem to him, 'Der Fremdling im Vaterland' ('The Stranger in his Native Country'). At the Englischer Hof he had hour-long conversations with one Gisella Nicoletti from Rome, a Rike von Hasse from Hamburg, and an Ada van Zuylen from Amsterdam. In such company he was able to talk, like a young man in love, about problems of logic such as the identity theorem of A=A. Schopenhauer's image of women began to be shaken. In conversation with Malwida von Meysenburg, the friend of Richard Wagner, he once admitted: 'I have not yet spoken my last word about women. I believe that if a woman succeeds in withdrawing from the mass, or rather raising herself above the mass, she grows ceaselessly and more than a man' (C, 376). His newly awakened sense for the feminine also made him susceptible to the charms of the young sculptress Elisabeth Ney, who came to Frankfurt in October 1859 in order to make a bust of him. For four weeks she worked in his apartment. Arthur was in a state of bliss. He told a visitor: 'She works all day at my place. When I get back from luncheon we have coffee together, we sit together on the sofa, and I feel as if I were married' (C, 225).

Even those who did not read philosophy knew the walker with the inevitable poodle. Frankfurters were increasingly copying him and buying poodles for themselves.

In the winter of 1857 Schopenhauer had a fall while out walking. This was considered newsworthy by the Frankfurt press: 'The philosopher Schopenhauer, who lives here, suffered a not inconsiderable injury to his forehead as a result of a fall. However (as we learned upon inquiry) he is sure to be restored shortly.'

On one of the last days of April 1860, as he was walking home from his midday meal, he experienced a shortage of breath and palpitations; there were recurrences during the next few months. As he was unwilling to abandon his custom of walking briskly he shortened his walks. But he did not change his lifestyle in any other way; he did not even give up his habit of cold bathing in the river Main. On 18 September he suffered another attack of choking. Wilhelm Gwinner visited him. He was the last person to have a conversation with Schopenhauer. The subject was the mystic Jakob Böhme and his own life's work.

'That his body would now soon be gnawed by the worms was not a distressing thought to him; on the other hand he reflected with horror on how his spirit would be butchered at the hands of the "philosophy professors" ' (C, 394).

Schopenhauer recalled his youth, the period of 'inspired conception' and expressed satisfaction at the fact that the last additions, made in his seventieth year, still displayed 'the same freshness' and the same 'lively flow'. During their conversation it got dark. The housekeeper lit a candle. Schopenhauer mellowed. Gwinner: 'I was still able to rejoice in his clear eyes, in which there was nothing to be seen of sickness or old age. It would be a pity, he observed, if he were now to die: he still had some important additions to make to his *Parerga*' (C, 395). Gwinner took his leave. Schopenhauer dismissed him with the words that 'it would only be a kindness to him to attain absolute nothingness, but unfortunately death did not offer any such prospect. Still, whatever happened, he had "at least a clear intellectual conscience" ' (C, 396).

Three days later, on 21 September – a Friday, like the day he was born – Schopenhauer got up somewhat later than usual. His housekeeper opened the window to let in the fresh autumnal morning air. Then she left. Shortly afterwards the doctor arrived. Arthur Schopenhauer was leaning back in the corner of his sofa. He was dead, his face undisfigured, without a trace of agony.

The Nile had reached Cairo.

CHRONOLOGY

1788 22 February: Arthur Schopenhauer is born in Danzig, the son of the patrician merchant Heinrich Floris Schopenhauer and his wife Johanna, *née* Trosiener.

1793 Shortly before the city's occupation by the Prussians the family moves to Hamburg.

1797 Adele Schopenhauer is born.
July: Arthur travels to Paris and Le Havre with his father. In Le Havre he stays for two years with the Grégoire de Blésimaire family. Friendship with Anthime, the son of the family.

1799 August: Return to Hamburg. Arthur attends Runge's private school (until 1803).

1803 March: Arthur – complying with his father's wish – decides against grammar-school study and a career as a scholar, and in favour of training as a merchant. As a reward he is allowed to accompany his parents on a tour of Europe (Holland, England, France, Switzerland, Austria).
3 May: start of the journey.

1804 25 August: end of the journey.
September: apprenticed to the merchant Kabrun in Danzig (until December).

1805 Apprenticed to the merchant Jenisch in Hamburg.
20 April: suicide (?) of his father.

1806 September: Having wound up the family business his mother, with Adele, moves to Weimar.
October: beginning of the friendship between Johanna Schopenhauer and Goethe. Johanna establishes her tea parties.

1807 May: Arthur, with his mother's support, terminates his merchant apprenticeship. He leaves Hamburg to acquire university entrance qualifications at the Gotha *Gymnasium*.

December: because of a poetic lampoon he has to leave the school. He moves to Weimar but does not live at his mother's house. Private tuition. Falls in love with Karoline Jagemann.

1809 Concludes his school studies. Has his paternal inheritance paid out to him, but his mother administers it.

9 October: starts his studies in Göttingen.

1809–11 Studies in Göttingen: natural sciences, Plato, Kant.

1811 Easter: visits Weimar. Schopenhauer to Wieland: 'Life is a sorry affair, I have resolved to spend it reflecting upon it.'

Autumn: Berlin University.

1811–13 Studies in Berlin. Attends lectures by Fichte, Schleiermacher, Wolf.

1813 2 May: Schopenhauer flees from Berlin because of the war. Short stay in Weimar. Quarrels with his mother. Withdraws to nearby Rudolstadt.

July – November: Writes his dissertation *On the Fourfold Root of the Principle of Sufficient Reason*.

5 November: returns to his mother's house.

Winter: conversations with Goethe on colour theory.

1814 April: culmination of arguments between Schopenhauer, his mother and her friend Gerstenbergk.

May: final break with his mother. Schopenhauer leaves Weimar.

1814–18 Lives in Dresden.

1815 *On Seeing and Colours*.

Draft and execution of the first version of his principal work, *The World as Will and Representation*.

1818 March: completion of manuscript. Brockhaus to be the publisher.

Autumn: start of his Italian journey (Florence, Rome, Naples, Venice).

1819 January: *The World as Will and Representation* is published.

Summer: family financial crisis owing to the collapse of the Danzig banking house of Muhl. Schopenhauer therefore returns to Germany. New tensions between him and his mother. Quarrels also with his sister Adele.

25 August: back in Dresden.

Applies for a lectureship at Berlin University. He is accepted.

1820 29 March: start of lectures. Very few students attend his lectures.

1821 Falls in love with the singer Caroline Medon. Beginning of the 'Marquet affair' (physical assault against a seamstress and suit for damages).

1822 22 May: second Italian journey (Milan, Florence, Venice).

1823 May: return. Arrival in Munich. Serious illness, depression (his philosophy is ignored).

1824 Stays at Bad Gastein, in Mannheim and in Dresden.

1825 April: back to Berlin. Once more, but unsuccessfully, attempts to give lectures. Tries to establish himself as a translator, also unsuccessfully.

1831 August: flees from Berlin because of a cholera epidemic. Moves first to Frankfurt-am-Main.

1832–3 Lives in Mannheim (July 1832–June 1833).

1833 6 July: settles in Frankfurt for the next twenty-eight years, until the end of his life.

1835 *On the Will in Nature.*

1838 Death of his mother.

1839 Competition essay 'On the Freedom of Human Will', awarded first prize.

1840 Competition essay 'On the Foundations of Morality', not awarded a prize.

1844 *The World as Will and Representation*: second edition, amplified by a volume.

1849 Death of his sister Adele.

1851 *Parerga and Paralipomena.*

1853 Beginning of Schopenhauer's fame.

1859 Third edition of *The World as Will and Representation.*

1860 21 September: death of Arthur Schopenhauer.

EDITIONS OF SCHOPENHAUER'S WORKS, SOURCES, ABBREVIATIONS

The references to Schopenhauer's works and the source editions are given wherever possible to English translations of the texts. Where these do not exist, the German reference has been retained. The following abbreviations have been used:

WWR I *The World as Will and Representation*, trans. E. F. J. Payne, vol. I: Cambridge, Mass., 1958

WWR II *The World as Will and Representation*, trans. E. F. J. Payne, vol. II: Cambridge, Mass., 1958

PP I *Parerga and Paralipomena*, trans. E. F. J. Payne, vol. I: Oxford, 1974

PP II *Parerga and Paralipomena*, trans. E. F. J. Payne, vol. II: Oxford, 1974

MW Minor Works: Volume III of the *Complete Works*, ed. Wolfgang Freiherr von Löhneysen: Frankfurt, 1986. Some of the contents of this volume have been translated into English, and references to these English editions are as follows:

FR 'On the Fourfold Root of the Principle of Sufficient Reason' in Arthur Schopenhauer, *Two Essays*: London, 1889

VC *On Vision and Colour*: London, 1942

WN 'On the Will in Nature' in *Two Essays*: London, 1889

FHW 'On the Freedom of Human Will' in *The Wisdom of Schopenhauer*: London, 1911

BE 'The Basis of Ethics', extracts in *The Wisdom of Schopenhauer*: London, 1911

FM 'On the Foundations of Morality', translated as extracts from 'The Basis of Ethics' in *The Wisdom of Schopenhauer*: London, 1911

P Papers: A. Hübscher, ed., *Der handschriftliche Nachlass*, 5 vols.: Frankfurt/Nachdruck, 1968–85

P I Early manuscripts

P II Critical discussions

P III Berlin manuscripts

P IV, 1 Manuscript books 1830–52

P iv, 2   Late manuscripts, *Gracian's Hand-Oracle*
P v   Marginalia
CL   Collected letters: A. Hübscher, ed., *Gesammelte Briefe*: Bonn, 1978
Corr   Correspondence: C. Gebhardt and A. Hübscher, eds., 3 vols. in Paul Deussen, ed., *Collected Works*: Munich, 1929ff
Corr 14   1st vol. of correspondence (1799–1849)
Corr 15   2nd vol. of correspondence (1849–60)
Corr 16   3rd vol. of correspondence (addenda, notes)
C   Conversations: A. Hübscher, ed., *Gespräche*: Stuttgart, 1971
TD   Travel diaries: Charlotte von Gwinner, ed., *Reisetagebücher aus den Jahren 1803 bis 1804*: Leipzig, 1923
D   Dissertation: original version of 'On the Fourfold Root of the Principle of Sufficient Reason', 1813. In A. Hübscher, ed., *Complete Works*, 7 vols.: Wiesbaden, 1950
LTR   Lecture: On the Theory of Whole Representation, Cogitation and Perception;
LMN   Lecture: On the Metaphysics of Nature;
LMA   Lecture: On the Metaphysics of Aesthetics;
LMM   Lecture: On the Metaphysics of Mores: All in Volker Spierling, ed., *Philosophische Vorlesungen*, 4 vols.: Munich/Zurich 1985
JSS   *Journal of the Schopenhauer Society*, 1912–44; later *Schopenhauer-Jahrbuch* (Paul Deussen, ed.), Frankfurt; year references given

NOTES

CHAPTER 1

7: 'Few, indeed . . .': see W. Gwinner,
Schopenhauers Leben, 349
8: 'The Nile . . .': see A. Hübscher,
Lebensbild, 115
8: 'I was . . .': J. Schopenhauer, *Ihr
glücklichen Augen*, 204
8: 'Here . . .': see E. Keyser,
Geschichte der Stadt Danzig, 24
9: 'Indeed . . .': J. Schopenhauer, *Ihr
glücklichen Augen*, 83
9: 'Voilà . . .': ibid., 203
9: 'I thank . . .': ibid., 5
10: 'Herr M. . . .': ibid., 82
10: 'If our . . .': see E. Keyser,
Geschichte der Stadt Danzig, 180
11: 'That my husband . . .': J.
Schopenhauer, *Ihr glücklichen
Augen*, 241
12: 'From all sides . . .': ibid., 242
12: 'And now . . .': ibid., 243
12: 'My quiet . . .': ibid., 243
13: 'My husband . . .': ibid., 189
13: 'I never . . .': ibid., 189
13: 'I no more . . .': ibid., 177
13: 'the tender . . .': ibid., 172
13: 'I believed . . .': ibid., 177
14: 'Splendour . . .': ibid., 146
14: 'My parents . . .': ibid., 177
15: 'Like all . . .': ibid., 253
15: 'magnificent garden . . .': ibid.,
190
15: 'Jameson . . .': ibid., 261

15: 'many a gap . . .': ibid., 262
15: 'a semblance . . .': ibid., 261
15: 'In the light . . .': ibid., 190
16: 'Good posture . . .': Corr 14, 15

CHAPTER 2

19: 'most important . . .': see B. Studt
and H. Olsen, *Hamburg*, 159
19: 'Hamburg's flag . . .': ibid., 128
20: 'far above . . .': see JSS 1932, 210
20: 'The Constitution . . .': see B. Studt
and H. Olsen, *Hamburg*, 120
21: 'Thrice happy . . .': see ibid., 156
21: 'Hamburg may . . .': see ibid., 155
21: 'Is it not . . .': see H. K. Röthel, *Die
Hansestädte*, 95
22: 'What is earning . . .': see ibid.,
327
22: 'Madame Chevalier . . .': see JSS
1932, 218
22: 'The sky . . .': H. Heine, *Schriften*
I, 515
22: 'And as . . .': ibid., 516
23: 'If such . . .': Corr 14, 109
23: 'Scholarship . . .': see B. Studt and
H. Olsen, *Hamburg*, 253
24: 'to be a record . . .': G. E. Lessing,
Werke 4, 233
24: 'The gallery . . .': ibid., 257
24: 'If a troupe . . .': see F. Kopitzsch,
Lessing und Hamburg, 60
24: 'I am withdrawing . . .': see B.
Studt and H. Olsen, *Hamburg*, 153

24: 'downright pickled-herring . . .':
see H. K. Röthel, *Die Hansestädte*,
325

24: 'What stands . . .': see ibid., 314

25: 'The production . . .': see B. Studt
and H. Olsen, *Hamburg*, 151

25: 'Admiration . . .': see ibid., 151

26: 'There is nothing . . .': see H. K.
Röthel, *Die Hansestädte*, 325

27: 'You regret . . .': Corr 14, 19

27: 'nothing but . . .': see K. Pişa,
Schopenhauer, 81

29: 'You will soon . . .': Corr 14, 5

29: 'Your father . . .': JSS 1971, 84

29: 'I understand . . .': JSS 1970, 32

29: 'For you too . . .': ibid., 33

30: 'You made me . . .': Corr 14, 3

31: 'Thereupon Herr Runge . . .': JSS
1968, 102

31: 'that these . . .': ibid., 102

31: 'the manner . . .': ibid., 103

31: 'of how . . .': ibid., 103

31: 'how in . . .': ibid., 104

31: 'Herr Runge . . .': ibid., 108

32: 'In the evening . . .': ibid., 103

32: 'In the evening . . .': ibid., 105

CHAPTER 3

34: 'that they . . .': see K. H. Röthel,
Die Hansestädte, 115

35: 'Yesterday . . .': see JSS 1932, 211

36: 'not to stay . . .': see JSS 1968, 99

37: 'I would altogether . . .': JSS 1971,
88

40: 'Little though . . .': JSS 1971, 85

40: 'I would wish . . .': Corr 14, 16

44: 'dangerous general . . .': J.
Schopenhauer, *Reise durch England
und Schottland*, 168

45: 'I am sorry . . .': see K. Pisa,
Schopenhauer, 120

45: 'How can . . .': JSS 1971, 88

47: 'I live . . .': F. Hölderlin, *Werke* 2,
931

47: 'But on holidays . . .': F.
Hölderlin, *Werke* 1, 389

CHAPTER 4

52: 'I will therefore . . .': Corr 14, 14

52: 'And with reference . . .': Corr
14, 16

53: 'Dancing and riding . . .': Corr
14, 16

53: 'I wish . . .': ibid., 16

53: 'You should . . .': see K. Pisa,
Schopenhauer, 136

53: 'I don't . . .': see W. Gwinner,
Schopenhauers Leben, 27

53: 'As you know . . .': JSS 1971, 86

53: 'You know . . .': JSS 1971, 89

54: 'I hereby discharge . . .': see K.
Pisa, *Schopenhauer*, 142

55: 'She found . . .': Adele
Schopenhauer, *Tagebücher* 2, 32

55: 'On such cruel . . .': Corr 14, 18

55: 'It is my wish . . .': Corr 14, 19

56: 'Existence here . . .': Corr 14, 27

56: 'Melancholic withdrawal . . .':
see W. Lepenies, *Melancholie und
Gesellschaft*, 103

57: 'The time . . .': M. Claudius,
Sämtliche Werke, 507

57: 'Man is not . . .': ibid., 506

57: 'Be honest . . .': ibid., 507

58: 'Whatever . . .': ibid., 506

62: 'As if dimly . . .': see K. Günzel,
König der Romantik, 63

62: 'the wheel . . .': W. H.
Wackenroder, *Schriften*, 153

64: 'grave . . .': ibid., 171

64: 'holy music': Novalis, *Werke* 2,
749

64: 'mediation of . . .': see E. Friedell,
Kulturgeschichte der Neuzeit, 920

64: 'God is . . .': see G. Schulz, *Die
deutsche Literatur zwischen
Französischer Revolution und
Restauration*, 211

64: 'Not he . . .': see ibid., 209

64: '*salto mortale* . . .': see ibid., 208

64: 'One must . . .': W. H.
Wackenroder, *Schriften*, 156

65: 'If such . . .': L. Tieck, *Werke* 1, 238

65: 'Music is . . .': W. H. Wackenroder, *Schriften*, 156

66: 'embraces . . .': JSS 1932, 217

66: 'these days . . .': ibid., 217

CHAPTER 5

68: 'You left . . .': Corr 14, 34

68: 'too determined . . .': Corr 14, 130

69: 'Thank God . . .': ibid., 110

69: 'I always . . .': ibid., 91

69: 'not forgetting . . .': ibid., 91

69: 'Dear friend . . .': ibid., 108

69: 'At last . . .': Jean Paul, *Briefe* 3, 236

70: 'Upon his entry . . .': see H. Pleticha (ed.), *Das klassische Weimar*, 16

70: 'You get . . .': see ibid., 12

71: 'The excrement . . .': see G. Günther and L. Wallraf (eds.), *Geschichte der Stadt Weimar*, 231

71: 'unless at least . . .': J. W. Goethe, *Werke (Weimarer Ausgabe)*, Abt. 4, 12, 50

71: 'some consideration . . .': see G. Günther and L. Wallraf (eds.), *Geschichte der Stadt Weimar*, 238

72: 'Although . . .': see H. Pleticha (ed.), *Das klassische Weimar*, 13

72: 'Among the people . . .': see ibid., 13

72: 'In vain . . .': see ibid., 18

73: 'You visit . . .': see ibid., 13

73: 'Send your wench . . .': see R. Friedenthal, *Goethe*, 397

73: 'When I arrived . . .': see H. Pleticha (ed.), *Das klassische Weimar*, 287

74: 'What struck . . .': see ibid., 65

74: 'A bourgeois . . .': see ibid., 17

74: 'Between the two . . .': see ibid., 17

74: 'I prefer . . .': see R. Friedenthal, *Goethe*, 417

74: 'If it were . . .': see ibid., 399

74: 'My existence . . .': Corr 14, 64

74: 'more at home . . .': ibid., 69

75: 'Goethe said . . .': ibid., 69

75: 'Here everyone . . .': ibid., 36

76: 'Although the world . . .': J. W. Goethe, *Werke* 10, 491

76: 'Every heart . . .': Corr 14, 42

76: 'Then the drum . . .': ibid., 46

77: 'Now the cannon . . .': ibid., 49

77: 'Necessity extinguishes . . .': ibid., 50

77: 'Just imagine . . .': ibid., 52

77: 'quite sweetly . . .': ibid., 52

78: 'never seen . . .': ibid., 56

78: 'I could . . .': ibid., 63

78: 'death is helping . . .': ibid., 63

78: 'I am glad . . .': ibid., 63

79: 'Now that winter . . .': ibid., 64

79: 'A stranger . . .': ibid., 43

79: 'Yet in . . .': see H. Blumenberg, *Arbeit am Mythos*, 535

79: 'Still you . . .': J. W. Goethe, *Werke* 1, 45

79: 'One would . . .': see H. H. Houben, *Damals in Weimar*, 47

79: 'Although already . . .': see H. Pleticha (ed.), *Das klassische Weimar*, 264

80: 'an object . . .': see H. Blumenberg, *Arbeit am Mythos*, 535

80: 'in peacetime . . .': Corr 14, 69

80: 'Amidst the thundering . . .': see R. Friedenthal, *Goethe*, 438

80: 'making a point . . .': see H. Pleticha (ed.), *Das klassische Weimar*, 289

80: 'That same . . .': Corr 14, 69

80: 'The circle . . .': ibid., 87

81: 'That you . . .': ibid., 130

81: 'I often . . .': ibid., 116

82: 'When everything . . .': ibid., 125

82: 'He spoke . . .': ibid., 120

82: 'long, serious . . .': ibid., 125

82: 'with tears . . .': ibid., 135
82: 'I know . . .': ibid., 130
82: 'hope of becoming . . .': ibid., 132
82: 'a moderately . . .': ibid., 132
83: 'so that you . . .': ibid., 132
83: 'When you . . .': ibid., 132
83: 'But such . . .': see W. Gwinner, *Schopenhauers Leben*, 44

CHAPTER 6
84: 'That you . . .': Corr 14, 137
84: 'You can . . .': ibid., 138
84: 'that I did . . .': ibid., 138
85: 'I live . . .': Corr 16, 620
85: 'As an old . . .': ibid., 620
85: 'without deriving . . .': ibid., 620
85: 'Make one's entry . . .': see W. Gwinner, *Schopenhauers Leben*, 289
88: 'Your enormous . . .': Corr 16, 4
88: 'That you . . .': JSS 1971, 92
88: 'I envy . . .': Corr 16, 4
88: 'I do not . . .': JSS 1971, 94
88: 'to present . . .': ibid., 94
89: 'to spend . . .': ibid., 104
89: 'if I die . . .': Corr 14, 134
89: 'Once you see . . .': JSS 1971, 94
89: 'I always . . .': Corr 14, 72
89: 'Myself . . .': JSS 1971, 94
89: 'I have no . . .': Corr 14, 124
90: 'kind of . . .': JSS 1971, 99
91: 'You are not . . .': JSS 1971, 97
92: 'bring with you . . .': ibid., 95
92: 'violent scenes': ibid., 99
92: 'impairing the freedom . . .': ibid., 101
92: 'I think . . .': ibid., 103
94: 'Mark now . . .': JSS 1971, 104
95: 'Of all . . .': ibid., 104
95: 'always a little . . .': Corr 14, 88
95: 'One would feel . . .': see H. H. Houben, *Damals in Weimar*, 56
96: 'to recite . . .': see ibid., 91
96: 'Hilla, Lilla . . .': see ibid., 91

96: 'When the people . . .': see ibid., 91
98: 'You are probably . . .': see H. Pleticha (ed.), *Das klassische Weimar*, 105
98: 'that which . . .': see H. H. Houben, *Damals in Weimar*, 176
98: 'the common bipeds': see H. Pleticha (ed.), *Das klassische Weimar*, 106
99: 'it was impossible . . .': see ibid., 187
99: 'His elegant . . .': JSS 1971, 92

CHAPTER 7
101: 'centre of . . .': see K. Pisa, *Schopenhauer*, 200
102: 'lumps of flesh . . .': H. A. Oppermann, *Hundert Jahre*, Teil 5, 272
102: 'Some people . . .': H. Heine, *Schriften* 3, 104
102: 'His debating . . .': see W. Schneider, *Schopenhauer*, 126
102: 'The city . . .': H. Heine, *Schriften* 3, 103
104: 'the most perfect . . .': see W. Schneider, *Schopenhauer*, 123
104: 'peak of all . . .': see ibid., 123
104: 'bold step': see A. Hübscher, *Denker gegen den Strom*, 111
106: 'Until now . . .': I. Kant, *Werke* 3, 25
109: 'not so much . . .': ibid., 63
109: 'paint in . . .': ibid., 120
110: 'productive imagination': ibid., 149
110: 'That this . . .': ibid., 176
111: 'highest point . . .': ibid., 136
112: 'The land . . .': ibid., 267
112: 'It is the peculiar . . .': ibid., 11
113: 'There is something . . .': G. Büchner, *Werke*, 33
114: 'If I now . . .': I. Kant, *Werke* 4, 432

114: 'Man is free': see A. Gulyga, *Immanuel Kant*, 143

114: 'You will ask . . .': J.-J. Rousseau, *Emile* (p. 557 Stuttgart 1963 edn)

115: 'there are . . .': see A. Gulyga, *Immanuel Kant*, 186

116: 'Gladly I serve . . .': see ibid., 187

116: 'between spirit . . .': H. Heine, *Schriften* 5, 531

116: 'monument to . . .': ibid., 532

117: 'Act only . . .': I. Kant, *Werke* 7, 51

118: 'It is wise . . .': see A. Gulyga, *Immanuel Kant*, 249

118: 'It may sound . . .': ibid., 243

118: 'Here even . . .': ibid., 243

CHAPTER 8

121: 'The fine dust . . .': see R. Köhler and W. Richter (eds.), *Berliner Leben 1806 bis 1847*, 301

121: 'In Berlin . . .': see ibid., 308

121: 'a living . . .': P. D. Atterbom, *Reisebilder aus dem romantischen Deutschland*, 48

122: 'Berlin is . . .': G. de Staël, *Germany* (p. 101 in Stuttgart 1962 edn)

123: 'a practical . . .': see W. G. Jacobs, *Johann Gottlieb Fichte*, 122

123: 'conflict between . . .': see M. Lenz, *Geschichte der Kgl. Friedrich Wilhelm-Universität zu Berlin* 1, 416

124: 'We consider . . .': see W. G. Jacobs, *Fichte*, 34

125: 'The "I think" . . .': I. Kant, *Werke* 3, 136

125: 'The source . . .': J. G. Fichte, *Grundlage der gesamten Wissenschaftslehre als Handschrift für seine Zuhörer*, 55

126: 'Well, if . . .': J. Paul, *Siebenkäs*

127: 'I alone . . .': J.-J. Rousseau, *Confessions* (p. 9 in Munich 1981 edn)

127: 'Who can keep . . .': F. Hölderlin, *Werke* 2, 743

128: 'I, a refugee . . .': M. Preitz, *Friedrich Schlegel und Novalis: Biographie einer Romantiker-freundschaft in Briefen*, 43

128: 'They had concluded . . .': see D. Arendt (ed.), *Nihilismus*, 33

129: The fantast . . .': F. Schiller, *Werke* 12, 263

129: 'Fly with me . . .': L. Tieck, *Werke* 1, 670

129: 'It follows . . .': J. Paul, *Vorschule der Ästhetik*

129: 'The mysterious . . .': Novalis, *Werke* 2, 201ff

130: 'then everyone . . .': see H. A. Korff, *Geist der Goethezeit*, 3, 253

CHAPTER 9

134: 'And I will . . .': J. Eichendorff, *Werke*, 9

137: 'Sex has gradually . . .': M. Foucault, *Sexuality and Truth* (p. 89 Frankfurt 1979 edn)

138: 'it is a fact . . .': T. Mann, *Doktor Faustus*, 197

CHAPTER 10

142: 'Wherever one . . .': Varnhagen von Ense, *Denkwürdigkeiten* 1, 244

142: 'Here everything . . .': see M. Lenz, *Geschichte der Kgl. Friedrich Wilhelm-Universität zu Berlin* 1, 469

143: 'Our institutions . . .': see ibid., 469

143: 'smell of corpses': see ibid., 471

143: 'it is a gruesome . . .': see ibid., 482

144: 'The remnants . . .': see ibid., 482

146: 'If the experiment . . .': see ibid., 499

146: 'In devout . . .': see ibid., 495

146: 'For while . . .': see ibid.

146: 'I cannot now . . .': see ibid., 496

147: 'While *Landsturm* . . .': see ibid., 505

CHAPTER 12

165: 'The Schopenhauer . . .': see H. H. Houben, *Damals in Weimar*, 183

165: 'I turned . . .': Adele Schopenhauer, *Tagebücher* 1, 128

168: 'You irritate . . .': JSS 1973, 125

168: 'Gans is . . .': ibid.

168: 'Over me . . .': K. Pisa, *Schopenhauer*, 264

168: 'You seem . . .': ibid., 125

169: 'I wanted . . .': ibid., 124

169: 'If I were . . .': ibid., 125

169: 'Do not answer . . .': ibid., 126

170: 'The door . . .': ibid., 128

171: 'You have often . . .': ibid., 126

172: 'Adele is . . .': see Adele Schopenhauer, *Tagebuch einer Einsamen* (ed. H. H. Houben), XIV

172: 'From Adele's . . .': ibid., XV

172: 'appallingly rattling . . .': ibid., XIX

173: 'Who could . . .': Adele Schopenhauer, *Tagebücher* 2, 46

173: 'Every vacuous . . .': Adele Schopenhauer, *Tagebuch einer Einsamen* (ed. H. H. Houben), 132

173: 'As the voice . . .': ibid., 98

173: 'My days . . .': Adele Schopenhauer, *Tagebücher* 2, 5

174: '*Finding* meant . . .': Adele Schopenhauer, *Tagebücher* 1, 148

175: 'We really are . . .': Adele Schopenhauer, *Tagebuch einer Einsamen* (ed. H. H. Houben), 290

175: 'Ferdinand . . .': Adele Schopenhauer, *Tagebücher* 1, 85

175: 'but if . . .': ibid., 93

175: 'I now think . . .': Adele Schopenhauer, *Tagebuch einer Einsamen* (ed. H. H. Houben), 49

175: 'My brother . . .': JSS 1977, 133

176: 'I know . . .': JSS 1977, 134

CHAPTER 13

177: 'the senses . . .': J. W. Goethe, *Werke* 12, 406

177: 'Young Schopenhauer . . .': C (A. Schopenhauer, *Gespräche*), 28

178: 'With others . . .': C (A. Schopenhauer, *Gespräche*), 27

178: 'This is not . . .': J. W. Goethe, *Werke* 13, 318

179: 'No matter . . .': see R. Friedenthal, *Goethe*, 456

179: 'Of whatever . . .': see ibid., 455

179: 'that the colours . . .': J. W. Goethe, *Werke* 14, 256

180: 'a revelation . . .': see E. Heller, *Enterbter Geist*, 56

181: 'the phenomena . . .': see ibid., 44

182: 'I shall not . . .': see H. Blumenberg, *Die Lesbarkeit der Welt*, 215

182: 'Friends . . .': J. W. Goethe, *Werke* 13, 614

183: 'Chromatic reflections . . .': ibid., 629

183: 'We believe . . .': ibid., 337

183: 'For here too . . .': ibid., 324

184: 'Gladly I'd continue . . .': ibid., 622

190: 'Dr Schopenhauer . . .': J. W. Goethe, *Werke* (*Weimarer Ausgabe*) 36, 112

CHAPTER 14

192: 'all good manners . . .': see E. Haenel and E. Kalkschmidt, *Das alte Dresden*, 165

192: 'There was a house . . .': L. Richter, *Lebenserinnerungen*, 40

192: 'those soft wordmongers . . .': see E. Haenel and E. Kalkschmidt, *Das alte Dresden*, 151

195: 'When tired . . .': see ibid., 245
198: '*natural* and . . .': I. Kant, *Werke* 3, 311
202: 'inperience, inspirituation': see H. v. Glasenapp, *Das Indienbild deutscher Denker*, 65

CHAPTER 15
216: 'tell': see M. Proust, *Remembrance of Things Past*, vol. 1 (p. 185 in Frankfurt 1964 edn)
221: 'It is a fact . . .': G. W. F. Hegel, *Werke* 4, 23
221: 'fashioner of his happiness': G. W. F. Hegel, *Werke* 2, 244
222: 'Massive impression . . .': see M. Riedel, *Theorie und Praxis im Denken Hegels*, 219
222: 'Let us not . . .': see ibid., 223

CHAPTER 16
228: 'Whose heart . . .': Novalis, *Werke* 1, 227
228: 'Yet our earth . . .': H. Steffens, *Anthropologie*, 14
231: 'Whoever regards . . .': F. Schleiermacher, *Monologen*

CHAPTER 17
241: 'Sailing across . . .': J. W. Goethe, *Werke* 11, 87
242: 'As the poet . . .': see A. Hübscher, *Denker gegen den Strom*, 78
243: 'I have seen . . .': A. Schopenhauer, *Gespräche*, 44
243: 'They are frightful . . .': see H. Kesten, *Dichter im Café*, 316
245: 'Dear friend . . .': JSS 1975, 189
245: 'May you not . . .': JSS 1977, 160
245: 'some inward pain': ibid., 160
245: 'My brother . . .': ibid., 133
245: 'I know nothing . . .': Adele Schopenhauer, *Tagebücher* 1, 12
245: 'Arthur has written . . .': JSS 1977, 134

245: 'I ought . . .': JSS 1977, 134
246: 'outrageous answer': Adele Schopenhauer, *Tagebücher* 1, 12
246: 'You may lose . . .': ibid., 63
246: 'This morning . . .': JSS 1977, 137
246: 'His girl . . .': Adele Schopenhauer, *Tagebücher* 2, 20
246: 'Do not accept . . .': JSS 1977, 157
246: 'If there is . . .': ibid., 157
247: 'I am sorry . . .': ibid., 182
247: 'overthrow . . .': ibid., 161
247: 'It pains me . . .': ibid., 164
247: 'My plans . . .': ibid., 168
247: 'Accept the firm . . .': ibid., 169
248: 'even though neither . . .': ibid., 140
248: 'She spoke . . .': ibid., 140
248: 'To die . . .': Adele Schopenhauer, *Tagebücher* 2, 32
248: 'by way of . . .': JSS 1977, 142
248: 'I do not wish . . .': ibid., 173
249: 'At last . . .': Adele Schopenhauer, *Tagebücher* 2, 42

CHAPTER 18
251: 'how he . . .': C (A. Schopenhauer, *Gespräche*), 35
251: 'received a letter . . .': Adele Schopenhauer, *Tagebücher* 2, 35
251: 'A visit . . .': see A. Schopenhauer, *Gespräche*, 35
252: 'that another . . .': Corr 14, 276
252: 'I am not . . .': Corr 14, 272
252: 'Since Hegel . . .': Corr 14, 272
253: 'It seems to me . . .': see A. Gulyga, *Hegel*, 167
253: 'warlord . . .': see ibid., 163
253: 'As long . . .': Hegel, *Werke* 11, 556
254: 'I cling . . .': see M. Lenz, *Geschichte der Kgl. Friedrich Wilhelm-Universität zu Berlin* 2, 220

254: 'The *goal* . . .': G. W. F. Hegel, *Phänomenologie des Geistes*, 564
255: 'I saw . . .': see A. Gulyga, *Hegel*, 81
255: 'The True . . .': see J. E. Erdmann, *Philosophie der Neuzeit* 7, 168
255: 'rakes through . . .': G. W. F. Hegel, *Werke* 2, 191
256: 'The ideas . . .': G. W. F. Hegel, *Werke*
256: 'One has to recall . . .': R. Haym, *Hegel und seine Zeit*, 4
256: 'His prematurely . . .': see A. Gulyga, *Hegel*, 246
257: 'Your looking . . .': see ibid., 279
257: 'There is probably . . .': see M. Lenz, *Geschichte der Kgl. Friedrich Wilhelm-Universität zu Berlin* II, 1, 183
257: 'A city . . .': see M. v. Böhn, *Biedermeier*, 440
257: 'After all . . .': see ibid., 440
258: 'dancing world history': see ibid., 454
261: 'Philosophy has . . .': G. W. F. Hegel, *Werke* 16, 353
261: 'which, with . . .': see M. Lenz, *Geschichte der Kgl. Friedrich Wilhelm-Universität zu Berlin* II, 1, 118

CHAPTER 19
270: 'that I have . . .': JSS 1974, 47
270: 'that I am . . .': ibid., 47
276: 'Schopenhauer's World . . .': see K. Pisa, *Schopenhauer*, 342
276: 'I took . . .': A. Schopenhauer, *Gespräche*, 53
276: 'metaphysics without . . .': see A. Gulyga, *Hegel*, 272
279: 'felt such violent . . .': C (A. Schopenhauer, *Gespräche*), 59

CHAPTER 20
281: 'You are less . . .': see W.

Gwinner, *Schopenhauers Leben*, 242
281: 'Money is . . .': see F. Bothe, *Geschichte der Stadt Frankfurt am Main*, 273
282: 'everything comes . . .': JSS 1968, 112
282: 'It is a small . . .': see ibid., 112
282: 'rare natural . . .': see ibid.
284: 'He was . . .': C (A. Schopenhauer, *Gespräche*), 88
285: 'We were engaged . . .': ibid., 62
288: 'Lead an orderly . . .': JSS 1976, 112
288: 'Two months . . .': ibid., 114
289: 'Listen, Sophie . . .': JSS 1978, 114
290: 'not a single . . .': ibid., 133
290: 'Virtually no one . . .': ibid., 134
291: 'Do not . . .': ibid., 134
291: 'That you should . . .': ibid., 136
291: 'I am certain . . .': ibid., 137
291: 'Permit me . . .': Adele Schopenhauer, *Tagebuch einer Einsamen* (ed. H. H. Houben), LXI

CHAPTER 21
298: 'The 3rd August . . .': see M. Lenz, *Geschichte der Kgl. Friedrich Wilhelm-Universität zu Berlin* II, 1, 395
298: 'At present . . .': Hegel, *Briefe* 3, 323
299: 'I can . . .': H. Heine, *Schriften* 7, 55
299: 'Philosophy cannot . . .': Marx-Engels *Werke* 1, 391
299: 'And now . . .': see T. Ziegler, *Die geistigen und sozialen Strömungen des 19. Jahrhunderts*, 179
299: 'I have . . .': see J. Hermand (ed.), *Das Junge Deutschland: Texte und Dokumente*, 185
300: 'Party! Party! . . .': see F. Vassen (ed.), *Die deutsche Literatur in Text*

*und Darstellung: Restauration,
Vormärz und 48er Revolution*, 174
300: 'Show me . . .': K. Gutzkow,
Wally – Die Zweiflerin, 114
300: 'We shall not . . .': ibid., 302
301: 'God become man . . .': see T.
Ziegler, *Die geistigen und sozialen
Strömungen des 19. Jahrhunderts*,
195
302: 'systematic philistinism . . .': F.
Nietzsche, *Werke* 1, 143
302: 'tiptoeing carpet-slipper
enthusiasm': ibid., 157
302: 'We demand . . .': ibid., 163
303: 'the supreme . . .': L. Feuerbach,
Der Anfang der Philosophie, 152
303: 'it is in . . .': L. Feuerbach,
*Grundsätze der Philosophie der
Zukunft*, 62 n.
303: 'The individual . . .': ibid., 61 n.
303: 'God was . . .': see T. Ziegler, *Die
geistigen und sozialen Strömungen
des 19. Jahrhunderts*, 203
304: 'Solitariness is . . .': L. Feuerbach,
*Grundsätze der Philosophie der
Zukunft*, 62 n.
304: 'The philosophers . . .': *Marx-
Engels Werke* 3, 7
305: 'Platonic and . . .': *Marx-Engels
Werke* 1, 267
305: 'It is therefore . . .': *Marx-Engels
Werke* 1, 379
305: 'Critique . . .': *Marx-Engels
Werke* 1, 379
305: 'The reform . . .': *Marx-Engels
Werke* 1, 346

CHAPTER 22
308: 'What the bourgeoisie . . .':
Marx-Engels Werke 4, 474
312: 'But he who . . .': J. G. Fichte,
Werke 1, 433

312: 'Unconditional is . . .': F. W. J.
Schelling, *Werke* 1, 56
313: 'that everything . . .': F. W. J.
Schelling, *Über das Wesen der
menschlichen Freiheit*, 46
313: 'everything is rule . . .': ibid., 54
314: 'Volition is . . .': ibid., 46
314: 'Yet love . . .': ibid., 97
321: 'Be mistrustful . . .': M.
Horkheimer, *Dämmerungen*, 251
322: 'The German workers . . .': see F.
Bothe, *Geschichte der Stadt
Frankfurt*, 295
324: 'The flood . . .': see ibid., 296

CHAPTER 23
328: 'To my regret . . .': Corr 14, 609
328: 'I cannot . . .': see A. Hübscher,
Lebensbild, 107
328: 'Schopenhauer, to . . .': ibid., 107
331: 'It is simply . . .': see F. A. Lange,
Geschichte des Materialismus 2, 557
332: 'Realism is . . .': see A. Huyssen
(ed.), *Die Deutsche Literatur in Text
und Darstellung: Bürgerlicher
Realismus*, 52
332: 'If a man . . .': see T. Nipperdey,
Deutsche Geschichte 1800–1866,
488
339: 'Anthropofugal thought': see U.
Horstmann, *Das Untier*
339: 'Finally, after . . .': see JSS 1970,
155
340: 'One can train . . .': see ibid., 158
341: *'Circulus vitiosus . . .'*: F.
Nietzsche, *Werke* 3, 617
342: 'As yet . . .': E. v. Hartmann,
Philosophie des Unbewussten 2, 222
342: 'Theoretical pessimism . . .': JSS
1971, 6
343: 'Works of art . . .': T. W. Adorno,
Ästhetische Theorie, 190

BIBLIOGRAPHY

From the listed bibliography I should like to highlight the following titles which have especially inspired me:

Anders, Günther, *Die Antiquiertheit des Menschen*, 2 vols.: Munich, 1956 and 1980

Foucault, Michel, *Théorie d'ensemble*: Paris, 1968

Heidegger, Martin, *Über den Humanismus*: Frankfurt, 1947

Henrich, Dieter, *Selbstverhältnisse*: Stuttgart, 1982

Lem, Stanislaw, *Solaris*: Düsseldorf, 1972

Marquard, Odo, *Abschied vom Prinzipiellen*: Stuttgart, 1981

Sartre, Jean-Paul, *The Transcendence of the Ego* in *Recherches Philosophiques*: Paris, 1936

Sloterdijk, Peter, *Der Denker auf der Bühne: Nietzsches Materialismus*: Frankfurt, 1986

BIBLIOGRAPHY:

Hübscher, Arthur, *Schopenhauer-Bibliographie*: Stuttgart, 1981

ON SCHOPENHAUER:

Abendroth, Walter, *Schopenhauer*: Reinbek b. Hamburg, 1967

Autrum, Hansjochen, 'Der Wille in der Natur und die Biologie heute': in JSS 1969

Bahr, Hans Dieter, *Das gefesselte Engagement: Zur Ideologie der kontemplativen Ästhetik Schopenhauers*: Bonn, 1970

Becker, Aloys, 'Arthur Schopenhauer und Sigmund Freud: Historische und charakterologische Grundlagen ihrer gemeinsamen Denkstrukturen': in JSS 1971

Borch, Rudolf, *Schopenhauer: Sein Leben in Selbstzeugnissen, Briefen und Berichten*: Berlin, 1941

'Schopenhauer in Gotha': in JSS 1944

Bröcking, W., 'Schopenhauer und die Frankfurter Strassenkämpfe am 18.9.1848': in JSS 1922

Bucher, Ewald (ed.), *Von der Aktualität Arthur Schopenhauers: Festschrift für A. Hübscher*: Frankfurt, 1972

Cassirer, Ernst, *Das Erkenntnisproblem in der Philosophie und Wissenschaft der neueren Zeit*, 3 vols.: Darmstadt, 1971

Diemer, Alwin, 'Schopenhauer und die moderne Existenzphilosophie': in JSS 1962

Dorguth, Friedrich, *Schopenhauer in seiner Wahrheit*: Magdeburg, 1845

Ebeling, Hans and Lütkehaus, Ludger (eds.), *Schopenhauer und Marx: Philosophie des Elends*, in *Elend der Philosophie*: Königstein/Ts., 1980

Ehrlich, Walter, *Der Freiheitsbegriff bei Kant und Schopenhauer*: Berlin, 1920

Fischer, Kuno, *Schopenhauers Leben, Werk und Lehre*: 4th edn Heidelberg, 1934

Frauenstädt, Julius, *Briefe über die Schopenhauersche Philosophie*: Leipzig, 1854

Neue Briefe über die Schopenhauersche Philosophie: Leipzig, 1876

Frost, Laura, *Johanna Schopenhauer: Ein Frauenleben aus der klassischen Zeit*: Leipzig, 1920

von Glasenapp, Helmuth, *Das Indienbild deutscher Denker*: Stuttgart, 1960

von Gwinner, Wilhelm, *Schopenhauers Leben*: Leipzig, 1910

Harich, Wolfgang (ed.), *Schopenhauer*: East Berlin, 1955

Hartmann, Hermann, 'Schopenhauer und die heutige Naturwissenschaft': in JSS 1964

Hasse, Heinrich, *Arthur Schopenhauer*: Munich, 1926

Schopenhauers Erkenntnislehre als System einer Gemeinschaft des Rationalen und Irrationalen: Ein historisch-kritischer Versuch: Leipzig, 1913

Schopenhauers Religionsphilosophie: Frankfurt, 1924

Haym, Rudolf, *Schopenhauer*: Berlin, 1864

Heidtmann, Bernhard, *Pessimismus und Geschichte in der Philosophie Schopenhauers*: Berlin, 1969

Hoffmann, Paul T., 'Schopenhauer und Hamburg': in JSS 1932

Horkheimer, Max, 'Die Aktualität Schopenhauers': in JSS 1961

'Schopenhauer und die Gesellschaft': in JSS 1955

Houben, H. H., *Johanna Schopenhauer: Damals in Weimar*: Leipzig, 1924

Hübscher, Arthur, *Denker gegen den Strom: Arthur Schopenhauer gestern, heute, morgen*: Bonn, 1973

(ed.), 'Materialismus, Marxismus, Pessimismus': in JSS 1977

Arthur Schopenhauer: Biographie eines Weltbildes: Leipzig, 1952

Arthur Schopenhauer: Ein Lebensbild: Wiesbaden, 1949

Schopenhauers Anekdotenbüchlein: Frankfurt, 1981

'Schopenhauer und die Existenzphilosophie': in JSS 1962

'Schopenhauer als Hochschullehrer': in JSS 1958
'Ein vergessener Schulfreund Schopenhauers': in JSS 1965
Jaspers, Karl, 'Schopenhauer: Zu seinem 100. Todestag 1960', in Jaspers, Karl, *Aneignung und Polemik*: Munich, 1968
Krauss, Ingrid, *Studien über Schopenhauer und den Pessimismus in der deutschen Literatur des 19. Jahrhunderts*: Bern, 1931
Landmann, 'Schopenhauer heute': in JSS 1958
Lütkehaus, Ludger, *Schopenhauer: Metaphysischer Pessimismus und 'soziale Frage'*: Bonn, 1980
von Marchtaler, Hildegard, 'Lorenz Meyers Tagebücher': in JSS 1968
Mühlethaler, Jacob, *Die Mystik bei Schopenhauer*: Berlin, 1910
Pfeiffer-Belli, Wolfgang, *Schopenhauer und die Humanität des grossen Asiens*: Bad Wörishofen, 1948
Pisa, Karl, *Schopenhauer: Geist und Sinnlichkeit*: Munich, 1978 (Taschenbuchausgabe)
Pothast, Ulrich, *Die eigentlich metaphysische Tätigkeit: über Schopenhauers Ästhetik und ihre Anwendung durch Samuel Beckett*: Frankfurt, 1982
Salaquarda, Jörg, 'Erwägungen zur Ethik: Schopenhauers kritisches Gespräch mit Kant und die gegenwärtige Diskussion': in JSS 1975
'Zur gegenseitigen Verdrängung von Schopenhauer und Nietzsche': in JSS 1984
(ed.), *Wege der Forschung: Schopenhauer*: Darmstadt, 1985
Schöndorf, Harald, *Der Leib im Denken Schopenhauers und Fichtes*: Munich, 1982
Schopenhauer, Adele, *Gedichte und Scherenschnitte*, ed. H. H. Houben and H. Wahl: Leipzig, 1920
Tagebuch einer Einsamen, ed. H. H. Houben: Munich, 1985 (reprint)
Tagebücher, 2 vols.: Leipzig, 1909
Schopenhauer, Johanna, *Ihr glücklichen Augen: Jugenderinnerungen, Tagebücher, Briefe*, ed. R. Weber: East Berlin, 1978
Schopenhauer, Johanna, *Reise durch England und Schottland*: Frankfurt, 1980
Gabriele: Munich, 1985
Schirmacher, Wolfgang (ed.), 'Schopenhauer und Nietzsche – Wurzeln gegenwärtiger Vernunftkritik': JSS 1984
'Schopenhauer bei neueren Philosophen': in JSS 1983
(ed.), *Zeit der Ernte: Studien zum Stand der Schopenhauer-Forschung*: Stuttgart, 1982
Schmidt, Alfred, *Drei Studien über Materialismus: Schopenhauer – Horkheimer – Glücksproblem*: Frankfurt/Berlin/Vienna, 1979
Die Wahrheit im Gewande der Lüge: Schopenhauers Religionsphilosophie: Munich/Zürich 1986
Schneider, Walther, *Schopenhauer*: Vienna, 1937

Schulz, Walter, 'Bemerkungen zu Schopenhauer', in Schulz, Walter (ed.), *Natur und Geschichte: K. Löwith zum 70. Geburtstag*: Stuttgart, 1967
Simmel, Georg, *Schopenhauer und Nietzsche*: Munich/Leipzig, 1920
Sorg, Bernhard, *Zur literarischen Schopenhauer-Rezeption im 19. Jahrhundert*: Heidelberg, 1975
Spierling, Volker (ed.), *Materialien zu Schopenhauers 'Die Welt als Wille und Vorstellung'*: Frankfurt, 1984
Schopenhauers transzendentalidealistisches Selbstmissverständnis: Munich, 1977
Tengler, Richard, *Schopenhauer und die Romantik*: Berlin, 1923
Vaternahm, Theodor, 'Schopenhauers Frankfurter Jahre': in JSS 1968
Verrecchia, Anacleto, 'Schopenhauer e la vispa Theresa': in JSS 1975
Voigt, Hans, 'Wille und Energie': in JSS 1970
Volkelt, Johannes, *Schopenhauer: Seine Persönlichkeit, seine Lehre, sein Glaube*: Stuttgart, 1900
Weimar, Wolfgang, *Schopenhauer: Erträge der Forschung*: Darmstadt, 1982
Zimmer, Heinrich, 'Schopenhauer und Indien': in JSS, 1938

OTHER WORKS

Adorno, Theodor W., *Ästhetische Theorie*: Frankfurt, 1973
Negative Dialetik: Frankfurt, 1975
Adorno, Theodor W. and Horkheimer, Max, *Dialektik der Aufklärung*: Frankfurt, 1969
Anders, Günther, *Die Antiquiertheit des Menschen*, 2 vols.: Munich, 1956 and 1980
Arendt, Dieter (ed.), *Nihilismus: Die Anfänge − Von Jacobi bis Nietzsche*: Cologne, 1970
Atterbom, Per Daniel, *Reisebilder aus dem romantischen Deutschland*: Berlin, 1867 (Nachdruck Stuttgart, 1970)
Baum, Günther, 'Aenesidemus oder der Satz vom Grunde: Eine Studie zur Vorgeschichte der Wissenschaftstheorie': in *Zeitschrift für philosophische Forschung*, JSS 1979
Bloch, Ernst, *Das Materialismusproblem, seine Geschichte und Substanz*: Frankfurt, 1972
Blumenberg, Hans, *Arbeit am Mythos*: Frankfurt, 1981; translated as *Work on Myth*: Cambridge, Mass./London, 1985
Die Lesbarkeit der Welt: Frankfurt, 1986 (Taschenbuch)
Böhme, Hartmut and Böhme, Gernot, *Das Andere der Vernunft*: Frankfurt, 1985 (Taschenbuch)
Böhme, Jakob, *Von der Gnadenwahl*, ed. G. Wehr: Freiburg i. Br., 1978
von Böhn, Max, *Biedermeier*: Berlin, n.d.
Borch, Rudolf, 'Die Gothaer Lehrer': in JSS 1942
Bothe, Friedrich, *Geschichte der Stadt Frankfurt am Main*: Frankfurt, 1977

Brockhaus, Heinrich Eduard, *Friedrich Arnold Brockhaus: Sein Leben und Wirken nach Briefen und anderen Aufzeichnungen*: Leipzig, 1876
Bruford, W. H., *Die gesellschaftlichen Grundlagen der Goethezeit*: Frankfurt/Berlin/Vienna, 1975
Brunschwig, *Gesellschaft und Romantik in Preussen im 18. Jahrhundert: Die Krise des preussischen Staates am Ende des 18. Jahrhunderts und die Entstehung der romantischen Mentalität*: Frankfurt/Berlin/Vienna, 1975
Büchner, Georg, *Sämtliche Werke*, ed. P. Stapf: Berlin, 1963
Buddha, Gautama, *Die vier edlen Wahrheiten: Texte des ursprünglichen Buddhismus*, ed. K. Mylius: Munich, 1985; translated as 'The Four Noble Truths', see Snelling, John, *The Buddhist Handbook*: London, 1987
Cioran, E. M., *Lehre vom Zerfall*: Stuttgart, 1979
Claudius, Matthias, *Sämtliche Werke*, ed. H. Geiger: Berlin, 1964
Descartes, René, *Ausgewählte Schriften*, ed. I. Frenzel: Frankfurt, 1986; in English see *The Essential Works of Descartes*: London, 1966
von Ditfurth, Hoimar, *Der Geist fiel nicht vom Himmel: Die Evolution unseres Bewusstseins*: Munich, 1980
So lasst uns denn ein Apfelbäumchen pflanzen: Es ist so weit: Hamburg/Zürich, 1985
Eckhart, Meister, *Einheit im Sein und Wirken*, ed. D. Mieth: Munich, 1986
von Eichendorff, Joseph, *Werke*: Munich, 1966
Elias, Norbert, *Über den Prozess der Zivilisation*, 2 vols.: Frankfurt, 1976
Erdmann, Johann Eduard, *Philosophie der Neuzeit*: Reinbek b. Hamburg, 1971 (Rowohlts deutsche Enzyklopädie)
Feuerbach, Ludwig, *Gesammelte Werke*, ed. W. Schaffenhauer: East Berlin, 1971
Grundsätze der Philosophie der Zukunft: Frankfurt, 1983 (reprint)
Fichte, J. G., *Werke*, ed. I. H. Fichte: reprinted Berlin, 1971
Foucault, Michel, *Théorie d'ensemble*: Paris, 1968
The History of Sexuality, 3 vols., Harmondsworth: 1984, 1987 and 1988
Frank, Manfred, *Eine Einführung in Schellings Philosophie*: Frankfurt, 1985
Der unendliche Mangel an Sein: Frankfurt, 1975
Der kommende Gott: Vorlesungen über die Neue Mythologie: Frankfurt, 1982
Freud, Sigmund, *Fragen der Gesellschaft. Ursprünge der Religion*, vol. 9 of *Studienausgabe*: Frankfurt, 1974; translated as *The Standard Edition of the Complete Psychological Works of Sigmund Freud*: London, 1953
Freund, Michael, *Napoleon und die Deutschen: Despot oder Held der Freiheit*: Munich, 1969
Friedell, Egon, *Kulturgeschichte der Neuzeit*: Munich, 1965; translated as *A Cultural History of the Modern Age*: New York, 1930–2

Friedenthal, Richard, *Goethe: Sein Leben und seine Zeit*: Munich, 1963; translated as *Goethe: His Life and his Times*: London, 1963
Geiger, L., *Berlin 1688 bis 1840: Geschichte des geistigen Lebens der preussischen Hauptstadt*: Berlin, 1892
Geyer, Bernhard, *Das Stadtbild Alt-Dresdens*: Berlin, 1964
Goethe, Johann Wolfgang, *Werke* (Hamburg edn): Munich, 1981; translated as *Goethe's Works*: Cambridge, Mass., 1885
Gulyga, Arsenij, *Hegel*: Frankfurt, 1981
Immanuel Kant: Frankfurt, 1985
Günther, G. and Wallraf, L. (eds.), *Geschichte der Stadt Weimar*: Weimar, 1975
Günzel, Klaus, *König der Romantik: Das Leben des Dichters Ludwig Tieck in Briefen, Selbstzeugnissen und Berichten*: Tübingen, 1981
Gutzkow, Karl, *Wally – Die Zweiflerin*: reprinted Göttingen, 1965
Habermas, Jürgen, *Der philosophische Diskurs der Moderne*: Frankfurt, 1985
Haenel, E. and Kalkschmidt, E. (eds.), *Das alte Dresden*: reprinted Frankfurt, 1977
von Hartmann, Eduard, *Philosophie des Unbewussten*, 2 vols.: Leipzig, 1913
Hauser, Arnold, *Sozialgeschichte der Kunst und Literatur*: Munich, 1953
Haym, Rudolf, *Hegel und seine Zeit*: Berlin, 1857
Hegel, G. W. F., *Sämtliche Werke*, ed. H. Glockner: Stuttgart, 1927ff; in English see *The Phenomenology of Mind*: London/New York, 1931
Heidegger, Martin, *Über den Humanismus*: Frankfurt, 1947
Der Satz vom Grund: Pfullingen, 1957
Sein und Zeit: Tübingen, 1963
Gelassenheit: Pfullingen, 1959
Heine, Heinrich, *Sämtliche Schriften*, ed. K. Briegleb: Munich, 1976; translated as *The Works of Heinrich Heine*: London, 1892–1905
Heinrich, Klaus, *Vernunft und Mythos: Ausgewählte Texte*: Frankfurt, 1982
Heiss, Robert, *Der Gang des Geistes*: Berlin, 1959
Heller, Erich, *Enterbter Geist*: Frankfurt, 1981; English as *The Disinherited Mind*: London, 1975
Henrich, Dieter, *Selbstverhältnisse*: Stuttgart, 1982
Hermand, J. (ed.), *Der deutsche Vormärz: Texte und Dokumente*: Stuttgart, 1967
(ed.), *Das Junge Deutschland: Texte und Dokumente*: Stuttgart, 1966
Hölderlin, Friedrich, *Sämtliche Werke und Briefe*, ed. G. Mieth: Munich, 1970
Horkheimer, Max (H. Regius), *Dämmerungen: Notizen in Deutschland*: Zürich, 1934
Horstmann, Ulrich, *Das Untier: Konturen einer Philosophie der Menschenfluchte*: Frankfurt, 1985

Huyssen, A. (ed.), *Die deutsche Literatur in Text und Darstellung: Bürgerlicher Realismus*: Stuttgart, 1974

Jacobs, Wilhelm G., *Johann Gottlieb Fichte*: Reinbek b. Hamburg, 1984

Jaspers, Karl, *Psychologie der Weltanschauungen*: Berlin/Göttingen/ Heidelberg, 1960

Kamper, Dietmar, *Zur Geschichte der Einbildungskraft*: Munich, 1981

Kant, Immanuel, *Werke*, 12 vols., ed. W. Weischedel: Frankfurt, 1964

Kesten, Hermann, *Dichter im Café*: Frankfurt, 1983

Keyser, Erich, *Geschichte der Stadt Danzig*: Kitzingen, 1951

Klessmann, Eckart (ed.), *Die Befreiungskriege in Augenzeugenberichten*: Munich, 1973

Köhler, R. and Richter, W. (eds.), *Berliner Leben 1806 bis 1847: Erinnerungen, Berichte*: East Berlin, 1954

Kopitzsch, Franklin, 'Lessing und Hamburg' in *Wolfenbüttler Studien 2*, 1975

Korff, Hermann August, *Geist der Goethezeit*, 4 vols.: Leipzig, 1959

Koselleck, Reinhart, *Kritik und Krise*: Freiburg/Munich, 1959

Kraus, Wolfgang, *Nihilismus heute oder Die Geduld der Weltgeschichte*: Frankfurt, 1985

Lange, Friedrich Albert, *Geschichte des Materialismus*, 2 vols.: Frankfurt, 1974; translated as *History of Materialism, and Criticism of its Present Importance*: London, 1877

Lem, Stanislaw, *Solaris*: Düsseldorf, 1972

Lenz, Max, *Geschichte der Königlichen Friedrich Wilhelm-Universität zu Berlin*, 3 vols.: Halle, 1910

Lepenies, Wolf, *Melancholie und Gesellschaft*: Frankfurt, 1972

Lessing, G. E., *Werke*, ed. H. Göpfert: Munich, 1971ff

Lorenz, Konrad, *Die Rückseite des Spiegels: Versuch einer Naturgeschichte der menschlichen Erkenntnis*: Munich, 1973

Löwith, Karl, *Von Hegel zu Nietzsche: Der revolutionäre Bruch im Denken des 19. Jahrhunderts*: Stuttgart, 1953

Lukacs, Georg, *Die Zerstörung der Vernunft*: Berlin, 1954

Mader, Johann, *Zwischen Hegel und Marx: Zur Verwirklichung der Philosophie*: Vienna/Munich, 1975

Mainländer, Philipp, *Die Philosophie der Erlösung*: Berlin, 1879

Majer, Friedrich, *Brahma oder die Religion der Indier als Brahmanen*: Leipzig, 1818

Mann, Thomas, *Doktor Faustus*: Frankfurt, 1974; translated as *Doctor Faustus*: Harmondsworth, 1968

Marcuse, Ludwig, *Philosophie des Un-Glücks*: Zürich, 1981
Philosophie des Glücks: Zürich, 1972

Marquard, Odo, *Abschied vom Prinzipiellen*: Stuttgart, 1981

Marx, Karl and Engels, Friedrich, *Werke*: East Berlin, 1959ff

Maus, Heinz, *Kritik am Justemilieu: Eine sozialphilosophische Studie*: Bottrop, 1940

Migge, Walter, *Weimar zur Goethezeit*: Weimar, 1961

Montaigne, Michel de, *Essays*, trans. J. M. Cohen: Harmondsworth, 1958

Mühr, Alfred, *Rund um den Gendarmenmarkt*: Oldenburg, 1965

Nietzsche, Friedrich, *Werke*, ed. K. Schlechta: Frankfurt/Berlin/Vienna, 1979 (Taschenbuch); translated as *The Complete Works of Friedrich Nietzsche*: Edinburgh/London, 1909–13

Nipperdey, Thomas, *Deutsche Geschichte 1800–1866*: Munich, 1983

Nissen, Walter, *Göttingen heute und gestern*: Göttingen, 1972

Novalis, *Werke*, ed. H. J. Mähl and R. Samuel: Munich, 1978

Oppermann, Heinrich Albert, *Hundert Jahre 1770 bis 1870*: reprinted Frankfurt, 1982

Ostwald, Hans, *Kultur- und Sittengeschichte Berlins*: Berlin, 1924

Pascal, Blaise, *Pensées*; translated as *Thoughts*: New York, 1910

Paul, Jean, *Werke*, ed. N. Miller: Munich, 1960ff

Petraschek, K. O., *Die Rechtsphilosophie des Pessimismus*: Munich, 1929

Plato, *Works*, 10 vols.: London: 1914

Pleticha, H. (ed.), *Das klassische Weimar: Texte und Zeugnisse*: Munich, 1983

Popper, Karl v. and Eccles, John C., *Das Ich und sein Gehirn*: Munich/Zürich, 1982

Post, Werner, *Kritische Theorie und metaphysischer Pessimismus*: Munich, 1971

Preitz, Max, *Friedrich Schlegel und Novalis: Biographie einer Romantikerfreundschaft in Briefen*: Darmstadt, 1957

Proust, Marcel, *Remembrance of Things Past*: London, 1949

Reichel, Ortrud, *Zum Beispiel Dresden*: Frankfurt, 1964

Richter, Ludwig, *Lebenserinnerungen eines deutschen Malers*: Frankfurt, 1980

Riedel, Manfred, *Theorie und Praxis im Denken Hegels*: Frankfurt/Berlin/Vienna, 1976

Rorty, Richard, *Der Spiegel der Natur: Eine Kritik der Philosophie*: Frankfurt, 1981

Ross, Werner, *Der ängstliche Adler: Friedrich Nietzsches Leben*: Munich, 1984

Röthel, H. K., *Die Hansestädte*: Munich, 1955

Rousseau, Jean-Jacques, *The Confessions of Jean-Jacques Rousseau*: reprinted London, 1957
Emilius; or, An Essay on Education: London, 1763

Sartre, Jean-Paul, *Being and Nothingness* (trans. Hazel Barnes): New York, 1966
'The Transcendence of the Ego': in *Recherches Philosophiques*: Paris, 1936

Schelling, F. W. J., *Ausgewählte Schriften*, ed. M. Frank, 6 vols.: Frankfurt, 1985
Über das Wesen der menschlichen Freiheit: Frankfurt, 1975 (Taschenbuch); translated as *On Human Freedom*: Chicago, 1936
Schiller, Friedrich, *Sämtliche Werke: Säkular-Ausgabe*, ed. E. v. d. Hellen: Berlin, n.d.; translated as *Complete Works*: Philadelphia, 1870
Schlegel, Friedrich, *Über die Sprache und Weisheit der Indier*: Heidelberg, 1809
Schmidt, Alfred, *Emanzipatorische Sinnlichkeit*: Munich, 1973
Schmitz, Hermann, *System der Philosophie: Der Leib*: Bonn, 1965
Schnädelbach, Herbert, *Philosophie in Deutschland 1831–1933*: Frankfurt, 1983
Schneider, Franz, *Pressefreiheit und politische Öffentlichkeit*: Neuwied, 1966
Schulz, Gerhard, *Die deutsche Literatur zwischen Französischer Revolution und Restauration*: Munich, 1983
Schulz, Walter, *Philosophie in der veränderten Welt*: Pfullingen, 1974
Schulze, Friedrich, *Franzosenzeit in deutschen Landen*: Leipzig, 1908
Sennett, Richard, *Verfall und Ende des öffentlichen Lebens – Die Tyrannei der Intimität*: Frankfurt, 1983
Sloterdijk, Peter, *Der Denker auf der Bühne: Nietzsches Materialismus*: Frankfurt, 1986
Kritik der zynischen Vernunft, 2 vols.: Frankfurt, 1983
Solé, Jacques, *Liebe in der westlichen Kultur*: Frankfurt/Berlin/Vienna, 1979
Spaemann, Robert and Löw, Reinhard, *Die Frage Wozu?*: Munich/Zürich, 1985
de Staël, Germaine, *Germany*: London, 1813
Steffens, Heinrich, *Anthropologie*, vol. 1: Breslau, 1822
Stern, Adolf, *Der Einfluss der französischen Revolution auf das deutsche Geistesleben*: Stuttgart/Berlin, 1928
Studt, B. and Olsen, H., *Hamburg: Die Geschichte einer Stadt*: Hamburg, 1951
Tieck, Ludwig, *Werke in vier Bänden*, ed. M. Thalmann: Darmstadt, 1977
Tillich, Paul, 'Der Mut zum Sein': in Tillich, Paul, *Sein und Sinn*: Frankfurt, 1982
The Upanishads, translated from the Sanskrit with an introduction by Swami Nikhilananda: London, 1951
Vaihinger, Hans, *Die Philosophie des Als ob*: Berlin, 1913
Varnhagen von Ense, K. A., *Denkwürdigkeiten des eigenen Lebens*: Berlin, 1922
Vassen, Florian, ed., *Die deutsche Literatur in Text und Darstellung: Restauration, Vormärz und 48er Revolution*: Stuttgart, 1975
Wackenroder, Wilhelm Heinrich, *Schriften*: Reinbek b. Hamburg, 1968
Wiggershaus, Rolf, *Die Frankfurter Schule*: Munich, 1986

Wittgenstein, Ludwig, *Tractatus logico-philosophicus*, 5 vols.: London, 1961

Ziegler, Theobald, *Die geistigen und sozialen Strömungen des Neunzehnten Jahrhunderts*: Berlin, 1910

Zimmer, Heinrich, *Philosophie und Religion Indiens*: Frankfurt, 1973
Maya: Der indische Mythos: Frankfurt, 1978

INDEX